War *of* 1812 Soldiers
of
Maury County,
Tennessee

Compiled By:
Jill K. Garrett

Southern Historical Press, Inc.
Greenville, South Carolina

SOUTHERN HISTORICAL PRESS, INC.
PO BOX 1267
Greenville, SC   29601

ISBN #0-89308-525-1

Printed in the United States of America

CONTENTS

INTRODUCTION

Maury County, Tennessee, was established 16 Nov. 1807 and at the time of the American Revolution was still part of the vast Indian hunting grounds of Middle Tennessee. The first time the young men of the county were called to serve their country was during the War of 1812 and the Creek War.

Jane Knox Chapter, Daughters of the American Revolution, chose for the chapter's Bicentennial project a study and compilation of the soldiers and patriots of the War of 1812.

Tennessee became known as "The Volunteer State" during the War of 1812, and Maury County's contribution might be considered typical of the time. Ten companies were formed in the county which in 1812 had 1,864 free white males (1005 voters)—and this book contains the names of 1,335 soldiers and patriots from the county, 58 of whom died or were killed in service. Two men from Maury County were among the seven killed at the Battle of New Orleans on 8 Jan. 1815.

These men range from generals to privates, from future sheriffs to horse thieves, and include spies, ferriers, trumpeters, former Revolutionary War soldiers, future Confederate soldiers, the father of a President of the United States, two black slaves, one Indian, the richest man in the county, and possibly the poorest. From the birthdates available, the majority of these soldiers were fourteen and fifteen.

Companies formed in Maury County were headed by the following captains: Samuel Ashmore, James McMahan, John Looney, Benjamin Reynolds, Bird S. Hurt, John Chisholm William Dooley, John Gordon (which also included Hickman County men), Robert Campbell, and Samuel B. McKnight. The major participation of these companies was in the Creek War.

The county still has one place name, Rally Hill, dating from this time when soldiers on the way to Alabama rallied on a hillside on the old Elk Trace. A house in Columbia, the county seat, was also named Rally Hill as it too was the site or rallying point for soldiers of the War of 1812. Many homes, mostly log, built by these early warriors still stand in the county.

Information on some of these men is brief and represents all that the chapter could learn about these soldiers. A master list of soldiers was prepared and given to several local researchers who generously added information from their own files. An appeal was made to various organizations for information. Jane Knox Chapter wishes to thank each person who contributed toward this book and each contribution is noted with each entry in the book.

We also want to thank chapter members Virginia W. Alexander (Mrs. Charles C.) and Jane C. Luna (Mrs. John) for their work on this book, and Marise P. Lightfoot (Mrs. Jack), member of Thomas McKissack Chapter, DAR, for her contributions from her files.

The following symbols were used in the book:

> \+ - indicates that this man died in service
> ( ) - comments and explanatory notes
> [ ] - information in brackets may or may NOT pertain to this soldier—this information was found on a person of this name and included for interest.

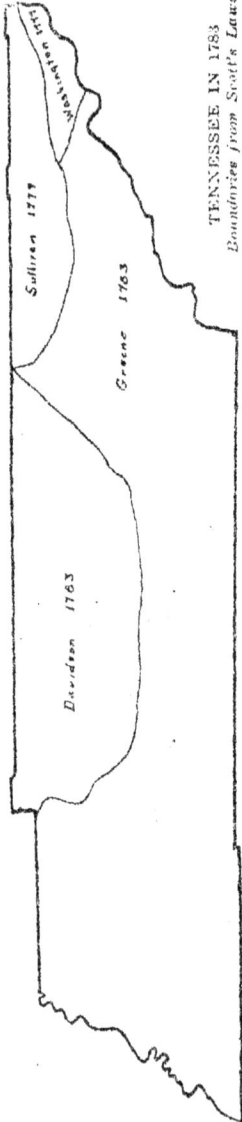

TENNESSEE IN 1783
Boundaries from Scott's Laws

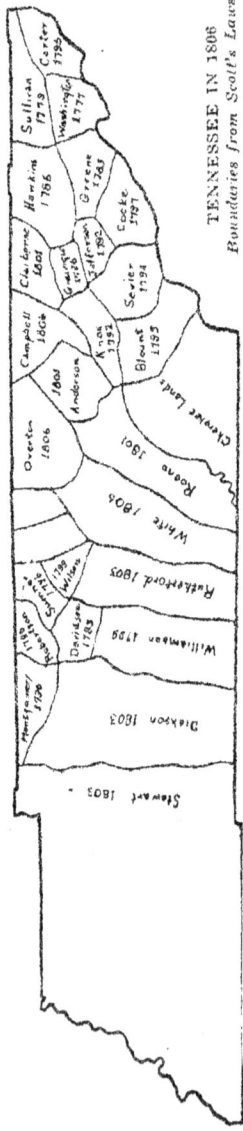

TENNESSEE IN 1806
Boundaries from Scott's Laws

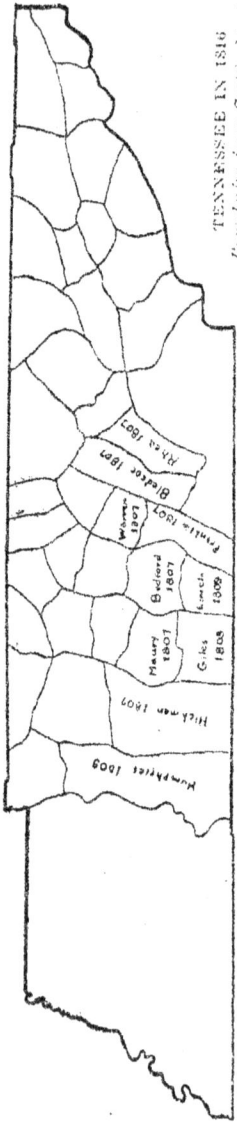

TENNESSEE IN 1816
Boundaries from Scott's Laws

WAR OF 1812 SOLDIERS OF MAURY COUNTY

LITTLETON ABERNATHY
Served in Samuel Bell McKnight's company. No further information.

ISAAC ACUFF
Enlisted 22 June 1812 as private in Capt. Benjamin Reynolds Company, Brig. General
Isaac B. Roberts Mounted Rangers. Enlisted 4 Oct. 1813 as sergeant in Capt. William
Dooley's Infantry, Col. Thomas McCrory. His wife's name was Polly and he got land
on Lytles Creek, part of the Breckenridge-Looney grant. (Maury County Deed Book
D, pages 111, 115, 143.) [No information on family. Abram Acuff, age 34 on the 185
Census is believed to be his son, but no proof; Abram named a son Isaac. [

JAMES ADAIR
Served in Captain John Looney's Company. No further information.

JOHN ADAIR
Served as private in Capt. James McMahon's Company, Tennessee Mounted Gunmen under
Col. Robert H. Dyer, private, enlisted 28 Sept. 1814, discharged 1 Jan. 1815. Born
in North Carolina.

Children of John Adair:
1. Lucretia, born 1812 at the Hunter Place at Mt. Pleasant; married J. D. Gardner.
2. No information on additional children.

(Source: Century Review of Maury County, page 268.)

JOHN ADAMS
Enlisted 4 Oct. 1813 as private in Capt. William Dooley's company, Col. Thomas
McCrory's infantry. No further information.

JOHN ADAMS
Enlisted as private in Capt. Benjamin Reynolds's first company. No further information.

WILLIAM ADAMS
Enlisted 28 Sept. 1814 as corporal in Capt. James McMahan's 1st Tennessee Volunteer
Gunmen, Col. R. H. Dyer; was sergeant on 27 Dec. 1814. No further information.

JOHN AKIN
Enlisted in Capt. Samuel B. McKnight's company. [This man has not been identified
as there were two of this name in the county. [[Possibly the son of the Rev. John
Akin, born 1756, died 1821, Revolutionary War soldier, whose will may be found in
the legislative petitions in the State Archives in Nashville. This John Akin married
Mrs. Mary Watson Howe and had the following children: 1. Robert, eldest son, born
3 Sept. 1784, died 18 March 1862; 1. Samuel Watson Akin, born 24 Feb. 1788, died
2 Nov. 1833; 3. John (possibly the War of 1812 soldier listed here); 4. Martha L.,
married __Grimes; 5. Permelia, married __Smith; 6. Eleanor, married __Biffle;
7. William V. Akin. [

WILLIAM AKIN
Enlisted in Capt. Robert Campbell's company. Muster roll shows his name as William
Akin; payroll of company shows his name as William Adkins. No further information.

JOHN D. ALDERSON
Enlisted in Capt. Robert Campbell's company. No further information.

ADAM RANKIN ALEXANDER

Enlisted as private in Capt. William Dooley's company. Born 1 Nov. 1781 in Washington County, Va.; died 1 Nov. 1848 at the age of 67 years; son of Oliver Alexander, Revolutionary War soldier; had brother Eben Alexander who lived in Knoxville, Tenn. He was the first white man to build a house in Jackson, Madison County, Tennessee; by 1834 he was in Shelby Co., Tenn.; was in Maury County at least as early as 1810.

Children of Adam Rankin Alexander:
1. Ebenezer Alexander - got land in Hardeman County, Tenn.
2. William Reagan - had land in Haywood County, Tenn.
3. No information on additional children.

(Source: Letter dated 29 Sept. 1971 from descendant Mrs. W. D. Brotherton, Cherokee, Alabama, to Mrs. Charles C. Alexander; also Alexander Kin, by Charles C. Alexander and Virginia W. Alexander, pages 86, 87.)

CYRUS ALEXANDER

Enlisted 18 Dec. 1813 as ensign in Capt. James McMahan's Mounted Gunmen, Col. N. T. Perkins. No further information.

JAMES ALEXANDER

Enlisted in Capt. John Looney's company. No correct identification on this man.

PETER B. ALEXANDER

Enlisted as ensign in Capt. John Looney's company. No further information.

SILAS ALEXANDER

Enlisted as private in Capt. William Dooley's company. [There were two men named Silas Alexander in Maury County; one the son of Daniel Alexander and nephew of a Silas Alexander; believed to be the younger Silas who was in War of 1812. The older Silas was at one time an ensign in the Tennessee Militia in Sumner County. Included below will be information on both men.]

Silas Alexander, the younger
Son of Daniel Alexander (born 9 July 1767), married Rachel Mauphet on 16 April 1794, C Cabarrus Co., N. C. Silas married 16 Oct. 1823 in Maury County, Tenn., to Mary Kennedy, died 1869 in Smith Co., Texas, buried in Chapel Hill Cemetery. Alexander Kin, page 38, says that he served in the War of 1812 first as a private, then as third sergeant, and in the navy.

Children of Silas Alexander, the younger:
1. Thomas Crawford Alexander, born 1824
2. Jane C. Alexander, born 1826
3. Marianne Alexander, born 1828
4. Newton F. Alexander, born 1829
5. Licus A. Alexander, born 1831
6. Robert K. Alexander, born 1834
7. William J. Alexander, born 1836
8. John D. Alexander, born 1838
9. Josiah H. Alexander, born 1840
10. Leonidas A. Alexander, born 1843
11. Linneaus C. Alexander, born 1846
12. Epaminondas M., born 1849.

(Source: Alexander Kin, by Charles C. Alexander and Virginia W. Alexander, page 38.)

Silas Alexander, the elder
Born Sept. 1777, married Sarah Reese. He was an ensign in the militia, commissioned
1798 in Sumner County; living in Maury County as early as 21 Dec. 1807 when he was
summoned for jury duty. Son of William Alexander. Removed to Fayette Co., Tenn.,
and died about 1829. His wife returned to Maury County where she died 22 Nov. 1839]
and is buried in Reese's Chapel Cemetery.

Children of Silas Alexander, the elder:
1. James Orville, born 12 July 1799, died 21 Sept. 1828, married Drucilla Abernathy.
2. William Reese, born 22 Jan. 1803.
3. George Logan Alexander, born 4 Jan. 1805, died 23 June 1887 in Graves Co., Ky.,
   married Martha Combs and Anna Peeler.
4. Matilda Sharp, born 18 July 1806, died 29 July 1856, married John Y. Abernathy.
5. Peggy Logan, born 19 Feb. 1808.
6. Elizabeth Caroline, born 19 Sept. 1809.
7. Daniel Americus, born 7 Sept. 1811, died 10 Nov. 1882, married Sophronia Yokley.
8. Silas Grandison, born 7 July 1813.
9. Sarah Louiza, born 7 Jan. 1815.
10. Esther Brown, born 20 Nov. 1816.
11. Franklin Houston, born 25 Nov. 1819.
12. Rachel Priscilla, born 15 Oct. 1821.

(Source: Alexander Kin, pages 34, 35, 36.)

BENJAMIN ALLEN
Enlisted 13 Nov. 1814 as private in Capt. Bird Hurt's company of infantry, Colonel
William Metcalf. No further information. [Marriage bond dated 10 Aug. 1811 for a
Benjamin Allen to marry Sally Voorhies, which may be for this man.]

CHARLES ALLEN
Enlisted 13 Nov. 1814 as private in Capt. Bird S. Hurt's company, Colonel William
Metcalf. Son of James Allen (born 1757, died 1829) and his wife Mary Tomlinson
(born 1757, died 1820). Born 1784 in Kentucky, married 1808 to Elizabeth Gill,
daughter of Thomas and Nancy Gill.) [Marriage bond dated 6 June 1808 with Nathaniel
Gholson, bondsman.] No information on children.

Brothers and sisters of Charles Allen:
1. Nancy Allen, married Jesse Tomlinson.
2. Catherine Allen, married Benjamin Reynolds.
3. William Allen, born 1772, married Nancy Quinn.
4. James Allen, married Elizabeth Reynolds.
5. Zachariah Allen.

(Source: Mrs. Leonard Gibson, Culleoka, Tenn., descendant of Nancy Allen Tomlinson.)

CHARLES ALLEN
Served as corporal in Capt. William Dooley's company. Name also appears to be
Allum on one roll of this company.

CHARLES REP. ALLEN
Enlisted 4 Oct. 1813 under Colonel Thomas McCrory.

CHARLES ALLEN
Served in Capt. Benjamin Reynolds' second company. This is possibly the same as
the Charles Allen above in Dooley's company as Reynolds was his brother-in-law.

GEORGE ALLEN
Served as first lieutenant in Capt. Dalton's company, Col. Williamson's regiment,
General Coffee's brigade; at Horseshoe Bend and at Pensacola when Spanish commander
surrendered; was at Battle of New Orleans; Born 1790 in S. C., died at Caney Spring

George Allen, continued:
"recently" at the age of 94 and left large family. (Columbia Herald and Mail, dated 5 June 1874.) [Note difference in age and birthdate.]

HENRY D. ALLEN

Commissioned captain 1813 in the 27th Regiment of Tennessee Militia; family says in "War of 1812". Born 26 March 1782, died 25 May 1873 in Lauderdale County, Ala. Married (1) 18 Dec. 1804 in Sumner Co., Tenn., to Polly Barnes, daughter of Joseph and Selah Barnes, born 15 Dec. 1781, died 11 Aug. 1856 in Lauderdale County, Ala., both are buried in Arkdel Cemetery near Lexington, Lauderdale County, Ala. Settled in Maury County near Mt. Pleasant, left April 1815 for Alabama. He married (2) to Marcy Rice Mayfield, widow of John Robinson; she was born 25 April 1820, died 28 April 1905 and buried in Granny Richardson Cemetery, Lauderdale Co., Alabama; they were married 16 Nov. 1857.

Children of Henry D. Allen:

1. Nancy
2. Robert
3. Bluford Turner
4. Nelson G.
5. Mary T.
6. Martha E.
7. Sara (Sally)
8. Eliza
9. Henry D., Jr.
10. Elizabeth A.
11. Margaret N.

(Source: "Some Lauderdale County, Ala., Cemetery Records," by Garrett and McClain.)

JAMES ALLEN

Commissioned lieutenant in 27th Regiment of Tennessee Militia in 1811. No further information.

JAMES ALLEN

Served as lieutenant in Capt. Benjamin Reynolds' second company; Reynolds was his brother-in-law; married Elizabeth Reynolds, marriage bond dated 26 March 1812, with Jesse Tomlinson, bondsman. [Refer to Charles Allen entry for parents.]

JAMES ALLEN

Enlisted as private 10 Nov. 1813 in Capt. William Dooley's company, Col. Thomas McCrory.

THOMAS ALLEN

Served in Capt. John Chisholm's company. No further information.

WILLIAM ALLEN

Enlisted in Capt. Benjamin Reynolds' first company and also in Reynolds' second company. Believed to be son of James Allen [see Charles Allen entry] and brother-in-law of Reynolds.

WILLIAM ALLEN

Born 18 Feb. 1773, died 4 Sept. 1859, buried in Allen Cemetery; wife Elizabeth, born 10 Jan. 1775, died 7 Feb. 1818, buried in Allen Cemetery. Known as Captain Allen. No further information.

ZACHARIAH ALLEN

Enlisted as private 13 Nov. 1814 in Capt. Bird S. Hurt's company; son of James Allen. [Refer to Charles Allen entry.]

THOMAS ALSUP

Commissioned captain in 27th Regiment, Maury County, in 1809. Between 1819 and 1825 got land in Lawrence County, Tenn. No further information.

WILLIAM B. AMONDS
Served in Capt. John Gordon's company; transferred to Capt. Williamson's company; no further information.

DAVID ANDERS
Enlisted as private 4 Oct. 1813 in Capt. Samuel B. McKnight's company, Col. Thomas McCrory. One muster roll gives his name as Davis Anders. No further information.

ROBERT ANDERSON
Commissioned captain in the 27th regiment, Maury County militia, 1811. No further information.

ADAM ANDREWS
Enlisted in Captain Samuel Ashmore's company. No further information.

LAZARUS ANDREWS
Enlisted as private 20 Sept. 1814 in Capt. Thomas Wells company, Col. Leroy Hammonds and was left at Fort Montgomery in December 1814. He was in Maury County in 1807 as he was a signer of a petition to form the county; lived on McGee's Road to Mount Pleasant; married Margaret Stockard, daughter of James Stockard (born 1741 Orange Co., N. C.) and his wife Ellen Trousdale (born 1751, died 1810.)

SAMUEL ANGLIN
Served in Capt. John Chisholm's company; no further information.

HIRAM ANTHONY
Served in Capt. Bird S. Hurt's company. Born about 1796 in S. C., living in District 6 of Maury in 1850; Lois, born 1800 in S. C., possibly his wife from census. No further information. [Early Maury marriages for Milton Anthony to Polly B. Glover, 2 Nov. 1815; Fanny Anthony to Hugh McWilliams, 29 July 1814 in Maury.]

DAVIS W. ARMER
Served in Capt. John Looney's company. No further information.

ROBERT ARMER
Served in Capt. John Looney's company. No further information. (Robert Armir appears on 1812 tax list of Stewart County; Robert Armour on 1820 census of Dickson County.)

ALEXANDER ARMSTRONG
Served in Capt. Samuel B. McKnight's company; on one muster roll of this company his name appears to be Abram Armstrong. No further information.

JOHN ARMSTRONG
Enlisted 4 Oct. 1813 as private in Capt. William Dooley's company, Col. Thomas McCrory; discharged 16 Dec. 1813. Enlisted 25 Sept. 1814 in Capt. McMahan's company of 1st Tennessee Gunmen, Col. Robert H. Dyer. No further information.

JOHN ARMSTRONG
Served as private in Capt. McMahon's company. No further information.

JOSEPH ARMSTRONG
Enlisted and served in Capt. Samuel B. McKnight's company. No further information.

BENJAMIN ARNOLD
Served in Capt. John Looney's company. No further information.

DAVID T. ARNOLD
Served in Capt. William Dooley's company as private. David Arnold took out marriage bond 14 Dec. 1814 to marry Polly M. Powell; William Nix was bondsman. In 1820 a

David Arnold, continued:

deed of gift was made by Thomas Arnold for land on Silver Creek in Maury County and the Thomas Arnold children were listed: William Arnold, Betsy Nix, David Arnold, Francis Nix, John Arnold, Polly Arnold, Rhoda Arnold, and Agnes Arnold.

FRANCIS ARNOLD

Enlisted 20 Sept. 1814 as private in Capt. Thomas Wells' company, Col. Leroy Hammonds. No further information.

ROBERT ARNOLD

Commissioned lieutenant in 27th regiment, Maury County militia, 1813; marriage bond to marry Polly Gordon dated 6 Dec. 1810, with Moses Arnold, bondsman.

SAMUEL ASHMORE

Commissioned as officer in militia in 1810; captain of 27th regiment, Maury County militia in 1811; 1812 had land near head of Lytles Creek. Mentioned in 1812 as a trustee of Ebenezer Presbyterian Church. (Maury County Deed Book E, Vol. 1, page 55.)

JESSE ATKINSON

Enlisted as private 18 Dec. 1813 in Capt. James McMahan's militia infantry, Col. N. T. Perkins. No further information. [Mrs. Marise Lightfoot believes that this man might be the son of John Atkinson, Sr., Revolutionary War soldier of Cumberland County, Va., born 18 Sept. 1755, died 2 April 1837, who had a son Jesse Atkinson. John Sr. was married in Cumberland County 6 Nov 1777 to Mary Armistead, born 17 Feb. 1758, still living in 1839.]

JOHN ATKINSON

Enlisted 18 Dec. 1813 in Capt. James McMahan's militia infantry, Col. N. T. Perkins. [Believed to be John Atkinson, Jr., son of John and Mary Armistead Atkinson. John Atkinson, Jr., came to Maury County from Pittsylvania Co., Va., in 1811, and moved to Williamson County, Tenn., about two years later.]

JOHN AVERITT

Served in Captain John Looney's company. In 1811 he paid taxes in Maury County for land on Fountain Creek. No further information.

+ARTHUR AYDELOTTE

Enlisted 21 Nov. 1812 as first corporal in Capt. Robert Cannon's company, Col. Thomas Benton. Enlisted as private 20 Sept. 1814 in Capt. John Looney's company, 2d regiment of Tennessee militia, Col. Alexander Loury. Died 18 March 1815. (This deathdate is from muster roll.) However, on 25 Feb. 1815 letters of administration on his estate were given by the Maury County court to Jedeah Aydellott, indicating that his death took place earlier than given on muster roll.

THOMAS W. AYDOLOTT

Commissioned ensign in the 46th regiment, Maury County, 1813. [A Thomas Aydelott will be found on Maury County tax lists in 1811 and one of this same name on the 1807 tax list of Williamson County. This man lived along Snow Creek and was often assigned to work on the road that led from the Natchez Trace to the Suck Island in Duck River.]

JAMES AYRES

Served in Capt. John Chisholm's company; name found as John Ayres on one roll of this company. [James Ayres marriage bond to Tabitha Williams, 8 Feb. 1817, with Arthur Ayres, bondsman.]

JOSEPH AYRES

Enlisted as private 20 Sept. 1814 in Capt. John Looney's company, 2d West Tennessee militia, Col. Alxander Loury. Ayres ex parte 1854 says: "died some years ago." In 1810 had land on Snow Creek. (Deed Book D, Vol. 1, page 229.) He was often assigned to work on the road leading to Hunter's Ford on Duck River. Married 23 Dec. 1818 to Alma Holliman.

Children of Joseph Ayres:
1. Mary J.   (The oldest of these three children described as 12 years old
2. Margaret   in 1854, but not identified.)
3. Thomas

(Source: Maury County 1818 marriages; Ayres Ex Parte, 1854.)

JOHN BACHELOR

Pension application, dated 28 Sept. 1850, Stoddard County, Mo.: John Bachelor, age 56, resident of Stoddard County, was trumpeter in a company commanded by Capt. John Baseowell in the Middle Tennessee Light Horse Volunteer commanded by Colonels Coffee and Alcorn in War of 1812; volunteered as substitute for a Mr. Steel at Nashville on 15 Dec. 1812 for term of two years, out of which he was to serve one year and continued in active service for twelve months in the war; never received discharge but twelve months subsequent to dismissal General William Carroll paid the deponent and his company in Gallatin, Sumner County, Tenn., for as soon as this term of service expired he and his company started directly for home about Dec. 15.

Appeared 9 June 1855, John Bachelor, aged about 65 years, resident of Stoddard Co., Mo., who said he was in Capt. John Baseowell's company in War of 1812. Got land warrant in 1850 for 80 acres which he has legally transferred and disposed of; now asks for more land. Signed: John (X) Bachelor, (Batchelor).

On 27 April 1878, at Stoddard County, Mo., Jane Batchelor, aged 68 years, says she is widow of John Batcbelor, who enlisted under Capt. John Baskwell under General Coffee. John died in Stoddard County, Mo., 8 Aug. 1868; he served as private. She married John Batchelor in Bedford Co., Tenn., in or about July 1839 by James Smith, J. P., there being no legal barrier to such marriage and that her husband had been previously married but his first wife was dead before said marriage and that she had not been previously married and her maiden name was Jane Lenesett (?). Signed Jane X Batchelor.

12 Dec. 1892 Jane Bachelor, widow of 1812 soldier, was dropped because of her death; she was last paid 18 April 1892, $12.

Bachelor, Jr., versus Bachelor, Sr., 1846, in Maury County chancery court gives further information on this soldier (not genealogical). He owned land on Rutherford Creek in Maury County in 1840.

(Source: Pension record of John Bachelor, widow's pension of Jane Bachelor.)

JAMES A. BAILES

Served in Captain Bird S. Hurt's company. No further information.

ANDREW BAKER

Commissioned ensign in 27th regiment, Maury County militia, 1811. He lived in the Snow Creek area of Maury County.

ISAIAH BAKER

Enlisted 13 Nov. 1814 as private in Capt. Bird S. Hurt's company, Col. William Metcalf infantry regiment. No further information.

JOHN BAKER
Enlisted 20 Sept. 1814 as private in Capt. Thomas Well's company; Colonel Leroy Hammond and Colonel Alexander Loury. No further information.

AMOS P. BALCH
Commissioned lieutenant in 27th regiment, Maury County militia, in 1812. [The only man of this name in the county was Amos Balch, who lived at Zion in 1811. He and his wife Patsy were members of this church and their children were Selina, Livinia, and John Witherspoon Balch.]

(Source: "Zion Presbyterian Church, Columbia, Tenn., Serving Christ and Community since 1907", souvenir booklet published 1957, page 13.)

JAMES BALGRAVE
Served in Capt. John Looney's company. No further information.

JOSEPH BALLANFANT
Service not determined; was stationed in Norfolk, Va., during War of 1812 and his wife drew a widow's pension for his service. He was born 14 Nov. 1790 at Halifax County, Va., died 9 Nov. 1869 at 79; eldest son of John Ballanfant of France. He married 22 April 1819 in Williamson County, Tenn., to Sally Turner, fifth daughter of James Turner (Revolutionary War soldier of Williamson County), who was born 7 August 1801 in Caswell Co., N. C., and died 18 April 1876 at 75. They are buried in the Ballanfant Cemetery at Culleoka, Tennessee.

Children of Joseph Ballanfant:
1. John Ballanfant, born 7 March 1820, Williamson County, married first cousin Eliza Estes Turner. (Bible record gives his birth year as 1821.)
2. No information on other children available to the chapter.

(Source: Maury County Cousins, published by Maury County Historical Society, 1967, pages 290-292; They Passed This Way, by Marise P. Lightfoot and Evelyn Shackelford, published 1965, page D-208; Columbia Herald and Mail, 21 April 1876.)

GEORGE BANKHEAD
Commissioned lieutenant, 27th regiment, Maury County militia, 1813. No further information.

ALEXANDER A. BARNES
Served in Capt. Bird S. Hurt's company. No further information.

ALEXANDER S. BARNES
Enlisted 13 Nov. 1814 as private in Capt. Bird Hurt's company, Colonel William Metcalfe's infantry. No further information. [Maybe the same as the one above.]

JOHN W. BARR
Commissioned ensign in 27th regiment, Maury County militia, 1812. No further information.

KINCHEN T. BASS
Served in Capt. John Looney's company; by 1830 was in Giles County. No further information.

HOSEAH R. BATEMAN
Served as private in Capt. Robert Evans company, 28 Sept. 1814 to 28 March 1815. Hosea Bateman will be found on 1840 census of Maury County. No further information available on this man.

SIMON BATEMAN

Enlisted 18 June 1812 in Capt. David Mason's company, militia cavalry, in Williamson County; served until 31 July 1812. He married 4 Nov. 1807 (date of bond) to Penny Brady in Williamson County. Penelope Bateman sued her husband Simon Bateman for a divorce in Maury County in 1832 charging desertion in 1826.

An advertisement in Independent Gazette, Franklin, Tenn., dated 2 Feb. 1822: "I have rented for five years the ferry at Reynoldsburgh...There is now a road opened around what is called the 3 mile slew only a small distance farther than the public way so that high water will never be any obstruction to passengers. Signed, Simon Bateman."

Penelope Bateman will be found on the 1830 Lincoln County census; one "S. Bateman" will be found in Shelby County on 1830 census.

THOMAS H. BATY

Reported as War of 1812 soldier; however service for him found in Seminole War when he enlisted 31 Jan. 1818 at Columbia as private in Capt. John A. Chapman's company, Thomas Williamson, colonel, regiment of Volunteered Mounted Gunmen. He died April 1857 and was buried in the Baty Cemetery on the Scribner Mill Road in Maury County.

JAMES BAXTER

"Served as lieutenant at New Orleans, one of the youngest officers in service." No definite service record established. He was the son of Jeremiah Baxter (born 4 Nov. 1777, died 20 August 1833) and his wife Catherine Baldwin (born 20 March 1778, died 21 Sept. 1844). The Baxters came to Tennessee in 1810, first settling in Nashville, then in Dickson County, and eventually in Maury. (In the part that became Marshall County.) James Baxter was born 15 August 1798. The Baxter Cemetery is located on Silver Creek in Marshall County.

Brothers and sisters of James Baxter:
1. Nancy Baxter, born 18 Sept. 1800, married Edward Woodward.
2. Lucy Baxter, born 9 Jan. 1803, married William Armstrong and lived in Calloway County, Missouri.
3. Sally Baxter, born 29 April 1805, married Edward B. Smith.
4. Elizabeth Baxter, born 16 July 1808, married Joseph Highland.
5. Nathaniel Baxter, Sr., born 13 Nov. 1812 in Charlotte, Tenn., married Mary L. Jones.
6. Evaline Baxter, born 11 Jan. 1815.
7. Montgomery Baxter, born 15 April 1817, killed 1836 in the Battle of San Jacinto.
8. William Fletcher Baxter, born 5 May 1820, died 28 Oct. 1898, married 1. Sara C. Harris; married 2. Martha J. Harris; he is buried in Harris Cemetery in Marshall County.
9. Amanda Baxter, born 10 April 1822; married a Nunn.

Sources: John Trotwood Moore, Tennessee the Volunteer State, Volume 2, page 786; Maury County Cousins, page 122; Maury County Neighbors, by Marise P. Lightfoot and Evelyn Shackelford, page 80; Maury County Chancery Court Records, by Jill K. Garrett and Marise P. Lightfoot, page 9. Jeremiah Baxter's will is recorded in Maury County.

+EDWARD W. BEANLAND

Enlisted 20 Sept. 1814 as fourth corporal in Capt. John Looney's company, Colonel Alexander Loury, 2d Regiment West Tennessee Militia; died 17 March 1815. He had been a constable in 1809, resigning in March of that year. He married Mary _____; she later married Peter Williams, who was on the first court of Marshall County. His son Ephraim was overseer for James K. Polk's property in Mississippi and there has been much published correspondence between the two men.
Continued on next page.

Children of Edward Beanland:
1. Edward Gibson Beanland
2. Priscilla Beanland, married 19 Aug. 1828 to Thomas B. Kennelly.
3. Leonard W. Beanland married 28 Oct. 1824 Matilda Bowden.
4. Druscilla or Matilda Beanland (name found as both in separate accounts)
5. Fennell (or Fenwell) Beanland
6. Ephraim (or Eppa) Beanland.
7. Matilda Beanland — name found on a list of Beanland's children dated 19 July 1819. May be the same as Druscilla.

All children were minors at father's death as Mary Beanland was appointed guardian. Mary Beanland was also called Polly Beanland.

(Sources: Maury County court minutes, Book 5, page 99; Correspondence of James K. Polk, Volume 2, pages 442-443; Maury County court minutes and estate settlements for 1815; 1817 deeds.)

ALEXANDER BEARD
No service established; drew pension; lived in Mt. Pleasant. Columbia Herald and Mail, 6 Aug. 1875, says "has lived in present home forty years."

ARTHUR BEATY
Served in Capt. John Looney's company. No further information.

JOHN BEATY
Commissioned ensign 1812 in 27th regiment of Maury County militia; served as a sergeant in Capt. Samuel B. McKnight's company.

RICHARD BEATY
Served in Capt. John Looney's company. No further information.

ABRAHAM BEAVERS
Served in Capt. Robert Campbell's company. No further information.

JAMES BEAVERS
Served in Captain John Gordon's company.

THOMAS BEDFORD
No service established; one source says served in War of 1812; another says in the Florida War. Lived in the Cathey's Creek area. No further information.

JOHN BELL
Enlisted as private in company of spies commanded by Captain John Gordon. Marriage bond dated 17 Sept. 1814 to Polly Alexander with Thomas Bell as bondsman. He kept a small diary while in service, entries follow:

Volunteered: William Kirk of comming with him to John Gordin spy Company for a six week touer. 1813   1814

1. Thomas Shoate
2. George Isom
3. Thomas Cats
4. John Bell
5. James Lagfort
6. Alexander Wiley
7. John Faris
8. Andrew Blair
9. Blank
10. Sam Perry
11. Homes H. Hopkins
12. Walker Knox
13. John Hudleston

State of Tennessee, Maury County
December the sixth day 1813 — Started from home on the six day and traveled at the

John Bell, continued:
distance of about sixteen miles to the town of Columbia, rendvoused at Chiton, and
had a very pleasant night with my neighbors and fellow soldiers—

on the seventh we commence our march about two oclock under the command of William
Kirk at which we traveled about ten miles and we camped.

on the eight we traveled up fountain Creek and crest a ridg traveled down lin Creek
and crossed richland creek & down it throug Pulsky and traveled with in about four
miles of elk river & camp.

on the ninth we marched on with in about three miles of huntsville and camp.

on the tenth we marched on to tennessee and thare we campt at Dettos landing.

on the eleventh we crest tennessee at Dettos landing and traveled till we came to fort
Deposit and campt.

on sunday the twelth we left fort Deposit and marched at the distance of about
twenty four miles camped at Sam Dinisian house.

on monday the thirteenth we traveled on til we came to fort Strother on Coosa at
the ilant and there we campt.

on tuesday the fourteenth wednesday the fifteenth, thursday the sixteenth, friday
the seventeeth Saturday the eighteenth we lay at fort Strother.

on sunday the nineteenth munday the twentieth we marched to little fuchee and there
we reconertered about and found some corn and a great many other indian utensials.

on tuesday the twentifirst we came to fort Strother — on wednesday the twentsecond
we marched back and brought back the ballance of the corn. on thursday the twent-
thurd on the twenty fourth and twenty fifth we lay at camp. Chrismas cave there was
the greatest fireing of guns that I ever heard in my life. on Sunday the twenty
sixth, munday the twenty seventh, tuesday the twenty eight, wednesday the twenty
nineth, thursday the thirth. We arrived at Cahaula river there was hostile Indians
villag but they had vachuated their houses and had camp down the river about two
miles. We marched down there but was gone. We came back and camp in the town all
night, burnt houses and marched on friday thirty first about sixteen miles and campt.

On Saturday the first day of January 1814, on Sunday the second we arrived at fort
Strother, monday the third, tuesday the fourth, wednesday the fifth, thursday the
sixth, Friday the seventh, Saturday the eight, Sunday the ninth, monday the tenth,
tuesday the eleventh, wednesday the twelvth, thursday the thirteenth, friday the
fourteenth, Saturday the fifteenth we commence our march to the fish pond. on Sunday we lay on tallashatha Creek. Monday we camp at Shoal Creek. on tuesday we camp
tallidego.

on wednesday, thursday, friday, we campt on ilant. on saturday January 22, 1814,
the indians attacked us and the battle lasted about half hour and the indians re-
treated that day we had two more attacks by the indians but we repulsed them both
times. on our march back on the 24th day we had another attack and beet indians
again.

(Source: Historic Maury, published 1965 by the Maury County Historical Society. Some
explanatory notes were included: "This diary lay dormant in the Spencer family all
these years until recently when Sam Spencer of Detroit sent a photostat copy to Mrs.
Ethel Jones Whiteside of Hampshire." The copy was furnished to the Maury County
Historical Society by Paul Delk of Hampshire, Tennessee.)

STEPHENSON BELL
Commissioned ensign in Maury County militia in 1810—name also found as Stinson Bell.
Had brothers Sterling, James, Thomas, and John Bell. Lived in Cathey's Creek area.

THOMAS HART BENTON
Born 14 March 1782 in Hillsboro, N. C., died of cancer of stomach 10 April 1858 at
Washington, D. C.; served as colonel in War of 1812. Admitted to practice law in
Maury County and Maury County Court Minutes, Book 2, page 101, has the following
item of interest: "Ordered that Thomas H. Benton be fined $1 for profane swearing
in presence of the court and he paid the fine to the clerk." His residency was brief
and he is more closely identified with Williamson County. He was son of Jesse and
Ann Gooch Benton. Later senator from Missouri; married 1821 Elizabeth McDowell,
daughter of James and Sarah McDowell of Rockbridge County, Virginia; she died in
1854.

Children of Thomas Hart Benton:
1. Randolph Benton, died young.
2. James McDowell Benton, died young.
3. Eliza Benton
4. Sarah Benton.
5. Susan Benton.
6. Jessie Benton married John Charles Fremont.

Brothers and sisters of Thomas Hart Benton:
1. Jesse Benton, had notable fight with Andrew Jackson in Nashville in 1813.
2. Five of his brothers and sisters died of tuberculosis.
3. An eighth child, no information.

Sources: Clarksville Jeffersonian, 14 April 1858; Maury County Court Minutes, Book 2,
entry for 20 June 1810; Historic Williamson County, by Virginia McDaniel Bowman, published 1971, page 170.)

SAMUEL BERRY
Served in Capt. John Gordon's company. No further information.

ALFRED BESON
Served in Capt. James McMahan's company. No further information.

JOHN BIFFLE
Served in Capt. Samuel B. McKnight's company; died before 1844. Marriage bond to
Polly Chambers dated 17 May 1814; believed to have died in Wayne County, Tennessee;
son of Jacob Biffle, Revolutionary War soldier.

Children of John Biffle:
1. Col. Jacob B. Biffle, born about 1828, died 1 Jan. 1877 in Texas. Famous
   Confederate Cavalry officer.
2. Mary Ann Biffle, born about 1826, died 1860, married Amos T. Hassell.
3. Nathan Fletcher Biffle, born about 1828, buried in Reed Cemetery, Myra, Texas.
4. James C. Biffle, born about 1820.
5. William D. Biffle.

Brothers and sisters of John Biffle:
1. Valentine Biffle, believed to have lived in Wayne County.
2. Nathan Biffle, born 16 March 1792, died 3 May 1853, buried at Ashland, Wayne
   County, Tenn. Married Ursula.
3. Catherine married John Akin.
4. Elizabeth married William Burns.
5. Emily, born 1 June 1795, died 28 March 1871, married Samuel Akin. Continued.

John Biffle, continued:
6. William Biffle, born 31 July 1803, died 31 Aug. 1885, married Frances Isom.
7. Susan Biffle married Miles Burns.
8. Jacob Biffle, Jr., died 29 Sept. 1830.

(Sources: Nashville Banner and Nashville Whig, 14 Oct. 1830; Mrs. Jo Ann Biffle
Sterling, Lawton, Oklahoma, descendant of Nathan Fletcher Biffle; Maury County
Neighbors, Marise P. Lightfoot and Evelyn B. Shackelford, quoting Lewis County
Circuit Court Minute Book 1, pages 7, 11, 17, 25, and Lewis County Enrollment
Book, March 1845, page 4.)

ISAAC BILLS

Commissioned captain of 27th regiment, Maury County militia, 1808; constable of
Maury County 1809. He was born 10 or 19 Nov. 1773 or 1775, died 24 Aug. 1821, buried in Bills Cemetery on Mooresville Pike; married Lillias Houston, born 6 Nov. 1773,
died 26 Feb. 1850; her tombstone in same cemetery says they were married 27 years.
Son of Daniel Bills (born 28 Sept. 1840 in Coon, died 18 March 1829, Maury County,
now the part that is Marshall) and his wife Deborah Denman, died 26 March 1819.

Children of Isaac Bills:
1. Alvin W. Bills.
2. John H. Bills.
3. Placebo M. Bills, born 1803, died 1828. (Dates in question as stone is worn.)
4. Sarah E. Bills.
5. Oliva L. Bills.
6. Isaac Newton Bills, born 1812, died 1854.
7. Martha E. Bills.

Brothers and sisters of Isaac Bills:
1. William Bills married Susannah Hutchins.
2. Rachel Bills married James Jackson.
3. Gersham Bills married Polly Hutchins.
4. Hannah Bills married William Marshall.
5. Sallie Bills married Amos London.
6. Patience Bills married James Houston.
7. Thomas Bills married Mary Collins.
8. Jonathan Bills married 1. _____, 2. Kate Royal.
9. Daniel Bills, born 1789, died 1845, married Mary Ketchum.
10. John Bills married Susan Powell.

Sources: Maury County Cousins, pages 202, 209; Tennessee Historical Quarterly,
March 1959, pages 54-68; They Passed This Way, Marise P. Lightfoot and Evelyn B.
Shackelford, page D-144; Roster of Soldiers and Patriots of the American Revolution
Buried in Tennessee, published 1974, Lucy Womack Bates, chairman, page 37.

JAMES BIRMINGHAM (Also spelled Burmingham)

Enlisted as private 20 Dec. 1813 in Capt. John Doak's company, Col. N. T. Perkins.
In 1811 he was assigned to take taxes in Maury County in Captain Scott's militia
company; in Dec. 1809 assigned to work on road leading from Natchez Trace to Suck
Island of Duck River.

LEVI H. BLACKARD

Served in Captain Bird S. Hurt's company. No further information. One Levy Blackard
appears on 1820 census of Lawrence County, Tenn.

ELIJAH BLOCKER

born about 1792, died 12 June _____; commissioned captain in 27th regiment of Maury
Militia in 1812; blacksmith. He married Susan Priscilla Winn, born 1793, daughter
of General Richard Winn. There is some question about his birthdate as one source
says his son Richard R. was born 1796. The old Blocker Cemetery near Sawdust was

Elijah Blocker continued:
destroyed around 1918. Sawdust was at one time known as Blocker's Shop for this man.

Children of Elijah Blocker:
1. Samuel A. Blocker, died in Missouri, married 22 Oct. 1839 to Margaret J. Laird.
2. Thomas Pinkney Blocker, killed in Civil War; married 23 June 1839 Julia Farrell.
3. Eliza Christine Blocker, married 29 July 1847 to Thomas L. Huckaby.
4. Mary Caroline Blocker, died in Missouri, marriage license issued 3 April 1839 to Willie R. Lamb.
5. Susan Roxanna Blocker, died 1871, married 21 Sept. 1841 Allen P. Nicks of Hickman County.
6. Sarah Selina Blocker, died 1894, married 2 March 1843 to George W. Young of Winnsboro.
7. Margaret S. Blocker, married 15 June 1845 to Dr. Absalom O. Nicks.
8. Martha Jane Blocker, born 22 Dec. 1834, died 27 Oct. 1908, married William Riley Conner 14 June 1852.
9. Richard R. Blocker. Century Review, page 299, says he was born 1796, however, he is shown as 36 on the 1850 census of Maury County.

Sources: 1850 Census, Maury County; Century Review, History and Directory of Maury County, published 1907, page 299; Frank H. Smith's History of Maury County, published by the Maury County Historical Society.

ANDREW BLAIR
Served in Capt. John Gordon's spy company; born 22 Nov. 1792, died 12 Oct. 1828, buried in Blair Cemetery near Hampshire; married 7 Jan. 1819 to Harriet Walker, born 19 Jan. 1796, died 27 Oct. 1819, buried Blair Cemetery.

Children of Andrew Blair:
1. Harriet Walker Blair, born 27 Sept. 1819, married 17 Aug. 1837 to George P. Webster.

WILLIAM BOAZ
Commissioned ensign 1814 in militia in Pittsylvania Co., Va., born 27 June 1783, died 27 Oct. 1852 at New Ramia Cemetery, Stiversville; married Mariah Bullington, born 3 May 1785, died 23 Aug. 1852 in Maury County.

Children of William Boaz:
1. Robert Boaz, born 14 June 1807.
2. Elizabeth Boaz, born 1809, died 21 Oct. 1887, married Allen Richardson.
3. Louras (?) Boaz, born 20 May 1810.
4. John Boaz, born 28 Oct. 1811, died 17 March 1854.
5. Polly Boaz, born 10 March 1813, died 8 May 1821.
6. David Boaz, born 26 March 1814, died 13 March 1855.
7. William Boaz, born 23 Aug. 1816.
8. George Boaz, born 9 Jan. 1818, died 4 April 1821.
9. Lydia Boaz, born 16 March 1819, died 7 April 1819.
10. Julia Ann Boaz, born 17 Dec. 1820, died 28 Dec. 1865.
11. Daniel Boaz, born 4 Oct. 1822.
12. Rebecca Boaz, born 1 May 1824.
13. Nancy P. Boaz, born 1 March 1826.

Sources: Descendant, Barry Brown, Spring Hill, Tenn.; Century Review of Maury County, page 307; Maury County Cousins, published by Maury County Historical Society, quoting Richardson Bible, page 293.

WILLIAM BOGARD

Served in Capt. John Gordon's company of spies. Son of Jacob Bogard, who died 1820, survived by a widow Susannah Board. No further information on the soldier.

Brothers and sisters of William Bogard:
1. James Bogard
2. John J. Bogard, married 11 Jan. 1822 to Nancy Hickman.
3. Abraham Bogard, married 1820 to Sarah Porter.
4. Polly Bogard married 1820 to Thomas Tidwell.
5. Alexander A. Bogard, minor heir of Jacob in 1821.
6. Susannah Bogard, minor heir of Jacob in 1821.

Source: January 1821 Circuit Court, Case 55, William and Jacob Bogard vs T. C. Gholson, Elliott and others when death of Jacob suggested to court; petition of Susannah Bogard, widow and relict of Jacob Bogard.

JOHN BOOKER

born about 1776 in N. C., commissioned ensign in 27th regiment, Maury County militia in 1808; still living in 1850; married Susanna _____. His age was given as between 25 and 45 in 1820 and his household contained three males and four females, possibly his children and one female aged between 26 and 45. On 20 May 1816 he got license to keep ordinary in county with William Yancy and John Muse as his securities.

PETER RICHARDSON BOOKER

County solicitor during War of 1812; born in Virginia; died 10 May 1839 in Somerville, Tenn., and buried there. He married 16 April 1806 in Williamson County to Susan Gray, who died in 1829; he married second to Mrs. Cynthia Holland Rodes in Giles County.

Children of Peter R. Booker:
1. Richard M. Booker, born 14 July 1808, died 14 Nov. 1831.
2. James Gray Booker, born 4 Nov. 1809, died 19 Aug. 1846, married Ellen Smiser.
3. Henry Leonidas Booker, born 9 Aug. 1814 died 31 March 1841, married Mary Ann H. Porter, daughter of Nimrod Porter.
4. Martha Elizabeth Booker, born about 1816, married Adam Dickey and Armstead Bracken.
5. Albert Booker, born 22 April 1820, died 25 June 1856, married Ruth A. Johnson.
6. Susan M. Booker, born 23 July 1823, married Oliver P. Catron.
7. Mary Florida Booker, born 12 March 1825, married Lewis M. Scott.
8. Peter R. Booker, Jr., born 12 Oct. 1827, died 11 March 1849, married 11 Nov. 1847 in Williamson County to Mary T. Garland.
9. Cornelia L. Booker, born 5 (or 3) June 1829, married Joseph R. Moseley.

Brothers and sisters of Peter R. Booker:
1. Richard M. Booker.
2. Possibly others, no further information.
3. Merrit H. Booker, born 1787, died 1839.

Letter from James Dick, dated 17 Feb. 1839, New Orleans, to his sister Mrs. Sarah Todd, Columbia, Tenn.: "Mr. Peter R. Booker is gaining strength slowly. He improve in walking and rides out in a carriage an hour or two every day that is fine."

Letter from James Dick, dated 29 May 1839, New Orleans, to his sister Mrs. Sarah Todd: "We had heard the day previous of the death of Mr. Peter R. Booker. He had left here very feeble, but we had strong hopes that he could be able to reach home. His own over anxiety perhaps caused him to make over exertions to get on, and he sunk under them." (Abstracted from family letters belonging to Mrs. Thornton Ryan, Columbia, Tenn.) Sources: Maury County chancery court records, Vol. 1 and Vol. Maury County Cousins.

GEORGE C. BOOTHE
Served in Capt. Robert Campbell's company. No further information. [A George C. Boothe, born 1756, died after 1840, served on the Virginia line during the American Revolution; drew pension in Rutherford County, Tenn.]

WILLIAM BOYAKIN
Served in Capt. Robert Campbell's company as an ensign. Name also found as Willie Boyakin. A man of this name was in the county and signed the petition to form the county in 1807.

ELIJAH BOYD
Served in Capt. Samuel Ashmore's company. No further information.

JAMES BOYD
Commissioned lieutenant in 27th Regiment of Maury County militia in 1812. No further information.

JAMES BOYD
Served as private in Capt. William Dooley's company.
[One James Boyd in the county was the son of Andrew Boyd and James died 15 Sept. 1825 in the county. Dower was set aside for Elizabeth P. Boyd, widow of James Boyd in 1826.]

JOHN BOYD
Served in Capt. Samuel Ashmore's company. No further information. [Andrew Boyd, soldier of the American Revolution, mentions in his will, recorded 29 Aug. 1829, his wife Sarah and his children: John R. Boyd, Winifred Boyd, Sally Boyd, Mrs. Thomas P. McKnight of Lauderdale County, Ala., and Mrs. Lewis Glass.]

JAMES R. BOYLE
Served in Capt. Robert Campbell's company. One roll of same company gives his name as John Boyle. No further information.

GEORGE BRADBURY
Resigned as constable in Maury County in Sept. 1808; he was still living in the county at least as late as 1811. No further information.

HUGH BRADFORD
Served in Capt. Andrew McCarty's company. No further information. [A Hugh Bradford appears on the 1820 census of Hickman County.]

WILLIAM R. BRADLEY
Served in Capt. James McMahan's second company. No further information.

ELI G. BRADSHAW
Served as private in Capt. William Dooley's company; born 2 July 1791, died 7 Feb. 1872, buried at Evergreen Cemetery near Campbell Station. His wife Sarah N., also buried there, was born 14 Sept. 1787, died 15 Dec. 1852. Eli Bradshaw gave the land for Evergreen Church, located one mile south of Campbell Station.

Sources: Tombstone inscriptions from "They Passed This Way"; Columbia Herald and Mail, 11 Aug. 1876.

JOHN BRADSHAW
Commissioned ensign 1812 in 27th regiment of Maury County militia. No further information.

SOLOMON BRADSHAW
Mustered 28 Jan. 1814 in Capt. Samuel Ashmore's company, Col. R. C. Napier's regiment

Solomon Bradshaw continued:

and mustered out and discharged 10 May 1814. He owned land on Fountain Creek and is said to have settled near Campbell Station between 1806 and 1810.

WILLIAM BRADSHAW

Third sheriff of Maury County, serving during the War of 1812. Born Dec. 1777, died at the age of 47 (his tombstone is shaled and difficult to read); buried in Bradshaw Cemetery; married Elizabeth _____, born Dec. 1785, died 30 Jan. 1832, also buried in Bradshaw Cemetery on Lytles Creek.

Children of William Bradshaw:
1. Hugh, born 1804, died 1866, married Caroline C. Gwinn Ford.
2. Americus, died 4 Aug. 176 at the age of 74, married Mary A. C. Martin, born 1817, died 1848, daughter of David and Sarah Martin. He was the last of the four brothers.
3. William Bradshaw.
4. Thomas Bradshaw, died Feb. 1875 at the age of 67; never married.
5. Edward Bradshaw.
6. Martha H. Bradshaw, born 1809, died 1840, married William P. Martin.
7. Elizabeth Bradshaw married George W. Gordon.
8. Margaret Bradshaw married Bernard Myers.

Sources: Nathan Vaught, "Youth and Old Age", (unpublished), page 63; "They Passed This Way", page D-141; Columbia Herald and Mail 26 Feb. 1875; Maury Intelligencer, 30 Nov. 1848, 1 Feb. 1849.

SANFORD BRAMLET

Enlisted 13 Nov. 1814 in Capt. James Gray's company, Col. John Cook's regiment, and served until 10 May 1815. On 18 Nov. 1816 a pillory was ordered erected on the public square to carry out the execution of a sentence against Sanford Bramlet and Martin Gurley sentenced by circuit court for horse stealing. In 1839 he petitioned the state for the restoration of his citizenship. A man of this name is living in 1830 in Obion County, Tenn.

HENRY BRANCH

Served in Capt. James McMahan's company. In 1810 a man of this name was assigned to work on the road in the Knob Creek area. A man of this name also lived in the Pottsville area of the county. No further information.

CORNELIUS BREWER

Served in Capt. Benjamin Reynolds' second company. Later lived in Wayne County and still living there in the 1870s.

GEORGE BREWER

Served in Capt. Benjamin Reynolds' first company. Believed to be the one who went to Wayne County and was living there in 1850, age 62, born in Georgia, with Martha, age 52, born in S. C., in his household.

DRURY BRIDGES

Appointed constable in Maury County March 1811. He died 1812 when an inventory of his estate was recorded with wife Polly as executor; brother Daniel L. Bridges, also executor.

Source: Maury County Wills and Settlements.

RICHARD BRIDGEWATERS

Served as first lieutenant in Capt. Robert Campbell's company. Believed to be the same man who was commissioned lieutenant in 1813 in the 50th regiment from Montgomery County and may not have been from Maury County.

HENRY BROOKS
Served in Capt. James McMahan's company. No further information.

ISAAC BROOKS
Served in Capt. James McMahan's company. No further information.

JAMES BROOKS
Served in Capt. James McMahan's second company. Married 24 Nov. 1810 to Easther Hopkins in Maury County with Samuel Crawford as his bondsman. No further information.

SAMUEL BROOKS
Served as private in Capt. William Dooley's company. [The 1812 tax list of Maury County shows a Samuel Brooks, Sr. Letters of administration on his estate were given to Samuel Brooks, Jr. On 19 May 1815 an inventory of estate was returned to court. The soldier was possibly the son.]

SAMUEL T. BROOKS
Served as first lieutenant in Capt. James McMahan's company. Son of Hezekiah Brooks (died 1835) and his wife Elizabeth.

Brothers and sisters of Samuel T. Brooks:
1. Paulina Brooks married Peyton C. Smithson.
2. Sarah Brooks married Andrew J. Bynum.
3. Hawkins Brooks.
4. Mary Brooks.
5. Ruth Brooks married William W. Tarkington.
6. Hiram Brooks.
7. Nancy Brooks married Jacob S. Notgrass.
8. Parthenia Brooks married Josiah Butts.

Souce: Smith vs Chaffin 1848, unpublished chancery court records.

JONATHAN BROOM
Served in Capt. Robert Campbell's company. Year's support was given to his widow Mary (Polly) Broom on 15 Aug. 1814. Commisione appointed to settle his estate in Nov. 1816. This man lived around Williamsport. In an old abandoned cemetery there is a stone for a Mary E. Broom, born 25 June 1815, died 4 April 1836, possibly some member of his family.

ABRAHAM BROWN
Served in Capt. John Looney's company. No further information.

DANIEL BROWN
Served in Bird S. Hurt's company. [There were at least two Daniel Browns in the county and it has been impossible to determine which one was the soldier. One of these lived in 1811 on Rutherford Creek and died 8 May 1829. His children were Daniel C. and Nancy Brown and possibly others. Another was Daniel Brown, Sr., who had children: Sally Hill, Nancy Atkinson, Jesse Brown, and Daniel Brown, Jr.]

LEONARD BROWN
Served in Capt. John Looney's company. No further information.

JOSEPH BROWN
Served as private in Capt. William Dooley's company. No further information.

JOSEPH BROWN
Served as cornet in Capt. James McMahan's company. No further information.

JOSEPH BROWN

Colonel during the Creek War, 1813-1814. Born 2 August 1772 in Guilford County, North Carolina; died 4 Feb. 1868 in Giles County, buried at Mt. Moriah Cemetery; married 19 Jan. 1796 to Sarah Thomas, born 21 June 1774, died 19 June 1840. He was the son of James and Jane Gillespie Brown. The first court of Maury County met in his home in 1807. Brown School in Columbia (in 1975) was named for him.

Children of Joseph Brown:
1. James, born 25 Oct. 1796, died 16 Jan. 1880, married Mary Ann Strong.
2. John Thomas, born 26 Jan. 1799, died 18 Aug. 1848, married Nancy White.
3. Joseph Porter Brown, born 1808, died 30 Sept. 1844 in Galveston, Texas, of yellow fever, married Jane Stewart Frazier.
4. Dr. David Franklin Brown, born 17 March 1801, died 1869, married Jane Frances McNeal, born 11 May 1813, died 25 June 1852.
5. Sarah Minerva Brown married Dr. Zebina Conkey.
6. Esther Elizabeth Brown married Martin M. Lane.
7. Amelia Ann Brown, born 15 Nov. 1813, died 5 Sept. 1899, married John James Phillip Lindsay.
8. Jane Gillespie Brown, died 1826, married Dr. Elisha S. Hall.
9. [One source said he had a son Joshua T. Brown—the editors of this book made no attempt to document or disprove this child.]

Brothers and sisters of Joseph Brown:
1. James Brown, killed by Indians.
2. John Brown, killed by Indians.
3. Jane Brown married James Collinsworth.
4. George Brown.
5. Daniel Brown.
6. Elizabeth Brown, born 1781.
7. Mary (Polly) Brown born 1783.
8. William Brown.
9. Ann Brown married William Anderson.
10. Margaret Brown married James Hamilton
11. Thomas Brown.

Sources: Evelyn B. McAnally (Mrs. Paul), member of Jane Knox Chapter; Mrs. Reuben Algood, Columbia, Tenn.; Genealogical Register compiled by Stephen A. Brown of Columbus, Miss., no publication date; Maury County Cousins, published by Maury County Historical Society, pages 244, 245; A. C. Hall and Sterling Brown admrs. of E. S. Hall, deceased, versus Joseph Brown, 1827, unpublished circuit court records; Nathan Vaught, "Youth and Old Age", page 61; National Banner and Nashville Whig, 30 Sept. 1826.

THOMAS BROWN

Served in Capt. Bird S. Hurt's company. [Widow's provision made by county court in April 1828 for Lurena Brown.]

EDWARD BRYANT

Said to be War of 1812 soldier, no service definitely established. Born Granville Co., N. C., married Elizabeth Amis, who died in Granville County.

Children of Edward Bryant:
1. Thomas H. Bryant, born 19 Aug. 1839 in Maury.
2. No further information.

Source: Goodspeed's History of Maury County, page 911.

JOHN BULLOCK

Believed to have been a soldier although no record established; always known as Major Bullock. Born 1 Oct. 1768, died 3 Feb. 1850 in Lewis County, buried at the Williamsport Cemetery. He was twice married; married secondly Effa Huddleston of Hickman County. "John Bullock, the father of the Hon. Lee Bullock of Columbia, was an old merchant of Centreville, a man of immense physical power and of great native intellect. He was an old schoolmate of Wiley B. Mangrum of North Carolina and was at that time his superior in college, but unfortunately for Mr. Bullock, he quit school before he completed his education, and drifted to the then wilds of Tennessee and engaged in farming and other pursuits. He lived to quite an old age, and died on Cathey's Creek in Maury County." (Hickman Pioneer, published Centerville, 8 Feb. 1878.) "William Whitfield ran the hotel [at Centerville] for a year or two and then rented it to Major John Bullock, father of Hon. Lee Bullock of Columbia." (Hickman Pioneer, 20 March 1885.) In article about Williamsport, "The next house south was a log dwelling, which was burned in the forties, it was, at my earliest recollection, occupied by Major John Bullock, who was a merchant in the place, but afterwards moved to Centerville, Hickman County, and engaged in the dry goods business. He retired from the dry goods business and came back to the vicinity of Williamsport and bought a farm, upon which he lived until his death at the advanced age of 80. He was buried at the town graveyard by the Masons, I performing the burial service. He had two sons by his last wife, Lee and Howell, both are prominent lawyers." (Maury Democrat, 11 Feb. 1892.)

Children of John Bullock:
1. John Bullock
2. Jonathan Bullock
3. Allen C. Bullock [Maury marriage bonds: Allen Bullock to Lucinda Pruit, 24 Aug. 1827]
4. Sarah Bullock married Temple Hicks, 24 May 1814 in Maury County.
5. Mary Bullock married Joseph Harris, 27 July 1819.
6. Ann Bullock married Elias Butler, 30 Dec. 1823.
7. Jason Lee Bullock, born about 1835, died 1911; married Laura Voorhies; second marriage to a woman in Washington, D. C.
8. Howell Collier Bullock, born 25 June 1838, died 17 March 1909, buried at Williamsport.
9. Sophronia P. Bullock, married John Beakley.
10. Margaret E. Bullock, born about 1840.

Sources: Lewis County, Tenn., wills in "Maury County Neighbors" by Lightfoot and Shackelford; Columbia Herald, 4 May 1911; 1850 census of Lewis County; 1850 mortality schedule of Lewis County; Maury County marriage records; "They Passed This Way".

JONATHAN BULLOCK

Commissioned Lieutenant in 1812 in the 27th regiment of Maury County militia; married Penelope Fly 10 April 1821. Son of Major John Bullock and his first wife. He was an early merchant of Santa Fe.

Source: Century Review of Maury County, page 143; Maury County marriage records.

ELI BUNCH

War of 1812 soldier in the Battle of New Orleans. (Columbia Herald, 28 June 1872.) Born 27 June 1795 in N. C., died on June 20, 1872 at home of son in law Al Hughes, "lack 7 days being 77 years." His listing on the 1850 census of Maury County shows: Eli Bunch, 55, born N. C.; Nancy, 50, Va.; Sarah J., 21, Tenn.; Nimrod P., 22, Tenn.; Eppy, 21, Tenn.; Harriet, 19, Tenn; Harriet, 19, Tenn; James, 17, Tenn.; and Mary, 13, Tenn. [Presumably these are his children.]

WILLIAM BUNARD

Served in Capt. John Gordon's company. No further information.

NATHANIEL G. BURGESS

Served in the 1813 militia from Maury County; enlisted as private 28 Sept. 1814 in Capt. James McMahan's company of mounted volunteer gunmen under Col. R. H. Dyer. No further information.

ROBERT BURNEY

Served in Capt. John Looney's company. No further information.

THOMAS BURNETT

Service not known. His widow Francis drew pension at Columbia in 1883 as a widow of War of 1812 soldier. She is buried at Pisgah Cemetery: Francis Burnett, wife of Thomas Burnett, born 20 July 1801, died 26 Sept. 1887.

Source: "They Passed This Way", page A-128.

+RICHARD BUTLER

Enlisted as private on 20 Sept. 1814 in Capt. John Looney's 2d West Tennessee militia; died 7 Feb. 1815. Feb. 1816 court minutes show that "Rd. Butler died in the army, 1 cripple boy and three other children." No further information.

+JAMES BURNS

1819 court minutes has the following: "died a soldier in the militia in 1814." Inventory of estate returned Nov. 1816 by John McFall. He married Jane McFall, daughter of John McFall and Martha Hill. She married 30 Oct. 1823 to James Helm.

Children of James Burns:
1. Martha (Patsy) — was still living in Georgia in 1829.
2. William Burns.
3. Margaret Burns — was still living in Georgia in 1829.
4. John Burns.
5. Milton Burns.
6. James Burns.
7. Henry — was mentioned in lawsuit in 1829 at which time James was not listed. Might possibly be the same as James.

Sources: Maury Will Book B, page 36; Will Book D, pages 358, 404.

James Burns served as private in Capt. Samuel Ashmore's company.

JOHN BURNS

Served in Capt. Andrew McCarty's company. No further information.

MILES BURNS

Commissioned lieutenant 1809 in 27th regiment of Maury County militia; commissioned ensign in 1814 in volunteer rifle company, 51st regiment. He married Susan Biffle, daughter of Jacob Biffle.

SANDY BURROW

Served in Capt. James McMahan's company. No further information.

WILLIAM BURRUS

Served in Capt. Andrew McCarty's company. [Believed to be the man who is found on 1820 census of Lawrence County.] No further information.

JAMES BYARS

Commissioned captain 1809 in 27th regiment of Maury County militia. Name is sometimes found as James F. Byars; was later a major. Lived in District 23 in 1850, age 60, born in N. C.; Cassandra, age 57, born in N. C., possibly his wife. Others

James Byars, continued:
others in household were: Marshal, 34; Nelson, 32; William M., 29; Isaac, 36; and
Susan, 20.

WILLIAM BYERS
Commissioned cornet in 5th brigade of cavalry in 1812. No further information.

TURNER BYNUM
Served in Capt. Bird S. Hurt's company. No further information.

AMOS CALDWELL
Commissioned ensign 1808 in 27th regiment of Maury County militia; officer also in
1813. Born 7 March 1781 in Halifax Co., Va., died 1852 in Maury County; lived near
Santa Fe; son of John Caldwell, Jr.; married 14 Aug. 1809 in Maury County to Sarah
Dodson, born 15 May 1795 in Halifax Co., Va., died 1861 in Maury, daughter of Thomas
and Sarah Dodson.

Children of Amos Caldwell:
1. William H. Caldwell, born 26 April 1811, died 25 March 1864 in Fayetteville,
    Ark., married 8 July 1835 in Maury to Margaret B. Webber.
2. John H. Caldwell, born 15 Dec. 1812 in Maury, died 19 June 1845 in Maury,
    married 15 Sept. 1836 in Maury to Ruth Jones.
3. Nancy D. Caldwell, born 27 Aug. 1816 in Maury, died 8 March 1898 in Maury,
    married 6 Nov. 1832 to Ambrose Hadley.
4. Sarah Jane Caldwell, born 17 Sept. 1819 in Maury County, died 1891 in West
    Tennessee, married C. W. Vestal.
5. Ocindie M. Caldwell, born 6 Sept. 1822 in Maury County, died March 1823.
6. David Allen Caldwell, born 13 Sept. 1826 in Maury, died 11 April 1896 in Maury,
    married 19 Dec. 1849 to Louisa E. Moore.
7. Dianah E. Caldwell, born 18 Sept. 1829 in Maury, died 14 June 1832 in Maury.
8. Louisa Marion Caldwell, married 22 Sept. 1861 to James H. Gibson in Maury.

Brothers and sisters of Amos Caldwell:
1. William H. Caldwell married Elizabeth Standfield; he was born 21 Dec. 1766.
2. David Caldwell, born 24 June 1769, married Elizabeth Tanner.
3. Jane Caldwell married Othe Thorp.
4. Allen Caldwell, born 1 Sept. 1775 married Polly Tanner.
5. George Caldwell, married Juley Capell.
6. Sarah Caldwell, born 1785, married Daniel Everett.
7. John Caldwell, born 22 Feb. 1790, married Patsy C. Rutledge.

Source: Jane Caldwell Luna (Mrs. John W.); Caldwell Bible; Will of Amos Caldwell,
signed 7 May 1852; Maury County Will Book F (Book 12), page 8.

HENRY CALDWELL
Served in Capt. Robert Campbell's company. No further information. [On one roll
of this company his name is Henry Caldwell; on pay roll his name is given as
Eldridge Caldwell; typed listing of this company in State Archives gives his name
as Hardy Caldwell. There was a Hardy Caldwell, who lived in Sumner Co., but this
name has not been found as yet in Maury County.]

+JOHN CALDWELL
Said to have been killed in War of 1812, but no service record has been found to
date. He married Patsy Rutledge in Maury County on 5 June ____ (bond found in
1809 box).

THOMAS CALDWELL
Commissioned ensign in lightinfantryin 1812, 27th regiment. No further information.

JOHN D. CALVERT
Served in Capt. John Looney's company. [The Calvert family settled near Culleoka; but no information has been turned in which would link this soldier and the one following to that family.]

SAMUEL CALVERT
Served in Capt. John Chisholm's company as substitute for Jordan Dotson. No further information.

CHARLES CAMPBELL
Served as fifer in Capt. Samuel B. McKnight's company. No further information.

JAMES CAMPBELL
Served in Capt. James McMahan's company. No further information [See following.]

JAMES CAMPBELL
Served in Capt. Samuel B. McKnight's company. No further information. [One James Campbell lived on Globe Creek; two of this name appeared on 1812 tax list.]

JAMES CAMPBELL
[This information may apply to one of the two above James Campbells.] Son of Alexander Campbell (born between 1740 and 1750, died in Hawkins County, Tenn., at 35) and his wife Amy Eaton, born in Maryland, who died in 1831. James Campbell married Sally Humphrey in Maury County, removed to Mississippi where his wife died. He returned to Tennessee and settled near Columbia where he died about 1857. Had children who lived in Tennessee and Texas.

Source: By Mrs. Leonard Gibson, Culleoka, who furnished pages from "Notable Southern Families", page 191.

Brothers and sisters of James Campbell:
1. Robert, born 1772 in Hawkins Co., died July 1828 near Campbellsville, Giles Co. He married 1799 to his cousin Jennie Taylor, who died in 1875.
2. Ann Campbell, born Aug. 1778, married _____Graves and lived near Culleoka, Maury County.
3. John Campbell, born 1 Oct. 1780, died 6 April 1860. He married July 1813 in Giles County to Sally Kimbrough of Binetwater (?). He lived at Fountain Creek Post Office in Maury County and in 1975 his old home still stands at Campbell Station, which was named for his son Andrew Jackson Campbell.
4. Hamilton Crockett Campbell, born 25 Sept. 1786, died 11 March 1853. He was a soldier in the War of 1812 from Giles County. Married 14 Sept. 1815 to Mary Mitchel Dickey, born 21 Nov. 1798, died 19 June 1887. They are buried in the Campbell cemetery at the rear of the Sanders house in Campbellsville, Giles Co.
5. Leticia Campbell, no further information.

JOHN CAMPBELL
Served as private in Sherman's Company, Virginia militia, War of 1812, and was granted 80 acres of land in Springfield, Mo., and land was assigned to Ezekiel M. Campbell. [He is also found as a Revolutionary War soldier; but some family members question this service. His service in the Revolution is given as second lieutenant of artillery in Capt. Mott's company of 2d N. C. Regiment.] Born Pennsylvania, 2 Feb. 1758 [another source says 1768], died 1816 "being lost on a trading trip (on which cotton and molasses were loaded on barges) going down the Miss." His will was dated 21 April 1816, and is recorded in Maury County; he died two months after making this will. He married Matilda Golden Polk, born 5 Dec. 1770, died in Springfield, Mo., 20 Sept. 1853, daughter of Ezekiel Polk. She was an aunt of James Knox Polk, eleventh President of the United States. She later married Philip Jenkins.

Children of John Campbell:
1. Mary Wilson Campbell, born N. C., 21 March 1795, married Joseph Miller.
2. Robert Bruce Campbell, born Mecklenburg Co., N. C., 5 July 1797, died at Columbia 1 Dec. 1852, married his second cousin Elizabeth Polk, born 9 Oct. 1796, died 8 July 1856 at Columbia, daughter of John and Elizabeth Alderson Polk.
3. Eliza Eugenia Campbell, born 24 May 1800 at Mecklenburg Co., N. C., died on Carters Creek 27 July 1856, married 8 Jan. 1819 Abdon Independence Alexander.
4. Ezekiel Madison Campbell, born 21 July 1802 in Mecklenburg Co., N. C., died in Polk Co., Missouri, 22 Sept. 1874, married 1821 in Maury to Rebecca Patton Adkins.
5. John Polk Campbell, born 29 March 1804 in Mecklenburg Co., N. C., died 28 May 1852 in Tallequah, Indian Territory, Oil Springs, Cherokee Nation; married in Maury, 28 May 1827 to Louise Terrill Cheairs, daughter of Nathaniel Cheairs.
6. William St. Clair Campbell, born 16 May 1808 in Maury County, died near Humbolt River Nevada while en route to California on 24 July 1852, married (1) 1826 to Mildred Ann Blackman, and (2) 1848 to Sarah Nichol.
7. Matilda Golden Campbell, born 14 April 1809 in Maury, died Nov. 1870 in Springfield, Mo., married Stephen Blackman.
8. Junius Tennessee Campbell, born 24 June 1812 in Maury, died 16 March 1877 in Springfield, Mo., married 1832 to Mary Ann Blackwell.
9. Caroline Huntley Campbell, born 14 March 1814 in Maury, married _____ Hardeman.
10. Samuel Polk Campbell, born 4 May 1816 in Maury, died unmarried at Springfield, Missouri, of cholera in July 1835.

Sources: Maury County Cousins, pages 244-246; Mrs. Frank Angelotti, "The Polks of North Carolina and Tennessee," pages 141-142; will of John Campbell in Maury County records; will of Matilda G. Jenkins in Springfield, Mo.

Brothers and sisters of John Campbell:
1. Robert Campbell - known as Robert Campbell Sr. at times to separate him from his nephew Robert Campbell, above.
2. Polly Campbell married Ezekiel Polk as his second wife. [This is established by the will of her father Robert Campbell which calls Ezekiel Polk his son-in-law.]

+JOHN CAMPBELL
In Oct. 1820 the Maury County court recognized the following as children of "John Campbell, deceased, late soldier in U. S. Army...begotten on body of his wife Ellen Campbell." Ellen is later found as Elenor Campbell, daughter of Joseph Denton, and is mentioned in Denton's will written 30 July 1818, recorded Jan. 1824.

Children of John Campbell:
1. Joseph D. Campbell "will be 15 on 13 Dec. 1817"
2. Elizabeth Campbell "will be 13 on 13 Dec. 1817."
3. Susannah Campbell "will be 11 on 16 Feb. 1818."
4. John Campbell "will be 9 on 10 Feb. 1818."
5. William Campbell "will be 5 on 30 Nov. 1817."

Sources: Will Book C, page 227; county court minutes for 1817 and 1820.

LUCINDA CAMPBELL
She drew pension in 1883 as widow of soldier in War of 1812. No further information.

MICHAEL CAMPBELL
Served in Capt. James McMahan's company. No further information.

MICHAEL CAMPBELL
Served in Capt. Andrew McCarty's company. No further information.

ROBERT CAMPBELL
Served in Capt. McMahan's second company. No further information. [Might be the son of John Campbell and Matilda G. Polk.]

CAPT. ROBERT CAMPBELL
Captain of a company formed in Maury County; early settler; died 16 Sept. 1847 at the age of 72.

Children of Capt. Robert Campbell:
1. Edward, died 1834 at the age of 18 in Maury County.
2. No further information.   3. Daughter married R. M. Dick.

Source: National Banner and Nashville Whig, 21 Nov. 1834.

WILLIAM CAMPBELL
Served in Capt. John Looney's company. No further information.

HOWARD CANNON
Served in Capt. Samuel Ashmore's company; married Lucretia Richardson, daughter of Thomas Richardson. No further information. ["Might" be son of Pugh Cannon, Revolutionary War soldier who lived in Maury County.]

JANE CAPPY
Drew widow's pension in 1883 in Columbia as widow of soldier in War of 1812. No further information.

ANDREW CARLINS
Served in Capt. Bird S. Hurt's company; no further information.

JOSEPH CARLOCK
Served as private in Capt. William Dooley's company. No further information.

JAMES CARNAHAN
Served in Capt. John Chisholm's company. No further information. On one roll of this company his name is found as John Carnahan.

WILLIAM CARR
Served in Capt. John Gordon's mounted spies, enlisted as private 24 Sept. 1813 and discharged 4 April 1814. [In June 1827 Susan D. Carr sues in circuit court for a divorce from her husband William Carr. John F. Carr, Revolutionary War soldier of Maury County, had a son named William Carr. No positive identification on this soldier.]

REUBEN CARTER
Served as corporal in Capt. William Dooley's company. No further information.

WILLIAM CARTER
Drew pension in 1883 in Santa Fe as a surviving soldier of the War of 1812. No further information.

JOSEPH MOREHEAD CARTHEL
Commissioned Lieutenant 1814 in 27th regiment of Maury County militia. Born 2 June 1794 (or 1791), died 4 Aug. 1849 in West Tennessee in family cemetery on his old farm which has been plowed and stones moved to a corner; married in Maury County on 11 Dec. 1825 to Rachel Jones, died 22 June 1888 at the age of 87, daughter of Thomas Jones and Catherine Shaw Jones. She is buried in the Oakland Cemetery, Trenton, Tenn. He was the son of Josiah W. Carthell and his wife Sarah Morehead. Josiah Carthell's will is recorded in Maury County Will Book D, page 371. (continued

Children of Joseph Morehead Carthel:
1. Sarah Catherine Carthel, born 25 Feb. 1827, married (1) Niles S. McCulloch, died 9 May 1851; (2) Capt. Thomas J. Carter on Nov. 1861, he was born 1803, died 1882.
2. Thomas Josiah Carthel, born 25 Aug. 1828, killed in battle of Atlanta during Civil War; married 18 July 1859 Mary Frierson, born 1833. They had two children: Joseph Morehead Carthel, born 1860, and Virginia, who married Charles Gray.
3. Jonathan Turner Carthel, born 14 May 1831, died 1912, married 13 May 1857 to Mary Neely, born 1837, died 1891.
4. Almira Lucretia Carthel, born 23 July 1834, died 18 Dec. 1925, married William Elder, born 1831, died 1887.
5. Elizabeth Frances Carthel, born 7 Aug. 1836, died 15 Sept. 1837.
6. Sophonia Ruth Carthel, born 23 Aug. 1837, died 17 Dec. 1840.
7. Emily Letitia Carthel, born 11 Dec. 1840, died 7 Sept. 1898, married 13 Oct. 1858 to William Thomas Byars, born 1836, died 1890.
8. Rachel Moselle Carthel, born 26 Dec. 1844, died 1908, married Eugene H. Elder and Thomas S. Watkins.
9. Joseph Norman Carthel, born 20 Oct. 1847, died 2 April 1862.

Brothers and sisters of Joseph M. Carthel:
1. Elizabeth Carthel, died single.
2. Nancy Carthel, married A. Kirkpatrick, lived in Victoria, Texas.
3. No further information.

Sources: Maury County Will Book D, page 371; The Jones Family History, pages 66, 73; Mid-South Bible Records, published by Fort Assumption Chapter, DAR, Memphis, pages 47, 48, 49.

JOHN CARUTHERS

Served in Capt. Benjamin Reynolds' first company. No further information. [This man could be the John Caruthers, born about 1788, died unmarried in Maury in Nov. 1840, who was a son of Robert Caruthers, Rev. War soldier, born 3 May 1758, died 4 Oct. 1828, and his wife Elizabeth Pattilo.]

MADISON CARUTHERS

"Paymaster in the army before he was twenty-one"1 died in New Orleans 27 Dec. 1847, born Rockbridge Co., Virginia; was 54 years at his death; once practiced law in Maury County. He was cashier of a bank while in Columbia. (The Columbia Beacon, 7 Jan. 1848.)

ROBERT CARUTHERS

Served in Capt. Samuel Ashmore's company; born 1 Feb. 1791, died March 1829, married 9 July 1812 to Elizabeth Brown Porter, born 1 July 1795 died 3 Nov. 1881. She drew pension for his wartime service. He was son of Robert Caruthers, Rev. War soldier, and his wife Elizabeth Pattilo.

Children of Robert Caruthers:
1. Eliza T., born 1812, died 1838, married R. G. Looney.
2. Sarah H., married Leonard D. Myers.
3. Susan, married William J. Sykes.
4. Robert A.
5. James M., died Jan. 1848.
6. Mary L., married William Mitchell Davidson.
7. Joseph P., born 26 Jan. 1821, died 14 Sept. 1823.

Brothers and sisters of Robert Caruthers: John (died Nov. 1840), Samuel, Mary (married a Patton), Susanna (married John D. Love), Elizabeth P. (married John D. Love and lived in Henry Co., Tenn.). Sources include Galloway vs Caruthers, 1859, Maury Co. Chancery Court Records, and tombstone inscriptions from "They Passed This Way."

THOMAS CASEBIER (or COXBIER)
Served in Capt. James McMahan's company. No further information.

THOMAS GATES
Served in Capt. John Gordon's company of spies. On 21 Sept. 1809 he was ordered to work on road leading from Natchez Road across Swan Creek to intersect road leading from Columbia to the Pond Spring. He had daughter who married Charles Wilson, whose estate was being settled in 1824.

JONATHAN CATHELL
Served in Capt. Samuel Ashmore's company. Son of Josiah W. Carthell (born in France, Revolutionary War soldier) and his wife Sarah Morehead, daughter of Joseph M Morehead and his wife Elizabeth Turner (she died 24 April 1819 at the age of 92). Refer also to Carthell. Jonathan Carthel married 7 Jan. 1819 to Mary _____.

Source: Mid South Bible Records, 48, 49.

ALEXANDER CATHEY
Justice of the peace in Maury County from 1810 to 1811. Both Alexander Cathey Sr. and Alexander Cathey Jr. appear in early records. No further information.

MATTHEW BRANDON CATHEY
Served in Capt. James McMahan's company. Born 1782, son of William and Alice Hayes Cathey; married Matilda Dalton; moved to Mississippi in 1836 and died there. He enlisted as private 29 Sept. 1814 in Capt. James McMahan's 1st Tennessee Volunteer Gunmen, Col. Robert Dyer.

Source: Kennedy-Cathey Book, page 39.

WILLIAM CATHEY
Commissioned captain in volunteer rifle company in 51 Regiment in 1814. [There were two men of this name in the county about the same time. Information on both will be given.]

William Cathey, one of the five sons of William Cathey. The father entered 4000 acres of land giving to four of his sons 1000 acres each. These sons were:
1. James Cathey [father of A. B. Cathey]
2. Dickey Cathey
3. William Cathey
4. Alexander Cathey
5. Matthew Cathey

William Cathey, son of Griffith Cathey (1776-1854) who married his cousin Susannah Cathey (died 1833) and Rebecca Finley. Griffith Cathey's children are as follows:
1. Rutherford Cathey married a Bingham.
2. William Cathey.
3. John Griffy Cathey.
4. James Cathey.
5. Polly Cathey.
6. Alice A. Cathey, born 1836, died 1855.

William Cathey, son of Griffith Cathey and his wife Susannah, married Emily Brown. His children were:
1. Jethro Cathey married Isabelle Anderson and Fannie Wilhelm.
2. Rutherford Cathey married Molly Miller.
3. Jim A. Cathey married Lizzie Worley.
4. Olivia Cathey married Richard Anderson.
5. Sarah Jane Cathey married Barkley Dicky.
6. Billie Cathey married Mary Tredway.

Source: The Cathey family by Miss Mary Norfleet and given to Snow Anderson, Alma, Ark., many years ago, furnished by Mrs. Mathew M. Rayburn, Thompson Station, Tenn.

GEORGE CAVELL
Served in Capt. Robert Campbell's company. Name given as Cavett on one roll. No further information.

AMANDA CECIL
She drew pension as widow of War of 1812 soldier in Mt. Pleasant in 1883. No further information.

JOSEPH CECIL
He drew pension as surviving soldier of War of 1812 in 1883 in Columbia; he was wounded in right ankle in the war. No further information.

EDWARD H. CHAFFIN
Enlisted 24 Sept. 1813 in Capt. William Mitchell's spies, a Rutherford County unit, before he came to Maury County. Born 30 Aug. 1791 in Virginia, died 6 Nov. 1856, buried in Greenwood Cemetery. He was son of Jesse Chaffin and his wife Henrietta Hatchett. Married 23 Sept. 1821 in Maury County to Mrs. Ruth Malinda Davidson Whiteside, widow of Dr. Abraham Whiteside. She died 12 May 1847. They had no children.

Brothers and sisters of Edward Chaffin:
1. Archer Chaffin, died in West Tennessee. In 1830 he was living in Hardeman County.
2. Nathan Chaffin married 24 Dec. 1811 to his cousin Harriet Hatchett and they lived in Bedford County, Tenn.
3. Phoebe Chaffin, born about 1793, died 1831, married Joel Dyer Harris.
4. Nancy Chaffin married Dr. Jonathan Burford and they lived in Whiteville, Tenn.
5. Sally Chaffin married Judge Lewis B. Tully.

Source: Tombstone record in "They Passed This Way"; Maury Democrat, 15 Feb. 1894; Lucille Frizzell Jacobs, "Duck River Valley in Tennessee and its Pioneers", published 1968, pages 72, 73; William L. Chaffin, "History of Robert Chaffin and his descendants and of the other Chaffins in America", published 1912, 259-263.

MOSES CHAFFIN
Served in Capt. Samuel Ashmore's company. Born about 1783 in Charlotte Co., Va.; died about 1824 when an inventory of his estate was being made in Maury County; his burial place is not known; son of Thomas and Elizabeth Chaffin of Charlotte Co., Va.; married 9 Aug. 1808 in Davidson County to Jane Jones, born about 1780 in Virginia, still living on 1850 census of Maury County. She was originally from Raleigh, N.C. She married her husband's brother Rowland Chaffin about 1825.

Children of Moses Chaffin:
1. Garland Chaffin, born 9 Oct. 1810. He was killed in a storm during the 1850s while traveling in a boat down the Mississippi River. He had an interest in the boat and in property in Natchez, Miss., to which place he was going at the time of his death.
2. William Benjamin Chaffin, born 25 April 1813, died at 82 years in Columbia. He married (1) Amanda Adkisson and (2) Margaret Martin.
3. Mary Elizabeth Chaffin, born 30 Dec. 1816, died in Huntsville, Alabama, 11 May 1872, married William Weaver.

Sources: Chaffin, "History of Robert Chaffin...", pages 259, 260; will of Thomas Chaffin, Charlotte Co., Va.; Davidson County marriages; Maury County Deed C, page 86; Maury County Will Book B, page 235, 327; Nathan Vaught, "Youth and Old Age", page 109. Vaught says of Garland Chaffin's death: "Moved to Natchez in 1834 or 1835 and there was lost in storm in the Missipia River. He never married."

ROWLAND CHAFFIN

Service record not found; family history says he served with Andrew Jackson at New Orleans. Born 1790 in Virginia, death unknown; lived one mile north of General Isaac Roberts in the Rutherford Hills. No cemetery was found in this area. Son of Thomas and Elizabeth Chaffin of Charlotte Co., Va. He married before 1825 to Jane Jones Chaffin, widow of his brother Moses Chaffin.

Children of Rowland Chaffin:
1. Green T. Chaffin, born 1825, died 1893, married Nancy A. Dowell and Sally Cunningham.

Brothers and sisters of Rowland Chaffin:
1. Littleberry Chaffin, died about 1835 when sale of his estate was being made in Maury County. He owned land on the Double Branches in Maury County. He had daughters Julia Ann and Lucretia T. Chaffin.
2. Isham Chaffin.
3. Thomas Chaffin, Jr., married 17 March 1803 in Charlotte Co., Va., to Nancy Mayes; died 1848.
4. Banister Chaffin; it is believed that he came to Maury County.
5. Coleman Chaffin, died about 1845, married Susan Weatherford. Deed Book 10, page 174 in Maury mentions his father Thomas Chaffin in Va. He was in Maury County at least by 1825.
6. Moses Chaffin, deceased by 1824. At his death he owned 20 acres on Little Bigby Creek in Maury County. See his listing.
7. Lina Chaffin, married 4 March 1805 to Samuel Weatherford.

Sources: William L. Chaffin, "History of Robert Chaffin...", pages 259, 260; will of Thomas Chaffin, Charlotte Co., Va.

HENRY CHAMBERS

Served in Capt. Robert Campbell's company. No further information.

ROBERT CHAMP

Enlisted as private 4 Oct. 1813 in Capt. William Dooley's company, Col. T. McCrory. His age was given as between 26 and 45 on 1820 census of Maury, and he died in Columbia in 1826 and is buried in an unmarked grave in Greenwood Cemetery. Maury Democrat, 15 Feb. 1894: "I must tell you about an old woman who lived at the old bridge, her name was Champ; she got drunk occasionally and threw rocks at everybody who passed. She had a pretty daughter by the uphonious name of Peggy Champ. Miss Peg did not become intoxicated, but would get far enough along sometimes to jump astride her pony and ornament the municipality vermilion; paint the town red for a few hours..."

State Docket, 1808-1821, April term 1819, case 9: Champ & wife indicted for malicious mischief on prosecuting James Brown. R. Champ found not guilty; Polly Champ found guilty and fined $5 and 2 hours imprisonment.

An unpublished chancery court case, in equity in 1818, shows that she was related in some way to one Zachariah Wilbourn. Court minutes for 21 Feb. 1815 show that Robert Champ was charged with trespass by William L. Armstrong.

Children:
1. Elizabeth Champ married 1 Sept. 1818 to Nathaniel Rogers.
2. Peggy Champ.
3. No information on others. 1820 census shows 4 young males and 2 young females in his household.

Sources: National Banner and Nashville Whig, 26 Aug. 1826; 1820 census of Maury; records cited in his listing above.

ELIZABETH S. CHAPMAN
She drew pension as widow of War of 1812 soldier in Spring Hill Tm.1883. No further information.

JOHN N. CHARTER
Served in Capt. John Gordon's spy company. No further information.

WILLIAM CHARTER
Enlisted 28 Sept. 1814 in Capt. Robert Evans' company of Tennessee Mounted Volunteer Gunmen, discharged 28 March 1815. This man has also been identified with Hickman County; in 1816 a lawsuit in Maury County involved land on Leatherwood Creek. He also served in the first Seminole War from Hickman County. No further information.

THOMAS CHEATHAM
Enlisted 24 Sept. 1813 in Capt. Arch McKinney's company, Col. R. H. Dyer, in the Williamson County troops. Married in Williamson County to Faney Gentry on 24 Aug. 1818. [This man has been identified by some as the same Thomas Cheatham who later lived in Maury County; no proof; no further information.]

JEREMIAH CHERRY
Appointed constable in Maury County Sept. 1809 and Sept. 1811. Also ran a tavern in Columbia. Born 1 April 1766, died 29 Jan. 1821; married Mary (Polly) _____, born 12 Jan. 1776, died 15 May 1832; they are both buried in Greenwood Cemetery.

Children of Jeremiah Cherry:
1. Kenneth, died 1829 at the age of 39.
2. Jeremiah, born 1797, died Oct. 1855, married 1819 to Mary Cooper.
3. William, born 1820, died 1821.
4. Daughter married _____ Hyde.
5. Polly, born 1795, died 1870, married 1814 to Joshua Guest.
6. Elizabeth (Betsy), born 1799, married 1815 to Pleasant Nelson.
7. Nancy, born 1802, died 1871, married Thomas Keef, born 1804, died 1852.
8. Rosey, married _____ Smith.

Sources: Maury County Cousins, pages 339, 341; Nathan Vaught, "Youth and Old Age", pages 64, 102; "They Passed This Way", D-2.

JOHN CHISHOLM
Captain of a company formed in Maury County in the War of 1812. He later moved to Lauderdale County, Alabama, where he died. Born 22 Nov. 1775, died 30 July 1847, buried in Chisholm Cemetery on the Chisholm Road out from Florence. His wife Ester, born 25 Nov. 1780, died 27 Sept. 1852. He was the son of John Chisholm, Sr., born 1 Aug. 1738, died 9 Oct. 1828 and his wife Mary, born 10 Aug. 1748, died 6 March 1827.

Children of John Chisholm:
1. Ester, born 19 Aug. 1819, died 28 May 1859.
2. James Gum, born 1 April 1812, died 26 Aug. 1844.
3. Others, but no further information.
4. Rachel, born 22 Oct. 1821, died 20 Dec. 1859, married Thomas Johnson.

Sources: Dr. Maurice Pruitt, Chattanooga, Tenn.; Chisholm tombstone inscriptions.

THOMAS CHOATE
Served in Capt. John Gordon's company of spies and mentioned in John Bell's diary. Married 12 March 1816 in Maury County to Naomi Choate. Will be found on 1820 census of Lawrence County. [See also Will Book B, 1829-1847, Lawrence Co., pages 147, 390, 429.]

NATHANIEL CHRISTIAN

Served as private in Capt. William Dooley's company, enlisted 4 Oct. 1813. He also enlisted as private 10 Dec. 1812 in Capt. Benjamin Reynolds' company, Col. T. H. Benton, volunteer infantry and was marked "refused to march". The 8th district surveyors book shows that Nathan Christian and Isom Christian got 320 acres in Lawrence County on Buffalo River on 22 Nov. 1820. [page 30 of this book]   In 1820 he is found on the Lawrence County census and no Christians are left in Maury County He was the son of Isham Christian and his wife Nancy. Sale was made of Isham's estate in Maury County in 1814. On 1820 census Nathaniel is found as between 26 and 45 years.

Children of Isham Christian; brothers and sisters of Nathaniel:
1. Martha (Patsy), married 6 Feb. 1828 Lawrence Co. to Elisha Pollock.
2. Nancy, born about 1794, married 2 July 1817 in Maury to Robert Payton.
3. Jane, married 15 Aug. 1823 Lawrence County to Thomas Wallace.
4. Betsy, married 9 Jan. 1817 in Maury County to John Perry.
5. Isham (aged between 18 and 26 in 1820) (age 52 in 1850 census of Lawrence Co.) married Betsy_____, age 30 in 1850, native of Virginia.
6. Charles.
7. Zelpha (Zilphy), married 30 May 1822 to Richard Ramsey in Lawrence County.
8. Rhody married 9 Oct. 1827 in Lawrence County to Daniel Pollock.

Sources: 1820 and 1850 census records of Lawrence County; Lawrence and Maury Counties, marriage records; estate settlement of Isham Christian in Maury County; 8th District Surveyors Book in Maury County register's office.

+JOHN CHURCHWELL

Enlisted 13 Nov. 1813 as private in Capt. John Jackson's company, Col. William Metcalf, Maj. Gen. William Carroll's infantry. Died 4 Feb. 1815. An inventory of his estate is listed in Maury County Will Book A, page 153, made 24 Aug. 1815 with Elizabeth Churchwell as administratrix, and one item listed "his discharge not known". [The Churchwell family in Maury County originally came from Pulaski Co., Kentucky.]

WILLIAM CHURCHWELL

Enlisted as private 18 Dec. 1813 in Capt. James McMahan's mounted gunmen, Col. N.T. Perkins. No further information.

WILLIAM CHURCHWELL

Enlisted as private 28 Sept. 1814 in Capt. James McMahan's 1st Tennessee Mounted Volunteer Gunmen, Col. Robert H. Dyer. [This may be the same man as above.] No further information.

[John Trotwood Moore's Tennessee, the Volunteer State, page 840, gives a brief resume of Richard Churchwell's family. He married 9 June 1792 in Lincoln Co., Ky., to Nancy Napier. They were the parents of: Bill, Dick, Jesse, Lias, Feal, June, Peg, Minerva, Lucinda, Ollie, Sophronia, and Robert Anderson Churchwell. It has been impossible to determine if these children are any of the above.]

BAYZE CLAYTON

Served in Capt. John Chisholm's company. No further information.

JOHN CLAYTON

Served in Capt. John Looney's company. No further information.

HENRY CLAPP

Columbia Herald and Mail, 5 June 1874: "Henry Clapp, now oldest resident of Rally Hill, was 38 during the War of 1812 and drew for a draft but got a blank."

ABNER CLEVELAND
Commissioned ensign in 46th regiment, Maury County militia, in 1814. No further information.

JAMES COCHRAN
Served in War of 1812; no record found. Born 2 May 1781, died 30 June 1859; married Jane Miligan; settled in Georgia, then to Tennessee, moved back to Georgia where he married, and finally to Maury County.

Children of James Cochran:
1. William J., born 7 June 1811 in Maury County.
2. No further information.

Source: Goodspeed's History of Maury County, p. 913.

GEORGE COCKBURN
Served as private in Capt. William Dooley's company; commissioned ensign in 27th regiment in 1809; appointed constable of Maury County in 1808, resigned March 1810; enlisted as private 4 Oct. 1813 in Dooley's company; ensign in Capt. Bird S. Hurt's company, enlisting 13 Nov. 1814. On 1820 census age is given as between 26-45. Some deed records for him: 5 April 1819 bought lot 41 from Joseph B. Porter, bounded on south by Free Street, running north to the river. By 5 April 1848 he sold lot 41 to William Galloway and called George Cockburn of Lauderdale County, Ala. (Maury Deed Book C, page 289) On 1837 deed, witness for George Cockburn was George Wesley Cockburn.

Nathan Vaught wrote of him: "This ferry house was at the river at the north east margin of town. This house was a one and half story high with 2 rooms and a large open hall between and the saim above stars and a very rough concern built of very rough logs and it was a very rough place indeed. All kinds of wickedness indulged in this place. This house was put up late in 1806 or quite early in 1807 by a Mr. Geo. Cockburn (pronounced Coburn) he had no Family and was a man of very bad morals. He was the owner of the Ferry for a long time..."

After his move to Alabama he also ran a ferry across the Tennessee River and some members of a Cockburn family are buried in a cemetery on the TVA reservation near the river on the Colbert County side. He will be found in Franklin Co., Ala., on the 1830 census—Colbert was later taken from Franklin County.

Acts of Alabama for 4 Jan. 1832, page 109, 13th session held at Tuscaloosa: "The illegitmate children (not named) of George Cockburn, now of Franklin County, are hereby legitimated..."

Sources: Nathan Vaught, "Youth and Old Age", page 46; Maury County Deed Book C, page 289; 1820 census of Maury; 1830 census of Franklin Co., Ala.

HENRY COCKBURN
Enlisted as private 28 Jan. 1814 in Capt. Robert Campbell's infantry company, Col. Robert Steele. No further information.

JOSEPH COE
Enlisted 4 Oct. 1813 as sergeant in Capt. William Dooley's company; born about 1784, died about 1850. In 1816 he had land on Fountain Creek and Little Bigby. He was born in Maryland and came in 1806 to Maury County, moving in 1829 to Fayette County. He served in the 20th General Assembly from Fayette County. He married Margaret_____.

Children of Joseph Coe:
1. Levin Hudson Coe, born 1807, died 1850, married 1832 in Maury County to Mary J. Lindsey.   continued

Children of Joseph Coe continued:
2. son, no further information.
3. son, no further information.

Source: Biographical Directory of the Tennessee General Assembly, Preliminary No.46 page 5.

JOEL COFFEE
Commissioned ensign in 27th regiment of Maury County militia in 1813. Married 9 Apr. 1818 to Sarah Mackey in Maury County. No further information.

JOHN COFFEE
Enlisted as private 28 Jan. 1814 in Capt. Andrew McCarty's militia infantry, Col. R. C. Napier. [One John Coffee was charged and found guilty in Oct. 1831 of the murder of his wife. On 15 March 1831 the Maury County court pays for an inquest held over the body of Bersheba Coffey. This murder trial was heard also in the supreme court.]

PERRY COHEA
Appointed patrolee for Columbia in Sept. and Dec. 1808. Was given a license to keep an ordinary in 1808. Born 1758, died 26 June 1821, buried in Greenwood Cemetery. He married Martha _____, born 2 June 1784, died 26 July 1821, also buried in Greenwood Cemetery.

Children of Perry Cohea:
1. Alexander
2. John (Jack)
3. Mary, born 2 July 1798, died 2 Aug. 1822.
4. James Calvin, born 5 Sept. 1819, died 30 Nov. 1819.
5. [Ann Cohea married 1817 to Elisha Uzzell in Maury County. Some believe that she may also be another child. No further information on this.]
6. [Perry Cohea, born 1796 in Tenn., married Mary J. _____, born 1801 in Tenn. This man later lived in Miss. and some believe that he is another child of Maury County's Perry Cohea. No further information on this.]

Sources: Nathan Vaught, "Youth and Old Age", page 68, 71; Maury County marriages; "They Passed This Way", D-3; Norman Gillis, Abstracts of Goodspeed's of Miss., p.116.

+HENRY COLEMAN
Enlisted as private 20 Sept. 1814 in Capt. John Looney's company, 2d West Tennessee militia under Col. A. Loury; also enlisted in Capt. Thomas Wells' company. Died by accident 7 Nov. 1814.

+JOHN COLEMAN
Mustered 27 Aug. 1814, served under Cadwallader Claiborne; died 12 Dec. 1814.

Children of John Coleman:
1. Thomas B. Coleman, living in Spring Hill in 1831.
2. Other children, no further information.

Source: Herbert Weaver, editor, Correspondence of James K. Polk, Vol. 1, pages 429-430. [This man may have served from Lincoln County.]

THOMAS COLEMAN
Served in Capt. John Chisholm's company; no further information.

THOMAS COLEMAN

(Possibly the same as the one before) Served as sergeant in Capt. John Chism's company, Col. R. C. Napier's regiment from 28 Jan. 1814 to 16 May 1814. Born 30 June 1770 in Virginia, died 15 Nov. 1826 at Williamsport, Tenn., buried at Coleman Cemetery on Emory Ladd home; married about 1789 in Salisbury, N. C., to Clarissa White born 22 Jan. 1777, died 11 July 1852. (She was twelve at the marriage.) He was the son of Thomas and Elizabeth Coleman.

Children of Thomas Coleman:
1. Nancy Coleman, born 27 May 1792, married James Josey
2. Thomas Buchell Coleman, born 8 Feb. 1794, never married, died Huntsville, Ala.
3. Sophia Betsy Coleman, born 17 May 1796, married Joseph H. McEwen, died in Nashville, Tenn.
4. Clarissa Coleman, born 7 April 1799, married John D. Alderson and James McEwen. No issue.
5. Julia Coleman, born 19 Nov. 1800, married John Edward, died in Texas, leaving several children.
6. Sallie Theresa Coleman, born 18 Nov. 1802, married Thomas Johnson.
7. Eliza Panthea Coleman, born 21 Nov. 1804, married Robert Crosby of Ireland.
8. William White Coleman, born 14 May 1807, married 1. Miss Johnson, 2. Jeanette Frierson.
9. Caroline Mary Coleman, born 12 Sept. 1809, married Powhattan Gordon.
10. Rufus Coleman, born 21 Jan. 1812, died 1890 in Hickman County.
11. Walter Coleman, born 4 May 1814, died and buried in Memphis where he practiced law.
12. Elvira Bouchell Coleman, born 12 Jan. 1817, married William Berry, died 20 July 1832, leaving one son William Berry of Nashville.

Brothers and sisters of Thomas Coleman:
1. Lucy Coleman, born 1 March 1759, married 1779 William Falkner.
2. Richard Coleman, born 22 April 1761, married 1779 to Lucy Sydnor, 1761-1810.
3. Betty Coleman, born 26 Jan. 1763, married Benjamin Routt.
4. Robert Coleman, born 15 Aug. 1772; had son Henry; descendants in Georgia.
5. Sarah Coleman, born 19 May 1775, married 1793 to Thomas Walker.
6. James Coleman, born 4 Jan. 1778.
7. Mary (Molly) Coleman, born 23 April 1780, married Oliver Stott.

Source: Coleman-White-Crosby papers of Mrs. Campbell Sowell, Sr., quoting Will Book No. 9, page 369, of Gloucester Co., Va., 1758; Coleman Cemetery records in "They Passed This Way", page B-4; Octavia Zollicoffer Bond, "Kinship Book".

THOMAS B. COLEMAN

Enlisted 28 Sept. 1814 in Capt. James McMahan's Tennessee Mounted Volunteer Gunmen, Col. R. H. Dyer. No further information.

BARTLET COLLINS

Served in Capt. Robert Campbell's company. No further information.

MEREDITH COLLINS

Served in Capt. John Gordon's company. No further information.

NATHANIEL COLLINS

Served in Capt. James McMahan's company. No further information.

ALSTON COOK

Served in N. C. troops; in 1828 drew pension in Maury County. No further information.

ENOS COOK

Died 2 April 1875 at Santa Fe, age 82, was at Battle of New Orleans. He was the las pensioner at Santa Fe. His widow Percilla drew pension as widow in 1883 at Santa Fe. Precilla Cook died 10 July 1889 at the age of 95. The 1850 census gives his age as 55, born in Delaware, and Prescilla, age 55, born in Virginia. (Her name spelled three different ways.) The following are presumed to be their children, were listed with them on 1850 census:

1. Sidney C., age 23, born in Ky.
2. Mary A., age 21, born in Ky.
3. William K., age 17, born in Tenn.
4. Harriet D., age 15, born in Ky.
5. Enos W., age 11, born in Ky.
   (Enos Wesley Cook, born 20 July 1840, died 20 June 1861, buried in Cook-Caughron Cemetery was son of Enos and Priscilla Caughron Cook and was the first of the 1st Tennessee Infantry, C.S.A., to die.)

Source: 1850 census of Maury County; "Confederate Soldiers and Patriots of Maury County, Tenn.," published by Capt. James Madison Sparkman Chapter, U.D.C., page 65.

RICHARD COOK

Served as 4th sergeant in Capt. Robert Campbell's company. No further information. [Name also appeared to be Richard Cock.]

[Richard J. Cocke was in Maury County at least as early as 1811 and settled on the Bear Creek pike area. He was known to have the following children: Pleasant Cocke, Wheeler Cocke, and Martha Cocke, born about 1820, married 1838 to John Gant. He also was a signer of the petition to form Maury County. There is some question if he would have been a soldier as on 18 June 1811 he was excused from jury duty because of his deafness.]

THOMAS COOK

Enlisted as private 28 Sept. 1814 in Capt. James McMahan's Tennessee Volunteer Mounted Gunmen, Col. R. H. Dyer. No further information.

RICHARD FIELDING COOKE

Served as major in Col. Woolfork's battalion under General Andrew Jackson; later served two terms in Tennessee General Assembly. Son of Robert Cooke and Susannah Watson; born 8 Jan. 1787 in Va., died 15 Oct. 1870, married 1 April 1812 to Margaret Cox; settled first in Maury County, Tenn., about 1810 then settled near Double Springs in White, now Putnam Co., Tenn. Cookeville, county seat of Putname County, was named for him.

Source: Carson-Cooke family data sent in by Bill Randolph of Texas, quoting "The Carson Family History" published in 1956.

EDMUND COOPER

Enlisted as private on 4 Oct. 1813, Capt. William Dooley's company, Col. Thomas McCrory; born about 1785 in Va., son of William Cooper, Sr., married 19 Aug. 1824 to Nancy Hadley, daughter of Ambrose Hadley. His will was written in 1844 and probated in 1872.

Children of Edmund Cooper:
1. Fanny H. Cooper
2. No further information.

Additional information on Edmond Cooper will be found on page 43.

Brothers and sisters of Edmund Cooper:
1. Benjamin Cooper.
   continued on next page

Edmund Cooper, continued:

2. Polly Cooper, born 1774.
3. Nancy Cooper, born 1790. [married 20 Aug. 1816 to James Taylor]
4. Rebecca Cooper [marriage license issued 24 Nov. 1819 to John Jordan]
5. Frances Park Cooper, born 5 March 1799, died 2 August 1862, married Netherland Tait.
6. William Cooper, Jr., born 29 Jan. 1781, died 21 Oct. 1834.
   (Widow's provision made for Elizabeth Cooper, Dec. 1834; Minute Book 12, 405,413.

Sources: Maury County Will Book F-1, page 418; Will Book Y, page 189; Tait tombstone in Meriwether Lewis Park, Lewis County; miscellaneous Maury County marriages; and family information of Jane Luna (Mrs. John W.).

MATTHEW DELAMERE COOPER

Enlisted 1813, served as first lieutenant in Capt. Christopher E. McEwen's company, discharged 10 Dec. 1813, Williamson County troops. Nashville Union and American, 5 Nov. 1874: "Roster of regiment under Thomas H. Benton given to Tennessee Historical Society...on 10 Dec. 1812 this group went to Natchez, recalled Oct. 1813, was in battle of Talladega...only survivors still living of Christopher McEwen's company are M. D. Cooper of Columbia, William Turnridge of Clarksville, Texas, and John Boyd, now blind and in poor house of Henry County, Tenn." Born 30 Oct. 1792 in Chester District, S. C., died 20 Dec. 1878, buried at Zion Cemetery. He was married three times: 1. Mary Agnes Frierson, born 1801, died 1834; 2. 1835 Elizabeth Jane Frierson, born 1819, died 1838; 3. Mary Ann (or Marian) Witherspoon Brown.

Children by first marriage:
1. William Frierson Cooper, born 1820, died 1909, unmarried.
2. Edmund Cooper, born 1821, died 1911, married Mary Stephens.
3. Alfred Cooper, born 1823, never married.
4. Jane Cooper, born 1825, never married.
5. Henry Cooper, born 1827, died 1884, married Ann Eliza Strickler.
6. Mary Agnes Cooper, born 1829, married Richard Sansom.

Children by second marriage:
1. Flavel Frierson Cooper, born 1838, never married.

Children by third marriage:
1. Martha Ann Cooper, died 1861, never married.
2. Duncan Brown Cooper, born 21 Nov. 1845 (or 21 April 1843), died 4 Nov. 1922, married Florence Fleming and Mary Polk Jones.
3. Alice Jane Cooper, born 1846, died 1901, never married.
4. Addison Cooper, married Eva Campbell.
5. Emma Sweet Cooper, born 1850, died 1894, never married.
6. Fannie Cooper, born 1855, died 1881, married George Milner.
7. Eloise Cooper, born 1852, died 1876, married Albert W. Stockell.

Source: Theodore Frierson Stephenson, "The Friersons of Zion Church"; Zion Cemetery inscriptions from "They Passed this Way".

ROBERT MELVILLE COOPER

Served in Capt. Bird S. Hurt's company. Born 29 Dec. 1790 Chester District, S. C., died 9 Nov. 1878 in Maury County, buried in McClain Cemetery; married 28 March 1816 in Maury County to Catherine Cooper, born 5 Oct. 1799 in Smith Co., Tenn., died 16 April 1863 in Maury County. Son of Robert Cooper and Jane Hamilton Cooper.

continued on next page

Children of Robert M. Cooper:
1. Albert Gallatin Cooper, born 9 Feb. 1817, married Elizabeth E. Webb in 1838.
2. William McAdams Cooper, born 9 Feb. 1823, killed 5 July 1862 at Tupelo, Miss. CSA
3. James Carlisle Cooper, born 17 Nov. 1826, died 11 Nov. 1897.
4. Henry Augustus Cooper, born 14 Sept. 1830, killed at West Point, Miss. CSA
5. Robert Theodore Cooper, born 7 April 1832, killed 12 April 1863. CSA
6. Thomas Simpson Cooper, born 5 Sept. 1834, died 6 Feb. 1923.
7. Alexander Duval Cooper, born 11 Sept. 1838, died 10 July 1861. CSA
8. Samuel Gwin Cooper, twin, born 11 Sept. 1838, died 24 April 1862. CSA
9. Leander Bruce Cooper, born 2 Sept. 1841, died 28 March 1926, CSA.
10. Alfred Theodrick, born 18 Sept. 1844, died 22 April 1931, CSA.
11. There were five other children in this family, no further information.

Brothers and sisters of Robert M. Cooper:
1. Elizabeth Cooper, born 1769 Chester District, S. C., married John Patton.
2. Hugh Cooper, born 1771 Chester Dist., S. C., married Catherine Brakefield, died in Miss. between 1861-65.
3. John Cooper, born Chester District S. C., 1773, married Jane Campbell, died in Miss. between 1861-65.
4. Eleanor Cooper, born Chester Dist. S. C., 1775, married Robert Smith; she died in Tenn.
5. William Cooper, born 1777 in Chester District, S. C., died in Miss. before the Civil War; married Dempsey Donaho.
6. James Cooper, born 1780 in Chester Dist., S. C., died in Miss. between 1861-65; married Margaret Connard.
7. Jane Cooper, born 1782, Chester Dist.,S.C., died in Ala. before Civil War, married William Hemphill.
8. Mary Cooper, born 1784 in Chester Dist., S. C., died 1830 in Tenn., married David Anderson.
9. Jonathan Cooper, born 9 May 1785 in Chester District, S. C., married Elizabeth Duffe 12 Sept. 1809 in Williamson Co., Tenn., died 28 April 1882 in Maury.
10. Sarah Cooper, born 18 Feb. 1787 in Chester District, S. C., died 18 July 1879 in Tenn., married Hugh Barr.
11. Hamilton Cooper, born 1789 in Chester District, S. C., died in Texas, married Miss Stephens.
12. Robert Melville Cooper, subject of this sketch.
13. Matthew Delamare Cooper, subject of previous sketch.

Source: Marise P. Lightfoot and Evelyn Shackelford, "Maury County Neighbors", page 158; "Confederate Soldiers and Patriots of Maury County, Tenn.," page 66, quoting family records of Miss Juanita Keys, Mt. Pleasant.

ANTHONY M. COPELAND
Enlisted as private 4 Oct. 1813 in Capt. Samuel B. McKnight's company, Col. Thomas McCrory; served as officer in militia in 1813. Son of David Copeland, Sr., and his wife Jane Craig. No further information on his marriage and children.*

Brothers and sisters of Anthony M. Copeland:
1. Sarah, married _____Carswell.
2. James Copeland, born about 1775.
3. David Copeland, Jr., married 21 Sept. 1824 to Nancy Combs.
4. Mary (Polly), married 10 March 1812 to James Craig. [One source says she married Prof. James Alexander.]
5. Peggy married _____Dobson. [One source says she married 23 May 1808 to Samuel Thompson.]
6. Hezekiah Copeland.
7. Betsy Copeland married _____McCarnish

*Married 24 March 1806 to Nancy Craig.

Anthony M. Copeland, continued:
8. Sally Copeland.
Source: Will of David Copeland, Sr., recorded in Maury County. Book C-1, page 209;
Lucy Womack Bates, "Roster of Soldiers and Patriots of the American Revolution buried
in Tennessee," page 99.

JAMES COPELAND
Enlisted as private 4 Oct. 1812 in Capt. William Dooley's company, Col. Thomas
McCrory; born about 1775; son of David Copeland, Sr., and his wife Jane Craig. No
further information.

GARLAND COSBY
Served in War of 1812; no service established as yet; born 25 Jan. 1777; married
21 Feb. 1799. [His Bible record is given in Maury County Cousins, No. 2, page 1;
but it has been impossible to determine his wife's name and those of his children.]

RUSSELL R. COVEY
Served in Capt. Bird S. Hurt's company, enlisting 13 Nov. 1814 as first corporal;
married 21 Nov. 1810 to Rachel Davis. Later lived in Hardin County, Tenn., will be
found there on 1830 and 1840 census records.

DAVID CRAIG
Enlisted as private 4 Oct. 1813 in Capt. Samuel B. McKnight's company. No further
information.

DAVID CRAIG
Commissioned lieutenant of volunteer rifle company, 27th regiment, 1812. [One David
Craig was appointed justice of the peace in 1810.]

JAMES CRAIG
Enlisted as private 22 June 1812 in Capt. Benjamin Reynolds company under General
Isaac Roberts. [Name found on one roll as James B. Craig.] No further information.

JAMES CRAIG
Enlisted as private 4 Oct. 1813 in Capt. William Dooley's company. No further
information. [One James Craig married 10 March 1812 to Polly Copeland; it has been
impossible to tell which one this was.]

JOHN W. CRAIG
Appointed patrolee for Columbia Dec. 1808. No further information.
[Inventory of one John Craig was made 12 Dec. 1815 with Betsy Craig and Isaac Acuff
as administrators.]

ROBERT R. CRAIG
Served in War of 1812; born 15 Dec. 1786 in S. C., died 18 Nov. 1854 in Maury Co.,
married Rachel Miles, born 8 Dec. 1795, S. C.; son of Samuel Craig of South Caro-
lina and Elizabeth Anderson of Ireland; settled in the Hill Station-Groveland-
Silver Creek area; believed to have lived in Coffee County briefly before coming to
Maury County.

Children of Robert R. Craig:
1. John Craig, born 12 May 1815 Columbia, S. C., died 13 June 1896, buried Rose
   Hill, married 23 Jan. 1838 in Maury County to Sarah H. Gilliam, born 1808, died
   22 March 1893, buried Rose Hill.
2. James M. Craig.
3. Stephen Samuel Craig, born 14 Dec. 1833, died 22 Aug. 1916, married 1859 to
   Mary A. Sharber.
4. William D. Craig.
5. Matilda Craig

6. Martha Craig.

[Goodspeed's History of Maury County, 914, 915; Century Review of Maury County, pages 236, 255; Craig tombstones in Rose Hill; Craig family papers. Some discrepancies in dates in these records. Robert R. Craig had a brother Samuel Craig, born 1810, S. C., married Zillie Covey—yet this would make Samuel about 25 years younger than his brother Robert.]

WILLIAM CRAIG
Enlisted as private 22 June 1812 in Capt. Benjamin Reynolds Company, Brigadier General Isaac Roberts Mounted Rangers. No further information.

WILLIAM CRAIG
Enlisted as private 29 Sept. 1814 in Capt. James McMahan's mounted volunteers under Col. Robert H. Dyer. Transferred to Capt. Wyatt's company. No further information.

WILLIAM CRAIG
Commissioned captain of a militia company 1807; had land or lived on Lytles Creek. No further information. [At least three William Craigs in county; information following will be on these men, and it was impossible to determine which was the soldier.

William Craig, born 1773 in Orange Co., N. C., died 1838; son of David and Eleanor Craig. He married 1794 to Mary Blackwood, daughter of William Blackwood and Mary King, born 1777, died 31 Jan. 1835, buried at Hunter's Cemetery. They were said to have had 13 children, but only the names of the six following are known:
1. Eleanor Craig, born 1795, died 1824, married Alexander Johnston, son of John Johnson and Martha Allison.
2. William Craig married Sarah Walker. [Possibly one of the soldiers listed above.
3. David Johnston Craig, married Mary Ann Hunter, daughter of Col. William Hunter and Eleanor Stockard.
4. Samuel Craig, nothing much known about him.
5. Mary Craig married Lemuel Long.
Source: Mrs. Evelyn Shackelford, Mt. Pleasant, from the papers of Mrs. Mary McKennon

William Craig, listed as over 45 on 1820 census, lived in Carters Creek area of the county. His children:
1. John Craig
2. Maria Craig
3. Matilda Craig, married 25 Sept. 1827 Moses Latta.
4. Franklin Craig.
5. Jeannette (Janet) Craig.
6. Louise Craig, born 1814, died 20 Feb. 1873, married John Latta, 19 Oct. 1834.
7. Samuel Craig.
8. Adeline Craig married John Akin.
Source: Columbia Herald, 21 Feb. 1873; Family Favorite, 22 Feb. 1873; Maury County deed book F, page 79; Virginia Alexander, Maury Co., Tenn., Deed Abstracts, Books D, E, F, page 55.

William Craig, one of the 14 children of Johnson Craig (Rev. War soldier) and his wife Martha Blackwood.
Source: Goodspeed's History of Hickman County, page 912.
He is supposed to have moved to Laclede Co., Missouri in 1853, and died there in 1869. He married in Williamson County to Amanda Copeland, who died 1836 when her son Peyton H. Craig was only two weeks old. (Goodspeed's History of Wayne County, page 859.) One source gives this William Craig's birthdate as 1805, which would have made him too young to have been a soldier.

WILLIAM W. CRAIG

Enlisted as private 10 Feb. 1813 in Capt. Benjamin Reynolds company, Col. Thomas Benton; transferred to Williamson County cavalry as he had moved to Williamson Co. [National Republican Banner, 14 March 1871: W. W. Craig died last night after a long and painful illness.] (Name found as William B. Craig once.)

ARTHUR H. CRANFORD

Enlisted as private on 20 Sept. 1814 in Capt. John Looney's company, 2d regiment West Tennessee militia; born 19 Dec. 1790, died 3 March 1877, buried in Cranford Cemetery off Bear Creek Pike. Columbia Herald, 15 Dec. 1871: War of 1812 pensioner who lives in District 27. Columbia Herald, 9 March 1877: "Arthur H. Cranford of the headwaters of Bear Creek died Saturday night at the age of 88 years, War of 1812 soldier, never had a doctor in his family until last week...married second wife two years ago." Married Frances Barker, born 14 Nov. 1791, died 23 Feb. 1873, daughter of George Barker, Rev. War soldier. Married 1873 to Elizabeth Tucker. (Columbia Herald, 17 Sept. 1873, Arthur H. Cranford, 85, and Miss Elizabeth Tucker, age 70, were married Wednesday."

Children of Arthur H. Cranford:
1. Fannie, born 14 Oct. 1829, died 7 Feb. 1873, married James M. Tucker.
2. Lucinda, married W. D. Jackson; born 1 Dec. 1833.
3. Wesley, born about 1826.
4. Priscilla, born about 1831
5. Arthur, born about 1835, died 1865, married Hester Ann Journey.
6. [Margaret, married _____ Dyer, is said to have been a child.]
7. No further information.

DAVID B. CRANFORD

Maury County Court Minutes, Book 17, page 278: 2 Feb. 1855 – Abraham H. Cranford is guardian of Mary Angeline Cranford, minor of David B. Cranford, soldier of the War of 1812, who served six months in Capt. Patterson's company, General Carroll's Brigade, she is daughter of David B. Cranford. Minute Book 17, page 362: David B. Cranford died leaving no widow; was private in War of 1812 in militia; Mary Angeline Cranford is sole survivor.

HARRY CRANFORD

Served in Capt. John Chisholm's company. No further information.

JOHN CRAUGHROM

Served in Capt. John Chisholm's company. No further information.

ELIZABETH CRAWFORD

Drew pension 1883 in Columbia as widow of War of 1812 soldier.

ALEXANDER C. CRAWFORD

Enlisted as private 28 Sept. 1814 in Capt. James McMahan's Tennessee Volunteer Gunmen, Col. Robert H. Dyer. [A soldier of the American Revolution by this name lived in Maury County, but it has been impossible to determine if he is this soldier or not, or a son.]

HARDIN W. CRAWFORD *

Enlisted 28 Sept. 1814 in Capt. James McMahan's First Tennessee Mounted Volunteer Gunmen, Col. Robert Dyer. No further information.

JAMES L. CRAWFORD

Served as sergeant in the militia and drew invalid pension in Maury County in 1828.

Hardy W. Crawford marriage bond 26 Oct. 1819 to Mahaly Harper.

JAMES T. CRAWFORD - see James T. Crofford.

SAMUEL CRAWFORD
Commissioned lieutenant 27th Regiment 1808; commissioned second major in 46th regiment 1812; second lieutenant in Capt. James McMahan's company, 1st Tennessee Mounted Volunteer, promoted to captain 27 Dec. 1814. Also served in First Seminole War, enlisted 31 Jan. 1818, captain, 2nd Tennessee Volunteer Mounted Gunmen, under Col. Thomas Williamson. Later known as Colonel Crawford. Born 5 Jan. 1781 in Moore County, N. C., died 28 Nov. 1842 (killed) in Maury County; married (1) Anney Booker, born 26 Jan. 1782 in Chatham Co., N. C., died 26 Jan. 1828; (2) Sarah _____. Married Anney Booker 23 Feb. 1804.

Children of Samuel Crawford:
1. Patsy Patterson Crawford, born 25 Nov. 1805, married 1824 James Hutcheson.
2. Charles Daniel Crawford, born 23 April 1807, married 1830 to Susan Wantland and 1841 Elizabeth Barr.
3. Sarah Sellers Crawford, born 26 Oct. 1810, died 11 July 1845.
4. William McAuley Crawford, born 10 Jan. 1813.
5. Samuel James Crawford, born 5 Jan. 1815, died 3 Nov. 1816.
6. Elizabeth McAll Crawford, born 22 March 1817 married 1838 Thomas Holcomb.
7. John Booker Crawford, born 16 July 1819, died 26 Oct. 1823.
8. James Sellers Crawford, born 22 Jan. 1822, married 1841 Martha Jane Renfro.
9. Luke Bynum Crawford, born 28 March 1825.
10. Anney Booker Crawford, born 10 Sept. 1827, died 31 Jan. 1828.

July 1859 court minutes: "Mrs. Sarah Crawford wishes an allowance of $20, being destitute of nearly everything to eat and wear. She is widow of Col. Samuel Crawford who fought well for his country." W. B. Fulsom, Esquire, was her trustee.

Source: Crawford Bible record sent to Maury County Historical Society by the late Mrs. E. K. Boyd, Bolivar, Tenn.; additional information from family records of Don Simmons, Murray, Ky.

WILLIAM CRAWFORD
Commissioned lieutenant in 46th Regiment in 1813 and 1814. No further information.

WILLIAM CRAWFORD
Enlisted as private 22 June 1812 in Capt. Benjamin Reynolds company, Brig. General Isaac Roberts. No further information. [Bill of sale, dated 8 Dec. 1819, Samuel Crawford of Maury sells to William Crawford of Maury, a nego "my part of my deceased father's estate, also household furniture now in possession of William Crawford."]

JOHN CREASY
Commissioned lieutenant 27th regiment Maury County militia 1812. No further information.

CORNELIUS CRENSHAW
Service not determined. 9 June 1819 deed registered for land he got in 1816, $67\frac{1}{4}$ acres on Globe Creek.

Source: Maury County Deed Book G, Instrument 86.

GEORGE CRIPPIN
Enlisted 22 June 1812 in Capt. Benjamin Reynolds company, Brig. Gen. Isaac Roberts, Mounted rangers; enlisted 10 Feb. 1813 in Capt. Benjamin Reynolds Company, Col. Thomas Benton Volunteer Infantry; enlisted 10 Dec. 1812 in Capt. Benjamin Reynolds company, Col. Thomas Benton Volunteer Infantry. Still in county in 1820. No further information.

EDWARD CROCHRAM
Served in Capt. John Looney's company. No further information.

SAMUEL CROSBY (or COSBY)
Commissioned lieutenant in 27th Regiment in 1809. No further information.

JAMES T. CROFFORD
Served in Capt. John Looney's company. Born 11 Dec. 1796, died 17 Feb. 1883, buried Elmwood Cemetery, Memphis, on Lot 146-149, the Looney lot; married Jane B. Porter, daughter of William Porter; she was born 30 Dec. 1800, died 30 Aug. 1874, buried in Elmwood Cemetery, Memphis. Name is spelled Crofford on tombstone.

Children of James T. Crofford:
1. Mary Amanda Crofford, buried Elmwood Cemetery, no stone; married 8 Oct. 1840 to Brig. General Preston Smith, CSA, born 25 Dec. 1823 in Giles County, died 20 Sept. 1863. He was educated at Jackson College in Maury County.
2. Louisa M. Crofford, born 24 Oct. 1825, died 20 Aug. 1909, married Robert Fain Looney, Colonel, CSA, buried Elmwood Cemetery, Memphis.
3. Nimrod Crofford, died in infancy.
4. Caleb Crofford, died in infancy.
   (Nimrod Porter Diary 10 Oct. 1866, mentions that his sister Jane is having graves of Nimrod and Caleb moved from Bradshaw Cemetery to the Seminary Cemetery. Local historians cannot identify the Seminary Cemetery.)
5. No further information on additional children.

Source: Elmwood Cemetery inscriptions furnished by Virginia W. Alexander (Mrs. C.C.) and various entries in Nimrod Porter diary, a copy of which is in State Archives. Porter made this note on 20 May 1863—"Rec'd news of James T. Crofford's death Feby 15." (Note difference in tombstone inscription and the diary entry—we believe diary entry is correct.)

JOHN CRUTCHER
Served in Capt. Samuel Ashmore's company. No further information.

JONATHAN CUNDIFF
Served in War of 1812 in Virginia. Cundiff Ford on Duck River was named for this man. Died 5 Oct. 1855. He married 22 May 1815 to Sarah T. Squires, who died 17 Oct. 1855.

Source: Maury County Cousins, No. 1, page 96.

AARON P. CUNNINGHAM
Enlisted as private 4 Oct. 1813 in Capt. James Porter's company, Col. John Wynne; had originally enlisted in Capt. William Wilson's infantry and transferred on 4 Nov. 1813. Died in Tishomingo Co., Miss. In 1811 he purchased 500 acres on Rutherford Creek, part of the Doherty grant; sold some of this land in 1811 to Solomon Herring. An old house on the Green's Mill Road north of Columbia is said to be his home.

JOSEPH CURRY
Served in Capt. Andrew McCarty's company. No further information.

DANIEL CUTBURTH
Served in Capt. William Dooley's company. [Have been unable to determine if this is Daniel Cutbirth, Sr., or Daniel Cutbirth, Jr. The following information on the Cutbirths was sent in by Mrs. Nelle J. Smith of Pulaski.]

Draper Manuscript, 12 DD 53-56 – James Calloway, grandson of Benjamin Cutbirth, wrote to Draper in 1846, "my grandfather Benjamin Cutbirth and my uncle Daniel Cutbirth went

Daniel Cutburth, continued:

to Maury County, Tenn., and settled on land in Maury County, south of Duck River." Records that Mrs. Smith located show that this land was on Big Creek around Gibson- ville and Yokely, Giles County.

Giles County Minutes of Court, Book 1837-1838, page 250—Owing to the satisfaction of the court that Daniel Cutbirth died at his usual place of abode or home in Giles County, had died intestate; George T. Malone was named administrator and later made report to the court of the inventory. 1838.

Giles County Deed Book Q, page 533, dated 13 Nov. 1843: W. D. Benderman, (son in law of Daniel Cutbirth, Sr.) bought the land sold at public auction on courthouse yard in Pulaski and in this deed the place was described as being on Big Creek and there was mention made of the mill.

Decree of Chancery Court at March 1846 session, Elizabeth Cutbirth sold her dower interest to Alexander Scott. She was described as being the widow of Daniel Cut- birth, deceased. She in return was to make her home with Alexander Scott family. She is buried at the Old Well Cemetery in Maury County—Betsy Cutbirth, consort of Daniel Cutbirth, Sr., and her daughter who married Richard Anderson is also buried there.

Daniel Cutbirth, Jr., married first to Jane Reed 7 Oct. 1814 and they lived in Lawrence County where Jane died before 1823; on 6 Jan. 1823 Daniel Cutbirth married (2) Elizabeth Reed, sister of Jane. Daniel Cutbirth, Jr., went to Tippah County, Miss., for a few years and back to Tennessee near Bolivar where his daughter Eliza who married Jesse Tudor lived. Samson Cutbirth, son of Daniel Sr. on the 1840 census of Giles County, who married 1 Jan. 1829 to Harriett Halls and was in Cass County, Texas, by 1850.

George Cutbirth, son of Daniel and Betsy Cutbirth, married Sarah Foster, daughter of John Foster, and they lived in Lawrence County, Tenn., before 1850.

Daniel Cutbirth, Sr., had daughter Sarah Cutbirth, who married Frances M. Rose.

Source: Letter from Mrs. Nelle J. Smith, dated 7 May 1973. [It seems probable that the War of 1812 soldier was Daniel Cutbirth, Jr.]

EDMOND COOPER
Refer also to page 35. Born 1785 in Virginia, died Feb. 1872 in Maury County, married 19 Aug. 1824 in Maury County to Nancy Hadley, born 1804, died 5 March 1873 in Maury, daughter of Ambrose Hadley, Sr.

Children of Edmond Cooper:
1. Benjamin H., born 1827, married 7 Feb. 1851 to Judy Williams.
2. Fanny H., born 1827, married 4 Dec. 1851 to David G. Williams.
3. Rebecca, born 1829, married 24 Oct. 1849 to John B. Flowers.
4. Polly P., born 1833.
5. Ambrose, born 1835, married 27 Nov. 1867 to Mary Phillips.
6. Nancy E., born 1837, married 12 Aug. 1854 to Elis Flowes.
7. Louiza H., born 1839, married 14 Dec. 1856 to George F. Flowers.
8. Sarah E., born 1846, married 2 March 1865, to Martin V. B. Brown.
9. Martha J., born 1830, married 11 Oct. 1848 to James D. Carrigan.
10. Isabella, born 1843.

Brothers and sisters of Edmond Cooper:
1. Polly B. Cooper, born 1774, died 1853, did not marry.
2. Nancy B. Cooper, born 1790, died 1866, did not marry.   continued

Edmond Cooper, continued:

3. Benjamin Cooper.
4. Rebecca Cooper, married 24 Nov. 1819 to John Jordon.
5. Frances Park, born 1799, died Aug. 1862, married Netherland Tait.
6. William Cooper, Jr., born 29 Jan. 1781, died 21 Oct. 1834.
7. John F. Cooper, died 1869 Lawrence Co., Ala., married Jane _____.

Source: Jane Luna (Mrs. John W.) from her family papers and research.

JOEL DABBS
Commissioned ensign in 51st Regiment in 1814. No further information.

JOHN DAGBY (or Dagley)
Served in Capt. John Looney's company, enlisted 20 Sept. 1814, 2d Regiment of West Tennessee Militia. Marriage bond dated 29 Nov. 1808 John Dagley to Sarah Boyd. No further information.

ADAM DALE
Captain in Col. William Y. Higgins' 2d Regiment of West Tennessee Militia. Born 14 July 1768 in Worcester County, Maryland, died 14 Oct. 1851 in Hazel Green, Ala. He was buried in the Jeffries Cemetery there and his body was removed in 1850s to Rose Hill in Columbia, Tenn. There is still a stone for him in the Alabama cemetery. He was also a soldier during the American Revolution and is considered the first settler of Dekalb Co., Tenn. He married 24 Feb. 1790 to Mary Hall, born 27 Oct. 1772, died 10 March 1859.

Children of Adam Dale:
1. Edward Washington Dale, born 11 Nov. 1790 in Worcester Co., Md., died 1840 in Columbia, Tenn., married 1. Ann Lewis Moore, 2. Mrs. Fannie Baird.
2. Lemuel Hall Dale, born 30 April 1793 in Worcester Co., Md., died 27 Aug. 1796 at Liberty, Smith County, Tenn.
3. Elizabeth E. Evans Dale, born 28 Oct. 1795 in Worcester Co., Md., died 7 May 1866 in Marshall County, Miss. Married 1. Samuel G. Gibbons; 2. ____ Flanagan; 3. 1833 Alexander Jeffries; 4. ____ High; 5. Absalom Brown; 6. 1848 Willis Routt.
4. Thomas Dale, born 26 June 1798 in Davidson Co., Tenn., died 31 Aug. 1820 in Liberty, Smith County.
5. Peggy Hall Dale, born 19 Oct. 1800, Smith Co., Tenn., married 1815 to John Phillips; she died 24 Jan. 1836 in Centerville, Hickman Co., Tenn.
6. Sarah Hill Dale, born 25 Dec. 1802 in Smith Co., Tenn., married 8 April 1835 to Nathan Vaught. She died in Columbia, Tenn., and is buried at Rose Hill.
7. Sopha Woodson Dale, born 19 March 1805 in Smith County, married Dr. Robert Turner 15 April 1818.
8. Mary Hall Dale, born 25 May 1807 in Smith Co., Tenn., married 25 Dec. 1828 in Smith County to Thomas Baker, and secondly to John H. Edminston.
9. Nancy Stevenson Dale, born 21 July 1809 in Smith County, died 3 Aug. 1816.
10. William Jourdan Hall Dale, born 10 July 1811 in Smith County, died 20 April 1830 in Nashville, Tenn.

Source: Nathan Vaught, "Youth and Old Age", pages 111-157. The first part of this history of the Dale family in this book was written by Adam Dale himself.

HENRY DAIMWOOD
Commissioned lieutenant in 27th Regiment in 1808. No further information.

WILLIAM DANIEL

Commissioned captain of volunteer rifle company, 27th regiment, Maury County militia in 1812—had been commissioned captain of a company in 1807. [Muster rolls show that William Daniel served as private in Capt. William Dooley's company; we have been unable to ascertain if the militia company captain and the private in Dooley's company were the same person or not. The private enlisted 4 Oct. 1813.] Born 26 Aug. 1774, died 19 (or 12) Sept. 1826 in Maury County; married Mary Kirk, born 4 June 1781, died 20 June 1847, daughter of Isaac Kirk.

Children of William Daniel:
1. Isaac K. W., 21 March 1802 – 20 Feb. 1849.
2. Caroline N., 1 Aug. 1803 – 22 April 1832, married 21 Dec. 1826 Giles T. Harris.
3. M. G., M. D., born 28 Dec. 180_, died 1827.
4. Minerva married 5 April 1836 William B. Theobald.
5. William W., Jr., died Aug. 1833.
6. John J.
7. Elizabeth, born 8 Dec. 1818, died 15 June 185_, married Benjamin F. Smith.
8. Franklin O., born 4 May 1821, died 22 July 1896.
9. Martha Angeline, deceased by 1845, married Allen White.

Source: Smith vs Daniel, 1845-50, unpublished chancery court records; Circuit Court Minute Book 1834-37, page 1.

DAVID DARNELL

Commissioned ensign in 27th regiment, Maury County militia, 1808. No further information.

JOHN DARNELL

Commissioned ensign in 27th regiment, Maury County militia, 1811. No further information.

BRACKETT DAVIDSON

Enlisted as private 28 Sept. 1814 in Capt. James McMahan's company, Col. Robert Dyer. Drew pension for his services or land bounty 29 Feb. 1848, Rect. Wt. No. 19863. Born 17 Nov. 1796, died 29 Sept. 1863 in Boyd, Dallas Co., Missouri. He moved to Missouri in 1847. Married 8 Aug. 1817 in Maury to Delila Hardison, born 22 July 1802, died Feb. 1884, daughter of James Hardison, Revolutionary War soldier. He spelled his name both Davison and Davidson. He was wounded 23 Dec. 1814 near New Orleans.

Children of Brackett Davidson:
1. Thomas Mcdearman, born 11 May 1818.
2. George, born 22 Feb. 1820.
3. Fanny Manerva, born 27 Oct. 1821.
4. Lucrecia, born 23 July 1823.
5. James Hardison, born 28 Jan. 1825.
6. Milton McMacklen, born 9 Sept. 1826.
7. Margaret Catharine, born 13 July 1828.
8. Calvin Bracket, born 1 March 1830.
9. William H., born 5 Jan. 1821.
10. Sarah Elizabeth, born 6 Feb. 1834.
11. Joshua, born 13 Oct. 1835.
12. Mary Jane, born 30 July 1837.
13. John Humphreys, born 30 Oct. 1843.
14. Charles Isom Joel, born 25 Nov. 1846.

Source: Pension-land bounty application; family information furnished by the late Claude B. Carter, Koscuisko, Miss., published Sept. 1966, page 84, Historic Maury published by Maury County Historical Society.

EPHRAIM E. DAVIDSON

Commissioned lieutenant, 27th regiment, Maury County militia 1809; served as corporal in Capt. Benjamin Reynolds company. Born 17 May 1785 in Burke Co., N. C., died 22 Sept. 1850, Lafayette Co., Miss.; married Mary Brank, born 25 Dec. 1789, died 25 Dec. 1864, Lafayette Co., Miss. They are both buried in College Hill Cemetery in that county. Son of John Davidson (born 15 Feb. 1750 Rowan Co., N.C., died 28 Feb. 1825 in Maury County) and his first wife Ruth Clement. John Davidson was a soldier in the American Revolution.

Children of Ephraim E. Davison:
1. John Franklin Davidson, married 24 Dec. 1845 Mary M. Davidson.
2. Margaret Tennessee Davidson, married 19 Jan. 1836 John Neely.
3. Ruth Clemens Davidson, married 11 Dec. 1832, J. M. Thompson.
4. Robert B. Davidson.
5. Abraham W. Curren Davidson.
6. Junius Davidson, born 26 Feb. 1825.
7. George Washington Davidson, baptised June 1829.
8. Edward Chaffin Davidson, born 17 Dec. 1832.

Brothers and sisters of Ephraim E. Davidson:
1. Jennie Davidson married Andrew Neely.
2. Ruth Melinda Davidson, died 12 May 1847 at the age of 56 years; married (1) Dr. Abraham Whiteside; (2) Edward H. Chaffin.
3. Mary Davidson, married _____ Martin.
4. Thomas Davidson, born 1776 married Mary Kennard.
5. John O. Davidson, born 1791, died 1856; married Ruth Ragsdale.
6. (Half) Cynthia Eliza, born 16 March 1793 Burke Co., N. C., died 1862, Panola Co., Miss., married (1) Paris Dooley; (2) 4 July 1833 William Rutledge Caldwell, born 1810, died 1 May 1889.

Source: Virginia W. and Charles C. Alexander, "Historic Ebenezer, Reese's Chapel, Presbyterian Church and Cemetery", 1968, p. 31; Roster of Soldiers and Patriots of the American Revolution Buried in Tennessee, 1974, page 112.

EPHRAIM DAVIDSON

Enlisted 4 Oct. 1813 as private in Capt. William Dooley's company. (Possibly the same man as above.)

GEORGE DAVIDSON

Lived in Southport in 1883 and drew pension as War of 1812 soldier. [Buried at McCain's Cemetery is George Davidson, born 7 July 1792, died 4 Aug. 1876, and his wife Sarah A. Davidson, born 26 Sept. 1800, died 22 Jan. 1868; marriage records show George Davidson married Sally Howard, license issued 11 Nov. 1820.]

GEORGE DAVIDSON

One of this name appointed constable June 1809. Man of this name appointed patrolee Sept. 1808 in Capt. James Byers company. No further information.

GILBRETH FALLS DAVIDSON

Served in Capt. Benjamin Reynolds company. Died 2 Aug. 1822, buried in Elk Ridge Cemetery, just over line in Giles County; married Polly _____. He was son of George Davidson (whose estate was settled in Maury in 1813) and Rosanna Falls, died 1834 at the age of 69. The parents were married 13 Jan. 1784 in Rowan County, N. C.

Source: Maury County Will Book A-1, page 71; Maury County Neighbors, pages 20, 21.

JAMES L. DAVIDSON

Served as private in Capt. William Dooley's company. (Possibly the same as the one following.)

+JAMES L. DAVIDSON
Enlisted as private 20 Sept. 1814 in Capt. John Looney's company; died April 1815 on extra service. [He is believed to be the son of George and Rosanna Davidson. In a division of Davidson's estate made as late as 1823, mention was made of James L. Davidson, deceased.]

JAMES L. DAVIDSON
Commissioned ensign of a light infantry company, 27th regiment, Maury County militia in 1814. Believed to be the same as above.

JOHN E. DAVIDSON
Commissioned lieutenant in 27th regiment, Maury County militia in 1808. Enlisted as private 22 June 1812 in Capt. Benjamin Reynolds company, Gen. Isaac Roberts Mounted Rangers. No further information.

JOSHUA DAVIDSON
Enlisted as private 18 Dec. 1813 in Capt. James McMahan's mounted gunmen, Col. N. T. Perkins; enlisted as private 28 Sept. 1814 in Capt. James McMahan's company. No further information. [It is believed he was a brother of Brackett Davidson.]

JABEZ DAVIS
Served in Capt. John Chisholm's company. No further information.

JAMES DAVIS
Served in Capt. John Looney's company. No further information.

JAMES R. DAVIS
Served in Capt. Benjamin Reynolds' second company. No further information.

JOHN DAVIS
Served in Capt. John Chisholm's company. Born 1793 in Georgia, died 1856 in Hamilton County, Illinois; married 10 June 1809 in Maury County to Dicy Tombs, born 1795 in Va., died 1870 Hamilton Co., Illinois. They are both buried in Hickory Hill Cemetery.

Source: Mrs. Christine J. Felty, Champaign, Illinois.

JOSEPH DAVIS
Served as private in Capt. William Dooley's company. No further information.

MAJOR DAVIS
Served in Capt. Bird S. Hurt's company. He married March 1811 to Penelope Bird; she left him 1812 and sued for divorce in 1816. He married secondly 27 June 1818 to Hannah Crosthwait. By 1830 he is living in Franklin Co., Alabama.

Source: Davis vs Davis, Equity Causes, 1818, Maury County records.

WILLIS DAVIS
Appointed constable in March 1809 and in March 1811 in Maury County. No further information.

+THOMAS DAWSON
Enlisted 20 June 1814 as private in Capt. Henry Newlin's company, militia infantry, Col. Philip Pikin; died 10 Oct. 1814. Miscellaneous court minutes: "Thomas Dawson died in the army, 5 boys and 1 girl." Maury County Will Book A-1, page 195, has inventory of his estate, 18 Nov. 1814, "discharge for 6 months tour of military duty...Col. P. Pikin, 17 Jan. 1815." He is buried near Fort Williams, Alabama, about 15 miles southwest of Childersburg, Alabama. His grave is marked.

48

BENJAMIN DEBERRY
Enlisted 28 Sept. 1814 in Capt. James McMahan's Tennessee Volunteer Mounted Gunmen, Col. R. H. Dyer; dismissed 1 Jan. 1815. No further information.

THOMAS DEBMAN
Discharged from the 8th infantry 1817. No further information. [Thomas Debnam married 27 March 1818 Williamson County to Sarah McLemore, Atkins McLemore, bondsman.]

TIMOTHY DEMONBREUN
Served in Capt. John Gordon's company. No further information. [This man is thought to have been a member of the well known Demonbreun family of Davidson County.]

WILLIAM DENTON
Served in War of 1812 in North Carolina, died 1815 North Carolina, son of William Denton and Ann_____. He married Elizabeth (Betsy) Stiles, born in N. C., who died in Maury County.

Children of William Denton:
1. Williamson Denton, born 1 March 1813, buried at Friendship at Culleoka.
2. Corda Denton, born 23 March 1814, died 17 March 1864, buried Lindsey Cemetery near Culleoka, married Parthenia Collier, born 1817, died 1899.

Brothers and sisters of William Denton:
1. Nelson Denton.
2. Peter Denton.
3. Lucy Denton.
4. Cloe Denton.

Source: Information furnished by Mrs. Dorris Bryant Pennington; ancestor of Mrs. Harvell Ashton, member of Jane Knox Chapter. William Denton enlisted 14 Sept. 1814, Capt. Isaac Watkins company of infantry; rendezvous Gates Court House, N. C. He was discharged 5 Feb. 1815, sick in camp at Norfolk, Va. Total pay, $37.26.

WILLIAM DEVASUER
Served in Capt. John Looney's company. No further information.

WILLIAM DEWBERRY
Served in Capt. John Looney's company. No further information.

SAMUEL DEY
Served in Capt. John Looney's company. No further information.

JOSEPH DIAL
Enlisted 28 Sept. 1814 in Capt. William Martin's company, Williamson County troops, discharged 27 April 1815. Born about 1778, died 1818 in Maury County at Culleoka; married 3 May 1806 in Williamson County to Elizabeth Cole, born 1785 in Bedford Co., Pa., died about 1852 in Lawrence Co., Tenn. He was the son of Thomas Dial and Polly Finley (?). She was the daughter of Thomas Cole, born 1760, died 1815 in Williamson County.

Children of Joseph Dial:
1. Uriah, born 1807, died young.
2. Delilah, born 1809, died after 1820.
3. Robert Finley, born 13 April 1813, died 1895, buried Bethany Cemetery; married
   1. Dec. 1832 to Elizabeth Butler; 2. 11 Feb. 1845 to Mary Frances Rust;
   3. 25 July 1852 to Nancy Susan Barnett; 4. 1875 to Mariah Watson.
4. Nancy Stephenson, born 1815, died 22 Jan. 1834, married Nathaniel Lancaster.
continued on next page

Children of Joseph Dial, continued:
5. Joseph Ross Dial, born 11 Dec. 1819, died 24 Nov. 1864 in Lawrence Co., Tenn., married Sarah _____, born 18 Dec. 1819, died 26 Aug. 1910.

Source: Family papers of Mrs. Reuben Algood, descendant.

BENONI DICKEY

Commissioned first major in 51 Regiment, 1813. Enlisted as private 24 Sept. 1813, Capt. Robert Evans Company of Mounted Spies, discharged 24 Dec. 1813. Born 1785, deathdate not known; married 23 June 1809 (date of bond) to Margaret Gordon Frierson, born 5 April 1793, died 25 Sept. 1815, buried at Zion Cemetery; he was the son of John Dickey.

Children of Benoni Dickey:
1. Samuel Grandason Dickey, born 22 June 1819, died 7 Sept. 1841. [Note birthdate and mother's deathdate; these dates are in question.]
2. John Frierson Dickey.
3. Lawrence Ludlow Dickey, born 29 Oct. 1813, died Aug. 1828.
4. No further information on any additional children.

Brothers and sisters of Benoni Dickey:
1. Capt. George Dickey.
2. Mary Jane Dickey.
3. See listing of John Dickey.

Source: The Friersons of Zion Church and some of their descendants.

GEORGE DICKEY

Commissioned captain of light infantry company 1814, 51st regiment. Born 23 May 1778, died 30 Nov. 1847, buried Zion Cemetery; married 19 July 1810 to Sarah M. Armstrong, born 1791, died 1845. (His home was located about on the location of the Baker School property in 1975 and was known as Dingley Dell.) He was son of John Dickey.

Children of George Dickey:
1. Mary L., married David D. McFall.
2. Margaret Parmelia.
3. Harriet Jane Agnes.
4. James M. Dickey.
5. Samuel George Dickey. [The dates for Samuel G. Dickey above are believed to belong to this man.]
6. Martha Lenore married 1837 to William H. Crittenden.
7. Sarah Gordon married James Blakely.
8. Sallie K. Dickey.
9. Napoleon Dickey.
10. Kate Armstrong Dickey.

Source: The Friersons of Zion Church and some of their descendants, page 36. Nathan Vaught wrote that one of George Dickey's daughters married W. O. Ferguson, but we have been unable to established the daughter; They Passed This Way, page A-103.

JOHN DICKEY

Appointed Justice of the peace by the State Legislature late in 1807. His tombstone near Sharp's Spring, Franklin, Williamson County, gives the date of death as 11 Jan. 1807. Descendants believe that this date is in error and should be 11 Jan. 1808 as there is record that he was living past his presumed death date. He married Mary W. _____, born Jan. 1748, died 29 Dec. 1821. Children on following page.

Children of John Dickey:
1. Capt. George Dickey, born 23 May 1778, died 30 Nov. 1847, married Sarah Way Armstrong.
2. Benoni Dickey, born 1785, death not known, married 23 June 1809 to Margaret G. Frierson.
3. Mary Jean Dickey, born 1777, died 1862; married Moses Gordon Frierson.
4. [Samuel Edward Dickey, born 3 Sept. 1780, died 3 Sept. 1835, buried at Zion; married Elizabeth_____. Descendants of this man believe he is a son of John Dickey, but no documentation has been discovered as yet.]
5. No further information.

Source: Tombstone inscriptions at Zion Church, Maury County; tombstone inscriptions at Sharp's Spring, Williamson County; family information of Miss Emma Porter Armstrong, descendant of John Dickey, Esquire.

JOHN DILL
Commissioned ensign in volunteer rifle company, 27th regiment, Maury County militia in 1812; enlisted 2 Nov. 1812 as 2d lieutenant in Capt. Benjamin Reynolds company of volunteer infantry, Col. Thomas Benton. No further information.

WILLIAM DILL
Served in Capt. John Looney's company. No further information. [A Jobe Dill was an early settler in the county; he lost his land in the famous land suit Kendrick vs Dallam and by 1817 was living in Mississippi. This soldier and the one above could be members of his family; to date the only child for whom there is record is Elizabeth Dill, who married Enos Pipkin.]

ALEXANDER DICKSON
Served in Capt. Samuel Ashmore's company. No further information. His name is also found on one roll as Alexander Dicken.

CHARLES R. DILLON
Enlisted as private 10 Dec. 1812 in Capt. William Carroll's company, Maj. General Andrew Jackson's volunteer infantry; his widow Frances A. Dillon drew pension in 1883 in Columbia as widow of War of 1812 soldier. He came to Maury County between 1817 and 1818; married Frances America Alderson, daughter of John S. Alderson. She was born 7 Nov. 1802 in Lunenburg Co., Va., died 20 July 1883, buried at Greenwood Cemetery.

Children of Charles R. Dillon:
1. Thomas Dillon.
2. Charles R. Dillon, born about 1825.
3. William Dillon.
4. "Bud" Dillon.
5. "one or two others".

Source: Nathan Vaught, "Youth and Old Age", pages 75, 97; 1850 census; Greenwood Cemetery inscriptions.

ADAM DIXON
Served six months in War of 1812, stationed at Fort Norfolk, Va., came to Maury Co. in 1818. Born 10 March 1785 in Bedford Co., Va., died 22 Aug. 1870 of dropsy in Maury County; married 23 Oct. 1811 Bedford Co., Va., to Hannah L. Erwin, born 26 Nov. 1791, died 22 Feb. 1875. Both are buried in the Lytles Creek Cemetery. He was the son of George Dixon and his wife Rachael Beard. Nathan Vaught, page 96, says that Adam Dixon came between 1810-1811—this is believed to be in error as Dixon's service was in Virginia during the War of 1812. Children on the following page.

Children of Adam Dixon:
1. Mary Hamilton Dixon, born 1812, died 1841.
2. George Cardwell Dixon, born 1814, died 1899.
3. Eliza Ann Dixon, born 1816, married George W. C. Maxwell.
4. Rachel Jane Dixon, born 1818.
5. Martha Jane Dixon, born 1820, married Abner H. Hanna.
6. Thomas Jefferson Dixon, born 1822, died 1911, married Katherine C. Kinnard.
7. Margaret Melissa Dixon, born 1824, died 1851, married Rev. J. N. Edminston.
8. Jonas Erwin Dixon, born 1826, died 1851.
9. Nancy Mariah, born 1829, died 1917, married Thomas Hanna; both are buried in Giles County.
10. Joseph Edward Dixon, born 1831, died 1902.
11. Rachel Virginia Dixon, born 1833, died 10 Feb. 1848.

Brothers and sisters of Adam Dixon:
1. Elizabeth Dixon, born 1767, died 1809 in Virginia.
2. Thomas Dixon, born 1769, died 1851, never married, buried Lytle Creek Cemetery.
3. Mary Dixon, born 1772, died 1812 in Va., married John Patterson.
4. Rachel Dixon, born 1775, married Thomas Davis.
5. Anna Dixon, born 1778, married John Thomas.
6. George Dixon, Jr., born 1781, married Pamelia Leftwich; he died 2 Apr. 1804.

Source: Mrs. Nelle J. Smith, Pulaski, Tenn., descendant; Adam Dixon's will in Maury County, 12 Sept. 1870; Nathan Vaught, "Youth and Old Age"; Columbia Beacon, 18 Feb. 1848.

SAMUEL DIXON
Commissioned captain in 27th regiment, Maury County militia, 1813. No further information.

WILLIAM DIXON
Drew pension in 1828 in Maury County for his service in Tennessee militia. No further information.

ELIZA DIXON
Drew pension in 1883 in Mt. Pleasant as widow of War of 1812 soldier. No further information.

JAMES DOBBINS
Commissioned captain in 5th cavalry brigade in 1813; commissioned lieutenant in 27th regiment, Maury County militia in 1814. [Two James Dobbins in the county at the same time and it is impossible to determine the soldier. The following information is on both of these men.]

James Dobbins, born April 1776, died 24 Dec. 1862, buried at Zion Cemetery. He was always known as Captain Dobbins. Born in S. C.; married 5 Sept. 1810 to Mary Lenore Armstrong, born 26 Dec. 1789, died 5 July 1856.

Children of James Dobbins:
1. James Gardner Dobbins, born 1811, died 1886, married Martha Emily Bills.
2. Mary Agnes Pamela Dobbins, born 1813, died 1855, married 1834 Josiah O. Fulton.
3. Margaret Louisa Dobbins, born 1815, died 1901.
4. William Alexander Dobbins, born 1819, died 1836.
5. Robert Wilson Dobbins, born 1825, died 1854.
6. John David Dobbins, born 1828, died 1849.

Source: Dobbins Bible, page 51, Maury County Cousins; page 52, The Friersons of Zion Church and some of their descendants. James Dobbins' house was located about the same site as Dr. Langa's home is in 1975 on Cayce Lane. He had brother Alexander Dobbins, born 4 Aug. 1778, died 19 March 1840.

Colonel James Dobbins, born about 1789, died 1836, son of David Dobbins, American Revolution soldier; married 23 Feb. 1814 to Eliza Webster, born 8 Nof. 1795, died 1835, daughter of Jonathan Webster.

Children of Col. James Dobbins:
1. Adaline, born 1818, died 1878, married Lytle Dooley.
2. Joseph J., died 8 Jan. 1893 at 67, married Sallie Moore.
3. Mary Eliza, married Thomas J. Crosby.
4. Harriet, born 11 March 1820, died Sept. 1835.

Source: Webster tombstone inscriptions; Dooley vs Dobbins, 1841, Dooley vs Webster 1845, chancery court cases; Maury Democrat 12 Jan. 1893; information from Mrs. Marise P. Lightfoot.

JOHN DOBBINS
Commissioned lieutenant in Tennessee militia; born 1773 (some give N. C., and other England), (1850 census shows S. C.), died 1859 in Tennessee; married Nancy Herring, sister of Solomon Herring; attended Bethesda Presbyterian Church; lived between Bear Creek and the Double Branches. He was son of Mrs. Jeannette Dobbins, said to be buried at McConnico's meeting house in Williamson County.

Children:
1. William A. Dobbins, died 1902 at the age of 86, buried Blanton's Chapel; married (1) 1843 to Ellis Jane Lockridge; (2) 1857 to Sarinthia Harriet Crawford, daughter of John Crawford, born 29 March 1821, died 17 Aug. 1876, buried Blanton's Chapel.
2. John J. Dobbin, born 1813, died 1886, buried Rose Hill, married 23 Feb. 1841 to Ann Chappell, daughter of William and Sarah Palmer Chappell, born 1823, died 1888, buried Rose Hill.
3. David W. Dobbin, died 23 Feb. 1876 at 65, married 1840 to Eliza Lockridge, born 1821, died 1863.
4. Jeanette Agnes (alias Nancy), married John H. Neelley.

Source: Circuit Court Minutes Vol 3, No. 1, 1834; Deed Book E, Vol. 2, page 302; Century Review, page 262; Columbia Herald, 4 July 1902; various tombstone inscriptions; information also furnished by Mrs. Virginia W. Alexander.

JOHN DOBBS
Born 1773, died 1859 in Maury County; served as lieutenant in Capt. John Doak's company, 2d Regiment Tennessee militia; was in Battle of New Orleans. No further information.

Source: Soldiers of the War of 1812 buried in Tennessee, page 32.

+ABLE DOCKERY
Enlisted as private 20 June 1814 in Capt. Henry Newlin's company, Col. Philip Pipkin Militia Infantry; left sick at Fort Williams 4 Nov. 1814. Buried at or near Fort Williams, 15 miles southwest of Childersburg, Ala.

BALAAM DOCKERY
Said to be soldier in War of 1812; no service established. Born about 1782 in S. C. died 1858; married Abigail_____, born 1790 in S. C.

Children of Balaam Dockery:
1. William R. Dockery, born 1812, died 1844, married.
2. John J. Dockery, born 1815 in S. C., married Mahala ____; lived Hickman County
3. James Dockery, born 1820, married Martha _____.
4. Hiram Dockery, born 1816 in S. C., married Margaret _____.
Source: 1850 census of Maury; various chancery court records.

HIGHTOWER DODSON
Served in Capt. James McMahan's company. [One Hightower Dodson was the son of Green-ham Dodson and his wife Elinor Hightower of Pittsylvania County, Va. Several of this name found. Researchers are referred to Silas Emmett Lucas, The Dodson Family and its supplement for work on this family.]

JORDAN DODSON
Served in Capt. John Chisholm's company. [One of this name later appears in Giles County; Marriage Records of Maury County, Jordan Dodson marriage bond to Polly Etton, Elisha Dodson, bondsman.]

WILLIAM DODSON
Served in War of 1812 from Virginia.   . Born about 1794 in Virginia, died 1883; married Catherine Davis, born about 1805 in Virginia, died 1865. Served in War of 1812; 1828 living in Davidson County; lived 1829 for one year in Maury; 1830 lived in Hickman County, and finally settled 1833 in Dickson County.

Children of William Dodson:
1. Henry J. Dodson, age 18 in 1850.
2. Napoleon Dodson, age 15 in 1850.
3. J. A., born 11 Aug. 1827 in Halifax Co., Va., married Mary A. E. L____ad and Eliza C. Hopkins.
4. Jerome, age 11 in 1850.
5. Three other children. No further information.

Source: Goodspeed's History of Dickson County, page 1334; 1850 Census of Dickson County.

WILLIAM DODSON
Served in Capt. James McMahan's second company. No further information.

+JOSHUA DONAHO
Served in Capt. Bird S. Hurt' company. Died 16 Dec. 1814. [Early court minutes show a John Donaho living in 1809 on the road leading from Fountain Creek to the upper ford on McCutcheon's Trace.] No further information.

ROBERT DONELSON
Soldier of War of 1812 who lived in Maury County. Marriage bond 24 Dec. 1806 in Williamson County to marry Peggy Feres, with James Faris as bondsman. No further information.

ESOM BALLINGER DOOLEY
Born 20 Sept. 1793 in N. C., died 13 Feb. 1871, buried in College Hill Cemetery, Lafayette Co., Miss. Enlisted as private 4 Oct. 1813 in Capt. William Dooley's company, Col. T. McCrory. Marriage bond dated 2 March 1814 in Maury County to marry Patsy Caldwell, widow of William Caldwell. [Her maiden name was Rutledge.] He was son of James Dooley, born 1746 in Richmond, Va., died 7 June 1824 in Maury County.

Brothers and sisters of Esom B. Dooley:
1. William (half), born 1772, died 1822.
2. Benjamin (half).
3. Paris F. Dooley (whole blood), born 23 Aug. 1800, died 1830.

Children of Esom B. Dooley:
1. Isaac M. Dooley, married Susan_____.
2. No further information.

Source: DAR Roster No. 1, page 581; Ancestor Index, U.S.U.S. Daughters of 1812, edited by Eleanor Stevens Galvin, 1970, page 153; "They Passed This Way", A-91; several Dooley lawsuits in chancery court.

WILLIAM DOOLEY

Captain of a company formed in Maury County; also appointed justice of peace of
Maury County in 1807; born 1772, died 22 Feb. 1822, son of James Dooley, Rev. War
soldier, who married 1766 to Margaret McKinney (who was killed by the Indians).
He married 1801 to Jane Ferilda Rutledge, born 1783, died 27 Feb. 1847; both are
buried in Dooley cemetery in Columbia.

Children of William Dooley:
1. McKinney Dooley.
2. Lytle Dooley, married 1836 to Adaline W. Dobbins.
3. William Dooley.
4. Gilbert W. Dooley, died 16 Aug. 1839 at 25 years.
5. Martin P., born 14 April 1819, died 10 Sept. 1876.
6. John L. Dooley (unaccounted for in family records)
7. Pinkney Dooley, died young.
8. Thomas Dooley.
9. Allen Dooley.
10. Serilda Katherine Dooley married James Washington Matthews.
11. Cynthia Dooley married 1826 to James Kimes.
12. Levicy Dooley, born 15 Dec. 1804, died 23 March 1857, married John B. Brown,
    born 1802, died 1862.
13. Matilda Dooley, married John P. Beard in 1827.

Brothers and sisters of William Dooley:
1. James, born 1761, died in Missouri at the age of 106 years.
2. Benjamin Dooley.
3. Paris F. Dooley (half), born 23 Aug. 1800, died 1830, married 1822 to Cynthia
   Davidson.
4. Esom Ballinger Dooley (half) — see previous page.
5. No further information on other brothers and sisters.

Source: Nathan Vaught, "Youth and Old Age", page 67; "They Passed This Way," page
A-91; DAR Roster No. 1, page 581; various Maury County marriage records; information
by Mrs. Evelyn B. McAnally, descendant, member of Jane Knox Chapter.

JOHN DOUGLAS

Served in Capt. Bird S. Hurt's company. No further information.

WILLIAM L. DOW

Drew pension 1883 in Columbia as soldier of War of 1812; lost right arm above the
elbow. No further information.

BENJAMIN DOWELL, SR.

Enlisted as Ferrier on 10 Dec. 1812 in Capt. John Baskerville cavalry, Col. John
Coffee; died in Maury County about 1837 or 1839. He got 1500 acres in Maury County
on 10 Sept. 1819 from Armistead Flipping and his wife Franky of Smith County, land
located on north side of Duck River. He married Elizabeth "Betsy" Desha, born
Sumner Co., Tenn., 1793, died 7 Sept. 1876, youngest child of Robert and Ellen
Desha. She is buried on Dowell Branch of Knob Creek in Maury County.

Children of Benjamin Dowell:
1. Adeline Dowell, born 1820, married Isaac H. McLuney (McLarry, McEllery). [There
   is some indication that she also had another marriage.]
2. Benjamin F. Dowell, born 1822, died 1884, married Alpina M.____; buried in
   Williams Cemetery.
3. Nancy A. Dowell, born 1823, died 1863, buried Rose Hill Cemetery; married 1850
   Green T. Chaffin.
   continued on next page.

Children of Benjamin Dowell, continued:
4. Elizabeth J. Dowell, born 1827, never married.
5. Louisa Virginia Dowell, born 1829, died 1862, married 1847 John M. Witherspoon.
6. Pleasant Dowell, born 1835, died 1853.
7. Phoebe Dowell (a minor in 1851), married Beverly A. Dodson, bron 1836, died 1862.
   She was born 14 Jan. 1840, died 7 July 1861.

Source: Knob Creek Cemetery tombstone inscriptions; Williams Cemetery tombstone
inscriptions; Dowell vs. Witherspoon 1851, chancery court records.

PAULINE DOWEN
Drew pension in 1883 as widow of War of 1812 soldier; drew it at Park Station. No
further information.

JOHN DOXEY
Served in Capt. John Chisholm's company. No further information.

EDWARD DRAKE
Served in Capt. John Looney's company. No further information. On 1820 census.

JOHN DUCKWORTH
Commissioned ensign 1813 in 46th Regiment. No further information.

WILLIAM DUNN
Served as private in Capt. William Dooley's company. No further information.

JAMES DUNCAN
Served in Capt. Bird S. Hurt's company.

JAMES L. DUNCAN
Served in Capt. Bird S. Hurt's company. No further information. (Name appears to
be Dunwood on the payroll of this company.)

WILLIAM DUNCAN
Served in Capt. James McMahan's second company. No further information.

CHARLES DUNNY
Served in Capt. John Gordon's company. No further information. (Name appears to be
Durmy at one place.)

LITTLETON DUTY
Qualified as justice of the peace in 1809 in Maury County. No further information.
[Some believe this might be Littleton Dooley instead.]

JAMES DYER
Served as private in Capt. William Dooley's company. No further information.

JAMES DYER
Served in Capt. Benjamin Reynolds' second company. No further information.

+MILES EASOM
Enlisted as sergeant 28 Sept. 1814 in Capt. Cuthbert Hudson's company of volunteer
gunmen, Col. Robert Dyer. (This was an outfit with men from Dickson and Williamson
counties.) He died 23 Nov. 1814. In 1827 his widow Barthena Easom filed for her
claim as widow in Maury County and claim was settled by Edward H. Chaffin. (No
information about soldier's residency in the county.)

WILLIAM EASTHAM
Served in Capt. Samuel B. McKnight's company. Lived on the east fork of Big Bigby Creek. Tennessee Roper was appointed administrator of his estate 16 May 1831; and estate was settled 10 May 1832. (Will Book E, page 301.)

MOSES ECHOLS
Served in Capt. James McMahan's second company. No further information.

DAVID EDDLEMAN
Served in Capt. Bird S. Hurt's company. No further information.

JOHN EDGAR
Commissioned ensign in militia, 27 regiment, in 1808. No further information. [Som indication that this man may have lived in Hickman County later.]

ROBERT EDMISON
Served in Capt. John Gordon's company, transferred to Capt. Williamson's company. No further information.

ADONIJAH EDWARDS
Appointed constable in Maury County Dec. 1809. In 1834 his wife Elizabeth was living in Williamson County. No further information.

CHARLES EDWARDS
Served as private in Capt. William Dooley's company. No further information.

DAVID EDWARDS
Served as private in Capt. William Dooley's company. No further information.

JOHN EDWARDS
Served in Capt. William Dooley's company as private. This man figured in several circuit court cases in 1815. No further information.

RICHARDSON B. EDWARDS
Enlisted 19 Dec. 1813 as fourth sergeant in Capt. Philip Pipkin's mounted riflemen (Davidson County men), and served until 8 Feb. 1814. He married 25 Sept. 1805 or 1807 to Margaret Watton; they separated 27 March 1812 and he sued in Maury County for a divorce.

Source: Equity Causes, Maury County, 1818.

THOMAS EDWARDS
Appointed justice of peace of Maury County in 1810 and 1811. Letters of administration were given on his estate 22 Feb. 1814 and widow's provision made for widow Mary. He had only one child, Anna Edwards.

WILLIAM EDWARDS
Served in Capt. James McMahan's second company. No further information. [Maury County marriage bond, dated 28 Feb. 1811, William Edwards to Sarah Williams, with Adonijah Edwards, bondsman.]

WILLIAM EDWARDS
Served in Capt. John Gordon's company. No further information.

GEORGE M. EGNEW
Served in Capt. William Dooley's company. No further information.

JESSE W. EGNEW
Served in Capt. John Gordon's company. No further information.

JESSE W. EGNEW
Served in Capt. Benjamin Reynolds' first company. He was a lawyer and his name is sometimes found as Jesse M. Egnew, and might be the same person as the one before. He was not married while in Maury County and according to Nathan Vaught died 30 Oct. 1832 of yellow fever in New Orleans where he had moved.

ANDREW ELLIOTT
Served in Capt. John Looney's company. No further information.

JAMES ELLIOTT
Served as private in Capt. William Dooley's company. Maury County Deed Book S, Vol. 1, page 273, dated 25 April 1835, William Davidson of Mecklenburg Co., N. C., to Joseph Elliott, John Elliott, James Elliott, Sabra Hackney, Dedimi Elliott, Cornelius Elliott, Samuel J. Elliott, Eli Elliott, Lydia Arthur, Jane Fifer, Polly Elliott 305 acres on Rock Creek for $430.00.

JOHN ELLIOTT
Appointed lieutenant in 27th regiment in 1812. [One Jone Elliott was given license to keep ordinary in county in 1808. One John Elliott was appointed constable in 1809 in Maury County. One John Elliott will probated in Marshall County 5 July 1858—born 1798 according to 1850 census. One John Elliott and wife Sarah sell land on 13 Aug. 1826, to Henry J. Beaty on Fountain Creek, Maury County Deed Book M, Vol. 1, page 167.] (See also footnote)

ROBERT ELLIOTT
Enlisted 26 Sept. 1813 in Lt. Joseph Mason's company, Col. William Pillow, and discharged 10 Dec. 1813. He drew pension 1828 in Maury County as member of 17th U. S. Infantry.

HARRY EMERSON
Served in Capt. Benjamin Reynolds second company. No further information.

JAMES EMERSON
Commissioned lieutenant 1814 in 27th regiment, Maury County militia. Served in Capt. Bird S. Hurt's company, War of 1812. No further information.

JOHN EMERSON
(John M. Emerson) Commissioned lieutenant, 27th regiment, Tennessee militia, 23 July 1810; served also as ensign in company commanded by Capt. Benjamin Reynolds; enlisted in fall of 1812, served 5 months, 22 days, and honorably discharged at Columbia. Obtained Land Bounty Warrant for 80 acres before his death. Entered service 2 Nov. 1812, discharged 30 April 1813. He was born about 1786 in Va., died 26 Nov. 1854, 15th District of Giles County, Tenn. On 1850 census of Giles County he was listed as a faith doctor. He was probably the son of Reuben Emerson of Scott County, Ky. He married 25 Nov. 1806 in Scott County, Ky., Catherine "Kit" Reynolds (born 1789 Fayette Co., Ky., died March 1873 at Lynnville, Giles Co., Tenn.) daughter of Aaron Reynolds and his first wife Catherine Chambers of Orange Co., Va., Fayette, Woodford, and Scott Counties, Kentucky.

Brothers and sisters of John M. Emerson:
1. James H. Emerson, born about 1792 in Kentucky, living 1850 in Giles County; married as second wife Susan Galbraith, born about 1808 in Tenn., on 8 Sept. 1844 in Maury County.
2. No further information.
   continued on next page

Maury Co. Deed Book M, Vol. 1, page 485—17 Jan. 1828, John Elliott and wife Sally, formerly Sally Hendricks, sell part of Jones Kendrick tract where they now live. Book T, Vol. 1, page 380, John R. Elliott of Cooper Co., Mo., selling lot in Mt. Pleasant, Tenn. (Information by Virginia W. Alexander.)

Children of John M. Emerson:
1. Aaron B. Emerson, born 6 Sept. 1807, either Ky. or Tenn.
2. James H. Emerson, born 28 Nov. 1808 in Maury County, living 1850 in Giles Co.,
   married Nancy Puckett, born about 1814 in N. C.
3. William B. Emerson, born about 1811 in Tenn.
4. Buford T. Emerson, born about 1814 in Tenn.
5. Lemuel Montgomery Emerson, born about 1815 in Tenn.
6. Benjamin Reynolds Emerson, born about 1818 in Maury County, married 8 July 1839
   in Maury County to Permelia Bazzell, born about 1819 in N. C.
7. Marion T. Emerson, born about 1819 in Tenn.
8. John G. Emerson, born about 1821 in Tenn.
9. Sarah "Sally" F. Emerson, born about 1824 in Tenn.
10. Wiley W. Emerson, born about 1826 in Tenn.
11. Reuben E. Emerson, born about 1830, Tenn.
12. Mary "Polly" B. Emerson, born about 1833 in Tenn.
13. Henry N. Emerson, born about 1834 in Tenn., died as Confederate soldier.

Source: Monte Hugh Knight, Columbia, Tennessee, quoting also Widow's Pension WC2311.

THOMAS ENGLISH
Enlisted as first lieutenant 13 Nov. 1814 in Capt. Bird S. Hurt's militia infantry;
also commissioned lieutenant 1814 in 51st regiment. Born 12 Aug. 1790, died 25 Sept.
1827, buried in English Cemetery near Cross Bridges; married Susan____, 31 May 1809,
born 9 Sept. 1786, died 12 March 1857. He was the son of Edward and Jane Bradley
English.

Children of Thomas English:
1. Lavinia English, born 15 May 1810, died 20 July 1867, married 7 Oct. 1824 George
   Nixon; she died in Texas.
2. Martha English, born 25 May 1811, married Wesley Nixon.
3. Jane Bradley English, born 12 May 1812, died 3 Aug. 1860, married John J. Akin.
4. Charlotte English, born 31 July 1813, married Hugh W. Farris.
5. William H. English, born 14 Dec. 1814, died 4 June 1882, married Mary B. Farris.
6. Samuel J. English, born 27 March 1816.
7. Thomas H. English, born 28 Sept. 1818.
8. Susanna English married James A. Majors.
9. Edward English.
10. Elizabeth English, married Samuel Farris.

Brothers and sisters of Thomas English:
1. Mary B. English, born 10 Sept. 1795, died 22 Feb. 1874, married 1. Isaac
   Tomlinson, 2. Joseph Erwin, 3. ____Frierson.
2. Edward Flinn English, born 17 June 1798, died 6 April 1885, Methodist minister,
   married Mary Ann Harris.
3. Hester Shaw English, born 24 Oct. 1833, died 7 July 1854, married F. B. Russell.
4. Margaret F. English, born 23 Nov. 1835, died 20 April 1855.

Source: Information from Mrs. Marie P. Lightfoot, Mt. Pleasant. She noted that
two daughters of Thomas English married son of the Rev. John Nixon and that research
had failed to reveal the maiden name of his wife Susan.

WILLIAM ENGLISH
Served in Capt. John Chisholm's company. No further information.

EPHRAIM ERWIN
Commissioned captain in 27th regiment, Tenn. militia, 1814. Served as ensign in
Capt. William Dooley's company. Will Book E, page 378, will of Jonas Erwin, which
was recorded 1 Sept. 1831 mentions his wife Mary and Jane, wife of son Ephraim.
continued on next page

Children of Ephraim Erwin:
1. Mary J. Erwin married _____Kellam.
2. Susan A. Erwin.
3. Elizabeth J. Erwin.
4. William H. Erwin.
5. John F. Erwin.
6. Jonas N. Erwin.

JAMES R. ERWIN

Served in Capt. John Looney's company. No further information. [Records of two men of this name have been found in Maury County records. The following will be information on both of these men.]

James Erwin - 1818 got land on the east side of Cathey's Creek; married Jane Kennedy 7 July 1810.

James Erwin —— Maury County Deed Book G, Vol. 1, page 500, 19 Feb. 1813, Alexander Cathey sold 50 acres to James Erwin, both of Maury County. Book K, Vol. 1, page 414, 22 Feb. 1813, James Erwin "received of Alexander Cathey, guardian of my wife Jean."

James Erwin —— Deed Book H, Vol. 1, page 199, 29 June 1819, James Watts sells 18 acres on Cedar Creek of James Irwin and John Nesbit. Book L, Vol. 1, page 273, James Erwin owned land in Big Bigby Creek. Book Q, Vol. 1, page 526, 1831, James Erwin and Susannah Erwin, formerly Susannah Goff, of Henry Co., Tenn., sell to Archibald W. Winn [?] and R. A. L. Wilkes part of John Goff's land on Big Cedar Creek. Book R, Vol. 1, page 118, 4 Sept. 1818, James Erwin of Bedford Co. appoints A. Erwin, Jr., of Bedford Co., power of attorney. Book R, Vol. 1, page 118, 3 May 1833, James Erwin of Fayette Co., Ky., by his attorney Andrew Erwin, Jr., of Bedford County, Tenn., to sell land on Cedar Creek. Book S, Vol. 1, page 461, James Erwin sells one acre to William Eakin, both are of Maury County. Book T, Vol. 1, page 159, 23 Jan. 1835, James Erwin of Maury County sells part of Mark Mitchell grant, later deeded to Gen. Winn.

Source: Deed research contributed by Mrs. Virginia W. Alexander, member of Jane Knox Chapter.

JOHN ESTES

Served in Capt. John Looney's company. No further information.

JOHN A. ESTES

Served in Capt. Benjamin Reyholds' first company. No further information. (Name found on muster roll, but not on payroll of this company.)

JOHN H. ESTES

Served as private in Capt. William Dooley's company. No further information. [Records for three men of this name. The following is information on John Estes, an early settler of Maury County; we had no way to determine if this man is one of these soldiers or not.]

John Estes - born Feb. 1779 in N. C., reared in S. C., came to Tennessee in 1809; died 12 Oct. 1862 and buried in Estes Cemetery on St. John's Lane. He married Martha Jaggers, born 5 Jan. 1782, died 11 July 1849.

Children of John Estes:
1. Thrashley Allen Estes, born 28 March 1805 died 17 July 1856, married Sarah E._____.
2. Thomas W. Estes, born 5 Aug. 1810, died 10 Aug. 1878, married Martha _____.
3. Coleman C. Estes, born 18 Jan. 1813, died 10 June 1864 (or 6 Oct. 1861) married Sarah M. Matthews.
   continued on next page

Children of John Estes, continued:

4. Daniel J. Estes, born 6 April 1816, died 8 July 1895, married Nancy Bourbon Russell.
5. Hannah C. Estes, born 28 Sept. 1806, died 1 June 1868, married A. C. Rainy.
6. Hester L. Estes, born 28 Sept. 1806, died 30 July 1853, married E. J. Sealy.
7. Evaline Hackney Estes, born 4 Nov. 1818, died 9 Dec. 1889, married G. W. Mayberry.
8. William Estes, no further information.
9. Eight other children, but no information on them.

Source: Estes tombstone inscriptions; information from Mrs. Evelyn B. McAnally; letter from the late Miss Hugh Ella Estes, Primm Springs, Tenn.

LYDAL B. ESTES

Postmaster of Columbia during War of 1812; appointed Sept. 1809. He died Nov. 1814 at the age of 39 and was buried in cemetery on Lytles Creek. In 1875 his grave was marked only by five trees.

Children of Dr. L. B. Estes:
1. Edwin C. Estes.
2. Alston B. Estes.
3. Ludwell H. Estes.
4. Addison Estes.
5. Louisa Estes married ____Massey.

Source: Clarion and Tennessee States Gazette, 15 Nov. 1814; Nathan Vaught, "Youth and Old Age", page 67; 1814 wills and inventories of Maury County.

ROBERT ESTES

Served in Capt. Bird S. Hurt's company. No further information.

RACHEL EVAN

Drew pension as widow of War of 1812 soldier in Columbia in 1883. No further information.

DANIEL EVANS

Said to be soldier in War of 1812, probably in Davidson County company. He was in county as early as Dec. 1807 and served on jury March 1808; lived on Bear Creek; died between July and Oct. 1826; married 8 Feb. 1794 in Davidson County to Mrs. Elizabeth Johnston Courtney, widow of Nehemiah Courtney. She was a sister of Mrs. Isaac Roberts.

Children of Daniel Evans:
1. James R. Evans, eldest son.
2. David J. Evans.
3. Sinai Evans married Henry Smith.
4. Polly Evans married John Smith.
5. No information.

Step-daughter of Daniel Evans:
1. Nancy Courtney, married by 1808 to John Beasley.

HENRY EWING

Served in Capt. Samuel Ashmore's company. No further information.

TIMOTHY EZZELL

Commissioned ensign 1809 in 27th regiment, Maury County militia. Later lived in Giles County; originally from Mecklenburg Co., Va.; married Elizabeth Buchanan; died after 1840 in Okolona, Miss., at the age of 84; had daughter Caroline Ezzell.

ROBERT FANNING
Served in Capt. John Looney's company. No further information.

BENJAMIN FARMER
Served in Capt. Robert Campbell's company. No further information.

JOSEPH A. FARMER
Served as second sergeant in Capt. Robert Campbell's company. No further information. [Man of this name appears in early Lawrence County records. Lawrence County Deed Book A, page 30, 1819-1825, Joseph Farmer deed of gift to Eliza Farmer.]

SAMUEL FARMER
Served in Capt. Robert Campbell's company. No further information.

JOHN FARNEY
Commissioned captain in 27th regiment, Tenn. militia, 1814. Enlisted as sergeant or 4 Oct. 1813 in Capt. William Dooley's company. Age given as between 26-45 on the 1820 census of Maury County. Married 1814 to Sarah (Sally) Sanderson, daughter of William and Jemima Sanderson. She died 22 Dec. 1822. [John Farney married Lavinia Webb, 1 April 1824.]

Children of John Farney:
1. William Farney - was 21 on 14 Jan. 1827. [Age of this child indicates that John Farney had been married before his marriage to Sarah Sanderson.]
2. John Davis Farney - will be 21 in three years; item dated 1826. [However one lawsuit indicates that William and John Davis Farney were children of Sarah Sanderson.]

Source: Sanderson vs Farney, 1827, unpublished chancery court records.

JOHN FARRIS
Served in Capt. John Gordon's company. No further information.

MICAJAH FARRIS
Served in Capt. James McMahan's second company. No further information.

SAMUEL B. FARRIS
Served in Capt. John Looney's company. Age given as between 26-45 on 1850 census; lived in Cathey's Creek area. [Samuel Faris married 18 Sept. 1817 to Martha E. Osburn in Maury County.]

LEVI FERRELL
Served in Capt. Samuel B. McKnight's company. Age given as between 26-45 on 1820 census of Maury County. No further information.

JOHN L. FIELDER
Served in Capt. John Gordon's company of spies; was also at Battle of New Orleans in the artillery. Birth not known, but in Scotland; came to this country before the Revolution, settled in Virginia and then came to Tennessee; married   to 1. Mary Denton; 2. Mrs. Campbell [given name possibly Mary]. He died about 1835.

Children of John L. Fielder:
1. Benjamin F. Fielder, born 7 Feb. 1824, died 4 Dec. 1914, married 1. Mary Estes and 2. Mary S. Barnes Fielder, widow of his brother Samuel Fielder.
2. Martha P. Fielder, married William S. Speer.
3. Thompson Fielder (or Jason Thompson Fielder) married 1. Alice Kinzer, 2. Sarah Estes.
4. Samuel P. Fielder, born 18 Sept. 1830, married Mary S. Barnes.
5. Mary Fielder married James H. Wilkes.
6. Ellen Fielder married Hiram Webb.   (continued on next page)

Children of John L. Fielder, continued:
7. Louisa Fielder.
   (All children were by his marriage to Mary Denton.)

Source: Information furnished by H. C. Matthews, Hiram, Ohio.

HENRY FIELDS
Served in Capt. James McMahan's second company. No further information.

JOHN FIELDS
Commissioned officer in Maury County militia in 1814. Born between 1785-1790, died in Maury County, will dated 18 July 1844, probated February term 1845. He married 1. about 1810 to _____, born between 1790-95, died between 1822 and 1824; 2. about 1824 to _____, born between 1801-10 and died before 18 July 1844. (1840 census of Maury has John Fields with wife, age 30-39. His will names minor heirs, beginning with James, child 5. The first four children listed below were by his first wife.

Children of John Fields:
1. Margaret "Peggy" Fields, born about 1812 in Tenn., died after 1878 in Maury County; married Nathaniel King Fitzgerald on 18 Aug. 1831, as his second wife.
2. Elizabeth "Betsy" Fields, born about 1814 in Tenn., living 1850 in Maury; married 23 Dec. 1830 in Maury to William F. Fitzgerald, born 1808 in Tenn.
3. Abel Fields, born about 1819 in Tenn., living in 1850 in Maury; married 1846 in Maury to Virginia Thurman, born 1826 in Virginia.
4. William Henry H. Fields, born about 1822 in Tenn., living 1850 in Maury; married 18 Jan. 1843 in Maury to Martha Slayden, born 1823 in Tenn.
5. James F. Fields, born about 1825 in Tenn., living in Maury in 1850; married 1846 in Maury to Sarah J. (Southern) Dockery, born about 1820 in Tenn.
6. Edmond Fields.
7. Matilda Fields.
8. Louisa Fields.
9. Peter Fields, born about 1835 in Tenn.
10. Bill Fields, born about 1837 in Tenn.
11. Edward "Ned" Fields, born about 1838 in Tenn.
12. Richard Fields, born about 1839 in Tenn.

Source: Family research and information by Monte H. Knight, Columbia, Tenn. His wife Vickie Love Knight is great-great-great granddaughter of John Fields.

RICHARD FIELDS
Enlisted as private 20 June 1814 in Capt. Mebane's Militia infantry, Col. Pipkin. Drew pension in 1883, living on Carter's Creek, as War of 1812 soldier. No further information.

WILLIAM FIELDS
Served in Capt. John Gordon's company of spies. Died 20 April 1814 of wounds received at Battle of Thorea. No further information.

MAJOR WILLIAM FIELDS
Service not known—may not have been War of 1812. National Banner and Nashville Daily Advertiser, 19 June 1833: Mrs. Sarah Fields, wife of Major William Fields, died in Maury County on the 2d instant, age 54. National Banner and Nashville Whig, 4 July 1831: Miss Nancy C. Fields, daughter of Major William Fields, married in Maury County to Greenville Hanks. No further information.

JAMES FILES
Served in Capt. John Gordon's company of spies. No further information.

+JOHN FILES
Enlisted 28 Sept. 1814 as private in Capt. James McMahan's Tennessee Volunteer
Mounted Gunmen. No further information. [Possibly died in service.] Will Book B-1,
page 109: "discharge, borne on Capt. Crawford's pay." Court minutes, 15 May 1815,
letters of administration on his estate given to James Files.

+SAMUEL FINLEY
Served in Capt. Bird S. Hurt's company; died 27 Jan. 1815. No further information.

THOMAS FINLEY
Served in Capt. Andrew McCarty's company. No further information.

WILLIAM FINLEY
Served in Capt. Bird S. Hurt's company. Still in the county on 1820 census. No
further information.

JOHN FISHER
Served in Capt. James McMahan's company. No further information.

AMBROSE FITZGERALD
Served in Capt. John Looney's company. No further information.

LANGFORD FITZGERALD
Enlisted 4 Sept. under Capt. Benjamin Jones, 24 Regt., then under Capt. Stewart,
7th regiment, then Capt. Allison, 7th regiment; discharged 11 May 1819. Moved to
Giles County from Maury where he died and left large family.

Children of Langford Fitzgerald:
1. William Fitzgerald.
2. No information on other children.

MASTIN FITZGERALD
Enlisted as private 1 March 1814 in Lt. James Berry's mounted riflemen. Born 30
Dec. 1791 in Virginia, died 30 June 1878; married Margaret Harder, born 10 Nov.
1793, died 4 Oct. 1869, buried at Theta Baptist Church Cemetery.

Children of Mastin Fitzgerald:
1. William Jackson Fitzgerald, born 15 Sept. 1812, died 4 Oct. 1824.
2. Pleasant Willie Fitzgerald, born 17 Nov. 1814, died 23 Oct. 1829.
3. Delila Powell Fitzgerald, born 14 March 1817, died 11 Aug. 1841.
4. Eliza G. Fitzgerald, born 17 July 1819, died 18 Dec. 1819.
5. Louisa Jane Fitzgerald, born 23 April 1821, died 26 June 1854.
6. Carroll Green Fitzgerald, born 23 July 1823, died 13 Aug. 1893, married Frances
   Hart Thompson.
7. Sarah Harriet Fitzgerald, born 26 Jan. 1826, died 9 Aug. 1827.
8. Lorena Mary Malinda Fitzgerald, born 2 Nov. 1824, died 9 Aug. 1827.
9. James Mastin Fitzgerald, born 11 April 1831.
10. Frances Marion Fitzgerald, born 4 Oct. 1833, married 1857 Caroline Chandler.
11. Margaret Emerenthy Fitzgerald, born 24 March 1826.
12. Morgan Elmo Fitzgerald, born 5 Dec. 1839.

Source: Goodspeed History of Maury County, page 919; Fitzgerald Bible in Maury
County Cousins, No. 1, page 372.

NATHANIEL KING FITZGERALD
Served as private in company commanded by Capt. John Looney, 2nd regiment Tennessee
Militia, Col. Hammond; enlisted 20 Sept. 1814 in Maury County and served until
23 April 1815, when he was honorably discharged at Mobile, Alabama. He was born
about 1787, probably in Pittsylvania Co., Va., died 20 Jan. 1873 in District 18 of

Nathaniel King Fitzgerald, continued:
Maury County; married about 1809 in Maury County to _____, born 1794, died 1820-30; married (2) to Margaret "Peggy" Fields, born about 1812 in Tenn., died after 1878 in Maury County. (She was drawing pension in Santa Fe as late as 1883.) They were married at Santa Fe 18 Aug. 1831 by Squire James Hudspeth. She was daughter of John Fields, War of 1812 soldier. (See his listing).

Children of Nathaniel Fitzgerald by first marriage:
1. _____Fitzgerald, born about 1809, male.
2. Jesse H. Fitzgerald, born about 1810 in Maury, married Susan Dodson, born about 1815 in Virginia; married 1840 in Maury.
3. James Fitzgerald, born about 1813 in Maury, deceased by 29 Dec. 1871; married Margaret Thurman, born about 1812 in Va., died____; married 1834.
4. Mary Fitzgerald, born about 1818 in Maury County, living (unmarried) 1850 in Maury County.

Children of Nathaniel Fitzgerald by second marriage:
1. Edmund P. Fitzgerald, born about 1833 in Maury.
2. Rebecca Fitzgerald, born about 1836 in Maury.
3. Paralee Fitzgerald, born about 1839 in Maury.
4. Abel Fitzgerald, born 4 July 1840 in Maury, died 4 Nov. 1917 in Maury; marriage not known; served in Maury Light Artillery, Confederate Army.
5. Melissa "Siscey" Fitzgerald, born 16 June 1842 in Maury, died after 25 Nov. 1870 in Maury; married 23 Nov. 1865 Maury County to John Andrew Jackson Young, born 1842 Tenn., died 1929 in Maury as his first wife. He is buried at Zion Church.
6. Susan Fitzgerald, born about 1844 in Maury.
7. Margaret Fitzgerald, born about 1846 in Maury.
8. Thomas Fitzgerald, born about 1849 in Maury.
9. Caledonia Fitzgerald, born in Maury, date not known.

Nathaniel King Fitzgerald was son of Christopher and Elizabeth ____Fitzgerald. Christopher Fitzgerald was born about 1760 in Virginia, died 1829 in Maury County; was in the county before 1809 settling on Snow Creek; came here from Halifax-Pittsylvania counties, Virginia, area. Christopher Fitzgerald's will will be found in Will Book E, page 105.

Brothers and sisters of Nathaniel King Fitzgerald:
1. James Fitzgerald, born about 1781 in Va., died after 1850 in Maury County; married (1)____Vestal (?); (2) Polly Ladd on 23 Aug. 1819 in Maury County.
2. John Fitzgerald, born 28 Jan. 1785, Va., died about 1840 in Maury County; married Nancy Hanks on 2 Oct. 1809 in Maury County. She was related to the Reverend Elijah Hanks of Pittsylvania Co., Va., and Maury Co., Tenn.
3. Nancy Fitzgerald, born in Va., married _____Dodson.
4. Mary "Polly" Fitzgerald, born in Va.
5. Thomas Fitzgerald, born about 1795 in Va., died after 1850; married as his second wife Cynthia Fisher in 1842 in Maury County.

Columbia Herald, 2 June 1871: "There is an old man living near Santa Fe, Mr. Nathaniel Fitzgerald, who is 88 years old, still in good health and spirits, though he is blind. He nver took a dose of medicine in his life since he can remember and never was sick. He has lived in the same house 65 years. He was a soldier under Gen. Jackson in the War of 1812 and is now an applicant for the pension allowed survivors of that war. He has a son 63 years old..."

Source: Family information and research of Monte H. Knight, Columbia, Tennessee, whose wife, Vickie Lynn Love Knight, is great-great granddaughter of Nathaniel King Fitzgerald.

PLEASANT FITZGERALD

Enlisted 28 Sept. 1814 in Capt. James McMahan's company, 1st Tennessee Mounted Volunteer Gunmen, in battle of Horseshoe Bend and at New Orleans. Drew a pension for his service. Born about 1795 in Virginia. He married 1. Margaret Slayden, daughter of Daniel E. Slayden; 2. _____ Wilkes. His listing on 1850 census shows his wife Margaret, 46, born in Va., Sanna P., age 20; George W., age 17; Daniel E., age 14; Andrew J., age 12; Pleasant M., age 10; Dilly Ann Martha J., age 8, and Ellen P., age 4. No further information.

JOHN DICKEY FLEMING

Enlisted as private 20 Dec. 1813 in Capt. Johnson' militia infantry, Col. Perkins; commissioned ensign of light infantry company in 51st regiment, 1814. He was always called Major John Dickey Fleming. Born 2 March 1792 in Williamsburg District, S.C.; died 12 Aug. 1882, buried Zion Church; son of James Fleming and Mary Frierson—she was one of the early Zion colonists. Married Margaret M. Williams, born 8 Feb. 1801, died 30 Nov. 1842.

Children of John Dickey Fleming:
1. Mary R. B. Fleming, born 1840, died 1856.
2. Margaret M. W. Fleming, born 1842, died 1844.
Maury Democrat, 17 June 1897: "...John D., grew to middle age, fought the Indians under Jackson, then married, became the father of two girls and settled in sight of his birthplace; he was stripped by death of all his loved ones and lived on into the 'sore and yellow leaf'. standing like some sturdy oak amid life's storms, a very bulwark of truth, gallantry and justice. He died in his 91st year..."

Brothers and sisters of John Dickey Fleming:
1. Thomas F. Fleming.
2. William Stuart Fleming, born 1795 died 1816.
3. James Sidney Fleming, married Sarah Scott and Louisa Gee; he was born 1797, died 1886.

Half-sisters of John Dickey Fleming (by father's first marriage to Annie Witherspoon:
1. Daughter (twin) died in infancy.
2. Annie Fleming (twin) married David Wilson.

Source: Maury Democrat, 17 June 1897; Soldiers of the War of 1812 Buried in Tennessee, page 38.

THOMAS F. FLEMING

"In Indian wars under Jackson". Born 21 Aug. 1789, died 15 Nov. 1838; son of James and Mary Frierson Fleming; married Margaret Armstrong.

Children of Thomas F. Fleming:
1. Ann W. Fleming married M. J. Kittrell.
2. Martha Adeline Fleming born 1823, died 1843, married Leeman (Lemon) Oatman.
3. Rebecca Fleming, born 1830, died 1887, married John J. Wilson.
4. James A. Fleming, born 1820, died 1890, married Sarah Louisa Frierson, born 1826, died 1891.
5. John Whitney Fleming married Ann Wilson.
6. William Stuart Fleming, born 1816, died July 1896.

Source: Maury Democrat, 17 June 1897, "The Fleming Family" written by W. S. Fleming.

ELISHA FIX

Served in Capt. Robert Campbell's company. No further information.

JOHN FLY
Served in Capt. Robert Campbell's company. No further information. [This may be the man named John Fly, age 80, living in Maury on the 1850 census, who was listed a a faith doctor. Maury county marriages show that one John Fly married Lydia Newton 18 June 1811.]

WILLIAM FLY
Commissioned lieutenant in 46th Regiment in 1813. Lived on Snow Creek. He married 10 Nov. 1809 to Mary (Polly) Mitchell, daughter of Andrew Mitchell, who was a Revolutionary War soldier. Born about 1775 according to Goodspeed's history of Mississippi.

Children of William Fly:
1. A. T. M. Fly, born 1811 in Maury County, moved to Wilkinson Co., Miss., married Eliza Jones and Ellen Rabb.
2. No information on other children.

Source: Gillis's Abstract of Goodspeed's Mississippi Memoirs, page 198.

NATHAN FORD
Served in Capt. Robert Campbell's company. No further information.

+LEWIS FORKNER
Served in Capt. John Looney's company. Maury County Will Book A, Vol. 1, page 248, his will dated 17 April 1814: "As I am about to go in campaign to the Creek Nation. Mentions Sally, my wife, and if she remarries to have child's part. Will Book B-1, page 170 mentions "one discharge to a six months tour of duty in the militia."

Children of Lewis Forkner:
1. Mourning Fortner.
2. Carolina Fortner.
3. Wilford Fortner.
4. William P. Fortner.
5. Rebecca Fortner.

ALEXANDER M. FOSSETT
Served in Capt. James McMahan's company. No further information. [It is believed that the last name should be Faucett and there is a record of an Alexander Faucett in the county. Nathan Vaught, "Youth and Old Age", page 66, wrote of Richard Faucett, who came to Maury County between 1809 and 1810. He was the father of ten children: 1. Alexander; 2. David; 3. John; 4. William; 5. Eleanor married Alexander Baldridge; 6. Sallie married James Pursell; 7. Nancy, married Alexander Baldridge as his second wife; 8. Katherine married Aaron Steele; 9. Polly; 10. Mary.]

GEORGE W. FOSTER
Served in Capt. Bird S. Hurt's company. [One man of this name was living on Fountain Creek in 1811. G. W. Foster ran for trustee of Maury County in 1844 and his announcement in the Tennessee Democrat, 18 Jan. 1844, read: "I am a plain man, and a blacksmith by trade, but neither the learned or buckeye blacksmith."]

RICHARD FOSTER
Commissioned ensign 1814 in the 27th Regiment, Tennessee Militia. [This man is believed to be Richard Foster, born 15 Aug. 1784, son of George and Sara Wilkes Foster. He died in Maury County. Married 30 Aug. 1804 in Charlotte Co., Virginia, to Elizabeth M. Foster.]

Source: Mrs. Leonard Gibson, Culleoka, Tennessee.

JOSEPH FOX

Served in Capt. John Chisholm's company, Col. Napier's regiment. Born 1782 in N. C.; died 20 Nov. 1842, buried McKnight Cemetery, Maury County; son of John Fox (born 19 Feb. 1754, died 1 Sept. 1840, Revolutionary War soldier) and Elizabeth Loving (who died before 1804.) He married 27 Feb. 1811 in Maury County to Nancy Hannah Church, born 20 Nov. 1793 in N.C., died 6 Dec. 1877, buried in McKnight Cemetery. She was the daughter of Thomas Church (born 11 Nov. 1766, died 1 May 1849) and Elizabeth Collett Fox (born 1769, died 24 Jan. 1856.) Joseph Fox lived on Leiper's Creek near Bethel in Maury County.

Children of Joseph Fox:
1. Elizabeth Fox, born 11 Feb. 1812, died 3 Feb. 1862, married Wiley E. Beasley.
2. Thomas W. Fox, went to Missouri.
3. John P. Fox.
4. Nancy Fox, born about 1820, married 30 July 1837 to William Adkison.
5. Matilda Fox, married 30 Nov. 1843 to William Beasley.
6. Joseph Fox, born 31 Dec. 1823, died 14 Oct. 1851, married 19 Sept. 1846 to Frances E. Hight.
7. Margaret Fox, born 4 Feb. 1828, died 24 Oct. 1903, married 13 Jan. 1848 Robert Gaskill.
8. Austin Fox, born about 1829, married 27 Nov. 1851 to Martha Petty; in 1917 he was living in Springfield, Missouri.
9. James Fox, born 29 Dec. 1831, died 16 Oct. 1850, never married.
10. Mary Caroline Fox, born 27 July 1834, died 22 Jan. 1908, married 26 Jan. 1853 John Shannon McKnight.

Brothers and sisters of Joseph Fox:
1. Austin Fox.
2. Alfred Fox.
3. Cintha Fox married _____ Pratt.
4. Lucy Fox, married _____ Genty.
5. Nancy Fox, married _____ Wakefield.
6. William Fox.
7. James Fox, married _____ Church.
8. Matilda Fox, married _____ Walker.
9. Mary Fox, married _____ Pratt.

Half-brothers and sisters of Joseph Fox:
1. Stephen Fox.
2. Calton Fox.
3. Milton Fox.
4. Daniel Fox.
5. J. Wesley Fox.
6. Cora Fox.
7. Eliza Fox.
8. Easter Fox.

Source: Information supplied by Marise P. Lightfoot, great-great-granddaughter of Joseph Fox. She added that Joseph Fox's widow received 160 acres bounty land and a widow's pension. John Fox, father of Joseph Fox, was a soldier in the American Revolution and was "six feet six inches tall".

HENRY FRACK

Served in Capt. Robert Campbell's company. No further information.

SAMUEL B. FRANKS

Served in Capt. James McMahan's second company. [His middle name is believed to have been Boone. Elizabeth Franks, who married Jacob Daimwood of Maury County, was granddaughter of Samuel Boone, brother of Daniel Boone.] Samuel B. Franks married Lucretia Moore, 18 Nov. 1817, in Maury County. No further information.

JOHN H. FRASEUR
Served in Capt. John Looney's company. No further information.

ELIAS FRIERSON
Commissioned captain 1808 in 27th Regiment of Maury County Tennessee Militia; was commissioned major in 1810 militia. Lived on Green's Lick Creek; died 1819. He married Charlotte McCauley, born 1784, died 1819.

Children of Elias Frierson:
1. John McCauley Frierson, born 1802, died 1823.
2. Samuel G. Frierson married Mrs. Isaac Frierson.
3. Sarah McCauley Frierson, born 1807, married _____ Travis.
4. Gideon Blackburn Frierson, born 1809, married _____ Beck.
5. William Wilson Frierson, born 1811, died unmarried.
6. Joseph Henderson Frierson, born 1813, died unmarried.
7. Loveann Matilda Frierson, born 1815, no further record.
8. Some indication of another child, but no further information.

Source: Theodore Stephenson The Friersons of Zion Church and Their Descendants.

MOSES GORDON FRIERSON
Commissioned captain in 27th Regiment, 1809 Tennessee Militia; born 1775, died 1813; son of William and Margaret Gordon Frierson. He married 1797 to Mary Jane Dickey, born 1777, died 1863.

Children of Moses G. Frierson:
1. Edward Livingston Frierson, born 1798, married Sarah Elvira Stephenson.
2. Isaac Edwin Frierson, born 1799, married Fannie Hardin.
3. Amarintha Susan Frierson, born 1802, died 1875, married Wm. Gordon Armstrong.
4. Margaret Amelia Frierson, born 1805, died 1861, married James Armstrong Frierson, born 1802, died 1859.
5. John Dickey Frierson, born 1807, died unmarried.
6. Elias Currin Frierson, born 1807, died 1883, married Martha Wilson.
7. Charles Calvin Frierson, M. D., born 1811, married Mildred Payne.

WILLIAM FRIERSON
Appointed justice of the peace of first court of Maury County 1807. [We have been unable to determine which William Frierson this man was. Frierson researchers are referred to Theodore Stephenson's The Friersons of Zion Church and Their Descendants.]

RICHARD B. GAMBLE
Served in Capt. Andrew McCarty's company. No further information.

ANDREW GAMMILL
Enlisted as second corporal on 13 Nov. 1814 in Capt. Bird S. Hurt's Militia Infantry, Col. Metcalf. On 22 Aug. 1815 he makes a deposition that "he was in General Carrol's Division of Militia at Orleans or returning from there at the time taxable property was taken." He has been identified as the son of James Gammill, who died 1794 in Stokes Co., N. C. He had a brother James Gammill who lived also in Maury, Bedford, and Davidson Counties early. He will be found on the 1830 census of Hardin County, Tenn.

JAMES GANNAWAY
Served as private in Capt. William Dooley's company. On the 1820 census of Maury his age is given as between 26-45. He married 2 July 1818 in Maury County to Nancy Grimes. He was the son of Money (Edmond) Gannaway, who married 22 Nov. 1788 to Drucilla Walker in Cumberland County, Virginia. Money Gannaway's will is recorded in Maury County in Book B, Vol. 1, page 15, dated 24 March 1815. (cont'd)

Brothers and sisters of James Gannaway:
1. eldest, not named in father's will, but mentioned.
2. next to the eldest, not named in father's will, but mentioned.
3. Gregory Gannaway, between 26-45 on 1820 census of Maury County, married 12 Aug. 1819 in Maury County to Martha McConnell.
4. William Gannaway.
5. Jane Gannaway married Benjamin Gholson.
6. Mary (Polly) Gannaway married 13 Oct. 1818 in Maury County to James W. Ldgin.
7. Martha (Patsy) Gannaway married 5 Aug. 1822 to James Tomlinson.
8. Edmund Gannaway married 4 Feb. 1826 in Maury County to Sarah Tomlinson.

Source: Gannaway vs Walker, 1842, chancery court lawsuit, Maury County; Maury County Will Book B-1, page 15; some family information of Mrs. Robert Hadley, Windsor, Missouri.

JAMES GANT
Served in Capt. Samuel Ashmore's company. No further information.

JAMES GANT
Served in Capt. Samuel B. McKnight's company. No further information.

THOMAS GARRARD
Commissioned ensign in 1814 in 27th Regiment of Tennessee Militia. This man was in the county in 1811 at least. In 1815 the court bound out an orphan, Thomas Allington, age 4½ years, to him. No further information.

JAMES GARRETT
Served as private in Capt. Doak's company, Col. N. T. Perkins' 1st Regiment of West Tennessee Mounted Volunteers from 30 Dec. 1813 to 8 Feb. 1814. Born 1775, died 1852 in Maury County. His inventory was recorded in the county 18 Dec. 1854.

Source: Soldiers of the War of 1812 Buried in Tennessee, page 42.

LEVI GARRETT
"Was War of 1812 soldier". Found on the 1823 tax list of Maury County. Born 27 May 1790 in N. C.; married 17 Dec. 1840 in Marshall Co., Tenn., to Francis T. Davis.

Children of Levi Garrett:
1. Jesse J. Garrett, born 1 Oct. 1846, married Mary Ferguson.
2. George W. Garrett, born 27 Oct. 1852 in Marshall Co., married S. L. Neren.
3. No further information.

Brothers and sisters of Levi Garrett:
1. Sally Garrett, born 2 June 1784, married 16 Feb. 1807 to William Payne.
2. Margaret Garrett, born 15 May 1786, married 19 Dec. 1808, moved to Maury County. (Husband not named.)
3. Isaac Garrett, born 25 April 1788, married Elizabeth Ward.
4. James Garrett, born 5 Sept. 1792, married 9 Oct. 1823 Lauderdale Co., Ala., to Betsy Willett.
5. Jesse Garrett, born 17 Dec. 1794, married Zerah T. Jones, lived Warren Co., Mo.
6. John Garrett, born 31 Jan. 1797.
7. Annie J. Garrett, born 17 June 1801, married 21 May 1821 to James Haizlip.
8. Rebeckah Garrett, born 25 July 1803, married 15 Dec. 1823 Henry Jones and lived in Warren Co., Mo.
9. Elizabeth Garrett, born 16 Nov. 1805, married 27 April 1827, Clement S. Garmer.

Source: Goodspeed's History of Marshall Co., Tenn., page 1204; family information sent to the editor by Mrs. Phillip Harris, Orem, Utah. Levi Garrett was son of Thomas Garrett, Jr., and his wife Anne Curry.

JOHN GARRIGUS

Commissioned ensign in 1808 in 27th Regiment Tennessee militia; served in Capt. Bird S. Hurt's company during War of 1812. He married Jan. 1811 in Maury County to Polly Cash. William Garrigus was his bondsman.

WILLIAM GARRIGUS

Served in Capt. Bird S. Hurt's company. On 4 May 1815 in Maury County he married Nancy Carr. No further information.

ROBERT GASKILL

Served in Capt. Newlin's company, 1st Regiment of Tennessee Volunteers. Born 1 Mar 1793 in Virginia, died 26 March 1856 in Maury County and buried in Gaskill Cemetery; married 9 May 1816 in Maury County to Elizabeth Haynes, born 30 Dec. 1796 in Georgi died 12 Aug. 1874, buried Gaskill Cemetery, Maury County. He was son of Mrs. Hanna Gaskill. He lived on Gaskill Branch of Maury County.

Children of Robert Gaskill:
1. Mary Woodson Gaskill, born 30 Dec. 1816, died 14 Oct. 1830, married 29 Jan. 1830 to C. C. Walters.
2. Evan S. Gaskill, born 4 Nov. 1818, died 7 Sept. 1891 in Wright Co., Mo., married (1) Sarah Cathey on 25 March 1840; (2) Miss Morris.
3. William A. Gaskill, born 24 May 1820.
4. Elizabeth Jane Gaskill, born 11 May 1822, died 4 Feb. 1882, married 4 Feb. 1847 to Joe Walters.
5. Enoch C. Gaskill, born 29 Feb. 1824.
6. Robert J. Gaskill, born 22 Jan. 1826, died 17 Feb. 1879, married 13 Jan. 1848 to Margaret Fox.
7. Allifair H. Gaskill, born 22 Nov. 1827, died before 1856, never married.
8. Sarah Rebecca Gaskill, born 14 Oct. 1829, died 13 Nov. 1887, married 25 May 1849 Oliver Perry Hight.
9. Henry Gaskill, born 27 June 1831.
10. Arthur, born 20 April 1833, died before 1856.
11. John W. Gaskill, born 7 Jan. 1835.
12. James W. Gaskill, born 27 Feb. 1838.
13. Jacob M. Gaskill, born 15 April 1841.
14. Thomas C. Gaskill, born 25 Jan. 1843, died 5 Dec. 1915.

Source: Information furnished by Marise P. Lightfoot, Mt. Pleasant, great-great-granddaughter of Robert Gaskill. She added that six of Robert and Elizabeth Gaskill's sons served in Company D, 3rd Missouri Cavalry, C.S.A. Robert Gaskill's widow never applied for a pension or for bounty land.

JOHN H. GATLIN

Served in Capt. John Chisholm's company. No further information.

JOHN GENTRY

Served in Capt. Samuel Ashmore's company. No further information.

WILLIAM GENTRY

Served in Capt. Robert Campbell's company. No further information.

GEORGE

Served as waiter to Capt. John Looney in Looney's company. No further information.

BENJAMIN GHOLSON

Enlisted as private 10 Feb. 1813 in Capt. Benjamin Reynolds' company, Col. Thomas Benton; enlisted 4 Oct. 1813 in Capt. William Dooley's company, Col. T. McCrory, became corporal in Dooley's company; also in Capt. John Looney's company. Born 17 Dec. 1793 in Ky., son of Francis Gholson; married Jane Gannaway. (See addenda.)

JOHN CHOLSON

Enlisted 23 June 1812 in Capt. Benjamin Reynolds Mounted Rangers, Brig. Gen. Isaac Roberts; enlisted 24 Sept. 1813, discharged 4 April, Capt. John Gordon's Mounted Spies; enlisted 14 Oct. 1813 in Capt. William Dooley's company, transferred to Gordon's spies, 15 Oct. 1813. Born 8 Feb. 1785, Va., son of Francis Gholson, Revolutionary War soldier, and his wife Mary Craig. He was in the Battle of Horseshoe Bend; removed later to Hamilton Co., Illinois. He was commissioned ensign 1808 in 27th regiment; ensign 1812 in 27th regiment; captain, 27th regiment, 1814.

The Gholson family was in Maury County quite early. On 2 March 1809, Olsimus Kendrick sued Francis Gholson in circuit court. Kendrick was of lawful age and made the following deposition: "in spring of the year 1808 he cleared and settled upon a certain tract of land lying at this present time in the county of Murray which he claims by gift from his father Jones Kendrick, who claims the same as assignee of a certain entry made by James Williams, now deceased...the same land is also claimed by one Dellam...Francis Gohlson who is also settled near the same land and claims it by a purchase from the sd Dellam..."

Brothers and sisters of John Gholson:
1. Benjamin Gholson, born 17 Dec. 1793 in Ky., married June Gannaway.
2. Nathaniel Gholson, born 25 Feb. 1787.
3. William Gholson, born 20 April 1789.
4. No further information.

Source: James Saunders, Early Settlers of North Alabama, page 376; information from Marise P. Lightfoot.

NATHANIEL GHOLSON

Enlisted 22 June 1812 in Capt. Benjamin Reynolds' company, Brig. Gen. Isaac Roberts; as sergeant 4 Oct. 1813 in Capt. William Dooley's company. Born 25 Feb. 1787, son of Francis and Mary Craig Gholson; married 25 May 1808 Patsy Gill.

WILLIAM GHOLSON

Enlisted 10 Dec. 1812 in Capt. Benjamin Reynolds company, Col. Thomas Benton; enlisted as sergeant 10 Feb. 1813 in Capt. Benjamin Reynolds company; born 20 April 1789, son of Francis and Mary Craig Gholson; marriage bond dated 12 Nov. 1810 in Maury County to marry Sarah Thomas.

JOHN GIBSON

Served in Capt. John Gordon's company. No further information.

WILLIAM GIFFORD

Served in Capt. Samuel B. McKnight's company. Born in Rutherford County, lived 15 miles south of Columbia; buried at Mooresville or Silver Creek. Married Ruth Money.

Children of William Gifford:
1. Elizabeth Thompson married David Arnold and Edmund Gwynn.
2. Cynthia Gifford married Thomas Milligan of Maury County.
3. Mary Gifford married John Jones.
4. Joel Gifford married Elizabeth Steele.
5. Gideon J. Gifford married Susan Vaughan, moved to Illinois.
6. Americus Gifford married Caroline Gant.
7. Robert Gifford married Emma Fawcett of Fayette County.
8. Franklin Gifford, C.S.A., married Rebecca Davis.

Source: Conversation with descendant Benjamin D. Hill, Washington, D. C.

JOHN GILBERT

Served in Capt. John Looney's company. No further information.

JAMES GILBREATH

Columbia Herald and Mail, 10 Sept. 1875: was in War of 1812. No service established. Born 2 April 1792, died 26 Sept. 1845, buried Gilbreath-Coffee Cemetery. Son
of John Gilbreath, Sr., (1768-1850) and his wife Mary (1758-1843.) Married Elizabeth Baker.

Children of James Gilbreath:
1. Andrew J. Gilbreath, moved to Texas.
2. William Gilbreath.
3. John B. Gilbreath, bron 2 Dec. 1823, died 3 Oct. 1855.
4. James H. Gilbreath.
5. Isaiah R. Gilbreath, born 1 Dec. 1828, died 21 Nov. 1864, m. Mary L. Coffey.
6. Minerva E. Gilbreath, born 30 Nov. 1819, died 28 Sept. 1875, never married;
   buried Gilbreath-Coffee Cemetery.
7. Absolum M. Gilbreath, born about 1830, died 22 Nov. 1858; married Emily_____.

Brothers and sisters of James Gilbreath:
1. Jane Gilbreath, born 2 Oct. 1795, died 22 April 1852, married 13 Oct. 1821 to
   Leonard Morrow.
2. John Gilbreath, Jr., born 22 Sept. 1799, married Susan Stalcup.
3. Son, moved to Arkansas.
4. Son, moved to Missouri.
5. Son, moved to South America.

Source: Information furnished by Mrs. J. R. Gilbreath, Columbia, Tenn.

JOHN GILBREATH

Commissioned ensign 1814 in 46 Regiment, Tenn. Militia. Born 22 Sept. 1799, some
question about his death date; married Susan Stalcup.

Children of John Gilbreath:
1. William Gilbreath, born 24 Jan. 1827, married 1851 in Kentucky to Mary Jane
   Jackson.
2. Nancy Jane Gilbreath, born 3 Sept. 1830, married _____Cannon.
3. John Samuel Gilbreath, born 19 Sept. 1834.
4. Minerva Elizabeth Gilbreath, born 14 April 1837, married Benjamin Tarpley.
5. Lydyan Alyway Gilbreath, born 23 Aug. 1839, died 28 Oct. 1841.
6. Mary H. Gilbreath, married ____Hickman.
Source: Information furnished by Mrs. J. R. Gilbreath, Columbia, Tenn.

DUNCAN GILCHRIST

Commissioned lieutenant 1814 in 51 Regiment, Tenn. Militia. [Later lived in Wayne
County.] Son of Malcolm Gilchrist (born 1744 in Scotland, died 12 April 1821 in
Maury County) and his wife Catharine (born 1752, died 1839.)

Brothers and sisters of Duncan Gilchrist:
1. Archibald Gilchrist, born 1794, died 1852.
2. John Gilchrist.
3. Sarah Gilchrist married _____McMillan.
4. Ann "Nancy" Gilchrist married 6 Feb. 1817 David Leech.
5. Malcolm Gilchrist.
6. Catharine Gilchrist, born 1792, died 1881, married David Dobbins, 1783-1860.
7. Daniel Gilchrist.
8. William Gilchrist.

Source: Will of Malcolm Gilchrist recorded Book C, page 191, Maury County Will
Books.

JAMES GILES
Served as private in Capt. William Dooley's company. No further information.

THOMAS GILL
Served in Capt. Benjamin Reynolds' company. He married 31 Oct. 1820 in Maury County to Sally Williams, niece of Sarah Dickey, second or third wife of Thomas Gill, Sr.

Children of Thomas Gill, Jr.
1. Eldridge Gill.
2. Sarah Ann Gill.
3. Robert D. Gill.

Brothers and sisters of Thomas Gill:
1. Frances Gill married Thomas Shane.
2. Patsy Gill married 25 May 1808 to Nathaniel Gholson.
3. Betsy Gill married 6 June 1808 to Charles Allen.
4. William Gill.
5. Joseph Gill.
6. Polly Gill, married 23 Oct. 1817 to James Lane.
7. Sally Gill married 14 May 1835 to Thomas Nunn.
8. Isabella Gill.
9. Robert R. Gill married 25 April 1832 in Maury County to Sarah M. Johnson; by 1846 he is in Monroe Co., Miss.

Source: Will of Thomas Gill, Sr., Maury County wills; Gill, Perry & Co. versus Gill, 1838, chancery court records. Thomas Gill, Sr., born 24 Aug. 1769, died 6 Aug. 1839, and his wife Nancy, born 3 Feb. 1771, died 20 Dec. 1815, are buried in Gill Cemetery near Campbell Station. He married second 5 Oct. 1820 to Sarah Dickey.

WILLIAM GILL
Enlisted as private 4 Oct. 1813 in Capt. William Dooley's company. He was born 19 March 1795, died 2 Aug. 1871, buried at Rose Hill. His obituary noted that he was a veteran of the Creek and Florida Wars and that he asked to be buried in a winding sheet. [Maury County marriages, William Gill, 20 May 1817 to Sally Hamilton William Gill to Sarah Cooper, 15 March 1828.] [Mrs. Sarah E. Gill, age 85, died 30 Sept. 1891 of old age, buried at Rose Hill Cemetery, no stone.]

+JAMES T. GILLESPIE
Served in Capt. John Gordon's company. Was last on roll 4 Feb. 1814 and missing, supposed to be killed. (Muster roll)

JOHN GILLASPIE
Enlisted as private 28 Sept. 1814 in Capt. James McMahan's company. No further information.

THOMAS GILLELAND
Served in Capt. James McMahan's company. No further information.

ALEXANDER GLASS
Served as third lieutenant in Capt. James McMahan's company. Still in Maury County on 1820 census. No further information.

ROBERT GLASS
Served as sergeant in Capt. James McMahan's company. No further information.

THOMAS GLASS
Served as sergeant in Capt. Samuel B. McKnight's company. No further information.

WILLIAM GLASS

Enlisted in Capt. John Stephens company mounted gunmen as 5th sergeant, 6 Oct. 1814, Col. Sam Wear's regiment, served until 6 April 1815. Died in Maury County. Married 12 April 1811 to Nancy or Agnes McCollough.

Source: Soldiers of War of 1812 Buried in Tennessee, page 43.

JOSEPH GLAWSON

"Major Joseph Glawson, a pensioner of 1812, died recently in Mt. Pleasant."
(Nashville Union and American, 26 Jan. 1873.)

WILLIAM GLENN

Columbia Herald, 26 Sept. 1870: "born in Virginia during Revolution, 1803 came to Tennessee to Stewart County, 1810 to Williamson County, married in Stewart County, in War of 1812, father in Revolution, is now 101 years." He died 3 Jan. 1872 at the age of 104. Columbia Herald and Mail, 5 June 1874: William Glenn died two years ago at the age of 106. Married Dovey Armstrong.

Children of William Glenn:
1. Robert A. Glenn, died 28 May 1886, operated store which he opened in 1854 at Glenn's Chapel area; married Margaret Jane Hurt, daughter of Bird S. Hurt. [Possibly another marriage.]
2. John Glenn, born 1 Sept. 1808, died Aug. 1879, married Martha Jane Lockridge.
3. Rebecca Glenn married 1835 to J. A. Stephens.
4. No further information.

Source: Century Review, pages 157, 158, 285.

JOSHUA GLOVER

Served in Capt. Robert Campbell's company. No further information.

PETER GOAD

Served as private in Capt. James McMahan's 1st Tennessee Volunteer Mounted Gunmen, enlisted 28 Sept. 1814. No further information.

REUBEN GOAD

Served in Capt. Robert Campbell's company; name also appears as Richard on one muster roll. No further information.

HIRAM GOFORTH

Served in Capt. John Chisholm's company. Married 29 March 1815 to Priscy Halcomb, date of bond in Maury County. Still in the county in 1830. Will of Andrew Goforth, Will Book A, page 33, mentions his sons Andrew, William and Hiram. Jane Hood was to receive Andrew Goforth's furniture, but no relationship given. No further information.

THOMAS GOFORTH

Served in Capt. John Chisholm's company. No further information.

WILLIAM GOFORTH

Commissioned ensign in 1814 in 46th regiment. No further information. (Refer to Hiram Goforth entry above.)

FRANCIS GORDON

Served in Capt. Glen Owen's Mounted Gunmen, enlisted 28 Sept. 1814, discharged 28 March 1815. Lived in Maury County in 1820.

JAMES GORDON

Served as sergeant in Capt. Samuel B. McKnight's company. No further information.

JOHN GORDON

Captain of company of spies under General Andrew Jackson; first postmaster of Nashville, Tennessee; operated Gordon's Ferry on Natchez Trace in Hickman County. He was born 15 July 1763, died 1819, buried on his farm in Hickman County; later reburied at Rose Hill in Columbia. He married Dolly Cross on 15 July 1794; she was born 15 July 1779, died 5 Dec. 1859. Her burial was recorded 7 Dec. 1859 in St. Peter's Episcopal Church records, Columbia: "Mrs. Dolly Gordon of Williamsport, age 85 (a Cumberland Presbyterian). She was the widow of John Gordon, captin of the Spies in A. D., 1812-14, in the Creek war under Gen. Jackson. She was connected wit. some of the most stirring scenes in the early history of Tennessee."

Children of John Gordon:
1. John Gordon, born 1795 in Davidson Co., died about 1844 in Missouri; married Polly Compton.
2. Fielding Lewis Gordon, born about 1797 in Davidson Co., died 1835 in St. Louis; married in Louisiana to Lethia Waddell in 1829; she died in 1834 of yellow fever, in Clinton, East Feliciana Parish, La.
3. Captain William Gordon, born in Davidson Co., married Mrs. Jane_____ in 1839; his death not known.
4. Major Bolling Gordon, born 12 April 1801 in Davidson County, died 10 Dec. 1880 in Hickman County, buried Rose Hill, Columbia; married Mary Elizabeth Watkins, born 1811, died 1880.
5. Col. Powhatan Gordon, born 15 Nov. 1802 near Nashville, died 29 Jan. 1879 in Bryan, Texas, buried Rose Hill; married Caroline Mary Coleman, born 1809, died 1887, buried Rose Hill.
6. Mary Ann Gordon, born about 1807, died about 1845, married Reuben White in Williamsport, Tenn.
7. Anna (Nancy) Gordon, born in Hickman County about 1809, died in childhood.
8. Dorothy (Dolly) Cross Gordon, born 29 Nov. 1811 in Hickman County, died 4 Dec. 1880; married (1) Charles W. Webber, attorney, who died a few years later; (2) Augustus Sowell, born 1811, died 1870.
9. Andrew Gordon, born at Gordon's Ferry in 1813, died unmarried 2 Aug. 1888.
10. Lieutenant Richard Cross Gordon, born Gordon's Ferry 1817, died 20 Nov. 1863; married Miss Ann Boatner and Miss Tabitha Smith.
11. Louisa Pocahontas Gordon, born at Gordon's Ferry, four months before her father's death on 21 Feb. 1819, died 13 July 1857 in Nashville, married 1835 Felix Kirk Zollicoffer, Brigadier General in Confederate Army. She is buried in the City Cemetery in Nashville.

Source: Octavia Zollicoffer Bond, "Family Chronicle and Kinship Book", page 144-5; Columbia Observer, 19 Sept. 1834.

WILLIAM GORDON
Served as ensign in Capt. Andrew McCarty's company. No further information.

WILLIAM GORDON
Commissioned ensign 1812 in 27th regiment. No further information.

WILLIAM GORDON
Commissioned lieutenant in 1814 in 51st regiment. No further information. [These records may all be for the same man.]

FINELY GOTHREY
Drew pension in 1883 as War of 1812 soldier, lived in Mt. Pleasant; received an injury to the abdomen. No further information. [Record of a Jacob Finley Guthrie who owned and operated a large tanyard in Wayne County has been found. No information if it were the man who drew pension in Maury County.]

ALEXANDER GRAHAM
Served in Capt. Samuel B. McKnight's company. No further information. [Name appears as William Graham on the payroll.] Commissioned ensign in 1814 in the 51st regiment.

LLOYD GRAHAM
Served in Capt. Samuel B. McKnight's company. No further information.

NIMROD GRAHAM
Commissioned lieutenant in 1808 in 27th regiment. No further information.

BALIAS GRAVES
Maury County Will Book B, page 122, Inventory of property of Balias Graves, deceased 18 Feb. 1817 consisting of his bounty of land as an enlisted soldier during the war in the service of the U. S. No further information. [Some researchers believe that he had a son named Thomas Graves.] Jacob Graves was the administrator of his estate. [Some researchers believe that the correct name was Seagraves.]

CURTIS G. GRAY
Commissioned ensign 1812 in 27th regiment. No further information.

GEORGE GREEN
Served in Capt. Bird S. Hurt's company. No further information. [Man of this name, age 68, born in N. C., will be found on 1850 census of Maury County.]

WILLIAM GREEN
No service record given. He lived or had land on the road leading from Fountain Creek to the McCutcheon Trace. [Settlement of estate for a man of this name on 24 Feb. 1814; his minor heirs were P. W. Green, Sary C. Green, and Franky Green Cambridge.]

JACOB GREGORY
Served in Capt. Robert Campbell's company. No further information.

HUGH GRIFFIN
Enlisted as private 4 Oct. 1813 in company of Capt. William Dooley in the 2nd Regiment of Tennessee Volunteer Militia, commanded by Col. Thomas McCrory. He was mustered into service at Fayetteville, Tenn. "After muster in the command marched to Camp Coffee, Creek Nation, from thence to Fort Strother, Coosa River, where they fortified, from thence to Taladega, Ala., thence back to Fort Strother where he remained till near muster out." He was discharged on 4 Jan. 1814 at Fayetteville, Tenn. No paymaster was there to pay him so he assigned his claim and discharge to his brother-in-law, William A. Johnson. He understood that Johnson transferred said discharge to one William Crawford and that he (Griffin) had no knowledge of it, or what became of it. He received 40 acres on bounty land warrant, which he sold. He bought 100 acres in 1853 in the 24th District, and left 100 acres in the 24th District in his will. He was a member of the Maury County Home Guard during the Civil War.

He was born 1790 in North Carolina, and died in Maury County, Tenn., will was proved 6 Jan. 1874. He was buried in the Rieves Bend Cemetery and his grave is not marked. He was son of John Griffith (born 1752 in Perquimans Co., N. C., died 1829 in Maury County, buried near old Love's Mill on Fountain Creek, stone still standing.) John Griffith was a captain in the 4th Regiment, North Carolina Line, during the Revolution; His application for pension, No. 4312, was rejected, 1828, lack of evidence. Proof of service for John Griffith discovered 1970—Revolutionary Roucher No. 9, Hillsborough District, N. C., dated 17 April 1786, 317 pounds, 7 shillings, 5 pence. (N. C. State Archives, Raleigh). John Griffith married Jane____ who was born about 1760-65, died 1840 in Gibson Co., Tenn.; married 1783 in Orange

Hugh Griffin, continued:
County, N. C. John Griffin migrated to Maury County prior to 1811.

Hugh Griffin married Sarah "Sally" Reynolds on 22 Jan. 1824 at Fountain Creek, Tenn. in Maury County. She was born 1798 in Scott Co., Ky., daughter of Aaron Reynolds (1753, Va.–1833 Maury or Giles County) and his first wife, Catherine Chambers, married 13 Aug. 1784, Orange Co., Va. Sarah died before March 1876 in Maury. Aaron Reynolds was son of John Reynolds, Bristol Mariner and Elizabeth Mossom, born 21 Sept. 1722, died 1754, New Kent Co., Va. (tombstone, St. Peter's Parish churchyard), dau. of the Reverend David Mossom (1690-1767), Rector of St. Peter's for forty years, during which time he performed the marriage ceremony of George Washington and Martha Custis, 1759. Aaron Reynolds was promoted to corporal at Valley Forge, serving with the 3rd/4th Va. State Line. Noted Indian fighter in Ky., where at the Seige of Bryan Station (Fayette County), he bluffed the renegade, Simon Girty, into leaving the fort unmolested. Aaron Reynolds saved Col. Patterson's life at the Blue Lick Defeat (Fayette County), 1782, and was awarded 100 acres for this act, by the Colonel; he had settled in Maury County, Tenn., prior to 24 Dec. 1810, when on this date he married (2) Margaret Davis of Maury County.

Children of Hugh Griffin:
1. _____, male, born late 1824, early 1825.
2. John Griffin, born ca 1826, died between 1854/60; married Martha E. Rieves, born 1834, died 1894, daughter of Thomas Jefferson and Sarah Murphy Rieves on 29 Dec. 1853 in Maury County.
3. James Griffin, born about 1827 (Middle initial "R"—for Reynolds?), living in 1860. Probably named for mother's brother James Reynolds, 1803-1879.
4. Mary Jane Griffin, born about 1828, married as his second wife to Joseph K. Freeland (b. ca 1811 N.C.), 3 June 1850. Both living in 1876 in Obion Co., Tenn.
5. Ann M. Griffin, born about 1829, married Benjamin F. Christopher on 31 Dec. 1846 in Maury County.
6. Laodicea Griffin, born about 1831, married Fountain Polk Scott on 26 Aug. 1852, his first wife.
7. Milton J. Griffin, born about 1833, died 13 May 1862 Aberdeen, Miss., as Confederate soldier.
8. _____, male, born between 1830/35.
9. Hugh Griffin II, born about 1836, died 1874/76, married Mary Jane Rieves, born 1834, died 1919, on 29 March 1860; she was daughter of Elijah and Polly Stallings Rieves of Maury County. Confederate soldier.
10. Elizabeth T. Griffin, born about 1839, died 1897, married Theodore S. Speed, born 1837, died 1906, on 17 Oct. 1867 in Maury County. He was Confederate soldier.
11. Louisa Mossom Griffin, born about 1841, died 1874/76, unmarried; insane.
12. William H. Griffin, born about 1843, living 1876 in Obion Co., Tenn., married Lucinda Jane Carrigan on 22 Dec. 1868 in Maury County.

Brothers and sisters of Hugh Griffin:
1. _____ Griffin, died ante 1840. (John, Jr.?)
2. _____ Griffin, died ante 1840. (James?)
(Both born prior to Hugh Griffin, born 1790. Suit, 1825, Maury County: John and James Griffin versus John M. Daniel.)
3. Mary "Polly" Griffin, born 1792/93 N. C., died 1852 in McNairy Co., Tenn., married William A. Johnson (ca. 1790-1852), brother of Alex. Johnson of Maury.
4. Celia Griffin, born ca 1797, N. C., living 1853, married Matthew Cunningham of Maury County.
5. Elizabeth B. Griffin, born about 1799, N. C., living 1853 in Gibson Co., Tenn., married Alexander G. Hamilton of Maury County.
6. Margaret Griffin, born about 1802 in N. C., living 1853 in Gibson Co., Tenn., married _____ Pruitt.

continued on next page.

Hugh Griffin, continued:

7. Sibella Griffin, born about 1806, N. C., living 1853 in Gibson Co., Tenn., married David Porter Hamilton, brother of Alexander G. Hamilton, of Maury.

Source: Family research contributed by Monte Hugh Knight (great grandson of Elizabeth T. Griffin Speed), member of General Society of the War of 1812, Ky/Tenn., No. 3486, Philadelphia, Pa., who lives in Columbia.

OWEN GRIFFIN
Served in Capt. John Looney's company. No further information.

WILIE GRIFFIN
Enlisted as corporal 28 Sept. 1814 in Capt. James McMahan's Tennessee Volunteer Mounted Gunmen. In 1810 he lived on the road leading to Chambers Ferry on Duck River. No further information.

JAMES GRIMES
Served in Capt. Benjamin Reynolds company. No further information.

JAMES GRIMES
Served as sergeant in Capt. James McMahan's company. No further information.

WILLIAM GRIMES
Served in Capt. James McMahan's company. No further information. [Two men of this name lived in Maury County at the same time; impossible to determine which man was this soldier.]

WILLIAM GRIMMETT
Born 1792 in Georgia; died 8 Sept. 1884 at Isom's Store in Maury County, buried in old Jones Presbyterian Churchyard on Cathey's Creek; son of Josiah Grimmett (born 1765 in England, who fought on Virginia line 1781, Pension S3428, died at Centerville, Tenn., after 1837. His mother was born in Maryland. He served as a private in Capt. Cuthbert Hudson's company, enlisted 28 Sept. 1814, died 28 March 1815. He married Betsy McAnally (Elizabeth Margaret), born 1792 in N. C.

Children of William Grimmett:
1. Gillie, born 1823, married Ed (Ned) Anderson.
2. Benjamin E., born 1821.
3. Nancy M., born 1825.
4. Elizabeth M., born 1829, married William Crowder.
5. Lousinda T., born 1831, married Jas. A. Kirk. (One source says Jos. A. Kirk)
6. Mary Jane, born 1833, married M. H. Smith and John Simmons.
7. Jesse, born 1827, married Harriett Campbell.
8. No information on other children, if any.

Brothers and sisters of William Grimmett:
1. Benjamin Grimmitt, born 1794, married Mary McChlorie.
2. No information on other children, if any.

Spence's History of Hickman County, Tenn., has the following sketch: "While Jackson's Army did not in a body go over the trace to New Orleans, it returned this way, and during the Creek War many struggling detachments went and returned this way. A story of the return trip from New Orleans was told to the late Daniel Smith by William Grimmett, who lived on Smith's land on Dunlap Creek, and is yet remembered by citizens of the Third District.

Grimmett in connection with the story pointed out a hollow tree on a hill side near

William Grimmett, continued:

the trace. Grimmett, when he enlisted lived in Dickson County, Tenn., on his return from New Orleans in the spring of 1815 a former neighbor of his became seriously sick before they came to the Tennessee River and he was detailed to drop out of the ranks and care for his sick friend, owing to the sick man's condition, they traveled very slowly.

Other Dickson County soldiers reaching home told Grimmett's father that his son was in company with a sick man somewhere on the Natchez Trace this side of the Tennessee River. The father proceeded to find the trace and follow it in search of his son, when Grimmett and his sick companion were near the tree pointed out, a rain came up so he and his companion sought shelter in this hollow tree and remained until the rain ceased. Then continued on their journey, but after crossing the Duck River, the sick soldier became much worse and laying down by the side of the trace, soon expired. Securing assistance, the body was carried to the Dr. Long place, now known as the Rufe Puckett place, Jack Charter of Leatherwood made the coffin. Charter was father of Cave Charter, a well-informed citizen of the Thirteenth District.

The dead soldier was buried on the Long Place, and soon after friends and relatives came from Dickson County and placed a rock wall around his grave, on the same day of the burial Grimmett's father arrived with horses and they returned together to Dickson County. This is the story of the rockwalled grave of the unknown soldier on the Rufe Puckett place.

Grimmett, while he lived in Hickman County, Tenn., drew a pension as a soldier of the War of 1812, and part of his pension money was used to pay his burial expenses. He was buried in the old Presbyterian Churchyard on Cathey's Creek in Maury County, Tennessee. Soon perhaps his grave, too, will be marked "unknown" as no stone with an epitaph marks the last resting place of this old soldier of the War of 1812... [End of account in Spence's history.]

Grimmett's grave was unmarked until recent years when a descendant, Mrs. Paul Brown, had a stone placed at the grave.

Source: Family information furnished by Mrs. Paul Brown (Elois) of Columbia, Tenn., descendant of William Grimmett.

JOEL GUARD
Enlisted as private 28 Sept. 1814 in Capt. James McMahan's 1st Tennessee Mounted Gunmen. No further information.

JOSHUA GUEST
[Enlisted as private 10 Jan. 1812, Capt. Evans Company, 1st Regiment West Tennessee Volunteer Militia, discharged 20 April 1813. This record is ordinarily given for Joshua Guest or Gist of Maury County, who married Mary Cherry. However, Joshua Guest also enlisted as corporal on 10 Dec. 1812 in Capt. Benjamin Reynolds company, Col. T. H. Benton. As Reynolds' company was composed of Maury County men, it is possible that this is his true service.] Born 12 Jan. 1789, died 2 Feb. 1831, buried in Greenwood Cemetery; married 11 July 1814 to Mary Cherry, born 10 Oct. 1795 in N. C., died 13 Feb. 1870. National Banner and Nashville Whig, 11 Feb. 1831: "Major Joshua Guest died at Columbia."

Children of Joshua Guest:
1. James L. Guest, born 11 May 1819, died 25 May 1886; married 1839 Emily Jane Hill, born 1823, died 1869, and second to Jemima Ann Erwin. In 1834 he was appointed by James K. Polk to West Point, but it was found he was too young to enter the academy.
2. Elizabeth Guest, married A. G. Bailey.
continued on next page

Joshua Guest, continued:
Source: Nathan Vaught, "Youth and Old Age", page 70; Maury County Cousins, No. 1, page 341, quoting the Guest Bible; tombstone inscriptions from They Passed This Way.

DAVIS GURLEY

Enlisted 24 Sept. 1813 in Capt. Archibald McKinney's company, Co. R. H. Dyer, discharged 10 Jan. 1814. Born 7 April 1792 in Johnston Co., N. C., died 2 June 1861 in Waco, Texas; married 8 June 1823 in Lauderdale Co., Alabama, to Patience Bland Smith daughter of Joshua Smith, born 24 Oct. 1797 in Chester District, S. C., died 7 July 1885, Waco, Texas. He moved to Alabama from Tennessee where he ran hotel on the Military Road, lived in Franklin County (now Colbert County); son of Edwards Gurley and Mary Davis (she married secondly to Thomas Edwards, cousin of her first husband). In 1855 moved to McLendon Co., Texas. [Nathan Vaught tells that a Gurley sott... early at the place known today as the John Early place—Dr. Daniel place on the Hampshire Pike.] In 1814 Davis Gurley was assigned to work on the road from the Doublehead Trace to the Elk River Ridge in Maury County. In 1822 he was authorized by the State of Alabama to build a turnpike road in Franklin Co., Ala.

Source: Information supplied by Virginia Alexander from information given to her by Mrs. Ernest B. Meynard of Pittsburgh, Pa.

+JEREMIAH GURLEY

Served in 1810 militia in Maury County; in 1813 was commissioned lieutenant colonel of the 51st regiment—family records show colonel under General Andrew Jackson. He enlisted 24 Sept. 1813 in Capt. Arch McKinney's company. Born 17 May 1786 in Johnston Co., N. C., died 11 Jan. 1814 at Ten Islands, Alabama, of wounds. His brother Davis Gurley was detailed to drag him off the field and nurse him. He was an early school teacher in Maury County. Was wounded at the Battle of Tallahatchie. He was son of Edwards Gurley and wife Mary Davis (she married Thomas Edwards as her second husband, cousin of first husband; Thomas Edwards' estate was settled in Maury County with Davis Gurley as administrator.) Letters of administration were given on the estate of Jeremiah Gurley on 22 Sept. 1814 to Davis Gurley.

Source: Maury County Will Book B, pages 148, 204, 208; information supplied by Mrs. Virginia Alexander from information given to her by Mrs. Ernest B. Meynard of Pittsburgh, Pa.

MARTIN GURLEY

Enlisted 24 Sept. 1813 in Capt. Archibald McKinney's company, discharged 10 Jan. 1814. The following advertisement appeared in The Chronicle, 1 Aug. 1816, weekly paper published in Columbia, Tenn.: "PROCLAMATION—Whereas it has been represented to me by the Jailor of Maury County that on the night of the 10th of June 1816, the following named and described persons did break the jail of said county, to which they had been committed for safe keeping, and escaped therefrom & from justice... MARTIN GURLEY, about 25 years of age, 5 feet 7 inches high, stout made, sandy complexion, fair hair, and speaks quick in conversation, the aforesaid Martin Gurley, was recently suspected and charged with the crime of Horse Stealing and committed therefor, from which he escaped....Joseph McMinn, Governor of Tennessee." More information on his crime will be found in various circuit court minute books of Maury County. Case was transferred to Williamson County and Goodspeed's History of Williamson County, page 795, has the following: Martin Gurley was convicted of horse stealing and received 39 lashes on the bare back, branded H. T. and compelled to stand in the pillory two hours each day for three days, rendered infamous, and sentenced to jail for six months. Maury County State Causes show that on 13 July 1815 Martin Gurley took red roan mare owned by Burrel Johnson. Gurley asked that his trial be changed to Williamson County as "he has enemies in this county who are prejudicing the people against him."

EDMUND GWUINN (GUINN, GWYNN)

Born 1794, came to Maury County in 1834, had served in Virginia. Married 1835 to Elizabeth Gifford, daughter of William Gifford. (She had first been married to David Arnold.) He was the son of Jesse Guinn and Mary Burton. No further information.

JOHN HAIL

Served in Indian wars under General Jackson; took Indian boy in one battle, reared and educated him; practiced medicine in Maury County until his death in 1852 or 1853. Married Tolitha Badgett, died 1838 or 1835, they had nineteen children, fourteen lived to be grown. He married (2) to Martha Sullivan and they had five children.

Children of John Hail:
1. William F. Hail, born 1828 in Lawrence Co., Tenn., Confederate soldier, married 1851 to Mary A. Vaughn.
2. Sarah E. Hale, born 1830 in Tenn.
3. No information on the other children.

Source: Goodspeed's History of Lawrence County, Tenn., page 818, 831.

(UNKNOWN) HAISTEAD

In 1883 Calvin D. Haistead drew a pension in Maury County as a child of a soldier of the War of 1812.

HENRY HALL

Served in Capt. Bird S. Hurt's company. [Henry Hall, Jr., marriage bond to marry Sally Stokes, 14 April 1810 in Maury County.] This man lived on what was called Hall's Trace or the Hall's Ford Road as early as 1810. In 1823 a petition to the county court mentions that at one time a ferry had been at mouth of Flat Creek and there would never be one at Hall's Ford as the river and banks there were extremely difficult. In 1828 John Napier was appointed overseer of road which led from Hall's Ford to Isaac Hall's old place and one Joseph Hall lived at the mouth of Cedar Creek. In 1824 the Flat Creek Meeting House was mentioned in county road minutes as being near this Hall's Ford Road. In 1857 the road minutes refer to old Hall's Ford. No further information.

ISAAC HALL

Served in Capt. Robert Campbell's company. No further information. Refer to Henry Hall entry.

JOHN HALL

Served in Capt. John Looney's company. No further information. [Both John Hall, Sr., and John Hall, Jr., appear in early Maury records. John Hall, Jr., married Prudence McFall 23 April 1810 in Maury County.]

JAMES HAMBLET

Commissioned ensign 1814 in 46th regiment. No further information. [In the division of the estate of Littleberry Hamlett in Oct. 1818, his estate was divided into lots and the following received shares: James O'Neal, Berryman Hamblet, Martha Hamblet, William Hamblet, Kibble T. Hughes, and James G. Hamblet.]

ALEXANDER G. HAMILTON

Served in Capt. Bird S. Hurt's company. No further information. In 1815 he was assigned to work on the road leading from Love's Mill to the Lewis Road.

GEORGE HAMILTON

Served in Capt. Bird S. Hurt's company. No further information. In 1815 he was assigned to work on the road leading from Love's Mill to the Lewis Road.

HANCE HAMILTON

Served in Capt. John Chisholm's company. In service 14 days in Creek War. Wife received land bounty in 1855. Born 12 Aug. 1775 in S. C., died 26 Sept. 1843, buried Williamsport Cemetery; married 31 July 1798 in Chester District, S. C., to Nancy Bell, born 7 Feb. 1779, died 14 Feb. 1862.

Children of Hance Hamilton:
1. Elizabeth, born 28 March 1803, died 22 April 1830, married 28 Sept. 1818 to Beverly Dodson.
2. John Bell Hamilton, born 29 Oct. 1807 in S. C., died 14 March 1887, buried Rose Hill, Columbia; married 16 April 1829 to Sarah Ann Alderson.
3. Mary A. Hamilton, born 11 Sept. 1809, died 28 Aug. 1847, married 1830 to John A. Wilkins. (Middle name is Ann.)
4. Samuel Hamilton, born 20 March 1801, died 27 Feb. 1869, deaf mute.
5. Lelias (Lilles) Hamilton, born 2 Jan. 1805, died 1 Dec. 1846, buried Williamsport Cemetery, married 11 Jan. 1826 to Nathan Duncan (or Dunger).
6. Alexander C. Hamilton, born 1810, no other information.
7. No information on other children.

Source: They Passed This Way, A-160; Century Review, page 297; bounty land application of Nancy Hamilton furnished by Mrs. Evelyn B. McAnally; They Passed This Way, B-25. [One source says that Hance Hamilton was born in Ireland, however, his wife's bounty land application gave South Carolina. One source says that John Bell Hamilton had nephews named Jim Wilkins, John Neely and John Cooke, and that they were the sons of his sister Elizabeth Cooke. This information cannot be reconciled to information above which can be verified, with the exception of Jim Wilkins, who was the son of his sister Mary Ann Hamilton Wilkins.]

Brothers and sisters of Hance Hamilton:
1. Agnes Hamilton, born May 1769.
2. Lilley Hamilton, born March 1770.
3. Isabella Hamilton, born April 1772.
4. Mary Hamilton, born July 1777.

According to the DAR Roster, page 769, edited by Edithe Rucker Whitley, Hance Hamilton was the son of Dr. Samuel Hamilton, born 24 May 1732 in Scotland, died after 1777 in N. C., married Lilley Campbell, born 1734; Samuel Hamilton was a soldier in the American Revolution.

HENRY HAMILTON

Commissioned ensign 1808 in 27th Regiment; also commissioned again in 1809. No further information.

THOMAS HAMILTON

Commissioned lieutenant of cavalry in 5th Brigade in 1812. No further information.

THOMAS HAMILTON

Served in company from Humphreys County; lived briefly in Maury County. Born 10 April 1789, was ruling elder in Cumberland Presbyterian Church for over 70 years. Married 2 Jan. 1812 to Elizabeth Forrest. He was son of James Hamilton (soldier in the American Revolution) and his wife Jane Gwin.

Brothers and sisters of Thomas Hamilton:
1. Ann, born 1 March 1783, married 20 Mar. 1800 to Jacob Parks, b. 1777, d. 1841.
2. Jane, born 1 Oct. 1784, married James Latimer; they moved to Texas in 1834.
3. Elizabeth, born 27 Dec. 1786, married Jacob McKee. They lived in Maury County.
4. Polly (Mary), born 13 June 1792, married Lynde Latimer and ____ Madden.
continued on next page.

Thomas Hamilton, continued:
5. James, born 22 Nov. 1794, married Peggy Lankford.
6. Robert, born 5 June 1796, married Elizabeth Bethea.
7. Alexander, born 20 Oct. 1798.
8. John, born 1 March 1803.
9. Sally, born 22 Feb. 1806, married Henry Lankford.

Source: Pension application W155 of Jane Gwin Hamilton; "Our Old Men", Volume 1, published 1877.

MOODY E. HANES
Served in Capt. John Gordon's company, transferred to Capt. Lauderdale's company. No further information.

GEORGE HANKS
Commissioned captain 1813 in 46th regiment. Born 6 June 1773, died 1 Sept. 1859 in Texas; married (1), license issued 29 Oct. 1791 in Pittsylvania Co., Va., Lurane Hill, daughter of the Rev. Thomas Hill; married (2) Oct. 1846 to Angelina Sutton. He moved 1806 to Williamson County, then Maury County; 1817 to Lawrence County, and in 1826 to Hardeman County. He was the son of Moses Hanks (soldier of the American Revolution) and his wife Agatha Dodson.

Children of George Hanks:
1. Frances Hanks, born Va., marriage license 7 Aug. 1807 in Williamson County to marry James Fitzgerald.
2. Nancy Hanks, born 5 Jan. 1795 in Va., married 1. 1809 John Fitzgerald, and 2. David Dodson.
3. Sarah Hanks, born 1797 in Va., never married.
4. Elizabeth Hanks, born 1798 in Ky., married 8 Nov. 1825 in Hardeman County to Uriah Stafford.
5. William Hanks.
6. George W. Hanks, born 1803 in Ky., married (1) Catherine Doty, (2)_____, (3) Louisa Sherwood.
7. Eli D. Hanks, born 1805 in Ky., married Mariah Ann _____; lived in Mississippi.
8. Hansford Hanks, born 1807 in Tenn., married 1828 Susan Foster; 1830 moved to Hardeman County; then to Texas.
9. Joicy Hanks, born 1808 in Tenn., married William Rogers.
10. Allen Hanks, born 1810 in Tenn., marriage license in 1833 in Hardeman County to marry Elizabeth Woolverton.
11. Elijah Hanks, born 1848 in Texas. (Child by second marriage.)

Brothers and sisters of George Hanks:
1. Moses Hanks, Jr., born 6 Jan. 1779, married 2 May 1808 to Mary Montgomery; by 1830 in Illinois.
2. Troy Hanks, born 2 March 1784.
3. Thomas Hanks, born 30 April 1786, died 28 Nov. 1857.
4. Elijah Hanks, born 12 Dec. 1793, died 12 Aug. 1871—noted Baptist minister in Maury County and Tennessee.

Source: "Our Hanks Family," by Gladys H. Johnson, pages 14, 42, 45, 48.

SAMUEL HANNA
Served in Capt. Samuel B. McKnight's company. [Cannot identify this man. The following information was sent in by Mrs. Nelle J. Smith, Pulaski, Tenn., and one of these men is believed to be the correct Samuel Hanna, who served in War of 1812.]

Maury County Wills, File "F to L", will of Samuel Hanna, 28 Nov. 1834, leaves his wearing apparel to his three sons: Andrew, Hamilton, and James Hanna. He mentions the children of Prudence and John Meadows, children of John and Jane Thompson, the children of Andrew Cauldwell and Thomas Cauldwell; daughter-in-law Marthy, wife of

Samuel Hanna, continued:
son James; grandson Abner H. Hanna [son of James Hanna, Sr.]; great granddaughter, Esther Elizabeth Thompson [daughter of Polly Thompson] Martha Agnes McCandless; James A. and Martha Jane [children of his grandson Samuel Hanna]; daughter Jane White. Executors of his will were John Matthews and his son James Hanna.

Maury County Wills, Will of James Hanna, Sr., dated 19 April 1853: to son Abner H. Hanna; Abner H. Hanna to pay all just debts of son Andrew Hanna, deceased; Naomi Hanna, wife of deceased son Andrew; land received from Samuel Hanna [father of James, Sr.]; sons Joseph, Andrew, deceased, Abner H., Samuel, James; daughters Margaret M. McCandless, Esther Murphy, Mary D. Alexander, and Prudence Meadows; a son John H. Hanna was mentioned in connection with a grandson Abner I. Hanna (the children by his second wife: Sarah J. and Abner I.); to each of the other children, Joseph, Andrew, Abner H., James, Margaret, Esther, Mary, and Prudence, to receive remaining 2/3s of property. Executors, Abner H. Hanna, Samuel Hanna.

First generation
Samuel Hanna, born 1741 in Virginia, died 1 Dec. 1834 in Maury County, Tenn. His children were:
1. Andrew Hanna
2. Hamilton Hanna
3. James Hanna
4. Jane Hanna
5. Polly Hanna
6. Esther Elizabeth Hanna

Second generation
James Hanna, Sr., son of Samuel Hanna; born in Virginia 25 Dec. 1768, married Martha Matthews, born 11 Dec. 1770, daughter of James and Mary Doak Matthews in Mecklenburg County, N. C. James Hanna died 16 Sept. 1854 and Martha died 19 Aug. 1835 and they are buried in John Matthews Cemetery, Maury County. Children of James Hanna, Sr.:
1. Andrew Hanna, born 1810, married 13 Nov. 1835 to Naomi Bryson.
2. Samuel Hanna, born 1791 in N. C., married 20 March 1821 to Hannah Robertson, born 1801 in S. C.
3. Abner H. Hanna, born 1813 in Tenn., married Martha Jane Dixon, 2 Feb. 1836.
4. Prudence Hanna, born 1807 in Tenn., married 4 Nov. 1829 to John Meadows.
5. Margaret M. Hanna, married _____ McCandless.
6. Esther Hanna, married _____ Murphy.
7. Mary D. Hanna, born 11 March 1806 in Tenn., married Ozni Alexander.
8. Joseph M. Hanna, born 1803, died 1888, married Martha Elizabeth [Betsy] Gilmer, born 26 Sept. 1804, died 22 Dec. 1877, both are buried at Pleasant Hill, District 3, Giles County, Tenn.
9. James Hanna, Jr., born 11 Oct. 1793, died 25 Aug. 1857, married Mary Cutbirth, born 11 July 1799, died Sept. 1876; both are buried in Mt. Carmel Cemetery, District 3 of Giles County, Tenn.

Third generation
Samuel Hanna, born 1791, married 20 March 1821 to Hannah Robertson. [This man is believed to be the War of 1812 soldier.] Children:
1. James Hanna, born 1826.
2. Margaret Hanna, born 1835.

Source: Family research contributed by Mrs. Nelle J. Smith, Pulaski, Tenn.

JAMES HARALSON
Enlisted as private 18 Sept. 1814, discharged 27 April 1815, Capt. James McMahan's Company, 1st Regiment of Tennessee Mounted Volunteer Gunmen. No further information.

CALLOWAY HARDIN
Enlisted 18 Dec. 1813 as first sergeant in Capt. James McMahan's Mounted Gunmen, Col. N. T. Perkins. Son of Martin Hardin. Marriage bond dated 28 April 1812 to marry Nancy McMahan, Richard McMahan, bondsman. [Lauderdale Co., Ala., marriages, Calloway Hardin to Louise McKinsey, 1823.] He later lived in Weakley County. Born 1791 in Georgia.

Source: Hardin information by Mrs. Jane Fullerton, Nashville.

HENRY H. HARDIN
Appointed constable in Maury County Dec. 1808. Son of William Hardin and his wife Sarah Bledsoe. Family records show that he died in Ashe Co., N. C., 23 Oct. 1856. Married Catherine Cox, died 1847.

Children of Henry Hardin:
1. No further information.

Brothers and sisters of Henry Hardin:
1. Mark Hardin.
2. Swan Hardin, born N. C., died in Texas 1838. [One source says he died in Tenn.]
3. Martin Hardin.
4. Richard Hardin, youngest son; lived in Maury briefly.
5. Cynthia Hardin, married _____Toney.
6. Sarah Hardin, born 1783, died 1863, married John F. Calloway.
7. Susan (Sucky) Hardin, born 1786, died 1842, married Alex Shaw.

Source: Hardin family material by Mrs. Jane Fullerton, Nashville; will of William Hardin, recorded 27 Jan. 1824, Book C, page 214. This family lived in Franklin Co., Ga., before coming to Maury County.

SWAN HARDIN
Early justice of the peace in Maury County: born in N. C., died about 1838 in Texas; married Jerusha Blackburn; son of William Hardin and Sarah Bledsoe. He left the county about 1825.

Children of Swan Hardin:
1. Benjamin W. Hardin, born 23 Jan. 1796 Franklin Co., Ga., died 2 Jan. 1850 in Liberty, Texas, married _____Gibson.
2. Augustine B. Hardin.
3. William Hardin, born 1801 in Franklin Co., Ga., died 25 June 1839 in Galveston, Texas. Married Sarah Ann_____.
4. Benjamin Franklin Hardin, born Jan. 1803 in Franklin Co., Ga., died 1878 in Liberty, Texas, married Cynthia O'Brien.
5. Milton A. Hardin.

Source: Hardin Family material by Mrs. Jane Fullerton, Nashville, Tenn.

THOMAS H. HARDIN
Appointed constable 1807 in Maury County. Married Lucy Nolen of Williamson County; later lived in Bedford County.

WILLIAM HARDIN
Served in Capt. James McMahan's company. Son of Martin Hardin; married 2 July 18_5 in Maury County to Elizabeth Pirtle. No further information.

Source: Hardin Family material contributed by Mrs. Jane Fullerton, Nashville, Tenn.

ABNER HARDISON
Served in Capt. Andrew McCarty's company. No further information.

CHARLES HARDISON

Enlisted as private 28 Sept. 1814 in Capt. James McMahan Tennessee Volunteer Mounted Gunmen, Col. Robert Dyer; born 16 Aug. 1795, died 4 Oct. 1878, buried in Morton Cemetery; married 1 Feb. 1821 to Hannah Daniel. He was son of the Revolutionary War soldier James Hardison and his first wife Mary Robertson.

Children of Charles Hardison:
1. Calvin Hardison, born 16 April 1824 in Marshall Co., married Sarah Wallace.
2. Mary Ann Hardison married Jesse Cheek.
3. No information on other children, if any.

Brothers and sisters of Charles Hardison:
1. Thomas B. Hardison, born 17 Nov. 1789 in N. C., married Mary Byrd Wilson on 30 Oct. 1813, he died 1876 in Marshall County.
2. Margaret Hardison, born 17 May 1791 in N. C., married _____Davidson.
3. William Hardison, born 17 Nov. 1793 in N. C., married Mary Hardison, daughter of Mark Hardison: married 27 Dec. 1812; died 26 Oct. 1830 in Maury County.
4. Fanny Hardison, born 15 July 1798 in N. C., married Nat Woolard.
5. Jool Hardison, born 5 Aug. 1800 in N. C., died 17 Dec. 1873 in Marshall Co., married 15 Oct. 1818 to Jane A. Long.
6. Humphrey Hardison, born 18 Aug. 1804 in N. C., married Harriett Woolard on 19 March 1826; he died 15 Oct. 1874 in Maury County.

Half-brothers and sisters of Charles Hardison:
(By father's second marriage to Mary Smythie.)
1. Ezra Hardison, born about 1809, married Serena Derryberry.
2. Asa Hardison, married Mary Dickson.
3. Richard B. Hardison, born about 1818, married _____Sowell.
4. James Y. Hardison married Dorothy Fonville.
5. Penelope Hardison, born about 1814, married Ira Hardison, son of Edward Hardison
6. Ive Hardison married Gabriel B. Morton.

Source: Columbia Herald and Mail, 21 July 1876; Century Review, 277, 278; Marshall County Historical Society Quarterly, Fall 1973, page 119; information from Mrs. H. P. Leeper, Nashville.

JOHN HARDISON

Served in Capt. Andrew McCarty's company. No further information.

JOSHUA HARDISON

Enlisted as private 18 Dec. 1813 in Capt. James McMahan's company. Born 6 Dec. 1793, died 11 July 1866, buried Hardison Cemetery; married 13 Oct. 1814 to Martha Long, daughter of David Long, born 17 Nov. 1795, died 25 July 1870.

Children of Joshua Hardison:
1. S. L. Hardison, born 1816, died 1901.
2. Robert H. Hardison, born 1825, died 1908.
3. No information on other children, if any.

COLEMAN HARDY

Served in Capt. John Looney's company. No further information.

(UNKNOWN) HARGROVE

Columbia Herald and Mail, 27 Aug. 1876: "Old Man Hargrove of Rally Hill was an old War of 1812 soldier." No further information. [Some indication that this might be Joseph Hargrove, who married Patsie Hartley. But no definite information on this man.]

MOSES D. HARPER

Served in Capt. Benjamin Reynolds company. He was grandson of Benjamin Harper; was member of Reece's Church, removed No. 1829 and by 1830 was in Obion County. He was appointed constable in Maury County 18 July 1825. He is said to have settled in the Bigtyville area as early as 1806. Married Mary_____.

Children of Moses Harper:
1. Elizabeth Lynn Harper, born 27 March 1814.
2. Martha Harper, born 7 July 1815.
3. Benjamin Harper, born 29 Oct. 1816.
4. Jane M. Bride Harper, born 19 Oct. 1818.
5. John Harper, born 18 Dec. 1819.
6. William Brown Harper, born 16 May 1821.
7. Samuel Lemmins Harper, born 2 Feb. 1823.
8. Mary Dickey Harper, baptised 6 March 1825.
9. James Blair Harper, born 23 Oct. 1826.
10. Agnes Missenah Harper, born 28 Dec. 1828.

Source: Historic Ebenezer Church, pages 30, 31; Maury County Deed Book B, Vol. 1, pages 229, 261; 1825 court minutes, page 69.

DAVID HARRIS

Served in Capt. Robert Campbell's company. No further information. [Name appears to be Daniel Hawley on one muster roll of this company.]

(UNKNOWN) HARRIS

Francis M. Harris drew pension as widow of War of 1812 soldier in 1883; her mailing address was River Station, Maury County. No further information.

EDMUND HARRIS

Appointed coroner of Maury County in 1807.

Children of Edmund Harris:
1. Dr. Giles T. Harris, born April 1806, died 16 May 1866; married Jane C. J. Steele, born 16 Nov. 1811, died 27 March 1891.
2. No further information.

Source: Maury County Cousins No. 1, page 253.

REUBEN HARRIS

Served in Capt. Samuel B. McKnight's company. No further information.

HENRY HART

Served as third sergeant in Capt. Robert Campbell's company. No further information.

JOHN HART

Served in Capt. Bird S. Hurt's company. No further information.

JOSEPH HART

Served in Capt. Bird S. Hurt's company. [There were two early Joseph Harts in Maury County. The following will be information on both of these men.]

Joseph Hart - tanner; Nathan Vaught said he came to county between 1816-1817. He was born 29 Dec. 1793, died 10 June 1833, buried Greenwood Cemetery. He married Frances Mary Alderson (daughter of Josiah Alderson) 21 Feb. 1822 (date of bond). When his estate was being settled, his heirs at law were: Francis M. Hart, Edward Hart, Thomas Hart, Gideon B. Hart, James K. Hart, Charles C. Hart, Samuel Hart, and Elizabeth Trotter, wife of William Trotter (no relationship given).
Source: Circuit court minute book 1834-1837, page 56.

Joseph Hart (second of this name) had his will recorded 29 Oct. 1828 in Maury County. His children were John L. Hart, Jesse Hart, James Hart, Nancy Hart, Jane M. Hart, and Sally W. Hart.

+ELIAS HASSELL
Columbia Herald and Mail, 15 Dec. 1876: "Elias Hassell was one of thirteen of Jackson's men killed at New Orleans on 8 Jan. 1815." Family lived in Rally Hill-Lasea area of Maury County. Muster rolls show that Elijah M. Hassell enlisted as private 20 Sept. 1814 in Capt. Thomas Well's company of infantry, Col. Leroy Hammonds, died 31 Jan. 1815 at Mardenville. (Battle of New Orleans was 8 Jan. 1815. Williamson County, Tenn., marriages: Elisha M. Hassell marriage bond to marry Nancy Hawkins, 18 Oct. 1809. Columbia Herald and Mail, 12 Dec. 1876: Mrs. Nancy Blackburn died Sunday in Williamson County, age 84, buried near Lasea; she married Elias Hassel who died 1815.

HENRY HASTINGS
Drew pension as soldier of War of 1812 in 1883, living at Santa Fe; was injured in left foot during the war. [Impossible to determine his service as several men of this name will be found on muster rolls in State Library and Archives.]

JOHN HATCHETT
Served in Capt. Bird S. Hurt's company. Born 26 Jan. 1784, died 8 Jan. 1848, buried in Mt. Carmel Cemetery in Marshall County; Hale and Merritt says that he was the first postmaster of Lewisburg, Tenn.

Source: Smith vs Osborne, 1840, chancery court records, John Hatchett, age 62, in 1845, of Marshall County; William M. West vs John Hatchett, for damages, Maury County Court Minutes, 20 Oct. 1825, page 161; Hale and Merritt, Tennessee and Tennesseans, Volume III, page 807; Marshall County, Tenn., Cemetery Records by Ralph Whitesell, page 34.

GRANT HAWKINS
Enlisted as private 13 Nov. 1814 in Capt. John Jackson's company; Col. William Metcalf, Maj. Gen. William Carroll. Inventory of estate of Grant Hawkins, deceased, recorded in Maury County and included: "Discharge for six months under command of General Jackson, Captain Jackson's company." William Hawkins was administrator and inventory recorded 17 Sept. 1816.

Source: Maury County Will Book A-1, page 182.

ANDREW HAYS
Served in Capt. John Gordon's company. No further information.

GEORGE HAYS
Commissioned lieutenant in 1811 in 27th regiment. No further information.

JONATHAN HAYS
Commissioned ensign in 27th regiment in 1811. No further information.

JOSEPH HAYS
Served in Capt. Robert Campbell's company. No further information. [The surname is in question, at one point it appeared to be Huper.]

WILLIAM HELMS
Served in Capt. Bird S. Hurt's company. No further information.

JAMES HENDERSON
Commissioned ensign in 51st regiment in 1814. No further information.

JAMES HENDERSON
Served in Capt. Samuel B. McKnight's company. No further information. [On one roll of this company the name is found as James Harderson.]

JAMES HENDERSON
Enlisted as private 4 Oct. 1813 in Capt. William Dooley's company. [At one place the name of Joseph Henderson is found as member of Dooley's company.] No further information.

JOSEPH H———SON
Served in Capt. Bird S. Hurt's company. No further information.

NATHANIEL HENDERSON
Served in Capt. John Looney's company. No further information. On 1820 census.

ROBERT HENDERSON
Commissioned lieutenant in 27th regiment in 1809. [Two men named Robert Henderson were in the county about the same time. One was the Rev. Robert Henderson, Presbyterian minister, and it is questionable that he served in the militia, as ministers were exempted from such service.]

WILLIAM HENDERSON
Enlisted as private 4 Oct. 1813 in Capt. Samuel B. McKnight's company. No further information. [It is believed by some researchers that this might be William Steele Henderson, son of William Henderson, connected with Reece's Chapel.] No identification possible.

WILLIAM HENDERSON
Served in Capt. John Looney's company. No further information.

(UNKNOWN) HENDERSON
James Norman Smith wrote in his memoirs that one of his neighbors, Henderson, was in the War of 1812 from the eastern part of the county. No identification and no further information.

ABNER HENDRICKS
Enlisted as private 28 Jan. 1814 in Capt. Andrew McCarty's company, Col. R. C. Napier's Militia Infantry. Also commissioned ensign in 1808 in 27th regiment. No further information. [This man has been identified by some researchers as the same Abner Hendricks who lived in Dickson County; was son of Elijah Hendricks of Humphreys County.]

JOHN HENDRICKS
Served in Capt. Bird S. Hurt's company. No further information.

CALEB HENLEY
(Or Caleb Hanley) Appointed constable in Maury County Sept. 1809. No further information.

WILLIAM HENLEY
Served in Capt. James McMahan's company. No further information.

JOHN HERALD
Served in Capt. John Gordon's company. No further information.

JOSEPH HERNDON
Appointed justice of the peace in Maury County in 1812. Came to county in 1807 and moved into Columbia in 1818. He died 1862 "the day Buell crossed the river." Son of Col. Benjamin Herndon; buried Rose Hill, no marker. Married Martha Coleman, who died 25 Feb. 1844, at the age of 66 years. Continued on next page.

Joseph Herndon, continued:
He came with his brother Benjamin Herndon, who later left the county.

Children of Joseph Herndon:
1. Benjamin Herndon married 1838 to Carolina M. Yates.
2. Joseph Herndon, born 1810, died 1849.
3. Wesley Herndon.
4. Stephen Decatur Herndon, born 1816, died 1902; married Mary Ellen Herndon, born 1819, died 1893.
5. Rebecca G. Herndon, born 19 June 1801, died 18 Sept. 1885, married Aug. 1819 to James B. Houston, and (2) John H. Dew, born 1803, died 5 March 1844.
6. Ann Herndon married 1823 to Rev. Hartwell H. Brown.

Source: DAR paper of Miss Camille Herndon, deceased member of Jane Knox Chapter; Nashville Gazette, 28 Aug. 1819; Tennessee Democrat, 7 March 1844; Maury Democrat, 11 Jan. 1894, 19 April 1894; Tennessee Democrat, 29 Feb. 1844; Nathan Vaught, "Youth and Old Age", page 86.

SOLOMON HERRING
Commissioned ensign 1813 in 46th regiment; served as corporal in Capt. James McMahan company; age given as between 26 and 45 on 1820 census of Maury County; married 4 July 1812 in Davidson County to Nancy Rains, she married (2) Laird B. Boyd.

Wayne County, N. C. wills—1789 will of Solomon Herring, mentions wife Jane, children Stephen, Solomon and Sally. Wayne Co., N. C., Jan. 1791 will of David Jernigan, mentions wife Alice and grandchildren Sally and Stephen Herring; Wayne Co. N. C., will, April 1784, will of Anthony Herring, mentions wife and son Solomon.

Maury County Deed Book N, Vol. 1, page 51—Jane (x) Herring of Boone Co., Mo., gives power of attorney to John Blackman, "my son in law" ot Maury County to collect what is due me from the estate of my son Solomon Herring, deceased, on 27 Jan. 1828, registered 29 July 1828.

His will is recorded Maury County Will Book D-1, page 78; written 30 Nov. 1824, recorded 4 June 1826 . He is buried in his family cemetery on the Green Mill Road and his son is broken and it is impossible to tell his dates. One source says he died in 1824.

Children of Solomon Herring:
1. Robert Herring, born 6 May 1813, died 14 July 1834 (without issue). (Only child)

Brothers and sisters of Solomon Herring:
1. Stephen Herring [died Jan. 1850 in Tipton County, age 65, born in N. C.]
2. Elizabeth Herring married John Blackman. [His name is also found as Blackburn.]
3. Jane Herring married Isaac Ford.
4. Anne Herring married Riley Slocum.
5. Nancy Herring, deceased by 1836, married John Dobbins.

Source: Maury County Circuit Court Minutes, May 1836, page 218; Davidson County marriage records; Herring Cemetery in "They Passed This Way"; Deed Book N-1, page 51

ABRAHAM HESTER
Served in Capt. Samuel Ashmore's company. No further information.

ELIJAH HICKS
Served in Capt. John Looney's company. No further information.

JOHN HICKS
Served in Capt. Bird S. Hunt's company. No further information.

(UNKNOWN) HIGDON
Vicey Higdon drew pension at Fountain Creek in 1883 as mother of a War of 1812 soldier. No further information.

JAMES HIGGS
Served in Capt. James McMahan's company. No further information.

ALEXANDER HILL
Served as private in Capt. William Dooley's company. No further information.

ROBERT HILL
Appointed justice of the peace in 1809 and still serving in 1811. No further information.

WILLIAM KENAN HILL
Enlisted in Fayetteville, Tenn., 20 Sept. 1814, private West Tennessee Infantry, Capt. John Looney's company, Col. Alexander Loury; was on muster roll on 5 Jan. 1815. Born 18 March 1794 in Duplin Co., N. C., died 1 Aug. 1841, Velasco, Brazoria County, Texas; son of John Hill (born about 1750 in Va., died 1807 in Duplin Co., N. C.) and his wife Jane Kenan (born about 1755, died 1819, Franklin County, Tenn.). He married Rebecca K. Harris, born 7 Oct. 1801 in Union County, S. C., died 29 Dec. 1860, buried in Columbia, Tenn., her remains were removed to Rose Hill Cemetery. She was the daughter of Richard C. Harris (born 18 Nov. 1763, died after 1834) and his wife Mary Burrow (born 12 Aug. 1777, S. C., died 1836, Columbia, Tenn.

Children of William Kenan Hill:
1. John Orlando Hill, born 18 Feb. 1819, Columbia, Tenn., died 3 April 1892, married 15 Nov. 1860 to Joanna Weaver, born 1843, died 1928.
2. Mary Jane Hill, born 14 March 1821, Columbia, Tenn., died 13 Aug. 1888, in Columbia, married 26 March 1839 to Dr. Alexander H. Brown.
3. Ann Eliza Hill, born 23 April 1824, died 28 Aug. 1854, married 21 April 1842 to Alexander Morgan.
4. William Kenan Hill, Jr., born 13 Dec. 1827, died 1 Sept. 1829.
5. Virginia Hill, born 7 Nov. 1830 in Columbia, died 9 Jan. 1859, married Calvin Morgan; both are buried at Rose Hill, Columbia, Tenn.
6. Octavine Hill, born 27 Aug. 1833 in Columbia, died 15 May 1913 in Columbia, buried Rose Hill Cemetery; married 22 Jan. 1852 to Dr. Jacob Hyleman Alison.
7. William Kenan Hill, born 25 Dec. 1839, died July 1890, unmarried.

Brothers and sisters of William Kenan Hill:
1. Felix Kenan Hill, born about 1774 Duplin Co., N. C., married 6 March 1797 to Sarah Beck.
2. Catherine Hill, born N. C., married (1) Kenan Love, (2) Curtis Hooks.
3. Sarah Hill, born N. C., married (1) William Beck, (2)_____Bracken.
4. John Hill—no record after 1810. From information in family, he may have been John Hill, who died in Maury County 1850, born N. C., age 72.
5. James Kenan Hill, born about 1792, died 18 Aug. 1848, Duplin Co., N. C., married 11 Feb. 1823 to Sarah Hann Hurst. He was in War of 1812.
6. Elizabeth Hill, born 20 July 1795 in Duplin Co., N. C., died 10 June 1869 in Tennessee, married James Davis, born 1790, died 1850.
7. Edward Blackmore Hill, born about 1797 Duplin Co., N. C., died after 1850 in Tenn., married Nancy_____(in Tenn. about 1819).

James Davis who married Elizabeth Hill is the same James Davis listed in Vol. 1, p. 91, Franklin County, Tennessee, Regiments as Capt. James Davis, 32nd Regiment Rifle Company, 23 July 1810. He moved to Holly Springs, Miss., and then to Texas where he served as General in war with Mexico; later served in Texas Legislature and the

William Kenan Hill, continued:
U. S. Senate.

So far as is known, James Kenan Hill was only brother or sister of the War of 1812 soldier, William Kenan Hill, who returned to his native Duplin Co., N. C. His obituary states that he served in War of 1812 but does not state where. He probably served from Tennessee, but if so the Kenan (or "k") doest not appear on the record.

Source: Information furnished by Mrs. Wallace A. Berryman (Allie Williams), great, great granddaughter of William Kenan Hill.

JOHN HILLIS
Served in Capt. John Looney's company. Born between 1794 and 1800. He was the son of Samuel Hillis (born 1759, died fall 1840 in Marshall County, Tenn.), Revolutionary War soldier, and his wife Elizabeth.

Brothers and sisters of John Hillis:
1. Mary Hillis married 2 May 1816 to Robert Osburn.
2. Samuel C. Hillis, born between 1794 and 1800, married 2 May 1816 to Elizabeth Osburn.
3. James Hillis, born between 1794/1900.
4. William Hillis, born between 1900/04.
5. Levi Hillis, born 1800/04, died July 1838.

Source: Marshall County Historical Society Quarterly, Summer 1973, page 70-71.

SAMUEL HILLIS
Served in Capt. John Looney's company, was in the Battle of New Orleans. Born between 1794/1800; married 2 May 1816 to Elizabeth Osburn. He was son of Samuel Hillis, Revolutionary War soldier (born 19 Feb. 1760 in Rowan Co., N. C., died between Oct. 1840 and April 1841) and his wife Elizabeth, who died March 1843. Refer to listing above.

Source: Hale and Merritt, Tennessee and Tennesseans, Vol. III, page 807; Marshall County Historical Society Quarterly, Summer 1973, page 70; information furnished by Mrs. Marise P. Lightfoot.

MICHAEL HINDSLEY
Enlisted 4 Oct. 1813 as private in Col. T. McCrory's regiment, Capt. T. K. Gordon Infantry company (a Giles county group). He had settled in Lawrence County when Maury's jurisdiction reached to the Alabama line. (Name is spelled Hynesly on one roll). Born about 1785, died 23 Oct. 1855 at 70 in Lawrence County, Tenn., married Mary _____, born 18 Dec. 1796, died 2 Dec. 1875. They are buried in the Hindsley Cemetery south of Lawrenceburg.

Children of Michael Hindsley:
1. Harwek Hindsley, born about 1824.
2. Elizabeth, Hindsley, born about 1822.
3. Mahulda Caroline Hindsley, born about 1830, married 14 Feb. 1855 to Thomas Jefferson Robertson; she died 7 Feb. 1886 in Mississippi, buried at Brooklyn Cemetery.
4. Emily J. Hindsley, born 1832, married 1855 to William C. Anderson.
5. John Hindlsey, born about 1835.
6. James Hindsley, born about 1838.
7. No information on other children, although there is indication that there were others.

Source: "At Rest, Cemetery Records of Lawrence County, Tenn." by Irene B. Alexander and Carrie Gresham, page 153; family records of T. T. Garrett, Jr.

DAVID HINES
Served in Capt. Robert Campbell's company. He and his wife Anne lived on the Chambers Ferry Road. No further information.

(UNKNOWN) HINES
Nancy R. Hines, widow of War of 1812 soldier, drew pension in Mt. Pleasant in 1883. No further information.

JAMES HINNEGAN
Commissioned lieutenant in 27th Regiment in 1808. No further information.

HENRY HOBSON
Enlisted 10 Feb. 1813 in Capt. Benjamin Reynolds company volunteer infantry as a private. No further information.

ISAAC HOBSON
Served in Capt. John Looney's company. No further information.

JOHN HOBSON
Served in Capt. John Looney's company. No further information.

JOHN HODGE
Appointed justice of the peace in Maury County in 1812. Born 14 May 1769, died 10 Oct. 1825, buried in Greenwood Cemetery; married Ann C. [Nancy] Lewis, born 1797, died 1848, buried in Greenwood Cemetery.

Children of John Hodge:
1. Mary E. Hodge, born 27 Feb. 1818, married Dr. Archibald H. Buchanan.
2. James L. Hodge, born 4 Aug. 1814, later lived in Wilkinson Co., Miss.
3. John J. Hodge, born 19 April 1816, living in New Orleans in 1843.
4. William J., born 14 April 1820, later in Wilkinson Co., Miss.
5. Robert J. Hodge, born 19 April 1822, later in Wilkinson Co., Miss.
6. Benjamin L. Hodge, born 21 Oct. 1824, later in Wilkinson Co., Miss.

Source: Hodge vs Brown, 1843, Maury County Chancery Court Records; Nathan Vaught, "Youth and Old Age", page 72.

WILLIAM HODGE
Served in Capt. Bird S. Hurt's company; died 15 April 1815. On 15 May 1815 letters of administration on his estate were given to David Love. Hodge had been assigned to work on road in 1809 which led from Joseph Brown's to Love's Mill. Left several children which the court appointed guardians for at several terms of court.

Children of William Hodge (1819 court minutes)
1. John Hodge
2. David Hodge
3. Cinthia Hodge
4. Alexander Hodge
5. James Hodge

1816 court minutes show the following Hodge orphans in the county: John Hodge, age 14 in 1816; William Hodge, age 17 on April 10, 1816; James Hodge, age 9, on 13 Nov. 1815. John Hodge, age 14, orphan, was bound in 1816 to Benjamin Thompson until he was twenty-one. (Some confusion in court records about his minor heirs.)

BENJAMIN HOGAN
Served in Capt. Robert Campbell's company. No further information. [On one roll his name appeared to be Anderson Hogan.]

ISAIAH HOGAN
Commissioned lieutenant in the 27th Regiment in 1811. No further information.

JOHN HOGAN
Commissioned ensign in 27th Regiment in 1811. Served in Capt. James McMahan's company. Lived on the road which led to Pond Spring. No further information.

JAMES HOLACE
Served in Capt. John Gordon's company. [This man is believed to have been James Hollis.]

DANIEL HOLCOMB
Served in Capt. John Looney's company. No further information.

SAM HOLDING
Columbia Herald, 25 April 1873: Capt. Sam Holding drew pension this year as War of 1812 soldier, age 83 years. He died 28 Aug. 1873; formerly lived in Marshall County. [Marriage bond to marry Elvria H. Gullett dated 13 Feb. 1827.]

EDWARD HOLLAWAY
Served in Capt. James McMahan's company. No further information.

SILAS HOLLIS
Served in Capt. Andrew McCarty's company. No further information. [A man of this name signed petition about 1819 as living in the Congressional Reservation.]

JAMES HOLMES
Served in Capt. Robert Campbell's company. No further information.

LEWIS (LEVIN) HOLMES
Served in Capt. Samuel B. McKnight's company. No further information.

DELANSON W. HOOD
Enlisted as private 13 Nov. 1814 in Capt. Bird S. Hurt's Militia Infantry, Col. William Metcalf. No further information.

JOHN HOOD
Served in Capt. John Looney's company. Paid taxes on land in the Rutherford Creek area. No further information.

ELI HOPE
Served as trumpeter in Capt. James McMahan's company, volunteer from Williamson County; was prisoner of war for 40 days. Born 1780 in S. C., death not known; he is believed to be buried in an unmarked grave in Jones Cemetery near Santa Fe. He married Ann Barnett, born 1777 in S. C., death not known.

Children of Eli Hope:
1. Rebecca A. Dodson, born 25 May 1816 in Williamson County, died 5 June 1898 according to tombstone; married James E. Dodson. (Maury Democrat, 14 Jan. 1892, says Rebecca A. Dodson, 74, has died.) She is said to be his only child. However the 1820 census of Maury County shows three males and three females in his household who could be his children. Mary J. Hope, born 1820, died 1884, is buried in the Jones Cemetery and is possibly his daughter.

Source: Century Review of Maury County, 270, 274; 1820 census of Maury County; Maury Democrat 14 Jan. 1892; information from descendant Burton Woody, Santa Fe.

HOLMES H. HOPKINS

Enlisted as private 1 Dec. 1813, discharged 4 April 1814 in Capt. John Gordon's Mounted Spies. He was son of Joseph Hopkins and his mother's name was possibly Sarah. Joseph Hopkins and wife Sarah came here from Davidson County and in 1812 he got 640 acres north of Duck River in the first big bend above John Gordon's ferry, adjoining Robert Hays' original tract. This bend was first known as Hopkins Bend and today is called Greenfield Bend.

Brothers and sisters of Holmes H. Hopkins:
1. Jason Hopkins.
2. Neal Hopkins.
3. Elizabeth Hopkins.
4. Avelina (Evelina) Hopkins married John Johns of Davidson County.

Source: Crofford vs McGaw, 1845, chancery court case in Maury County—this is the box in which case is filed and not name of case; The Clarion and States Gazette, 20 Sept. 1814.

JASON HOPKINS

Enlisted as private 24 Sept. 1813 in Capt. John Gordon's Mounted Spies, transferred to Capt. Lauderdale's company on 14 Dec. 1814. Married 18 April 1809 to Alsee Williams. Son of Joseph Hopkins.

Source: Davidson County, Tenn., Marriage Records.

NEAL HOPKINS

Enlisted as corporal 24 Sept. 1813 in Col. John Coffee's regiment, Capt. Daniel Ross Mounted Gunmen, transferred to Capt. John Gordon's company on 24 Oct. 1813. Son of Joseph Hopkins. Married 2 Sept. 1815 in Davidson County to Nancy Johns.

HENRY HOPSON

Served in Capt. James McMahan's company. No further information.

JAMES HOSSEY

Served in Capt. John Looney's company. No further information. [This is believed to be correctly James Jossey, see later.]

WILLIAM HOUSE

Served in Capt. Robert Campbell's company. No further information.

CALEB HOWELL

Served in Capt. John Looney's company. No further information.

JOHN HOWELL

Served in Capt. Andrew McCarty's company. In 1813 was assigned to work on a road in the Cathey's Creek area. No further information.

MALACHI HOWELL

Served in Capt. Samuel B. McKnight's company. No further information.

STEPHEN H. HOWELL

Drew pension in 1883 in Maury County as surviving soldier of the War of 1812—he was wounded in the heart. No further information.

ALLEN HOWARD

Served in Capt. Robert Campbell's company. No further information.

PERMENUS HOWARD

Served in Capt. Samuel Ashmore's company. No further information.

SHADRICK HOWARD
Commissioned ensign 1809 in 27th Regiment. No further information.

WILLIAM HOWARD
Served in Capt. John Looney's company. No further information.

WILLIAM B. HUBBELL
Drew pension 1883 as surviving soldier of the War of 1812; was wounded on right arm below shoulder; lived at Southport. No further information.

THOMAS HUD (or Hood)
Served in Capt. Robert Campbell's company. No further information.

DANIEL HUDDLESTON
Served in Capt. John Looney's company. No further information.

JOHN HUDDLESTON
Served in Capt. John Gordon's company. No further information.

EDWARD B. HUDSON
Appointed justice of the peace for Maury County in 1809 and 1810. Died 25 Feb. 1826, married Assenath Reese.

Children of Edward Hudson:
1. Prudence Hudson, born 24 Feb. 1800, died Oct. 1824.
2. Syrene Hudson, born 28 Nov. 1801.
3. Nancy Hudson, born 6 April 1803.
4. Richard Davis, born 23 Dec. 1805.
5. Elizabeth Brevard Hudson, born 3 Dec. 1807.
6. Charlotte McCauly Hudson, born 27 Nov. 1809, died 3 June 1833.
7. Greenup Hudson, born 27 Jan. 1812.
8. Assenath Reese Hudson, born 18 Nov. 1813.
9. Esther Hudson, born 18 May 1816.

Source: Historic Ebenezer Church, page 28.

JAMES HUEY
Commissioned coronet in 54th Brigade, cavalry, 1813. [One James Huey, whose estate was being settled circa 1824, was survived by wife Jane and the following children: James H., William G., Catherine (married Jonathan Mills), Parmelia (married John Underwood), Mary (married John Renfro), John, Elizabeth, Jane, and Andrew J.] No further information. [One of this name constable in Maury County in 1808.]

JOHN HUEY
Commissioned ensign 1813 in 46th regiment. Also served as farrier in Capt. James McMahan's company. No further information.

SOLOMON HUFFSTALLER
Served in Capt. James McMahan's company. No further information.

EUDDET HUGHES
Commissioned lieutenant of volunteer company of infantry in 1812. No further information.

DAVID HUGHES
Served in Capt. Andrew McCarty's company. No further information.

KIBBLE T. HUGHES
Served in Capt. James McMahan's company. On the 1823 tax list he paid taxes on

65-3/4 acres on Duck River in Capt. Fitzgerald's company along with men named
Hanks, McLeans, Coopers, Chappell, Desha, and Dowell.

DANIEL HUMPHREY
Served in Capt. Samuel Ashmore's company. [Name also appears to be David Humphrey.]
[At one point name appears to be David Murphy on one muster roll.]

OLIVER HUNT
Maury County Deed Book B-1, Oliver Hunt gives to friend David Craig, both of Maury
County, power of attorney to convey tract of land (160 acres) "it being bounty given
me by the U. S. for service in late war" to James Mitchell, Jr. Deed was dated
26 Aug. 1820, registered 18 April 1821, page 279.

+AARON HUNTER
Enlisted 13 Nov. 1814 as lieutenant in Capt. John Jackson's company, Col. William
Metcalf's Infantry, Maj. Gen. William Carroll, died 20 Feb. 1815. His will is recorded in Maury County, Will Book A, page 251. In 1810 he lived on road leading
from Columbia to Snow Creek. Maury Minute Book for 1815, page 289, mentions Mary
Hunter, widow of Aaron Hunter; 22 Aug. 1816 court minutes mentions that she was left
with eight children.

Children of Aaron Hunter:
1. Terrell Hunter.
2. Nancy Hunter.
3. Betsy Hunter.
4. Comfort Hunter.
5. James Hunter.
6. Sarah Hunter.
7. Hezekiah Hunter.
8. No further information.

JOHN HUNTER
Served in Capt. James McMahan's company as sergeant. Daily Herald dated 29 April
1938: "John Hunter had two sons, William and John, both of whom fought in the
Indian wars. One of these sons is reputedly the first white child born in that
section of the county. William was colonel in state militia and fought in the
Mexican War." The War of 1812 soldier is believed to be John Hunter, Jr., who died
in Illinois prior to 1853, leaving a widow and children. John Jr.'s share of his
father's estate was $5,879.50—estate was worth $30,720. His father John Hunter, Sr.,
was born 6 Dec. 1767, died 28 Oct. 1852, married 2 Jan. 1789 to Mary Gilbert, born
2 Feb. 1768, died 11 (?) Sept. 1839.

Children of John Hunter:
1. William C. Hunter—lived in Illinois with his mother.
2. Jason L. Hunter —lived in Illinois with his mother.
3. Emily Hunter married Albert Pamsey of Illinois.
4. Mary Hunter married Jesse Gay of Gentry Co., Mo.
5. James Hunter, deceased by 1853, leaving widow Emily Jane of Missouri.
6. Joseph Hunter, deceased by 1853.
7. John Hunter, lived in Missouri.

Brothers and sisters of John Hunter:
1. William Hunter.
2. Cely (or Dely) P. Hunter, married a Henry.

Source: Unpublished chancery court records abstracted and contributed by Marise P.
Lightfoot, Mt. Pleasant, Tennessee.

NICHOLAS HUNTER
Served in Capt. John Gordon's company. No further information.

+KEMP W. HURST
Served as sergeant in 35th Regiment of Infantry, died 19 Feb. 1815. His heirs were Sally A. and Smith W. Hurst of Maury County.

Source: Maury County 1818 Minutes, page 210; page 57, Soldiers of the War of 1812 Buried in Tennessee by Mary Hardin McCown and Inez E. Burns.

BIRD S. HURT
Captain of company under General William Carroll; muster rolls dated Nov. 1814 to May 1815; settled first in Columbia and later settled around Rally Hill or Hurt's Cross Roads; married Miss White according to Nathan Vaught. His widow was named Susan (born 1791 died 1854 buried in Hurt Cemetery). He died Oct. 1836 in Maury County. He had received a license to keep an ordinary in the county in 1811.

Children of Bird S. Hurt:
1. William S., born about 1811.
2. Elizabeth S., never married, deceased by 1841.
3. Margaret Jane Hurt married Robert A. Glenn, Tennessee legislator 1873-1878, son of William Glenn.
4. Susan M. Hurt (or Sarah M.—name hard to decipher).

Source: Century Review of Maury County, page 285; Will Book 8, pages 448, 449; miscellaneous chancery court records; Nathan Vaught, "Youth and Old Age", page 91. Conversation in 1975 with descendant James M. Hurt of Columbia: Mr. Hurt believes that Bird S. Hurt's full name was Bird Stratton Hurt.

JOHN HUTCHINSON
Advertisement in Nashville Whig, 4 March 1814: "$50 REWARD—deserted from garrison of Newport, Ky., 24th Regiment on the 5th instant, John Hutchinson, aged 27 years, 6 feet 2½ inches high, born in Virginia, dark complexion, blue eyes, brown hair, by profession a cooper, enlisted in Columbia, Tennessee."

PATRICK HUTTON
Enlisted 28 Jan. 1814 as private in Capt. Andrew McCarty's company, Col. R. C. Napier. [Marriage bond dated 22 March 1806 in Williamson County, Patrick Hutton to Eley Germain.]

ARTHUR T. ISOM
Enlisted 14 Feb. 1814 in Capt. John Gordon's Mounted Spies. [Name given as Arthur Isham.] Enlisted as private 28 Sept. 1814 in Capt. James McMahan's company. [Name given as Arthur T. Isom.] National Banner and Nashville Whig, 17 Oct. 1831: "Col. Arthur T. Isom of Maury County married 5 Oct. 1831 Miss Eleanor D. Goodall in Rutherford County." Columbia Herald and Mail, 22 Sept. 1876: Moved to Hinds Co., Mississippi, about 1835.

GEORGE ISOM
Commissioned cavalry lieutenant, 5th brigade, 1813. Possibly the same as the one following.

GEORGE ISOM
Enlisted 24 Feb. 1814 in Capt. John Gordon's mounted spies. Name is also found as Isham on these muster rolls. [There were two contemporaries named George Isom in the county. The will of William Isom, Sr., 1813 mentions the following children: William, Jr., Henry, Dudley, Charles, George, Arthur, and Jonathan. The will of Jonathan Isom, recorded 1813, mentions his wife Elizabeth and the following children: Ursula, John, Elizabeth, Sally, Jenney, Polly, George, and Jamey Isom. No identification of the soldier can be made from these wills.]

JAMES ISOM
Commissioned captain of 27th Regiment in 1809; commissioned second major of the 51st Regiment in 1813. [A man of this name signed the petition to establish the county; man of this name in the county who had brother John Isom; estate of James Isom was being inventoried June 1826 and his wife was named Polly.] No further information.

BOBBY JACKSON
Lived in District 27 in 1871 and was a War of 1812 pensioner. [Columbia Herald and Mail, 15 Dec. 1871.] Jackson Cemetery in Jackson Bend tombstone inscriptions: Robert Jackson, born 4 Feb. 1791, died 3 May 1877; Nancy W. Jackson, born 20 Sept. 1800, died 15 March 1873. Columbia Herald, 21 March 1873: Nancy Jackson, wife of Bobby Jackson of District 24 died Saturday, age 74 years, he is now 84.

Children of Bobby Jackson:
1. Elizabeth Jackson, born 4 Nov. 1826, died 12 Aug. 1903, married Thomas M. Primm.
2. R. C. Jackson married Sarah Daimwood.
3. No information on other children.

Source: Century Review of Maury County, pages 255, 256.

BRANCH JACKSON
Served in Capt. John Chisholm's company. His will, signed 30 March 1818, recorded 27 Jan. 1824, mentions his mother Henaretta Jackson and sister Polly Ann.

Source: Will Book C, page 220.

DANIEL JACKSON
Served in Capt. James McMahan's company. No further information.

NATHANIEL JACOBS
Served in Capt. John Looney's company. Mo further information.

JOHN JAGGERS
Served in Capt. Bird S. Hurt's company. Married 28 May 1816 in Maury County to Hollin Herrald. No further information.

SIMON JAGGERS
Served in Capt. Bird S. Hurt's company. [This man was twice married and after his second marriage moved to Okolona, Miss. He married 12 April 1836 in Maury County to Katherine J. Houston.]

DAVID JARREL
Commissioned lieutenant in cavalry, 5th brigade, 1811. No further information.

SIMEON JENKINS
Discharged from the 8th Infantry in Dec. 1817, from Maury County. No further information.

WALTER S. JENKINS
Enlisted 24 Jan. 1814 in Capt. Nathan Farmer's Mounted Riflemen. Son of Philip Jenkins (born about 1761, died 1835 in Maury) married 8 June 1779 to Elizabeth Hungerford. Philip Jenkins married second in Maury County to Matilda Polk Campbell in 1821. Maury County Minute Book 12, page 481, Sept. 1835, letters of administration on estate of Philip Jenkins were issued to Walter S. Jenkins. Walter S. was listed as being between 40 and 50 on the 1840 census of Maury County. He married 13 Nov. 1816 in Williamson County to Agnes P. Stone.

Brothers and sisters of Walter S. Jenkins:
1. Sarah Jenkins, died 1819, married 16 Jan. 1812 James Norman Smith.
2. Annie Jenkins, married Dr. Joseph G. Hall   continued on next page

Brothers and sisters of Wlater S. Jenkins, continued:
3. Barton W. Jenkins.
4. Jane Jenkins married Joseph Morehead. [Her first name in question.]

Source: Memoirs of James Norman Smith on microfilm in Maury County Public Library;
information of descendant Mrs. Louise M. Heaton, Clarksdale, Miss., contributed by
Virginia W. Alexander.

+JOHN JENNINGS
Enlisted as private 13 Nov. 1814 in Capt. Bird S. Hurt's company of militia infantry
Col. William Metcalf; died 31 Jan. 1815. Rock Creek Baptist Church Minutes for
March 1815 has this entry: "sickened & Died at N. Orleans in Maj. Genl Carroll's
Division in 1815."

ABRAHAM JOBE
Served in Capt. James McMahan's company. In 1822 Abraham, James, Jesse and Samuel
Jobe were in the county militia and lived in the area now along the Bear Creek Pike;
he was still living in this area on the 1840 census of Maury County.

JAMES JOBE
Commissioned lieutenant in 27th Regiment, Maury County Militia, in 1811. Born in
Virginia, died 1833; married Catharine Pitt, born in N. C. He was an early settler
of Rutherford County and later moved to Maury County and built one of the first
cotton gins in Maury County.

Children of James Jobe:
1. Elihu C. Jobe, born 1809 in Maury County, married Mary W. Smith. They were the
parents of Dewitt Smith Jobe, who was murdered during the Civil War. A marker
located between Truine and Nolensville in Williamson County has the following:
"Dewitt Smith Jobe, a member of Coleman's Scouts, CSA, he was captured in a corn-
field about 1½ mile W., Aug. 29, 1864, by a patrol from the 115th Ohio Cav.
Swallowing his dispatches, he was mutilated and tortured to make him reveal their
contents. Refusing he was dragged to death behind a galloping horse. He is
buried in the family cemetery 6 miles NE."
2. No further information.

Source: Williamson County Historical Society Publication No. 3; Goodspeed's History
of Rutherford County, page 1042; Tennessee Historical Markers, page 143.

ABNER JOHNSON
Enlisted as private 22 June 1813 in Capt. Benjamin Reynolds company, Brig. Gen.
Roberts Mounted Rangers; drew pension as serving in 39th Regiment U. S. Infantry;
pension list of 1828. [He is believed to be the son of Abner and Nancy Johnson; the
elder Abner was a soldier in the American Revolution. Abner Johnson married Polly
Mobley in Maury County 12 Nov. 1817.]

ABNER H. JOHNSON
Enlisted Jan. 1814 in Capt. Samuel Ashmore's company served until May 1814, no
further information.

ALEXANDER JOHNSTON
Served in Capt. Samuel B. McKnight's company. This man has been identified as the
son of John Johnston, Rev. War soldier, (born 5 Jan. 1753, died 5 Oct. 1818) and
his wife Martha Allison (born 1758 in Maryland), married in summer of 1774 in
Baltimore. He died 1832; his second wife was Lotty Stockard Mitchell, whom he had
married 3 May 1829. (She married 1838 to William Craig).

Children of Alexander Johnston: (continued on next page)
1. John C. Johnston, aged 20 in 1840.

Children of Alexander Johnston, continued:
2. Margaret Ellen Johnston.
3. Mary A. Johnston, born about 1820, married Burrell Walker of Wayne County.
4. William S. Johnston, born about 1830-1.
5. James A. Johnston, born about 1833.
6. Elizabeth Johnston, age 16 in 1840.

Source: Information by Mrs. Marise P. Lightfoot, Mt. Pleasant; Craig vs Johnson, 1840, Maury County Chancery Court Records.

AMOS JOHNSTON

Appointed justice of the peace of Maury County June 1809; died June 1829. He married Elizabeth_____, who later married Lemuel Prewitt.

Children of Amos Johnston:
1. Lewis Johnston.
2. Jacob Johnston.
3. Jesse Johnston.

Source: Mt. Pleasant Masonic Lodge resolution; Maury County Equity Causes, 1835.

ELIJAH JOHNSON

Served in Capt. James McMahan's company. No further information. [Johnson vs Brien, 1851, Maury County Chancery Records: Elijah Johnson, died intestate in Giles County and administrator appointed 3 Dec. 1830. His children were: William M., James E., Elizabeth, who married William M. Street, John H., and Emily J. Johnson, who married C. D. Brien of Davidson County.]

GARRETT JOHNSON

Served in Capt. Robert Campbell's company. No further information.

ISHAM JOHNSON

Served in Capt. James McMahan's company. Son of John Johnson, Rev. War soldier, and his wife Isabella Erwyn. On 15 Aug. 1814 James Johnson was given license to keep ferry at or near the Suck Island and Isham Johnson was his security. The George Hogue place on Knob Creek has been found as the place of the late Isham Johnson. He was living in Wayne County in 1834.

Brothers and sisters of Isham Johnson:
1. Matthew Johnson, living in Lawrence County in 1834.
2. Judith Johnson married Isaac Sellars.

Source: Records of Marise P. Lightfoot and unpublished Chancery Court records which she has abstracted.

JAMES JOHNSON

Served in Capt. Samuel Ashmore's company. [On one roll his name is given as Samuel Johnson.]

JAMES JOHNSON

Appointed constable in Maury County in June 1809. No further information. [In 1814 a man of this name given permission to keep ferry near Suck Island.] [In 1818 one Matthew Johnson was guardian for the minor heirs of a James Johnston, deceased. These heirs were: Sarah, Nancy, Joseph, Ester, and Elizabeth Johnston.]

JOHN JOHNSON

Served in Capt. Samuel Ashmore's company. No further information.

JOHN JOHNSON

Served in Capt. Andrew McCarty's company. No further information.

JOHN JOHNSON
Served in Capt. William Dooley's company. No further information.

JOHN JOHNSON
Served in Capt. Bird S. Hurt's company. No further information.

JOHN JOHNSON
Served in Capt. Bird S. Hurt's company. No further information. (Two of this name in this company.)

JOHN W. JOHNSON
Served in Capt. James McMahan's company. No further information.

JOHN JOHNSON Miscellany
As it was impossible for the editor of this book to separate the several men named John Johnson in the county, the following is information on men of this name who were of an age to be a War of 1812 soldier in the county:

John Johnson — Will signed 9 Sept. 1813, recorded in Book A, page 117; children mentioned in this will were: Elijah, Thomas, Nancy, Elizabeth, Polly, Joseph, and William.

John Johnson — Will signed 1 Feb. 1850, recorded in Book F (12), page 6; mentions wife and children: Allen, Sally White, Polly Polk, Mariah Pickard, Eliza Davis, Elizabeth Cambel, James, Richard, Allen, Mose (deceased), William; son and daughter of Mose Johnson, my son deceased; granddaughter Sophia E., daughter of my son Allen Johnson. Witnesses to will were Edward Davis and Andrew W. Hill.

John Johnson married Isabella Kerr 21 Feb. 1814.
John Johnson married 18 Feb. 1819 in Maury to Tabby Farmer, William Sharp, J. P.

ROBERT JOHNSON
Served as first lieutenant in Capt. Andrew McCarty's company. No further information. [Robert Johnson married Mary Murrell 29 April 1822 in Maury County.]

ROBERT JOHNSTON
Served in Capt. James McMahan's company. No further information. Man of this name was commissioned lieutenant in 1812 in 27th Regiment.

SAMUEL JOHNSON
Appointed justice of the peace in Maury County in 1812. No further information.

SAMUEL JOHNSTONE
Commissioned lieutenant colonel 1814 in 51st Regiment. No further information.

SAMUEL M. JOHNSON
Served in Capt. John Looney's company. No further information.

SIMON JOHNSON
Appointed justice of the peace in Maury County, resigned Dec. 1809. Married 6 Nov. 1816 to Keziah Barker in Maury County.

Children of Simon Johnson:
1. John Johnson married Ellen Kitrell, daughter of Samuel and Betsy Adkins Kittrell.
2. Thomas Johnson, lived in Missouri in 1841.
3. Joseph Johnson, lived in Fayette Co., Tenn., was not 21 in 1841.
4. Henry Johnson, lived in Maury, was not 21 in 1841.
continued on next page

Children of Simon Johnson, continued:
5. Robert Johnson, lived in Maury County.
6. Ferdinand Johnson, lived in Maury County.
7. Eliza Johnson, married Joel S. Reaves of Maury County.

Source: Century Review of Maury County, page 248; Tennessee Democrat, 6 May 1841; Maury County Settlements and Inventories, Book A, page 236. (This book is located in basement of courthouse and is not in clerk's office upstairs.)

THOMAS JOHNSON
Commissioned lieutenant 1812 in 27th Regiment. No further information.

THOMAS G. JOHNSON
Served in Capt. James McMahan's company. No further information.

WILLIAM JOHNSON
Served in Capt. James McMahan's company. No further information.

WILLIAM A. JOHNSON
Served as Major during the War of 1812. Born 1789 in Guilford Co., N. C., died 1852 in McNairy County, Tenn. He married about 1810 to Mary "Polly" Griffin, born about 1789 in N. C., died 1852 in McNairy County. She died three days after her husband. He was son of William and Sarah McClaren Johnson of Maury County.

Children of William A. Johnson:
1. Milton Hugh, born 17 July 1813 in Maury County, died 17 June 1897 in Humboldt, Gibson County, Tenn., buried Rosehill Cemetery; married (1) 2 Sept. 1834 to America J. Thomas; married (2) 8 Nov. 1864 to Mrs. M. I. M. Wrather.
2. Daughter, born between 1810 and 1820.
3. Daughter, born between 1810 and 1820.
4. Daughter, born between 1810 and 1820.
5. No further information; it is known that William A. Johnson had five children.

Brothers and sisters of William A. Johnson:
1. Alexander Johnson, born 14 April 1782, died 7 Feb. 1857 in Maury County; married 6 Aug. 1805 in Rockingham Co., N. C., to Mary Jane Ballanfant.
2. John Johnson.
3. Female - no further information.
4. Female - no further information.

Grandchildren of William A. Johnson through his son Milton Hugh Johnson include:
1. Hiram Thomas Johnson, born 27 Aug. 1836, died 24 July 1882. Attorney and Tennessee State Representative.
2. John P. Johnson, born about 1842, died 1879. Attorney, partner with his brother Hiram Thomas Johnson.

Source: Mrs. J. A. Cushman, 1120 Wade Drive, Bedford, Texas 76021, descendant; Goodspeed's History of Gibson County, page 892; 1820 and 1830 census records of Maury County.

ABNER JONES
Served in Capt. James McMahan's company. No further information.

ABNER JONES
Served in Capt. Andrew McCarty's company. No further information.

ALFRED JONES
Served in Capt. Robert Campbell's company. No further information. [At one point on one roll the name appears to be Alfred Ivey.]

CAROLINE JONES
Drew pension in Columbia in 1883 as widow of War of 1812 soldier. No further information.

BENJAMIN JONES
Served in Capt. Samuel Ashmore's company. No further information.

BENJAMIN JONES
Served in Capt. Samuel B. McKnight's company. No further information. [At one point the surname appeared to be James instead of Jones.]

HEZEKIAH JONES
Commissioned lieutenant in 27th Regiment in 1814. No further information.

JOHN JONES
Commissioned ensign in 27th Regiment in 1811. No further information.

JOHN JONES
Served in Capt. Benjamin Reynolds company. No further information.

SAMUEL JONES
Captain in Maury County militia, also served in Revolutionary War. Born 1755, died 1831 in Maury County; married 1790 Elizabeth Goodloe, born 17 Aug. 1772, died 1854.

Children of Samuel Jones:
1. Sarah Applewhite Jones, born 7 Nov. 1791, died before 1857, married James David Cockrill.
2. Robert G. Jones, married Candis Curtis; still living 1857.
3. Nancy M. Jones married James M. Jones.
4. Mary Jones married David Glass.
5. Edward D. Jones, born 31 March 1800, died 15 Feb. 1847, married Kitty Anne Edwards Willis.

Source: Information furnished by Mrs. Marise P. Lightfoot, Mt. Pleasant, from her files on Revolutionary War soldiers; page 60, Soldiers of the War of 1812 Buried in Tennessee.

THOMAS JONES
Service not determined. Born 2 Ja. 1771 in Wake County, N. C., died 1852 in Gibson County, Tennessee, buried in family cemetery on old homeplace; son of Capt. James Jones and his wife Charity Alston. He married 19 Nov. 1795 to Catherine Shaw, daughter of John Shaw, born 23 April 1781 in Wake Co., N. C., who died at 85. He moved 1804 to Smith County, Tenn., and then to Maury County, and in 1825 moved to Gibson County, Tennessee.

Children of Thomas Jones:
1. Elizabeth Jones, born 10 Sept. 1797 in Wake County, N. C., died 7 Sept. 1889; married 1. Rev. Alexander M. Williams, born 28 Jan. 1793, died 12 Jan. 1847; 2. John Barham.
2. Rev. John Washington Jones, born 27 March 1798 in Wake County, died 7 Oct. 1866; married Elizabeth Perry, born 1 Jan. 1799, died 5 May 1861, daughter of William and Elizabeth Shaw Perry.
3. James Jones, born 6 Jan. 1800, married Lucretia A. Williams, born 1804; went to Gibson County, but returned to Maury County.
4. Rachel Jones, born 17 Oct. 1801, died 7 Dec. 1888, married Joseph Morehead Carthel.
5. Frances Jones, born 17 Dec. 1803, died 1892, married William W. Hamon, born 1797 died 1836.
continued on next page

Children of Thomas Jones, continued:

6. Charity Jones, born 15 Feb. 1806, died 1871, married Hartwell S. Dickason, born 1801, died 1865.
7. Priscilla Jones, born 20 Feb. 1808, died 23 April 1858, married John H. Freeman, born 1797, died 1874.
8. Mary Jones, born 7 Feb. 1810, died 183?, married John Hancock Crisp, born 1810, died after 1865.
9. Solomon Jones, born 31 Oct. 1812, died as infant.
10. Willis Jones, born 3 June 1815, died 23 Jan. 1883, married Lou Ann Tindell, born 23 Nov. 1816, died 1 May 1857.
11. Aley Jones, born 19 June 1817, died 1 March 1872, married Hugh Douglas Neilson.
12. Ruth Jones, born 1 Feb. 1819, died 16 June 1899, married 1. William M. Irwin, born 1811, died 17 June 1864; 2. Henry Harper, born 1815.
13. Catharine Jones, born 9 June 1821, married James Madison Lassiter, born 15 Sept. 1815.
14. Thomas Wyly Jones, born 29 April 1824, died 1 April 1904, married Elizabeth R. Mitchell, born 8 May 1825, died 8 Dec. 1896.

Source: Page 34, History of the Jones Family, loaned for copying by Mrs. Anne P. Westbrook, Waverly, Tennessee.

WILLIAM JONES
Served in Capt. James McMahan's company. No further information.

WILLIS JONES
Enlisted 20 June 1814 as corporal in Capt. Mebane's company, Col. Philip Pipkin's 1st Regiment of West Tennessee Militia, discharged 21 Dec. 1814. Born 11 June 1784 in Orange County, N. C., died 23 Oct. 1834, buried family cemetery near Santa Fe, Tennessee; son of Edmund Jones (born 1749, died 1834) and his wife Rachel Alston (born 27 Sept. 1747, died before 1834); married Elizabeth Gee, born 25 March 1792 in Chatham County, N. C., died 9 Nov. 1834, buried family cemetery near Santa Fe, Tennessee. She was the daughter of George Gee (born 1 April 1767, died 9 July 1848, N. C.) and his wife Charity_____ (possibly Taylor), who died March 1840 in N. C. Willis Jones lived north of Duck River in Maury County near Santa Fe.

Children of Willis Jones:
1. Lemuel Jones, born 22 Dec. 1811, died 6 Aug. 1845, married Jane Latta.
2. Eliza Jones, born 28 Nov. 1813, died between 1834 and 1843, married Andrew Tate Mitchell Fly.
3. Martha (Patsy) Jones, born 10 Oct. 1815, death not known, married Peter Nash.
4. Ruth Jones, born 10 July 1817, died 27 Aug. 1853, married John H. Caldwell.
5. Charity Millinor Jones, born 18 Sept. 1819, died 25 Aug. 1848, married Washington Blackburn Russell.
6. Wiley Gabriel Jones, born 22 April 1821, died 10 Aug. 1868, married (1) Sarah Jane Dodson; (2) Martha A. Godwin.
7. William Joseph Jones, born 4 Nov. 1823, died 3 April 1909, married (1) Nancy Emeline Hanks; (2) Harriet J. Miller; (3) Sarah Margaret Williams; (4) Lucinda (Lou) Katherine McConnico; (5) Nannie H. Evans.
8. Rachel Alston Jones, born 2 Jan. 1825 died 20 Oct. 1902, married Madison Monroe Russell.
9. James Willis Jones, born 28 Jan. 1828, died 5 March 1904; married (1) Amanda America Dodson; (2) Rebecca A. Satterfield; (3) Sarah Ann Woody.
10. Mary Elizabeth Jones, born 20 April 1831, died 28 Jan. 1862, married John Shaw Perry.
11. Sarah Ellen Jones, born 26 Aug. 1834, died 5 June 1838.

Brothers and sisters of Willis Jones:
1. Lewis Jones - moved from N. C. to Maury County and Franklin County, Tenn., then to Mississippi.
continued on next page

Brothers and sisters of Willis Jones, continued:
2. Sugar Jones — moved to Maury County then to Mississippi.
3. Alston Jones — married (2) Polly Mayberry, Hickman County, Tenn.
4. James Jones (not mentioned in father's will), in his will mentions a debt to his father.
5. Nancy Jones married Thomas J. Brooks, Hickman and Maury Cos., Tenn.
6. Sally Jones, born 25 Jan. 1788, died 20 Feb. 1868 (from Maury County Cousins)

Source: Information supplied by Catherine Gilliam (Mrs. Richard) and Charlotte F. Shenk (Mrs. D. H.) of Huntsville, Alabama, from their family papers and research.

JAMES JORDAN
Served in Capt. James McMahan's company. No further information. [James Jordan, died 28 Feb. 1867, is buried in the Lytles Creek Meeting House Cemetery.]

+WILLIAM JORDAN
Enlisted as private 28 Sept. 1814 in Capt. James McMahan's Tennessee Volunteer Gunmen, Col. Robert H. Dyer; died at New Orleans 25 Feb. 1815. Thomas Jordan was administrator of his estate in Maury County.

JAMES JOSSEY
Served in Capt. John Looney's company. Commissioned lieutenant in 27th Regiment, 1813. Born 23 Nov. 1786 in Georgia, died 12 Dec. 1831 in Maury County, buried in the Webster Cemetery. Married Nancy Coleman, born 24 May 1792 died 18 Jan. 1873, buried in Webster Cemetery. (Her stone says born 27 May died 16 Jan.) Jossey was a friend of Albert Pike when he was in Maury County—Pike stole a canoe and went down the river to Jossey's according to Nat Jones. He was the son of Henry Jossey and his wife Mary Hill (daughter of Henry Hill and Sarah Cotton Hill.) (Mary Hill Jossey married as her second husband 18 April 1816 in Maury County to John L. Macon and is also buried in the Webster Cemetery.)

Children of James Jossey:
1. Mary Hill Macon Jossey, born 1818, died 1839, buried Crosby=Coleman Cemetery; married Oct. 1836 to D. D. Johns. They had a daughter Addie.
2. Sally Jossey, married (1) Wilks Walker, (2) George Stockard. She had sons Ellis (who disappeared) and Otey Walker (who married Laura Dorsett).
3. Sophie C. Jossey married 19 Nov. 1851 in Maury to William A. Baker. She had Fannie (married Sam Graham of Pinewood), Sallie, and a son.
4. Rowena E. Jossey married 17 Sept. 1850 to Nathaniel E. Griffin.
5. William Walker Jossey, born 26 Nov. 1813, died 28 June 1853, married Miss Littlefield, buried Webster Cemetery.

Brothers and sisters of James Jossey:
1. Sarah Jossey married Jonathan Webster.
2. Rowena Caroline Jossey married 9 Nov. 1821 to John W. McGimsey.
3. Christina Jossey (called Keddy and Kittie) married Col. Richard Willis of Greensboro, Georgia.
4. Henry Jossey, Jr.

Source: Letter written by Mary T. Seabright to Mrs. P. H. Southall, dated 12 March 1917 in Webster papers; also quoting "The Hills of Wilkes Co., Ga., and Allied Lines and Webster Cemetery inscriptions.

BENJAMIN JOURDAN
Served in Capt. Bird S. Hurt's company. No further information.

DIANA JUDD
Listed on the 1883 pension list as the mother of a soldier, living on Carter's Creek. Much conflicting information on this entry as dates do not match. See next page.

Diana Judd, continued:

Daniel Judd, born 5 Sept. 1800, died 11 July 1860, buried Pisgah Methodist Church Cemetery, Maury County, married Dinah Farray 18 Aug. 1824 in Lauderdale County, Ala. She is also buried at Pisgah and her stone reads: Diana Judd, born 18 Sept. 1804, died 4 Feb. 1882. Daniel Judd, born in Pa., was a Methodist minister.

Children of Diana Judd:
1. Nelson P. Judd, born 1825 in Alabama, married Martha Patillo.
2. Martha Judd, born 1826 in Tennessee.
3. Hannah J. Judd, born 22 Oct. 1831, married Enoch Galloway.
4. Johanna Judd, born 1840 in Tenn., married Manson Vestal.
5. John M. Judd, born 1843 in Tenn.
6. Daniel Judd, Jr., born 1847 in Tenn.
7. No information on other children if any.

Source: Century Review of Maury County, page 134; 1850 census of Maury County; Lauderdale Co., Ala., marriage records; Pisgah Cemetery inscriptions from "They Passed This Way."

HENRY KELLAM
Served in Capt. Benjamin Reynolds company. No further information.

JOHN KELLAM
Served in Capt. Benjamin Reynolds company. No further information.

EDWARD KELLY
Served in Capt. Robert Campbell's company. No further information.

JOHN KELLY
Appointed constable in Maury County June 1809. No further information.

JOSHUA KELLY
Served in Capt. John Gordon's company. No further information.

+WILLIAM KELLY
Enlisted as private 28 Sept. 1814 in Capt. James McMahan's Volunteer Mounted Gunmen, Col. R. H. Dyer; killed in battle 23 Dec. 1814. Maury County Will Book A-1, page 156, shows that his estate included "certificate for lost property in the army" and his wages for a tour of duty to New Orleans. Polly Kelly was administratrix of his estate in Aug. 1815 and bought all household items at the sale of estate.

Children of William Kelly:
1. Charles D. Kelly (minor in 1819)
2. Nancy Murray (minor in 1819)

Source: 1819 court minutes which gives his minors in 1819; Will Book A-1, page 156.

ROBERT G. KELSEY
Commissioned ensign in 51st Regiment in 1814. Kelsey's Cross Roads in Maury County was named for him—this place no longer has an identity in the county. He married Elizabeth Kelly, license issued 17 July 1820 in Maury County, and marriage was solemnized by Hugh Shaw.

WILLIAM KENAMORE
War of 1812 soldier, no service given. Born 1792 in N. C., died 1862 in Springfield, Missouri; married Polly Johnson, daughter of Abner Johnson (Revolutionary War soldier, born 1759, died 185), who was born 1782, and died 1870 in Missouri. In 1854 they moved to Springfield, Missouri.
(continued on next page)

Children of William Kenamore:
1. Grant Allen Kenamore, born 14 Feb. 1824 in Maury County, died 7 July 1885; moved to Greene Co., Mo., 1854, moved to Dent Co., Mo., 1856, married Emily Frances London, died 1874. They had George R., born 1846, and William B.
2. No information on other children, if any.

Source: Missouri Pioneers, Book 4, page 68.

JESSE KENDRICK
Commissioned ensign 51st Regiment, 1814. No further information.

JOHN KENDRICK
Commissioned lieutenant in 27th Regiment in 1813. No further information.

ANDREW KENNEDY
He was justice of the peace in Maury County in 1810, resigned December 1810. Maury Democrat, 16 April 1908: "Andrew Kennedy owned a store and 640 acres of land on the Dry Forks. He committed suicide by hanging, being the first case of suicide on Cathey's Creek." [Another source says that this Andrew Kennedy settled around Zion Church and was not the one on Cathey's Creek.]

EVANDER KENNEDY
Enlisted 28 Sept. 1814 in Capt. James McMahan's company, Col. R. H. Dyer; had been in Capt. Glen Owens' company and transferred; saddler while in service. [Evander Kennedy married Mary Goff, daughter of Andrew Goff of Williamson County.]

Children of Evander Kennedy:
1. Elizabeth G. Kennedy.
2. No information on other children if any.

Source: 1812 Ancestor Index, National Society, United States Daughters of 1812, page 288.

ELI M. C. KENNEDY
Served as private in Capt. William Dooley's company, enlisted 4 Oct. 1813. No further information.

ELI KENNEDY
Enlisted as private 22 June 1812 in Capt. Benjamin Reynolds' company of Mounted Rangers. No further information. [Eli Kennedy marriage bond dated 16 Aug. 1814 to marry Margaret J. Finley with Francis McBride as bondsman.] [Eli Kennedy marriage bond dated 23 Jan. 1823 to Elizabeth Currey.]

ELI KENNEDY
Enlisted 10 Feb. 1813 in Capt. Benjamin Reynolds company. No further information.

JAMES KENNEDY
Served in Capt. Robert Campbell's company. [Man of this name found on records in 1835 as being 56 years old.] No further information.

JOHN M. KENNEDY
Enlisted as private 28 Sept. 1814 in Capt. James McMahan's company, Col. R. H. Dyer, Tennessee Volunteer Mounted Gundmen.

(UNKNOWN) KENNEDY
Parthenia Kennedy drew pension in Columbia in 1883 as widow of War of 1812 soldier. No further information.

WILLIAM E. KENNEDY

"Was in the army with the president". (Correspondence of James K. Polk, edited by
Herbert Weaver, Volume II, page 10.) Possibly served in group from Fayetteville,
Tennessee. Born 18 April 1794, died 17 Dec. 1863 in Maury County and buried at Zion
Cemetery. [Deathdate is in question. His will was written 18 Oct. 1856 and he
freed his slaves and made some bequests which were in litigation before the Civil
War.] He married Elizabeth O., born 9 Dec. 1805, died 7 Oct. 1841. [One source
says he married daughter of Col. Nathaniel Willis and had several children, none of
whom lived.] He was circuit judge from 1828 to 1833. He was son of Robert Campbell
Kennedy (born 27 Aug. 1761, died 25 Feb. 1815 in Lincoln County, Rev. War soldier)
and his wife Esther Edmiston (born 13 April 1766, died 16 Aug. 1823). R.C. Kennedy
first settled in Davidson County on Murfreesboro Fork Road and moved to Lincoln
County between 1808 and 1809.

Children of William E. Kennedy:
1. Infant son, born and died 28 Sept. 1830.
2. William Edwin Kennedy, born 28 Nov. 1836 died 20 Aug. 1837.
3. Several more infants buried at Zion Cemetery which are believed to be his
   children.

Brothers and sisters of William E. Kennedy:
1. Sally Buchanan Kennedy, born 1 Aug. 1806, died 25 July 1818.
2. Hettie Kennedy married Robert Huston McEwen.
3. Margaret Montgomery Kennedy, born 13 Jan. 1786, died 6 April 1843, married 1803
   in Davidson County to George M. Martin, died 3 May 1873; they later lived in
   Maury County and their daughter married General G. J. Pillow.
4. Sister married Dr. Saunders.

Source: Clayton's History of Davidson County, pages 73, 106, 475; Williamson County
Historical Society Journal No. 3, page 2; Zion Cemetery inscriptions from "They
Passed This Way".

ELI KENNER

Commissioned ensign in 27th Regiment 1813. No further information. [This is
possibly Eli Kennedy but name was Kenner on the list.]

ROBERT KERR

Appointed patrolee in Capt. James Byers Company in Sept. 1808. No further information.

WILLIAM KERR

Served in Capt. McMahan's company. No further information. [One William Kerr died
2 Dec. 1853 in Maury County at the age of 72.] [One William Kerr was born 1780 in
the Carolinas, lived in Maury County, and was married to Margaret Mitchell, born 1807
in N. C.; she later married 1842 to William Yancey.]

DAVIS KILCREASE

Commissioned ensign in the light infantry, 46th Regiment, 1814; born in Edgefield
District, S. C., died 23 March 1821 in Hamilton, Monroe Co., Miss; married 9 Nov.
1817 in Williamson Co., Tenn., to Mahala Mandley. He was the son of William
Kilcrease and his wife Frances. Mahala Kilcrease later married Thomas Townsend. His
estate was also settled in Maury County as our court minutes dated 26 Oct. 1825 show
that Mahala Kilcrease was appointed administratrix of Davis Kilcrease.

Children of Davis Kilcrease:
1. Kelber Kilcrease.
2. Francis Kilcrease.
3. Harriett Kilcrease.

Source: Family records of Jane Luna (Mrs. John), member of Jane Knox Chapter.

JOHN KILCREASE
Commissioned lieutenant in light infantry, 27th Regiment, 1812. Bron 29 Sept. 1788 in Edgefield District, S. C., died 5 Sept. 1843, Maury County, buried Rose Hill in Columbia; married Susan_____, born 1 Feb. 1792 in Edgefield District, S. C., died 26 July 1870 in Maury County, buried Rose Hill. Son of William and Frances Kilcrease

Children of John Kilcrease:
1. Mary Frances Kilcrease, born 16 May 1824, died 16 June 1884, buried Rose Hill, married 5 June 1839 to Wilson Tucker.
2. Harriet S. Kilcrease, born 1817, died 1899, buried Rose Hill, married Isaac Foster.
3. Racheal Kilcrease, born 1835, died 1906, buried Rose Hill Cemetery, married (1) William C. D. Gill, born 1821, died 1852; (2) 1850 to Al..gelow Barr, born 1832, died 1901.
4. Nancy Kilcrease, born 28 Sept. 1813, died 2 Dec. 1875, buried Rose Hill, married Berry Folsom.

Source: Rose Hill Cemetery records, 1850 census; inventory of John Kilcrease's estate, Book Z, page 541; research and family records of Jane Luna [Mrs. John W.].

WILLIAM KILCREASE
Appointed justice of peace for first quarterly court of Maury County, resigned March 1810; born in S. C., came to Tennessee when he was eighteen; died 9 June 1843 in Maury County at the age of 78 years; married Frances_____, died 26 Nov. 1849.

Children of William Kilcrease:
1. John Kilcrease, born 29 Sept. 1788, died 5 Sept. 1843.
2. Davis Kilcrease, died 23 March 1821.
3. Nancy Kilcrease, born 17 Nov. 1795 in S. C., died 9 Nov. 1846 in Maury County; married 23 Dec. 1817 to Thomas S. Caldwell.
4. Elizabeth Kilcrease, born 1796 in Edgefield District, S. C., died 19 July 1853, married (1) 15 Jan. 1811 to James Hayes; (2) 1824 to Samuel Wheatley.
5. Rachel Kilcrease, born 4 March 1801, died 1 May 1846 married Col. Israel McCarroll.
6. Catherine Kilcrease, born 4 March 1815 in Tennessee, died 20 July 1851 in Maury County, married 21 Jan. 1835 to Nathaniel Nicholson.
7. William Kilcrease, Jr., died 9 April 1839.

Source: Will of William Kilcrease, Maury Will Book Z, page 514; family records of Jane Luna (Mrs. John W.), Bible records of Thomas S. Caldwell; records in family of Mr. Andy Hunter gives the deathdate for Elizabeth Wheatley as 5 Oct. 1859.

EBENEZER KILPATRICK
Commissioned captain in 27th Regiment in 1811. Maury County Deed Book E-1, page 86, Elihu Kilpatrick gets 200 acres from Joseph Kilpatrick, recorded 14 April 1813, land was on both sides of Duck River, mentions Ebenezer Kilpatrick's corner. Witnesses to deed were Jos. Carthel and Ebenezer Kilpatrick. On 1820 census of Maury County his name is found and his age is given as between 26-45. The surname also appears frequently as Kirkpatrick. Court minutes for 23 June 1809 shows that Ebenezer Kirkpatrick and Joseph Kirkpatrick were assigned to work on a road leading to the Bedford County line.

FELIX KILPATRICK
Enlisted as private 10 Dec. 1812 in Capt. Benjamin Reynolds Volunteer Infantry company. On 1811 tax list his name is found as Felix Kirkpatrick. No further information.

JAMES KILE
Served in Capt. Samuel R. McKnight's company. No further information.

JOSEPH KINCAID

Constable in Maury County in 1807. One of the first settlers of Maury County, came here from Kentucky. Married Eliza McLeece at the Clay home in Kentucky. On 1820 census his age is given as between 26-45. Inventory of his estate was made in Maury County 10 July 1824.

Children of Joseph Kincaid:
1. David Kincaid - mentioned as getting part of the estate.
2. Samuel Kincaid - mentioned as getting part of the estate.
3. Elizabeth Kincaid - mentioned as getting part of the estate.
4. Jane Kincaid - mentioned as getting part of the estate.
5. Polly Kincaid - mentioned as getting part of the estate.
6. Eliza Caroline Kincaid, born 1824 in Tennessee, died 1897, married 1833 to Henry Barrett Fussell, died 1895. [It was impossible to determine if she were the same as No. 3 child or not.] (Her dates as found, believed to be in error.)

Source: The Life of Captain Joe H. Fussell, by Mrs. Joe H. Fussell, page 4; Goodspeed's History of Maury County, page 921; Maury County Will Book D, page 237; Will Book D, page 292, 450.

WILLIAM KINDLE

Served in Captain John Gordon's company. No further information.

ABNER KING

Enlisted as private 28 Sept. 1814 in Capt. James McMahan's Tennessee Volunteer Mounted Gunmen; was killed in battle on night of 23 Dec. 1814. Maury County Will Book A, page 154: "his claim on the U. S. for his services in Capt. McMahan's company of mounted men from 28 Sept. until as will appear by the muster rolls." Will Book A, page 193: Rebecca, widow of Abner King.

AVERY KING

Served in Capt. Samuel B. McKnight's company as corporal. No further information.

LEWIS KIRK

Enlisted as sergeant 28 Jan. 1814 in Capt. Nathan Farmer's Mounted Riflemen (a Giles County group). Commissioned captain 1809 in 27th Regiment. No further information.

NATUS KIRK

Enlisted as private 22 June 1812 in Capt. Benjamin Reynolds Mounted Rangers; married Priscilla Knight in Maury County, daughter of Nancy Knight. He died 1829 in St. Clair County, Alabama; Priscilla Kirk is still in St. Clair County on the 1830 census. Maury County Deed Book E, page 82; Natus Kirk got 150 acres on Fountain Creek from James Knight, recorded 7 April 1813, part of Richard Dallam land on Fountain Creek, adjoins William Gilbert's land. Witnesses to the deed were William Weems and Money Gannaway. He possibly lost this land at the conclusion of the famous Kendrick-Dallam suit.

Children of Natus Kirk:
1. Nancy Kirk.
2. Harriet Kirk.
3. Hilliard Kirk.

Source: Will of Nancy Knight in St. Clair County, Alabama, dated 22 Feb. 1834. He is believed to have been son of Patience Kirk described as "very old" in Nov. 1811 in Maury County records and whose estate was settled 20 Feb. 1815.

WILLIAM KIRK

Commissioned ensign 27th Regiment in 1808. Enlisted 24 Sept. 1813 as sergeant in Capt. John Gordon's Mounted Spies. No further information.

EDWARD KIRKPATRICK
Served in Capt. Samuel Ashmore's company. No further information.

ELEAZOR KIRKPATRICK
Served in Capt. Samuel Ashmore's company. No further information. [The name is believed to be correctly Kilpatrick but shown as Kirkpatrick on muster roll. Maury County marriages shown Eleazer Kilpatrick marriage bond to marry Nancy Cathell with Josiah Cathell as bondsman on 4 June 1811. On 18 Sept. 1809 Eleasor Kirkpatrick applied to Maury County court to receive the tax list of Joseph Kirkpatrick. Eleazer Kilpatrick found on 1820 census of Maury County aged between 26 and 45.]

JOHN KIRKPATRICK
Served in Capt. Samuel Ashmore's company. No further information.

GEORGE KITTRELL
Service not stated; born 31 March 1796 N. C., died 4 Oct. 1868 in Maury County, buried Kittrell Cemetery; married 18 Feb. 1818 Elizabeth H. Rutherford, born 23 April 1798, died 7 Jan. 1865, buried Kittrell Cemetery. Came to Tennessee from N.C. about 1800 and first settled near Gallatin.

Children of George Kittrell:
1. George W., died Jan. 1912 at age of 87 in Maury County, married Mary Walker on 26 Nov. 1850; served in Mexican War.
2. Twelve other children, no information.

Source: Soldiers of the War of 1812 Buried in Tennessee, page 64; Kittrell Cemetery listing in "They Passed This Way", A-136; Maury Democrat, 1 Feb. 1912.

JAMES KNIGHT
Enlisted 10 Dec. 1912 as private in Capt. Benjamin Reynolds company, Col. Thomas Benton's Regiment of Volunteer Infantry. No further information.

WALKER KNOX
Enlisted as private 1 Dec. 1813 in Capt. John Gordon's company, discharged on 14 Feb. 1814. Son of James Knox; had brother James Knox, Jr.; his mother later married Ambrose Powell. Inventory of his estate recorded in Maury Will Book A-1, page 141: one discharge for tour of duty in Capt. John Gordon's Co. of "spiez" for term of 7 months; one discharge for a tour of 4 months and 15 days in the Tennessee militia under the command of Major General William Carroll.

Source: Smith vs Brown, 1834, chancery court cases in Maury County.

JAMES KYLE
Served in Capt. James McMahan's company. No further information.

DAVID KUTCH
Served in Capt. Robert Campbell's company. See following.

... In the old records it is impossible to tell if a name is David or Daniel. On the muster roll the name first appears to be David. To complicate the matter, there is record of both a David and a Daniel Kutch being in Maury County very early—in 1809 court minutes a Daniel Coatch is mentioned. Information on both names will be given. On 1823 tax list of Maury David Kutch is found; on 1824 tax list both David and Daniel Kutch are found; later a Daniel Kutch is found as a signer of the those who were living in the Congressional Reservation. Daniel Kutch, aged 50-60, will be found on 1830 census of Lawrence County, Tenn.

An old deed book, no page numbers, has the following entries of interest on this name:

David Kutch, continued:

Margaret Duncan, eldest daughter of Hannah Kutch, who was a daughter of George Whittey, deceased, received of George Mosteller by the hand of Daniel Kutch, "amount left to me by my grandfather." Signed 19 April 1819. Also William Martindale received from George Mosteller $50 left o him by grandfather, George Whittey, deceased. An examination was made of Mary Martindale and Hannah Kutch away from their husbands and they say they signed the deed of conveyance. Thomas Martindale and Daniel Kutch acknowledged the deed of conveyance, 19 April 1819. Daniel Kutch was appointed overseer of road from Williams Ferry to McLean's mill circa 1819.

CLAIBORNE LACEY
Served in Capt. Samuel B. McKnight's company. No further information.

CONSTANTINE LADD
Enlisted as private 18 Dec. 1818 in Capt. James McMahan's Mounted Gunmen, Col. N. T. Perkins. No further information. [Year of enlistment is in error but as it appears on list.]

+THOMAS LADD
Enlisted as private 28 Sept. 1814 in Capt. James McMahan's Tennessee Volunteer Mounted Gunmen, Col. R. H. Dyer; died 24 Jan. 1815. The memorandum of his sale is recorded in Will Book A-1, page 205 and among those buying was Jehosphat Ladd. His inventory was recorded 17 May 1815 and included "one discharge in the volunteer horse company commanded by General Coffee." (Will Book B-1, page 46) Jane Ladd was the administrator.

THOMAS LADD
Served in Capt. John Chisholm's company. No further information.

JESSE LAMB
Served in Capt. John Looney's company. No further information.

AARON LANCASTER
Enlisted as private 28 Sept. 1814 in Capt. James McMahan's Tennessee Volunteer Mounted Gunmen. A return was made on his land for taxes in 1815 for 100 acres and Lancaster wrote the court that "he was in the army at Orleans under the command of Genl Jackson at the time of giving in tax return."

The following advertisement appeared in The Columbia Beacon, 22 Oct. 1847: "Notice: I hereby forewarn all persons not to trade with my wife Minta Lancaster on my account as she has left my place of Residence without any just cuase—as I am determinted not to pay her contracts. Aaron Lancaster, 22 Oct. 1847."

JOSEPH LANCASTER
Served in Capt. Andrew McCarty's company. No further information.

MICHAEL LANCASTER
Enlisted as private 4 Oct. 1813 in Capt. William Dooley's company. Born 16 Dec. 1780, died 12 Aug. 1862, buried in Lancaster Cemetery; married Susan_____, born 12 March 1781, died 5 Nov. 1876, buried in Lancaster Cemetery. She was born in Buckingham County, Va.

Children of Michael Lancaster:
1. Elisha Lancaster, eldest, living Clifton, Tenn., in 1874.
2. Charles A., born about 1817, married 25 Nov. 1841 to Margaret Galloway.
3. W. W., born about 1815, married Adeline_____.
4. Mary Lancaster married 22 Dec. 1842 Marcus G. Dillehay.
5. They had nine children, no information on others.
Source: Lancaster Cemetery; Columbia Herald, 21 Aug. 1874, 7 July 1876, 30 June

JOHN LANE
Commissioned lieutenant in 27th Regiment in 1809. No further information. [This man might be John Lane, born 6 March 1775, early settler of Marshall County; son of Col. Joel Lane; married Sarah Elizabeth Jones. See Marshall County Historical Quarterly, Summer 1974, page 39.]

JOSEPH LANE
Commissioned ensign in 27th Regiment in 1809. No further information. [Maury County Court Minutes show Joseph Land was appointed constable in Sept. 1809.]

WILLIAM LANE
Appointed patrolee in Capt. James Byers Company Sept. 1808. No further information. [Century Review of Maury County, page 280: William Lane married Winnie Ingram; their only child given in this sketch was S. C. Lane.]

+JAMES LANGFORD
Served in Capt. John Gordon's company. Last on roll 9 Feb. 1814, "supposed to have died". No further information.

JOHN LANGFORD
Served in Capt. Bird S. Hurt's company. No further information. [John Langford married Betsy Grurdin, marriage bond dated 21 June 1814.]

JOHN M. LANKFORD
Served in Capt. Andrew McCarty's company. No further information. [See marriage bond in entry previous.]

JOHN LARD
Served in Capt. John Chisholm's company. No further information. [John J. Laird, born 25 Sept. 1797, died 17 Oct. 1819 is buried in the Old Lynnville Cemetery in Giles County.] [Nathaniel Laird, Revolutionary Soldier, who lived in Maury County, and his wife Agnes Scott had a son named John Laird, born 18 Feb. 1791.] [Nathan Vaught, "Youth and Old Age", page 71: Alexander Laird, bricklayer, came to Maury in 1812 or 1813. He had three children: John Laird, printer, Louisa, who married a Terrell, and another daughter.]

THOMAS LASLEY
Fought at New Orleans, no exact service record given. Born 20 June 1788, possibly in Orange County, N. C., died in Maury County, 1 May 1873, buried Lasley Cemetery in Sandy Hook Community. His family were members of Smith's Chapel Methodist Church and he was a trustee of the church. He married Catherine Pickard, also of Orange County, N. C., born 12 April 1791, died 5 Oct. 1860. It is believed that Thomas was the son of Thomas Lashley, who will was dated 19 April 1823, proven Feb. 1824 in Orange County, N. C., and that Catherine was the daughter of John Pickard, whose will was dated 15 Feb. 1812 in Orange County. If she was the daughter of John Pickard, she was possibly first married to an Efland as John Pickard named a daughter Catherine Efland.

Children of Thomas Lasley:
1. John H. Lasley, born 1818, died before 18 May 1898, married 7 Oct. 1840 in Maury County to Elizabeth Thompson, daughter of Thomas and Elizabeth Thompson. She was born 1823, died 1841. On 1 Jan. 1845 John H. Lasley married Isabella M. Baldridge in Gibson County, Tenn. She was born in Maury in 1819 and was daughter of James L. and Narcissa Henderson Baldridge. In 1877 John H. married Sarah J. Frazier Whittle, widow of Charles J. Whittle. John H. was a first lieutenant in 47th Tennessee Infantry, CSA.
2. Craig Lasley.
3. Rebecca Lasley, born 6 June 1820, died 10 June 1908, never married, buried Lasley Cemetery. (continued on next page)

Children of Thomas Lasley, continued:

4. Martha (Patsy) Lasley, married 28 Jan. 1838 in Maury to James G. Shaw. She was deceased by 1850 census.
5. Medda Lasley, born 1 Feb. 1824, died 13 July 1891, buried Lasley Cemetery; married in Lewis County 28 June 1847 to Thomas J. Lasley.
6. Elizabeth Lasley, born 6 Nov. 1825, died 28 Nov. 1894, never married, buried in Lasley Cemetery.
7. Catherine Lasley, born 16 April 1832, married J. H. Himes.

Possible brothers and sisters of Thomas (from will of Thomas):
1. Fanny Lasley.
2. Hannah Lasley.
3. Nicy Lasley married Henry Ray.
4. Jean Lasley.
5. Rachel Lasley.
6. Elijah Lasley.
7. Alexander Lasley.
8. Betsy Lasley married David Ray.

Source: Information contributed by Virginia W. Alexander (Mrs. Charles C.) from her research on this family.

(UNKNOWN) LATTA
Rachel Latta of Santa Fe drew pension as widow of War of 1812 soldier in 1883. No further information.

THOMAS B. LATTA
Served in Capt. John Jackson's company, 1st Tennessee Militia; born 23 Nov. 1782 in North Carolina; died 13 Aug. 1848 in Kentucky, buried Pleasant Hill Cemetery, Graves County, Kentucky. Married Mary L. Moore, born 27 Sept. 1782 in N. C., died 23 June 1858, buried Pleasant Hill Cemetery, Graves County, Ky., daughter of James and Catherine Moore.

Children of Thomas B. Latta:
1. Elizabeth Latta, born 4 May 1805, died, unknown; married Hardy Kirby.
2. James Latta, born 1 Feb. 1807, married 20 Dec. 1830 to Nancy E. Butler.
3. Jane Latta, born 24 Feb. 1809, died 10 Aug. 1866 in Ky., married 19 Nov. 1829 to Sinnett Laffoon.
4. John Latta, born 13 July 1811 in Maury County, Tenn., died 9 July 1872 in Ky., married 16 Aug. 1835 to Mary Aydelott.
5. Catherine Latta, born 5 Nov. 1813 in Tenn., died 22 Nov. 1875 in Kentucky, married 7 May 1841 to James Boon.
6. William Henry Latta, born 5 May 1816 in Tenn., died 15 March 1891, married Nov. 1836 to Burnette Stokes. (Her name is Pernetta on census.)
7. Thomas Henderson Latta, born 29 Nov. 1818 in Tenn., died 4 Sept. 1896 in Ky., married 24 Oct. 1844 to Pernina Stokes.
8. Alexander Robertson Latta, born 22 Jan. 1821 in Tenn., died 21 April 1903 in Ky., married 23 Aug. _____ to Mary Fondville.
9. Selina Mary Latta, born 10 June 1823, died 14 Aug. 1858, Ky., never married.

Source: Information from Mrs. F. M. Gossum, Jr., Fulton, Kentucky, based on her research on this family.

WILLIAM LATTA
War of 1812 soldier at Santa Fe, died Oct. 1874 at the age of 80 years. His obituary says that he was survived by only two children and that he had had cherry plank for his coffin for thirty years. At his death only three War of 1812 soldiers remained in Maury County. (Columbia Herald and Mail, 10 Oct. 1874.)

JOHN LAWRENCE
Served in Capt. James McMahan's company. No further information.

SAMUEL LAWRENCE
Served in Capt. James McMahan's company. No further information.

(UNKNOWN) LAWRENCE
Venus Lawrence of Mt. Pleasant drew pension in 1883 as the mother of a War of 1812
soldier. No further information.

DAVID LEACH
Commissioned ensign in 27th Regiment 1812. Married Nancy Gilchrist 4 Feb. 1814 in
Maury County (date of marriage bond). In 1831 Nancy Leach was appointed guardian of
his five children. (Maury County Will Book 6, page 18.) In 1833 Nancy Leech made
a return to the court. (Maury County Will Book 6, page 139.)

WILLIAM D. LEIPER
Served in Capt. John Gordon's company. No further information. No further information.

JOHN W. LEMASTER
Served as private in Capt. William Dooley's company; later fought in Mexican War;
always known as Captain Lemaster. Born 21 Oct. 1793, died 9 Sept. 1876, buried in
Tabernacle Cemetery, Green Hill, Lauderdale County, Ala. He was son of Joseph
Lemaster, Revolutionary War soldier, (born 15 Nov. 1748 in Maryland, died 10 Aug.
1826 in Williamson County) married about 1792 in Abbeville District, S. C., to Mary
Waddell. He married Nancy L. Almond, born 21 Jan. 1801, died 14 March 1872, buried
Tabernacle Cemetery, Lauderdale County, Ala. Nathan Vaught wrote of him: "John W.
Leymaster, 80 odd, now lives in Lauderdale County, Alabama, blacksmith. Came to
Maury County 1808-09, married Miss Alman." Married 11 Oct. 1821.

Children of John W. Lemaster:
1. Sophronia A., born 5 Aug. 1827, died 7 Jan. 1879.
2. W. H. Lemaster, born 5 May 1836, died 26 Aug. 1919.
3. R. E. Lemaster, born 7 June 1845, died 7 Oct. 1905.
4. Samuel H. Lemaster.
5. Mary Elizabeth Lemaster, born 29 Aug. 1822.
6. Marcus Lefayett Lemaster, born 10 Dec. 1824, died 25 July 1825.
7. Charlotte Rebecca, born 9 March 1830
8. John Brown Lemaster, died 29 Aug. 1853 or 1833.
9. James Knox Polk Lemaster, died 28 May 1835.
10. No information on others, if any.

Brothers and sisters of John W. Lemaster:
1. Rebecca Lemaster, born 15 Jan. 1784 S. C., died 19 Feb. 1850, married Alexander
   McKay. (Half-sister by father's marriage to Hannah_____.)
2. Joseph M. Lemaster, born 1794-1802, married Elizabeth Miller.
3. Nancy Lemaster, born about 1785 (half)
4. Elizabeth Lemaster, born about 1788. (half)
5. Hannah Lemaster, born 26 March 1795 in S. C. died 1 Sept. 1853, married Joseph
   Polk.
6. Mary Lemaster, born about 1799, was unmarried in 1823.
7. Eliza Lemaster, born about 1807, married Wiley D. Brown.
8. Daughter, not named, who married William Pzant. (Surname in question as very
   hard to decipher.) (Found in Civil Causes ending 1832 in courthouse basement.)

Source: Tabernacle Cemetery inscriptions; Maury County Cousins, p. 152; Maury County
Cousins No. 2, page 285, quoting Bible Record found in Pension W797; information
from Mrs. Jack Lightfoot, Mrs. Horace Taylor, and Mrs. Gaines B. Norton, Jr.

BENJAMIN HERNDON LEWIS
Commissioned lieutenant in 5th Brigade of Cavalry, 1813. Died prior to 1843 "without wife or issue". Son of James Martin Lewis.

JAMES MARTIN LEWIS
Qualified as justice of the peace of Maury County Dec. 1809; Revolutionary War soldier; born 7 May 1762, died 2 April 1822, buried Greenwood Cemetery, Columbia; married Mary Boswell Herndon.

Children of James Martin Lewis:
1. Benjamin H. Lewis, see above.
2. William Terrell Lewis.
3. Micajah G. Lewis.
4. Frances Lewis, died 1797.
5. Sarah Pines Lewis married Isaac B. Hardin and Dr. William McNeil.
6. Nancy Lewis married John Hodge.
7. Eliza Lewis married Dr. Thomas Brown.

Source: Nathan Vaught, "Youth and Old Age", page 72; additional information supplied by Marise P. Lightfoot.

JOSEPH LINSEY
Served as private in Capt. William Dooley's company. No further information.

JOHN LINDSAY
One of first justices of the peace in Maury County, member of first court, and served many years on the court; minister. Born 30 May 1768, died 8 June 1828, son of John Lindsey and Mary Masterson of Halifac Co., N. C.; married Sarah Kearney, born 2 March 1774, died 16 Dec. 1840, daughter of Philip Kearney and Elizabeth Kinchen.

Children of the Rev. John Lindsay:
1. Joachim Lindsay, died young. [There is record that he lived to be married, however.]
2. John Lindsay married Ann Brown, daughter of Joseph Brown.
3. Maria Lindsay married General L. H. Coe of Memphis.
4. Elizabeth Lindsay married Dr. Benjamin Carter.
5. Sarah K. Lindsay married Russell Williamson.
6. Lucinda Lindsay married John Moore.
7. Mary Masterson Lindsay married Guston Kearney.

Source: Information from Mrs. Naomi Whitaker's family papers.

Brothers and sisters of Rev. John Lindsay:
1. Anna Lindsay, born 11 Nov. 1753, married 20 Oct. 1774 to George Zollicoffer. They were the grandparents of General Felix Kirk Zollicoffer. (Source: The Zollie Tree, page 142.)
2. No information on the others.

JOHN LIPSCOMB
Served in Capt. Samuel Ashmore's company. No further information.

GEORGE LISLE
Served in Capt. Bird S. Hurt's company. No further information.

POMEY LITTLE
War of 1812 pensioner, aged 93, living in Maury County. No further information. (Columbia Herald and Mail, 11 May 1877.)

JOHN LIVESAY

Served in Capt. John Looney's company. No further information. [John Liversay marriage bond dated 24 Aug. 1814 to marry Peggy Lyon.]

JOSEPH LOFTON

Served in Capt. Samuel B. McKnight's company. No further information.

MARTIN LOGGINS

Enlisted 4 Oct. 1813 in Capt. James Shannon's company, Col. Thomas McCrory, served until 4 Jan. 1814. No further information.

AMOS LONDON

Served in the 1st Regiment (Pipkin's) West Tennessee Militia. Information sent by Mrs. Opal Cox, who has researched this line, indicates that this is the same Amos London who married Sarah Bills and was on the 1840 census of Giles County—Sarah London being in that county on the 1850 census. There is also a record that Amos London served under Captain Samuel Crawford in the 2nd Regiment of Tennessee Mounted Gunmen, Col. Thomas Williamson, in the Seminole War—volunteering at Fayetteville, Tenn., on or about 30 Jan. 1818, discharged at Columbia 30 June 1818.

MATTHEW P. LONG

Commissioned lieutenant in 27th Regiment in 1811. No further information.

+WILLIAM LONG

Enlisted as private 28 Sept. 1814 in Capt. James McMahan's company, Col. Robert H. Dyer, died 21 Jan. 1815. Married in Orange County, N. C., 29 Aug. 1806 to Peggy Blackwood. His estate was settled in Maury County Will Book A-1, p. 145 and 192, property being sold 26 Sept. 1815. Will Book B-1, page 112, adds "one note for $6 his services in a tour to New Orleans."

WILLIAM C. LONG

Served as private in Capt. William Dooley's company. No further information.

ISAAC A. LOONEY

Commissioned captain of light infantry 27th Regiment 1814. No further information.

JOHN LOONEY

Commissioned captain 1813 in 27th Regiment; also commanded a company of men from Maury County. He later lived in St. Clair County, Alabama, and his pioneer home there was opened to the public in 1974. He left Maury County about 1816 when he was selling his land here and by 1818 was in St. Clair County when he built his log cabin. His wife Rebecca died about 1840 in St. Clair.

JOHN LOONEY

Served as sergeant in Capt. John Gordon's company. No further information.

EDOM C. LOVE

Served in Capt. Andrew McCarty's company, mustered 28 Jan. 1814, discharged at Fayetteville 15 May 1814; born 1795/96 in Chester Co., S. C., died 25 July 1871 at Love's Branch in Maury County. He was son of John Love, who estate was settled in Maury County in 1814, and his wife Jane. (It is believed that Jane was either a Kendrick or Cathey, and that she might have been his second wife.) John Love was son of Robert Love and Violet Wilson of Chester County, Pa., and Chester Co., S.C., who married 1738 at the Forks of the Brandywine; removed from Pennsylvania about 1762 to the area of Anson County, N. C. (the part which later became Chester, York, and Lancaster counties in South Carolina) and died in Lancaster Co., S. C., in 1786. John Love (son) received grant of land in Mecklenburg Co., N. C. (just across the line) in 1783 and he is found in that county 1790 as are the Catheys and Kendricks; removed to Maury County about 1806 and settled on or near the Cathey grant.

Edom C. Love, continued:

Edom C. Love married about 1816 in Maury County to (1) Ann Strickland, born between 1795/1800; and (2) 1837/38 in Maury County to Celia Ramsey Love, born 22 March 1813 in N. C., died after 1879, Maury County, who was the widow of Nathan Love (Edom's brother) to whom she was married 7 April 1833 in Maury County. Celia was the daughter of Jeremiah Ramsey, born 14 Sept. 1768, and his wife Elizabeth, born 3 Sept. 1770, of Maury County.

Children of Edom C. Love and wife Ann Strickland:
1. Virginia Jane Love, born 15 Jan. 1817 in Maury County, died Oct. 1876 in Maury or Hickman County, Tenn., married 27 Nov. 1838 in Maury County to Thomas Kendrick Love, born 11 Jan. 1817 in Maury, died after 1864 in Hickman County, first cousin, son of Joel Love and his wife _____ Carlock.
2. Daughter, born between 1815/20 in Maury County.
3. John Love, born between 1820 and 1825 in Maury County, married Frances Bailey.
4. Edom Love, Jr., born between 1820 and 1825 in Maury County, married Susan Curry.
5. Son, born between 1825 and 1830 in Maury County.
6. Daughter, born between 1825 and 1830 in Maury County.

Children of Edom C. Love and wife Celia Ramsey:
1. Nathan Love, born 11 June 1839 in Maury, died before 1879.
2. Henry Love, born 27 May 1840 in Maury County.
3. William Love, born Aug. 1842 in Maury County, died before 1879.
4. Sarah Ann Love, born 14 Nov. 1844 in Maury County.
5. Eli David Love, born 28 Feb. 1847, probably Lewis County, Tenn.
6. Andrew Jackson Love, born 10 June 1850, probably Lewis County, Tenn.
7. James Houston Thomas Love, born 4 Aug. 1852, probably Lewis County, Tenn.
8. Celia Alice Artimesia Love, born 3 June 1856, probably in Lewis County, Tenn., died 30 Nov. 1923 in Maury County, married J. L. Smith, born 1858, died 1938.

Brothers and sisters of Edom C. Love:
1. Robert Love, birth not known, probably in Chester Co., S. C.
2. John Love, Jr., probably born in Chester Co., S. C., married 25 May 1805 in Williamson County, Tenn., to Mary Agnes Hays.
3. Elizabeth "Betsy" Love, probably born in Chester Co., S. C., married 26 Jan.181: in Maury County to David Terry.
4. Joel Love, born about 1790, probably Chester Co., S. C., or Mecklenburg Co., N. C., married _____ Carlock. (ggg great grandparents of Vickie Lynn Love Knight.)
5. Eli Love, born about 1798 S. C., died after 1850 possibly Lewis County, Tenn., married Celia Skipper, born about 1806 in N. C. Married 4 Jan. 1821.
6. Wilson Love, born about 1800, probably Mecklenburg Co., N. C., living in Maury in 1830.
7. Nathan Love, born about 1802 in Mecklenburg Co., N. C., died before 1837 in Maury, married 7 April 1833 to Celia Ramsey as her first husband.
8. Easter (Esther) Love, dates not known, married 24 Jan. 1832 in Maury County to David Ramsey.

Information supplied by Monte H. Knight from his research on the Love family.

JAMES LOVE
Appointed justice of the peace of Maury County in 1807 and served for number of years on the court. No further information.

JOHN LOVE
Name appears in 1810 court minutes as justice of the peace. No further information or identification.

MATTHEW LOVE

Private in Capt. Brice Martin's 2nd Regt. of Tennessee Volunteers, commanded by Col. William Martin, enlisted at Brevard's in Smith County, Tennessee, served from 21 Nov. 1812 until 22 April 1813. He received a bounty land grant for his service, Warrant No. 27071, for 182 acres of land in Greene County, Ark. This land was assigned to his two sons James Wylie Love and Matthew Young Love. Born 1 Jan. 1772 in County Antrim, Ireland, died 1 Nov. 1858 in Greene County, Arkansas, buried old Love Cemetery near Jonesboro, Ark. He lives in Ireland, South Carolina, Tennessee, Mississippi, and Arkansas. Married Jennette Wylie on 1 Oct. 1804 at Charleston, S. C., born 31 March 1784 in South Carolina, daughter of Dr. James Wylie of Scotland. She died 16 Aug. 1846 in Greene County, Arkansas, and was the first person buried in the old Love Cemetery.

Children of Matthew Love:
1. Nancy Love, born 19 Aug. 1805 in S. C., married John Martin Francis, lived in Russellville, Ala.
2. Jane Love, born 12 July 1810 in Smith County, Tenn., married (1) Elisha Augustus Quarles 25 Dec. 1833 at Pontotoc Co., Miss.; (2) 1859 Poinsett Co., Ark., to Asa Dodson Puckett, Sr., she died in the fall of 1868 in Bernie, Missouri.
3. Frances Love, born 8 May 1814 in Smith County, Tenn., married (2) John Puckett after the Civil War in Arkansas.
4. Elizabeth Love, born 9 Feb. 1812 in Smith County, Tenn., married Joseph Cooper and lived in Pontotoc County, Miss.
5. James Wylie Love, born 3 May 1819 in Hickman County, Tenn., died Nov. 1859 in Greene County, Arkansas, married Molly Brown.
6. Matthew Young Love, born 28 March 1821, Hickman County, Tenn., married Mary Jane Hollister in Greene Co., Tenn., died in 1889.
7. Robert Love, died 6 Nov. 1823 in Hickman County, Tenn.

Source: Information furnished by descendant Mrs. A. W. Hicks, Amarillo, Texas.

ADAM LOWRY

Served in Capt. Samuel Ashmore's company. No further information.

WILLIAM C. LUCKETT

Columbia Herald, 31 Jan. 1873: "William C. Luckett has left us; War of 1812 pensioner; only five soldiers remain." Whig and Tribune, Jackson, Tenn., 8 Feb. 1873: "William C. Luckett, War of 1812 soldier, died near Santa Fe last week." No further information.

JAMES LYNCH

Commissioned lieutenant in 27th Regiment in 1812. No further information.

PETER LYONS, JR.

Served in General Coffee's troops during War of 1812; by 1813 was in Giles County; married Elizabeth Seale, daughter of Jarvis Seale, Rev. War soldier. The will of Peter Lyons, Sr., is in Maury County, recorded 9 Jan. 1824, and his wife's name is given as Elizabeth.

Brothers and sisters of Peter Lyons, Jr.:
1. Caty Lyons married _____ Malone.
2. John Lyons.
3. James Lyons.
4. William Lyons.
5. Jenny Lyons, deceased by 1824, married _____ Sanders.
6. Elizabeth Lyons married _____ Hunt.

Source: Maury County Will Book C-1, page 151; and information from Virginia W. Alexander (Mrs. Charles C.), member of Jane Knox Chapter.

JAMES H. MACK

Served in Capt. Samuel Ashmore's company. Son of John Mack, Revolutionary War soldier (born 1740 in Scotland, died 1814 in Maury County, will dated 31 May 1813.) John Mack's wife Sarah was born in Pennsylvania and died in Maury at the age of 83. James H. Mack was listed on the 1820 census of Maury as being between 26 and 45.

Brothers and sisters of James H. Mack:
1. Constantine Mack, aged between 26 and 45 on 1820 census of Maury County.
2. John Mack, Jr.
3. Polly Mack married Nathaniel Murphy.
4. Judge Robert Mack, born 2 Aug. 1773 in Virginia, died 17 Oct. 1865 in Maury, married Sarah M. Brown, died 7 May 1877, sister of Governor Aaron V. Brown.
5. William Mack, born 29 Dec. 1775 in Pittsylvania Co., Va., died 25 Dec. 1861, married Mary Blair.
6. Sally Mack married _____ Nance.
7. "my other children" were mentioned but not named in John Mack's will.

Source: Maury County Will Book B-1, page 6; "O Brave Pioneer" by Sara Sprott Morrow, privately printed 1973; tombstone inscriptions from "They Passed This Way."

PETER MAIX

Served in Capt. Benjmain Reynolds company; no further information.

EPHRAIM MANNING

Served in Capt. John Gordon's company. No further information.

JOHN MANSHER (or MANSKER)

Served in Capt. John Gordon's company. No further information.

PHILIP MARCUS

Served in Capt. John Looney's company. No further information. Still in county on 1820 census.

GEORGE MARTIN

Warrant No. 7133 for bounty land by U. S. to George Martin, deceased, for his enlistment in service of U. S. during late war is recorded in Maury County Deed Book B-1, page 173, recorded 26 April 1819. The land was being conveyed to Samuel Craig by Robert Martin, Dosha Segraves, Vincent Segraves, and Sally Andrews by power of attorney to Horatio Depriest. Probate deeds show his name as George W. Martin.

JOHN MARTIN

Served in Capt. John Chisholm's company. No further information. [Name appears to be James Martin on a second muster roll of this company.]

ROADHAM MARTIN

Maury County Deed Book B-1, page 160: Roadham Martin of Maury County gives power of attorney to his friend Horatio Depriest to convey to Samuel Craig 160 acres in the Missouri Territory "my bounty land due from U. S. for enlistment in service of U. S. during the late war." Warrant No. 7134, dated Jan. 1818, registered Jan. 1818. An old probate deed book for this period, page 192, shows him as heir of George W. Martin, deceased, and in 1819 is selling land in Missouri. Rodham Martin married Fanny Sherman in Maury County 13 March 1818.

ROBERT MARTIN

Drew pension 1883 in Columbia as War of 1812 soldier, lost left leg. No further information.

SAMUEL MARTIN

Served in Capt. James McMahan's company. No further information.

OBEDIAH MASH

Served in Capt. William Dooley's company as a private. Born before 1775 in N. C., died about 1823-1824 in Maury County. Inventory of his estate recorded 18 Oct. 1824 in Maury Will Book D, page 138. He married Elizabeth_____, born about 1785 in N.C. died after 1850 in Maury County.

Children of Obediah Mash:
1. Susan G. Mash, born 1804 in N. C., married Gabriel Brown.
2. Leonard "Jack" Mash, born about 1824 married Sarah B. Scribner.
3. At least four other children, no further information.

Source: Mash Family Bulletin, 1969, page 20, edited by Robert M. Hess, Houston, Tex.

ABNER MATTHEWS

Commissioned ensign 27th Regiment 1812. Son of James Matthews, Rev. War soldier, who was born 1739 in Antrim County, Ireland, died 1825, and his wife Mary Doak, born 1749, died 1833. Abner was born 21 Nov. 1792.

Brothers and sisters of Abner Matthews:
1. James Matthews, Jr., born 23 Oct. 1766, died young.
2. John Matthews, born 24 Oct. 1768.
3. Martha, born 11 Dec. 1770.
4. Mary Matthews, born 17 Oct. 1772.
5. Robert Matthews, born 20 Oct. 1774, died young.
6. William Doak Matthews, born 18 March 1777 died young.
7. Margaret Matthews, born 27 June 1781.
8. Samuel Matthews, born 27 Dec. 1782.
9. Prudence Matthews, born 23 March 1789, died young.
10. Joseph Matthews, born 13 Jan. 1779, married Sarah Walker.
11. Agnes Matthews, born 8 Sept. 1786.

Source: Family information contributed by Mrs. Nelle J. Smith, Pulaski, Tenn.; also Maury County Cousins, published by Maury County Historical Society.

ALEXANDER MATTHEWS

Served in Capt. Samuel Ashmore's company. No further information.

JOHN MATTHEWS

Served as justice of the peace of Maury County, qualified June 1809. Born 24 Oct. 1768, died 20 July 1839, buried in Matthews Cemetery. No information on children.

Source: They Passed This Way, page A-88.

LEWIS MATTHEWS

Served in Capt. Samuel B. McKnight's company. No further information.

LEWIS MATTHEWS

Served in Capt. James McMahan's company. No further information.

ROBERT MATTHEWS

Served in War of 1812, no service given. Born 1773, presumably in North Ireland, died 1839 in Maury County and buried near McCain's; cabinet maker. He married Mary Ann Stewart, born about 1775 in Ballymacashen County Down Ireland, died near Columbia, daughter of Sampson and Catherine Wiley Stewart. Her cabin burned in 1938. The family history gives her death as about 1864. However, her son W. L. Matthews wrote in his medical journal on 10 March 1879: "Our Mother died."

Children of Robert Matthews:
1. Jane Matthews, born about 1802 in Maury, still living 1839; never married. (cont'd

Children of Robert Matthews, continued:

2. Patricia (Patsy) born 1804 in Maury County, married about 1824 to James (Joe) Matthews, cousin; she died 1888 in Spring Hill, Texas.
3. Sampson Stewart Matthews, born 1808, died 1883 in Navarro County, Texas, married 1834 Sarah Reece, born 1808.
4. William Newton Matthews, born 7 July 1810, died 21 March 1886, married about 183?, Eliza Mack, granddaughter of John Mack, she was born 17 March 1811, died 7 Nov. 1895. (The family history gives his name this way. However, Maury Democrat, April 1889 gives his name as Newton H. Matthew married 1834 to Eliza L. Mack and had eight children. Also buried as Newton H. Matthews in cemetery in "They Passed This Way" page A-68. Eliza Mack Matthews' death was reported in a newspaper as 22 March 1886, dying of heart disease.)
5. Minerva Katherine Matthews, born 23 Sept. 1812 died 24 April 1871 at Navarro C. Texas, married (1) 1834 Frank Slaughter; married (2) Dr. George Washington Hill in Texas.
6. Robert Harrill, born 1814, died 1894 in Navarro, Texas; married at the age of 7? to Betty Priddy, age 28.
7. Prudence Shaw Matthews, born 31 Dec. 1816, died 15 Nov. 1906 in Hubbard, Texas, married 14 Sept. 1836 to Samuel Wright.
8. John Matthews, born about 1818, married Sarah Covey.
9. Elizabeth Matthews, born 26 May 1819, died 30 Nov. 1917 in Maury County, buried McCain's C. P. Church Cemetery; married 1846 to Henry Caleb Estes.
10. W. Lafayette Matthews, born 20 Jan. 1825 died 29 Jan. 1900, buried Rose Hill in Columbia; practiced medicine in county for 50 years. (Family history gives his birthdate as 1820, the 1825 date comes from his tombstone.) Never married.

Source: "Sampson Stewart, His Royal Ancestors and Some of His Descendants", by Sidney Wright Blount, 1961, page 14.

CHARLES P. MAY
Commissioned lieutenant in 27th Regiment 1812. Also served in Capt. William Dooley's company. No further information. No further information.

WILLIAM MAY
Served in Capt. Bird S. Hurt's company. No further information.

DAVID MAYBERRY
Served in Capt. James McMahan's company. No further information.

(UNKNOWN) MAYBERRY
Jennett Mayberry drew pension in Columbia in 1883 as widow of War of 1812 soldier. No further information.

DAVID MAYES
Served in Capt. John Chisholm's company. No further information.

ISAAC MAYES
Served in Capt. John Chisholm's company. No further information.

A. B. MAYFIELD
Served as private in Capt. William Dooley's company. Also a man of this same name served as sergeant in Capt. John Gordon's company. Also commissioned captain in 5th Brigade of cavalry in 1812. Born 1782, died in 1850s in Monroe County, Miss. His name is given as A. B. John Mayfield on his tombstone. He ran a trading post in that county in Mississippi and had one of the first cotton gins in that section. He had a son Isaac Mayfield. No further information available on other children.

GEORGE MAYFIELD
Served in Capt. John Gordon's company. No further information.

JOHN MAYFIELD
Served in Capt. John Gordon's company. No further information.

NIMROD MAYFIELD
Served in Capt. John Gordon's company. No further information.

WILLIAM MAYFIELD
Served in Capt. Bird S. Hurt's company. No further information.

+JESSE MAYS
On 16 Aug. 1819 the Maury County court allows tuition for the two minor children and heirs of Jesse Mays "who fell in the late war."

CAPTAIN MAYS
In 1807 a Captain Mays headed a militia company in Maury County; men who served in his company lived between Big Bigby Creek and Lick Creek. No further information.

GEORGE McADAMS
Commissioned ensign 1814 in 51st Regiment. Also man of this name served in Captain James McMahan's company. No further information.

WILLIAM B. McADAMS
Served as sergeant in Capt. John Gordon's company. No further information.

HIRAM McALEB
Served in Capt. John Chisholm's company as substitute for Thomas Stone. No further information.

FRANCIS McBRIDE
Served as corpl. in Capt. William Dooley's company. Commissioned ensign in 22d Regt. Militia on 16 Oct. 1807; lieutenant on 21 Oct. 1808. Born 1788 in Rockingham Co., N. C., died after 1851 in Wayne County, Tenn. Married 16 March 1814 in Maury County to Margaret Perry, born about 1790. He was the son of Isaiah McBride (born 1760 in Virginia, died 1815) and his wife Jane McClain; married 10 Aug. 1779 in Guilford County, N. C. Jane McClain McBride died in Wayne County, Tenn. Francis McBride moved about 1810 to Maury County and lived in the Bigbyville area. Later lived in District 6 of Wayne County.

Children of Francis McBride:
1. William C. McBride, born 1817 in Maury County, died 1850-51 in Wayne County; married Mary____, born 1823; they had at least four children.
2. Mary McBride, born about 1820-21, never married, lived until 1880.
3. Five other children; no other information.

Brothers and sisters of Francis McBride:
1. Samuel McBride.
2. Elizabeth McBride, born 1798 in Rockingham Co., N. C., married 13 Nov. 1817 to David Voorhies; moved to Wayne County; mother of nine children.
3. Six other children, no further information.

Source: "The McBride Family of Rutherford County, Tennessee," by Robert Martin McBride, Nashville, 1963; pages 7-8.

JOHN M. McBRIDE
Served as private in Capt. William Dooley's company, 2nd Regiment of Tennessee Volunteers. Born 24 July 1791 in N. C., died 8 Dec. 1857 in Maury County; said to be buried at Mt. Nebo Methodist Church Cemetery. He married (1) 12 March 1810 in Maury County to Mary (Polly) Jaggers, born 9 Dec. 1800, died 14 April 1836 in Maury
continued on next page

John M. McBride, continued:
County. Married (2) 24 Feb. 1837 to Hannah C. Kinzer, born 1814, died 1889, daughter of Henry Kinzer and Elizabeth Mayberry. Hannah drew pension as widow of War of 1812 soldier in 1883 and her mailing address was Sawdust, Maury County, Tenn.

Children of John M. McBride by first marriage:
1. William S. McBride, born 16 March 1819 in Maury, died 26 April 1875 in Maury, married 12 March 1839 in Maury to Rosannah Kinzer.
2. James D. McBride, born 17 May 1821 in Maury County.
3. John P. McBride, born 14 May 1823 in Maury, died in Missouri (possibly Sedali), married 21 July 1845 to Emily Stanfield Lawson.
4. Jesse S. McBride, born 18 Jan. 1825, married 25 Dec. 1844 to Martha J. McBride.
5. Mary T. (or J.) McBride, born 12 Nov. 1826 in Maury County.
6. David A. McBride, born 7 Oct. 1828 in Maury, died 16 Aug. 1852.
7. Hester J. McBride, born 28 Dec. 1830 in Maury County, married E. T. Estes.
8. Sara A. McBride, born 16 Nov. 1832 in Maury County.
9. Martha Elizabeth McBride, born 16 Sept. 1834 in Maury, died 1 Feb. 1910, married William Richard McKennon.

Children of John M. McBride by second marriage:
1. Eliza A. McBride, born 4 Oct. 1837 in Maury County.
2. Cornelia McBride, born 22 Aug. 1840 in Maury County.
3. Robert Nathaniel McBride, born 31 Aug. 1841 in Maury County, died 15 July 1890, married 12 May 1871 to Helena Williams, born 1851 died 1920.
4. Charles W. McBride, born 16 Aug. 1843 in Maury, died 21 May 1862, married 14 May 1861 to Mary B. Healey, born 1845.
5. Benjamin Franklin McBride, born 6 March 1845, married 12 Jan. 1870 to Ellen M. Gray, born 1847, died 1894; Confederate Soldier. He married (2) Anna Belle Brown.
6. Catherine Tennessee McBride, born 22 Aug. 1847 in Maury County, died 17 Feb. 1848.
7. Sophrona C. McBride, born 5 Dec. 1849 in Maury, married April 1868 to William Temple.
8. Mack Henry Bascomb McBride, born 31 Dec. 1851 in Maury County, died 2 April 1889, buried at Mt. Nebo.

Source: Family information contributed by descendant Mrs. Evelyn B. Shackelford, Mt. Pleasant. She noted that John M. McBride was described by his wife Hannah in her pension application as being "6 feet high, dark hair, fair complexion, gray eyes."

JOHN McBRIDE
Served in Capt. John Looney's company. No further information.

SAMUEL McBRIDE
Served in Capt. Samuel Ashmore's company. Born 30 March 1791 in Rockingham Co., N.C died 17 Oct. 1870 in Lawrence County, buried in Pleasant Garden, Lawrence County; married 4 April 1816 in Maury County to Mary Voorhies, born 1 April 1795 in N. C., died 28 June 1869, buried in Pleasant Garden Cemetery, Lawrence County. He was the son of Isaiah McBride and his wife Jane McClain. Lived District 11, Lawrence Co.

Children of Samuel McBride:
1. Sarah McBride, born 1825.
2. Rebecca A. McBride, born 1827.
3. William McBride, born 1832.
4. Mary E. McBride, born 1836.
5. Three other children, no further information.

Source: "The McBride Family of Rutherford County, Tennessee," by Robert Martin McBride, Nashville, 1963, pages 7-8.

+SAMUEL B. McBRIDE
Served in Capt. Bird S. Hurt's company; died 4 March 1815. No further information.

SAMUEL McBRIDE
Served as second lieutenant in Capt. John Looney's company. No further information.
[May be the same as Samuel McBride, buried in Lawrence County.]

+WILLIAM McBRIDE
Commissioned ensign 1810 in Maury County militia. Enlisted 23 June 1813 at Columbia
(outfit not given), died in Detroit, Canada. His heirs were Francis McBride, Mary
Harper, Samuel McBride, Elizabeth McBride, Thomas J. McBride, and Agnes McBride.
Some of his heirs lived in Maury County and some in Wayne County. [This appears to
be the family of Isaiah McBride, father of Francis and Samuel, both of whom were
War of 1812 soldiers.]   Enlisted in Capt. Isaac L. Baker's company.

Source: "The Correspondence of James K. Polk", Volume 1, Herbert Weaver, editor,
pages 214, 215.

ELI McCAIN
Commissioned ensign in 27th Regiment in 1814. [Name also spelled McKean]. He
married 5 Nov. 1804 in Rutherford County, Tenn., to Polly M. McGahey, daughter of
William McGahey or McGaughey, Rev. War soldier. On 20 Dec. 1817 Eli McCain deeded
land to William Mack, John J. Zollicoffer, and Adam R. Alexander for a meeting
house on Little Bigby Creek. In 1818 he was selling land to William A. Maxwell on
Little Bigby before going to Alabama. [One Eli McCain is in 1820 and 1830 census of
Lawrence County, Alabama.] [John McCain's will probated 26 Nov. 1798 in Blount
County, Tenn., names his sons John, Eli, James, Robert and William; and his wife
Agnes. According to settlement he had daughters Agnes and Margaret.]

Source: Rutherford County marriage records; research from files of Virginia W.
Alexander.

THOMAS McCALL
Served in Capt. James McMahan's company. No further information.

JAMES McCALLY
Served in Capt. Bird S. Hurt's company. No further information.

ISRAEL McCARROLL
Service not determined; always called Colonel McCarroll. Whig and Tribune, Jackson,
Tenn., 1 Feb. 1873: "Col. Israel McCarroll, an old and honored citizen of Maury
County, died at Spring Hill about two weeks ago." Columbia Herald, 24 Jan. 1873:
"Col. Israel McCarroll died Friday; Methodist; Mason; buried Spring Hill Cemetery;
born in N. C. or East Tennessee about 1800, lived near Nolensville; 1830 moved to
Maury County, married Mrs. Giddings, now deceased; lived Spring Hill, died 10 Jan.
1873." He married Mrs. Rachel Kilcrease Giddens 1830 in Williamson County.

Children of Israel McCarroll:
1. William McCarroll, born 5 April 1832, died 30 April 1854.
2. John McCarroll, born 29 Oct. 1834, died 24 Jan. 1861.
3. James McCarroll, born 27 July 1836, died 12 May 1867.
4. No information on other children if any.

Source: Spring Hill Cemetery inscriptions in "They Passed This Way" and newspapers
quoted above; Williamson County marriage records.

ANDREW McCARTY

Commissioned captain of 27th Regiment in 1812. Headed a company from 28 Jan. 1814 to 10 May 1814 which served in Colonel Napier's regiment. He possibly removed from Maury County in 1824 when his name is removed from the rolls of Reece's Church. He married Ruthy Reece, daughter of James Reece; marriage bond is dated 11 Aug. 1808 with James Reece, Jr., as bondsman.

Children of Andrew McCarty:
1. Minerva Cowan McCarty, born 23 June 1809.
2. David Franklin McCarty, born 1 July 1810.
3. James Reese McCarty, born 12 Dec. 1811.
4. William Wriley McCarty, born 6 Jan. 1813.
5. Andrew Henry McCarty, born 9 March 1814.
6. Ruth Lovenah McCarty, born 4 Dec. 1815.
7. John Leroy McCarty, born 10 Jan. 1817.
8. Elizabeth L. McCarty, born 29 Sept. 1818.
9. Sarah Susannah McCarty, born 24 April 1820.
10. Nancy Caroline McCarty, born 2 Aug. 1821.
11. Jane Moriah McCarty, born 4 Sept. 1823.

Source: Historic Ebenezer Church, by Virginia W. and Charles C. Alexander, page 30.

JOHN McCLAIN

Was at the Battle of New Orleans in the Tennessee Militia. Born 16 March 1777 in N. C., died 5 April 1881 in Maury County, buried in McClain Cemetery on Lewis-Maury County line. He married 1808 in Warren Co., Tennessee, to Elizabeth McMillan, born 21 Jan. 1792 in Kentucky, died 26 June 1865 in Maury, buried in McClain Cemetery. (Pension gives her maiden name as Mullins.)

Children of John McClain:
1. Lucinda McClain, born about 1811 in Kentucky, married Samuel Dodson.
2. William T. McClain, born 29 Aug. 1820 in Bedford Co., Tenn., died 25 Oct. 1891, buried Mt. Joy; married 24 Aug. 1847 to (2) Martha Williams Dickson.
3. Godfrey McClain, born about 1823.
4. Matthew McClain, born about 1825.
5. Dr. Ephraim McClain, born 1827, died 1903, buried in Mimosa Cemetery, Lawrence County; married 2 Aug. 1849 to Telia Ann Clendenin.
6. Elizabeth McClain, born about 1828.
7. Mack McClain, born 1829, died 1895, buried McClain Cemetery, Mt. Joy.
8. Martha McClain, born 12 April 1831, died 22 Oct. 1892, buried Mt. Joy, Tenn., McClain Cemetery, married Joel Cox.
9. Martin McClain, born 22 March 1833, died 26 May 1916, buried McClain Cemetery, Mt. Joy, married 1 Sept. 1872 to Nancy Jane Beckum.

Brothers and sisters of John McClain:
1. Patsy McClain married John Mitchell.
2. Alney McClain.
3. Betsy McClain, married 7 May 1818 to John Boyd.
4. Cynthia McClain, born 2 June 1798, died 22 Aug. 1851, married (1) John Hill and (2) Richard Stockard.
5. Carvil B. McClain married 5 May 1831 to Lucretia A. Williams. (See entry for Cavell McLean, soldier, later in this book.)
6. Ephraim McClain, born 19 Jan. 1808, died 29 March 1865, buried McLean Cemetery in Marshall Co. Married 25 Aug. 1832 to Elizabeth S. Ogilvie.
7. James B. McClain, born 1814 in Tenn., married 23 March 1835 to Elizabeth Ricketts.

Source: Information contributed by descendant Mrs. Kay Neeley, Mt. Pleasant, Tenn.

JAMES D. McCLEAN
Commissioned captain in 46th Regiment 1812. No further information.

SAMUEL McCLUSKEY
In Dec. 1808 appointed patrollee for Columbia. No further information.

THRASHER McCOLLUM
Died 20 Nov. 1814 while serving with militia. Maury County Court Minutes 8 May 1815, Mary McCollum given letters of administration on estate of Thresher McCollum—name also found as Thrashley McCollum. Will Book D-1, page 451, mentions that Mary was administratrix and that there were eight children to be schooled. One place mentions seven children. Deed Book R-1, page 374, 1834, mentions eight children. In 1825 Mary T. McCollum sold land on Leiper's Creek to John McIntire and wife Lydia, Lydia was deceased by 1834. Thrasher McCollum had land on Leiper's Creek as early as 1814. [Williamson County Court Minutes, April 1805, page 128, an inquisition was ordered by court to see if Thrasher McCollum was a lunatic.]

Children of Thrasher McCollum:
1. John McCollum.
2. Sarah McCollum.
3. Ruth C. McCollum.
4. Lydia McCollum.
5. No information on other children.

Source: Maury County Will Book D-1, page 451; 1815 court minutes; Deed Book R-1, page 374.

ARCHIBALD McCONNELL
Served in Capt. Bird S. Hurt's company; born 29 Jan. 1795, died 15 March 1847, buried Houston Cemetery on Globe Road west of Lewisburg. "In Battle of New Orleans" is on his stone; married 20 April 1820 to Elizabeth M. Houston, born 31 Aug. 1799, died 14 Jan. 1884, Houston Cemetery. He was son of Samuel McConnell (born circa 1768/69, died in Marshall County 18 July 1839) and his first wife Mary Proctor.

Children of Archibald McConnell:
1. Willis Harvey McConnell, born 1822 died 1907 married Winnie E. Phillips and Mary Jane Alford.
2. James Carroll McConnell, born 1827, married F. A. McKenzie, later lived in McNairy County.
3. Alfred Marion McConnell, born 1829, died 1919 married Mary A. Collins and Margaret Hinson.
4. Cynthia Artimissa McConnell, born 1832, died 1912, married Nathan Berry London and Pervines Fox, Jr.
5. Samuel Patton McConnell, born 1834, married Martha Jane Lipscomb and Letha Cochran.
6. John Newton McConnell, born 1837, married Sarah Nancy Emaline London and Martha Caroline Routh. He died 1905.
7. Joseph Marshall McConnell, born 1839.
8. Archibald Simeon McConnell, born 1842, died 1909, married Mary Vine London.
9. William Jasper McConnell, born 1846, died 1904, married Pamelia Jane Elliott.

Brothers and sisters of Archibald McConnell:
1. John McConnell, married Sally Young in 1817, moved to Mississippi.
2. James McConnell, born 1793, married Nancy Davis and Mary_____.
4. Martha (Patsy) McConnell married 12 Aug. 1819 to Gregory Ganaway, son of Money Ganaway; later lived in Missouri.
5. Mary (Polly) McConnell married John Bennett Crafton; later moved to Arkansas.
6. Elizabeth McConnell, born 1805, married Squire Larue.
Source: Marshall County Historical Quarterly, Summer 1973, pages 67 and 68.

JAMES McCORD
Served in Capt. Robert Campbell's company. No further information.

(UNKNOWN) McCORD
Sarah McCord drew pension in 1883 as widow of War of 1812 soldier; her post office was Glenn's Store. No further information.

EPHRAIM McCRACKEN
Commissioned captain in 27th Regiment in 1811; marriage bond to marry Mary Mitchell in Maury County, dated 19 July 1811. The 1820 census of Maury County shows Ephraim McCracken, over 45 years, living in Hunter's Road area. [The Virginia Gazette, 14 April 1967: John McCracken, Revolutionary War soldier, served in a Maryland regiment as an officer in the Continental Army, moved to N. C., and later Tennessee, probably lived Williamson or Maury County; married ____ Lytle and had the following children: John, Ephraim, Joseph, Thomas, James, Samuel, Robert, Sallie, and Jennie.] The will of Joseph G. McCrackin, recorded Maury County in Will Book 6, page 331, mentions my beloved wife Elizabeth, my father Ephraim McCrackin and David R. Mitchell to be executors, executed 6 Aug. 1834.

SAMUEL McCRACKEN
Served in Capt. Robert Campbell's company. No further information. Man of this name found on 1820 census of Maury County age 26-45 with wife 26-45, living near Silas Caldwell, Solomon Herring and James T. Sandford. [Samuel McCracken, who lived in Maury County, moved to Illinois in 1832 and fought in Black Hawk War. He is known to have at least one son named Jonathan Eli McCracken, born 1816 on Duck River in Maury County.]

WILLIAM McCULLY
Served in Capt. John Gordon's company. No further information.

JOHN McCUTCHEON
Served in Capt. John Gordon's company. No further information. No further information. [This man might possibly be connected with the McCutcheon family of Williamson County.]

SQUIRE BELL McDANIEL
Served as private in Capt. William Dooley's company; also served in Capt. Benjamin Reynolds' company. No further information.

JOSEPH C. McDOWELL
Appointed patrollee for Columbia in Sept. 1808. McDowell Spring (now Burns Spring) in Columbia was named for him. He was described by Nathan Vaught as being a brother-in-law of John White. "Part owner of the land in the east part of town; had a family and some children, names of them not remembered; he moved away from here quite early."

Source: Nathan Vaught, "Youth and Old Age", page 100.

HUGH McDUGOLD
Served in Capt. Bird S. Hurt's company. No further information.

JOHN McELYEA
Served in Capt. Andrew McCarty's company. No further information.

ROBERT McELWEE
Served in Capt. John Chisholm's company. No further information.

THOMAS McELWEE
Served in Capt. John Chisholm's company. No further information.

GEORGE McFALL
Served in Capt. Robert Campbell's company. No further information.

JOHN McFALL
Commissioned lieutenant in light infantry company 51st Regiment in 1814. Born 1786 or 1787 in Georgia (age estimated from 1850 census), moved to Hickman County, Ky., after 1828 and died between 1860 and 1870. He married 28 May 1806 in Williamson County to Alsey Dobbins, daughter of David Dobbins, soldier of the American Revolution.

Children of John McFall:
1. David Dobbins McFall married Mary Dickey; lived in Maury County. Their old home Forest Home burned in 1925.
2. Augustine McFall, never married.
3. William Hill McFall, born 15 Sept. 1808 (another source says 1818), died 16 March 1895, buried Pleasant Hill Cemetery near Fulton, Ky., married Mary K. Hagan, born 4 Dec. 1809, died 26 June 1860; married (2) Francis C. Pigram.
4. Olivia McFall.
5. Oscar McFall, served in the Mexican War.
6. George McFall.
7. Martha McFall.
8. Alexander McFall.
9. Mary McFall.

Brothers and sisters of John McFall:
1. Thomas McFall.
2. No information on others if any.

Source: Family information of Mrs. Annie Barton Armstrong, descendant; research of Mrs. Virginia W. Alexander; McFall History from History of the Browder-McFall Families, compiled by Charles McFall Browder, 1963, contributed by Mrs. Mary Louise Gossum, Fulton, Ky.

GEORGE W. McGAUGHEY
Commissioned captain in 27th Regiment in 1808. He signed the petition to set up Maury County in 1807. [This soldier is believed to be the son of William McGaughey or Magahay, Rev. War Soldier, born 1740 in Scotland, died after 1812 near Duck River, Maury County, and his wife Elizabeth Lackey, born 1742, died 1804. The following information pertains to the children of that William McGaughey.]

Brothers and sisters of George McGaughey:
1. Samuel McGaughey, born 1763, died 1841, married Jane Laughlin.
2. Agney McGaughey, born 1765, married Archibald Alexander.
3. Margaret McGaughey, born 1767, married David Robinson.
4. Polly M. McGaughey married Eli McCain.
5. Elizabeth McGaughey married William Johnston.
6. William McGaughey, Jr., born 1773, died about 1820, married Margaret Boyd.
7. James McGaughey.
8. Anne McGaughey married _____ William.

Source: Roster and Soldiers The Tennessee Society of the Daughters of the American Revolution, 1894-1960, edited by Edythe R. Whitely, page 1182.

JAMES McGAUGHEY
Served in Capt. James McMahan's company. Married Margaret McCain, 12 April 1798 with William McGaughey as bondsman. [Believed to be son of the Revolutionary War soldier William McGaughey and brother of the soldier listed above.] James McGaughey was executor of the will of John McCain in Blount County, Tenn., in 1798. He later
continued on next page

James McGaughey, continued:
lived in Lawrence County, Alabama. Orphans Court Minutes, Book F, page 176, Law-rence County, Ala., Sept. 1839, lists the legatees of James P. McGaughey, deceased: John M., William M. D., Alfred D. F., Eli A., and Samuel M. McGaughey, and widow Margaret McGaughey. Margaret McGaughey, age 70, born in N. C., is on the 1850 census of Lawrence Co., Ala.; again on 1860 census, age 81; and finally on the 1870 cenus at age 91 years.

Source: Research by Mrs. Virginia W. Alexander from sources mentioned in the listing.

JAMES McGOWAN
Served in Capt. Andrew McCarty's company. No further information.

ELI McKEAN
Received commission in the 1814 militia in Maury County. [Believed to be the same as Eli McCain, see earlier.]

ROBERT McKEE
Served in Capt. Benjamin Reynolds company. No further information.

SAMUEL B. McKNIGHT
Captain of a company of Maury County soldiers; one of the first trustees of Reese's Church in Maury County; moved to Madison County, Tenn., in 1820s and finally to Cape Girardeau, Missouri, where he will be listed on the 1850 census of that county as age 65, born in Kentucky, with his wife Arabella, age 64, born in N. C. He marr-ied Arabella Hunter in Williamson County, Tenn., marriage bond dated 17 May 1806. She is mentioned in the will of William Henderson, probated in Maury County in 1824. He was later a judge in Missouri.

Source: Research by Mrs. Marise P. Lightfoot.

SAMUEL BELL McKNIGHT
Served as private under Lt. Mason in Col. Pillow's Volunteer Infantry and also in Capt. Cannon's company, Col. Benton's regiment. Born 4 March 1789 in Davidson Co., Tenn., died between 1840-50; son of William McKnight (born before 1766, died 3 Nov. 1805) who married Elizabeth _____ (possibly Bell), who died before 24 March 1827. He married 16 July 1812 to Jane Reid Shannon, born 27 April 1792 in Davidson Co., Tenn., (then N. C.), and died between 1834 and 1840. She was the daughter of David Shannon (died Sept. 1821) and his wife Jane _____ (possibly Crow), who died 1827-29. Samuel Bell McKnight lived in the Carter's Creek area of Maury County.

Children of Samuel Bell McKnight:
1. Robert McKnight, born before 1815, married Martha Whitaker; he died 1849.
2. Elizabeth McKnight born 22 Feb. 1815 died 27 Oct. 1822.
3. Louisa J. McKnight, born about 1819-20, died before 1859, married 23 June 1844 to Robert O. Jack.
4. Malinda Jane McKnight, born 11 June 1821, married 6 Oct. 1844 to William Maury Lockhart.
5. John Shannon McKnight, born 29 Jan. 1824, died 4 June 1885, married 26 Jan. 1853 to Mary Caroline Fox.
6. Lavicy Ann McKnight, born 2 Aug. 1825 died 4 Aug. 1901, never married.
7. William Porter McKnight, born 4 Aug. 1827 died 12 Aug. 1827.
8. Daughter born 1829, died in infancy.
9. Martha M. McKnight, born 29 April 1834 died 5 Dec. 1906, married 11 Oct. 1862 James M. Whitaker.

continued on next page

Samuel Bell McKnight, continued:

Brothers and sisters of Samuel Bell McKnight:
1. James McKnight, born 1 Oct. 1786.
2. Mary McKnight, born 8 Nov. 1790.
3. William McKnight, born 1 May 1792.
4. Robert McKnight, born 5 April 1794.
5. Nancy McKnight, born 3 March 1799.
6. John McKnight, born 8 Dec. 1802.

Source: Research and family information of Marise P. Lightfoot, great-great-grand-daughter of Samuel Bell McKnight.

JOSEPH McKNITT
Commissioned lieutenant in 27th Regiment in 1812. No further information. [This is believed to be really Joseph McNutt, who also was commissioned in 1814, as the name McKnitt does not appear to be an early Maury County name.]

JOHN McLEAN
Served in Capt. James McMahan's company. (Refer to John McClain.)

CAVELL B. McLEAN
War of 1812 soldier, service not given; lived in Maury County and later moved to Wayne County, Tennessee. He was the son of Ephraim McLean; married 5 May 1831 in Maury County to Lucretia Adams Williams, daughter of Joshua Williams of Maury Co. (Refer to John McClain entry.)

SAMUEL McLEAN
Appointed justice of the peace and qualified Sept. 1809. Born 27 Jan. 1775, died 10 April 1850 in Lawrence County, Tenn., buried in McLean Cemetery; married Elizabeth Irvine, born 1778, died 1846. He was the son of Ephraim McLean and Elizabeth Davidson.

Brothers and sisters of Samuel McLean:
1. John McLean, killed by Indians.
2. George McLean married daughter of Gen. William Davidson.
3. Ephraim McLean married _____ Vance, buried on Snow Creek in Maury County.
4. Charles McLean, died 1825, married 1799 Sallie Vance, died 1847; in 1811 he moved to Rutherford County, Tenn.
5. Alney McLean married _____ Vance.
6. William McLean, born 17 Feb. 1773, drowned in Duck River 23 July 1814, buried in McLean Cemetery, Snow Creek, Maury County, married Margaret Miller.
7. James McLean moved to Madison County, Tenn.
8. Robert McLean, born 1782 in Harrodsburg, Ky., married _____ Wilson.
9. Daughter married Robert Ewing.
10. Daughter married Robert Brank.
11. Daughter died in infancy.

Source: Marshall County Historical Quarterly, Spring 1975, pages 12, 13; Maury County Cousins, page 708-714; "They Passed This Way", page B-30; "At Rest, Lawrence County Cemetery Records", page 233.

JOHN McLISH
Served as private in Capt. Glen Owens company, Col. Robert H. Dyer's Mounted Gunmen. [This man has been identified as the famous John McLish, or McClish, the half-breed who lived on the Natchez Trace at one time. The following information will be about the Indian McLish.] Continued on the next page:

John McLish, continued:
Town Gazette and Farmers Register, Clarksville, Tenn., 12 Sept. 1819: At treaty of
Old Town held 19 Oct. 1818, a reservation was "secured to John M'Cleish on the north
side of a circutious river by consequence of his having been raised in the state of
Tennessee and marrying a white woman..."

"Stands and Travel Accommodations of the Natchez Trace", by Dawson A. Phelps, in the
Journal of Mississippi History, Vol. XI, Jan. 1949, page 49: McLish Stand: The
land on the north side of Buffalo River, where the Natchez Trace crosses, is identified as part of a section of 640 acres reserved to John McLish by the Treaty of the
Chickasaw Counsil House, 20 Sept. 1815 and confirmed by Treaty of Old Town, 19 Oct.
1818...McLish was a half-breed Indian and kept a stand.

Advertisement in The Clarion and Tenn. State Gazette, published in Nashville, 13
Sept. 1814: "John Graham, died at my house...a young man...left behind saddle bags,
some money, and clothing...had a brother Isaac Graham in Giles County..."Signed, J.
McCLISK, Big-Buffaloe, 13 Sept. 1814.

"Some Chickasaw Chiefs and Prominent Men", published by Mississippi Historical
Society in Publications, Vol. VIII, page 557: A daughter of Saleechie Colbert married John McLish (McCleish), a quarter half-breed and fine looking man. McLish was
quite a man of affairs, visited the Chickasaw Agency in Colbert County, Ala., nearly
every month, and ran a stand on the Natchez Trace in Lawrence County, Tenn.

ANDREW McMACKIN
Commissioned lieutenant in 51st Regiment in 1814; Served as second lieutenant in the
2nd Regiment of Tennessee Militia in Capt. John Looney's company. Born 8 Jan. 1776
in Maryland, died April 1853; received invalid pension in Lawrence County in 1851.
He married 16 June 1796 in Greene County, Tenn., to Mary Johnston.

Children of Andrew McMackin:
1. Hugh Allison McMackin, born 26 May 1799, died 17 Dec. 1850, buried Pisgah
   Cemetery; married Emily Pillow of Maury County; she was born 18 June 1797.
2. Martha Washington McMackin, born 1807, buried in Fall River Cemetery, Lawrence
   County, married Richard Choate.
3. Other children, but no further information.

Pension abstracts:
In 1851 John Simmons, Giles County, made deposition that he knew Andrew McMackin in
War of 1812, joined at Fayetteville 20 Sept. 1814...McMackin sprained leg which
caused his leg to dwindle and perish and totally disabled him.

Samuel McBride, first lieutenant in Capt. Looney's company, says that McMackin was
left in hospital 7 March 1815 in "Mobeal" when army disbanded.

McMackin, age 75 in 1851, says he was at Battle of Pensacola and while en route to
Mobeal he got ankle and knee dislocated; placed in hospital near Mobeal and stayed
here until spring of 1815; right leg is of no service; says went to Fayetteville to
Fort Deposit to Fort Strother to Fort Jackson. At Fort Jackson he was to guard
deserters and then Fort Claiborne; leg gave way on 30 Oct. 1814; Genl Andrew Jackson
gave him permission to go behind army. Jackson said, "hobble along the best he
could." Got to Pensacola 7 Nov. 1814 and to Fort Montgomery 13 Nov. 1814.

Joseph Inman, major in 2d Regiment, made deposition in Giles County and said that
McMackin's leg "swolen to enormous size".

Source: Family information from Mrs. Carrie Gresham, Lawrenceburg, Tenn., descendant
and the pension application of Andrew McMackin.

ELISHA McMACKIN
Served as first lieutenant in Capt. John Looney's company. No further information.

HUGH McMACKIN
Served as private in Capt. John Looney's company. No further information. [May be Hugh Allison McMackin, son of Andrew McMackin, on page 133.]

+JAMES McMAHAN
Captain of company of Maury County soldiers from 28 Sept. 1814 until 28 March 1815, according to muster rolls, however, he died before March. Maury County Court Minutes, 20 Feb. 1815, page 233, Richard McMahan and Calloway Hardin appointed administrators for James McMahan, deceased. Will Book B, page 246, Nov. 1817, inventory of his estate includes "wages while in service of U. S.—$280 amount collected for lost property while in service of U. S. $148.50." Will Book A-1, page 233, 20 Feb. 1815 Polly McMahan, wife of James McMahan. On 31 March 1815 she asks for her dower and at that time she is in Henderson County, Kentucky. Maury County Deed Book E-1, page 147, James McMahan got 151 acres on Rutherford Creek from Anthony I. Turner, recorded 14 July 1813; land was part of Charles Partee, Sr., land, bounded by Benton and Turner and included, "an improvement made by John Goodnight...including spring Goodnight used and where Willie Griffin now lives." Richard McMahan was a witness to the deed.

SAMUEL D. McMAHAN
Served as sergeant in Capt. James McMahan's company. Married 27 April 1811 in Maury County to Phebe Young. No further information.

JOHN McMANNIS
Served in Capt. John Looney's company. No further information.

ALLEN McMASTERS
Served in Capt. Andrew McCarty's company. No further information.

THOMAS McNEAL
Commissioned captain in 27th Regiment of Militia in 1813. Served in Capt. James McMahan's company. Later known as Colonel McNeal. Married about 1803 in Williamson County to Clarissa Polk, daughter of Ezekiel Polk; in 1822 moved to Hardeman County, Tennessee. His tombstone in the Polk Cemetery, Bolivar, Tenn., says Captain Thomas McNeal, born 19 June 1771, died 2 July 1830. His wife Clarissa, born 25 Dec. 1782, died 8 Dec. 1846.

Children of Thomas McNeal:
1. Ezekiel Polk McNeal, born 6 Sept. 1804, died 10 Dec. 1886, married Anne Williams.
2. Jane Frances McNeal married Dr. David Franklin Brown.
3. Prudence Tate McNeal, born 20 Jan. 1809 died Aug. 1840, married John Houston Bills
4. Mary Eliza McNeal, born 16 Sept. 1806, died 10 Sept. 1853, married Mark R. Roberts. She is buried Polk Cemetery, Bolivar.
5. Albert Thomas McNeal, born 28 Jan. 1811, died 3 Sept. 1844, married Mary Jane Dunlap.
6. Samuel L. McNeal, born 1 Dec. 1815 died 5 Sept. 1871, buried Polk Cemetery in Bolivar.
7. Evelina Louisa McNeal, born 26 July 1818, died 20 Oct. 1855, married Erasmus McDowell and Dr. George Boddie Peters.
8. William Wallace McNeal, born 23 Sept. 1821, died 7 April 1870, married Elizabeth Walker Barry.

Source: Cemetery Records of Hardeman County, Tenn., Vol. 2, page 13, compiled by Mrs. Robert S. Owens, Mrs. E. K. Boyd, and Mrs. Howell Lee Davidson; "The Polks of N. C. and Tennessee" by Mrs. Frank M. Angellotti, page 143.

JOSEPH McNUTT
Commissioned captain in 27th Regiment 1814; served in Capt. Benjamin Reynolds' company; also served as ensign in Capt. Samuel B. McKnight's company. No further information.

ROBERT McNUTT
Commissioned lieutenant in 27th Regiment in 1814; also appointed justice of the peace. Later moved to Texas where he was known as Major McNutt. Born 1 May 1795 in Tenn., died 31 Aug. 1853 in Hutto, Texas; married 24 Feb. 1818 in Maury County to Mary (Polly) Jackson, born 26 Oct. 1796 in N. C., died 28 Dec. 1867 in Hutto, Texas, daughter of Brice and Elizabeth Jackson.

Children of Robert McNutt:
1. Eliza McNutt, born 3 Oct. 1819 in Maury County, died 25 Jan. 1849 in Austin County, Texas, married Uriah Sanders and Nelson Morey.
2. Nancy McNutt, born 8 July 1821 in Maury County, died 31 Nov. 1855 in Hutto, Texas, married (1) James B. Allen and (2) Dr. Knight.
3. Martha McNutt, born 8 Sept. 1823 in Maury County, died 31 Nov. 1855 in Hutto, Texas, married Benjamin J. Allen.
4. Robert Brice McNutt, born 3 Feb. 1826 in Maury County, died 11 July 1860 in Austin Co., Texas, married Elizabeth T. Bush.
5. John William McNutt, born 7 Feb. 1828 in Maury, died 1 Sept. 1842 in Maury.
6. Mary Elizabeth McNutt, born 30 Jan. 1830 in Maury, died 26 June 1858 in Belton, Texas, married Parker M. Levi.
7. Jane Catherine McNutt, born 16 Jan. 1832 in Maury County, died 28 Oct. 1902 in Mexia, Texas, married Henry Martin Munger.
8. Son, born 5 Feb. 1834, died 19 Feb. 1834.
9. Tabitha Tennessee McNutt, born 6 Dec. 1835 in Austin County, Province of Mexico, died 4 Aug. 1853 in Hutto, Texas.
10. Hamilton M. McNutt, born 22 Dec. 1838 Austin County, Republic of Texas, died 14 July 1932 Goldthwaite, Texas, married 1866 to Mary Jane Harris Burrows.

Source: "Stirpes", Texas State Genealogical Society, Dec. 1972, pages 136-137.

JAMES McPEAK
Served in Capt. Samuel Ashmore's company; surname in question, could also be McCrack. No further information.

PLEASANT McQUARRY
Served in Capt. Benjamin Reynolds company; married 27 Sept. 1797 in Davidson County to Nancy McQuerry. He is listed on 1820 census of Maury County as being over 45. He was one of those who purchased land from Richard Dallam and eventually lost his land when the lawsuit was in favor of those who purchased land from Kendrick. The following was in the Columbia Herald and Mail, 14 July 1876: "The Delham (sic) party were financially ruined; had to give up their homes; and left exhausted. Mr. McQuary had bought from Delham the place, near Culleoka, where Mr. Tidwell lived, now owned by Mr. Ben Fitzpatrick. Many years after, I saw Mr. McQuary in Miss. He was not living in want, but reduced circumstances; was very old; hobbling with a stick; hand shaking with palsy. He had known my parents before my birth. My mother was still alive. He said to me, "Well, Billy, when will you go back to the old county." I answered that I expected to return that summer. He remarked, "When you see your Mama, tell her I say God Bless her." He then raised his head and with a high, shrill voice, from the very bottom of his heart he said, "If you see Dick Tidwell, tell him I say G____d___him," and, I, presume, carried that feeling to the grave. It made a very serious and lasting impression on me, and though I claim not to be superstitious, I would much dread the heartfelt curse of any old man."

JOHN McQUERTA
Served in Capt. Andrew McCarty's company. No further information.

JORDAN McVAY
Commissioned lieutenant in 27th Regiment in 1809. No further information.

HUGH McWILLIAMS
Served as private in Capt. Samuel Ashmore's company. Married 29 July 1814 in Maury County to Fanny Anthony. No further information.

THOMAS MERCER
Served in Capt. Robert Campbell's company. No further information.

JOHN MILIGIN
Served in Capt. Bird S. Hurt's company. No further information.

DANIEL B. MILLER
Commissioned lieutenant in 46th Regiment in 1813. Marriage bond dated 21 Jan. 1810 i. Maury County to marry Susanna Brown. [Researchers on this line believe he is the son of Harman Miller, Sr., whose will is in box M of Old Wills in the Maury County Courthouse.]

JACOB MILLER
Served in Capt. James McMahan's company. Married 18 Jan. 1816 in Maury County to Susanna Needham. No further information.

JOHN MILLER
One of the original justices of the peace of Maury County in 1807; served at least until 1812, possibly longer. He died 13 Nov. 1848. Three marriages have been found for him: 1. Catherine Hall, who died early; 2. 16 Dec. 1819 in Maury County to Polly McGee; 3. marriage bond 30 Sept. 1836 to Easter or Esther Mangrum, who died 29 Dec. 1868, later married E. Hanks. He is possibly buried in an unmarked grave in Miller Cemetery on Jack Baugus place. Columbia Herald, 1 June 1877: John Miller, early settler, married Polly McGee, widow of the Rev. McGee. They lived on Carter's Creek where they are buried.

Children of John Miller:
1. Washington W. Miller, born 1811, married Susan Hadley.
2. Mildred Miller married 14 July 1828 to Vincent Miller, son of Frederick Miller.
3. Susan Miller married David J. Evans.
4. Naomi Smith Miller, deceased by 1849.
5. Francis Virginia Miller, minor in 1849.
6. Wilmoth Miller married 10 Sept. 1823 to James R. Evans.
7. Sally Miller married James R. Evans, after her sister's death.
8. Harriet Miller married William J. Jones, she died June 1849.
9. Benjamin Harvey Miller, minor in 1849.
0. John Miller, Jr. (Nashville Banner and Nashville Whig, 4 Oct. 1830, John Miller, Jr., son of Esquire John, died in Maury County.)

Source: Smith vs Evans, 1849, Box S-2, chancery court records; Settlements, 1852-54, page 235; Goodspeed's History of Maury County, page 945.

JOSEPH H. MILLER
Commissioned lieutenant in 27th Regiment in 1811. Married 22 Feb. 1811, date of bond, to Maria W. Campbell. [Married 21 Oct. 1822 to Mary Roundtree.) No further information.

STEPHEN MILLER
Served in Capt. Bird S. Hurt's company; marriage bond dated 16 Feb. 1811 to marry Patsy Kennedy. No further information.

DAVIS MILLS
Served in Capt. Benjamin Reynolds' company. No further information.

GIDEON MILLS
Served in First Regiment Riflemen; drew pension as he lost an arm in War of 1812.
Born 1790, died Friday, 29 May 1829, buried at Reece's Chapel Cemetery, with stone;
married 29 Dec. 1821 to Rebecca Luellan in Maury County. Will Book E, page 464,
estate settlement finally made in 1832 and one of items paid was for trip to Nash-
ville "on pension business". Inventory of his estate was made 24 Oct. 1829 in
Maury County. Will Book E, page 66, mentions wife Rebecca and his children.
Francis S. Perry was administrator of his estate.

SAUNDERS MILLS
Served in Capt. Benjamin Reynolds company. Marriage license issued in Maury on
30 Aug. 1814 for him to marry Drucia Cannon. His age given on 1820 census of Maury
as between 26 and 45. No further information.

THOMAS MILLS
Served in Capt. Benjamin Reynolds company. At one time appointed overseer of the
road which led up Little Bigby Creek to the Giles County line. No further information.

NIMROD MINIFEE
Served in Capt. John Gordon's company. No further information.

ANDREW MITCHELL
Served in Capt. John Chisholm's company. No further information. [Andrew, James
and John Mitchell, all soldiers of the American Revolution, settled in Maury County
and all three of them had sons named James, John, and Andrew. It was impossible for
the correct Andrew Mitchell of the War of 1812 to be determined.]

JOHN MITCHELL
Served in Capt. Benjamin Reynolds company. No further information.

JOHN MITCHELL
Served in Capt. James McMahan's company. No further information.

JOHN MITCHELL
Commissioned captain in the 46th Regiment in 1813. No further information.

LITTLETON MITCHELL
Served in Capt. James McMahan's company. No further information. [Lessenberry
Mitchell to Avery Hill, marriage bond dated 24 Nov. 1823.]

BENJAMIN MONEY
Served in Capt. Benjamin Reynolds company; also served as private in Capt. William
Dooley's company. He is said to have drowned in Duck River, date not known. No
further information.

JOHN MONEY
Served in Capt. John Looney's company. No further information.

Brothers and sisters of John Money:
1. Ruth Money married _____ Gifford.

Source: Information from Benjamin D. Hill, Washington, D. C.

ALEXANDER MONTGOMERY
Commissioned 1807 as captain of militia company. No further information.

DAVID MONTGOMERY
Served in Capt. James McMahan's company. No further information.

JAMES MONTGOMERY
Commissioned second lieutenant in Capt. James McMahan's company. No further information. [Marriage bond to marry Susanna Craig, 19 June 1809 with John Craig as bondsman in Maury County.]

BENNETT MOORE
Served in Capt. John Chisholm's company; commissioned lieutenant in 46th Regiment in 1812. [Bennett W. Moore married Polly Rankin in Maury County 31 March 1816.] No further information.

ISAAC MOORE
War of 1812 soldier; by 1839 was in Tishomingo County, Miss. No further information.

JAMES MOORE
Served in Capt. John Looney's company. No further information.

+JAMES MOORE
According to Nashville Banner, 27 Jan. 1908, James Moore of Maury County was one of the six men killed in the Battle of New Orleans. Son of James Moore (1753-5 Jan. 1805) and his wife Catharine Robinson (died Sept. 1806.)

Brothers and sisters of James Moore:
1. John Moore, born 1780.
2. Mary Moore, born 1783, married Thomas Latta; she died in Kentucky.
3. Elizabeth Moore, born 1785, married Joe McAlister, died in Kentucky.
4. Alexander Moore, born 1789, married Sallie Latta.
5. Sarah Moore, twin, born 1795, married Jackson Fitzgerald, died in Texas.
6. Margaret Moore, twin, born 1795, married Benjamin Polk; lived in Texas.
7. Michael Robinson Moore, born 1800, married Nancy Miller.
8. Martha Moore, died when house burned.
9. James Moore, died when house burned. Two children named this.
10. Martha Moore, no further information. Two children named this.

Source: Maury County Cousins No. 2, page 23.

JOHN MOORE
Served as private in Capt. E. Robinson's company, 3rd Regt. U. S. Infantry from 13 Nov. 1813 to 13 May 1815; born 1780, died 1837 in Maury County; married 1806 to Nancy Ann Rogers, born 1790, died 26 Aug. 1846.

Source: Soldiers of the War of 1812 Buried in Tennessee, page 75.

SAMUEL MOORE
Served in Capt. John Gordon's company. No further information.

THOMAS MOORE
Served in Capt. John Looney's company. No further information.

(UNKNOWN) MOORE
Viney Moore in 1883 drew pension as widow of War of 1812 soldier; drew pension at Hurricane Switch in Maury County. No further information.

JOHN MOREHEAD
Commissioned captain 27th Regiment in 1809. In 1811 he sued his wife Martha for a divorce, in Maury County. Name often spelled Muirhead. [He might be the same as
continued on next page

John Morehead continued:
John W. Morehead who received part of the estate of Joseph Morehead in Maury County
8 March 1832.] Goodspeed's History of Maury, page 777, says that John Muirhead
lived south of Gordon's Ferry.

JOSEPH MORGAN
Served in Capt. James McMahan's company. No further information.

JAMES MORRIS
Served in Capt. Bird S. Hurt's company. No further information.

JAMES MORRISON
Commissioned coronet in 5th Brigade of cavalry in 1809. No further information.

GEORGE MURPHY
Served in Capt. Andrew McCarty's company. No further information.

JACKY MURPHY
No service found under this name. This is the same as John M. Murphy below.

+JOHN M. MURPHY
Maury County Will Book A-1, page 218, inventory of the sale of John M. Murphy,
deceased, included "Wages for a tour of duty to Orleans." No date, but others on
this page were for March 1815. Nathaniel Murphy was his administrator. He was
the son of Nathaniel Murphy and his wife Polly Mack, daughter of John Mack.

Brothers and sisters of John M. Murphy:
1. Sarah Bernetta Murphy married Thomas J. Rieves.
2. Miles P. Murphy, Sr. 1808-1875, married Eleanor Jacynthia Mack.
3. No information on others.

Source: Moore Questionnaire of E. N. B. Rieves in State Library and Archives;
Century Review, page 246; Maury County Will Book B, page 6.

+JOHN MURRIW (?)
Served in Capt. Bird S. Hurt's company; died 30 Dec. 1814. [This name was quite
hard to decipher and we believe that this is really the service record for John M.
Murphy above but the name appears to be Murriw. The name Murriw does not appear in
any early Maury County records.]

HARTWELL MYLES
Served in Capt. John Gordon's company. No further information.

JAMES C. NAIL
Served as private in Capt. William Dooley's company. No further information.

CHRISTOPHER NATIONS
Served in Capt. Bird S. Hurt's company. No further information.

ELI NATIONS
Served in Capt. Bird S. Hurt's company; by 1830 is in Lauderdale County, Alabama.
Married 24 Feb. 1816 in Maury to Polly Love. [Lauderdale County, Ala., marriages
show Eli Nations married 7 March 1827 to Sally Weathers.] He was the son of Thomas
Nations whose will is recorded in Maury Will Book A-1, page 245, 25 May 1816. Deceased, Thomas Nations, who had no pen and ink to make a will leaves estate to his
wife Nancy Nations and his lawful heirs Edward Nations, Thomas Nations, and Eli
Nations. The Nations family was in Maury County at least by 1813 and they lived
on the road which led from Duck River to Whitaker's Path.

THOMAS NATIONS
Served in Capt. John Looney's company; married 24 Nov. 1819 to Margaret Stephenson.
No further information.

ENOCH NEEDHAM
Served in Capt. Robert Campbell's company; still in county on 1820 census. [Could
be son of Lewis Needham, in the county in 1820, who is mentioned in Hale and Merritt
"Tennessee and Tennesseans", page 2276.]

ISAAC NEEDHAM
Served as corporal in Capt. Robert Campbell's company; married 7 Dec. 1814 to Susannah Eddleman; still in county in 1820; sometime later moved to Cape Girardeau, Mo.

CHARLES RUFUS NEELY
Commissioned captain in 5th Brigade of Cavalry in 1812. One source says he was
captain in War of 1812, with no further information. Born 1787 in Botetort Co., Va.,
died 1820 or 1821 near Tuscumbia, Alabama; moved to Tuscumbia about 1817; married
Louisa Polk, daughter of Ezekiel Polk, marriage bond dated 19 Jan. 1808 in Maury
County.

Children of Charles Rufus Neely:
1. Rufus P. Neely, born 26 Nov. 1808 in Maury County, died 1901; lived in Bolivar,
   Tennessee.
2. Mary Catherine Neely married William W. Atwood of Austin, Texas.
3. Adela Clarissa Neely married Thomas G. Bell, Thomas Chambliss and Col. John
   Pope.
4. James Jackson married Fannie Stephens, daughter of Dr. Daniel Stephens; lived
   in Bolivar.
5. Thomas Neely.
6. Fanny Neely.
7. William Neely.

Source: "The Polks of N. C. and Tennessee" by Mrs. Frank Angèllotti of San Rafael,
California.

GEORGE NEELY
Served in Capt. John Looney's company. No further information

GEORGE NEELY
Served in Capt. John Gordon's company. No further information.

JAMES NEELEY
Appointed constable in Maury County in March 1809. No further information.

JOHN NEELY
Commissioned ensign 1809 in 27th Regiment. No further information

JOHN NEELY
Served in Capt. John Gordon's company. No further information.

JOHN S. NEELLEY
Served in Capt. Samuel B. McKnight's company. No further information.

JOHN S. NEELLEY
Commissioned captain in 27th Regiment in 1811. No further information.

[It has been difficult to separate the several men named John Neely-Neelley in early
Maury County. The following will be information on men of this name and we do not
know which ones are the soldiers.]

John C. Neelley
Born 15 Oct. 1798, died 28 Oct. 1858, buried McCain Cemetery; married Parolee E.
Drake, born 29 Jan. 1819, died 19 Nov. 1889. Their children were:

1. John F. Neelley, lived on Campbellsville Pike, married Emma Neelley.
2. Permelia J. Neelley.
3. Andrew J. Neelley.
4. Whitfield Neelley.
5. Henry H. Neelley.
6. Martha Neelley.
7. Mary Neelley.
8. Ella Neelley.

Source: Century Review of Maury County, page 141.

John C. Neely
Born in Virginia, came to Tennessee 1800, served in War of 1812, died 1867, married
about 1814 to Elizabeth_____, born in North Carolina, died 1872; son of Isaac and
Fannie Neely. Parents of eleven children:

1. Isaac L. Neely, born 5 Feb. 1821 in Williamson County, third child.
2. No information on the others.

Source: Goodspeed's History of Williamson County, page 998.

John Neely
Living in Maury County in 1821. He was the son of Matthew and Margaret Neely of
York County, S. C. (For further information on this man's ancestry refer to
Bulletin of the Genealogical Society of Old Tryon County, N. C., May 1973 issue.)

PALLAS NEELY
Served as sergeant in Capt. Andrew McCarty's company. No further information.

ROBERT NEELY
Served in Capt. James McMahan's company. No further information. (See below)

ROBERT NEELY
Commissioned captain in 27th Regiment in 1812. No further information. [Anne
Neelly, wife of Major Robert Neelly died 21 March 1833, age 63 years, is buried in
Hunter's Cemetery in Mt. Pleasant.]

ROBERT NEELY
Maury Democrat, 2 April 1908: Arthur T. Isom, Matthew B. Cathey and Robert Neelsy
were in the Battle of New Orleans on the 8th of January 1815. Their Captain Mahon
(sic) was killed in the night attack Jackson made on the British during Christmas
week.

SAMUEL NEELY
Served in Capt. John Looney's company. Family Bible says died 4 Feb. 1815. Frank
H. Smith wrote that a Neely, brother of Simpson Neely and uncle of A. Elijah died
in service in War of 1812. Born 27 Sept. 1794 son of Robert Neely (born 26 Aug.
1768 died in Maury 8 May 1811) and his wife Margaret (born 24 Nov. 1765.) Inventory
of his estate was made in Maury on 17 Aug. 1815.

Brothers and sisters of Samuel F. Neely:
1. Hugh Neely, born 1792 died 6 March 1821.
2. Mary Neely, born 19 Nov. 1796, married William Whiteside and Michael Higgins.
3. Simpson Neely, born 20 July 1799 S. C., died 8 Sept. 1886, married 4 April 1820
   Elizabeth Denham, born 20 July 1797 N. C., died 8 April 1875, buried at Rose Hill
   continued

Brothers and sisters of Samuel F. Neely:
4. Thomas M. Neely, born 1801 died 1855.
5. James W. Neely, born 1804.
6. William Neely, born 1808 died 1831.

Source: Maury County Cousins, pages 55, 75, 336; Rose Hill Cemetery inscriptions.

THOMAS NEELLEY
Served as corporal in Capt. Samuel B. McKnight's company. [Maury County marriages: Thomas Neeley marriage bond to Synthia Read 20 Feb. 1817.]

JOHN NEIL
Served as second lieutenant in Capt. Benjamin Reynolds company. No further information.

PLEASANT NELSON
Commissioned captain in rifle company, 27th Regiment in 1814; first sergeant in Captain Benjamin Reynolds company. Born 29 June 1792, possibly in Halifax Co., Va., died 27 Feb. 1862, buried in Greenwood Cemetery in Columbia; married Elizabeth _____, born 15 Dec. 1799, died 15 March 1870, buried in Greenwood Cemetery. He was the son of John Nelson and was an innkeeper in Columbia. The hotel he built in the 1820s still stands in downtown Columbia.

Children of Pleasant Nelson:
1. Adeline Nelson married Joseph A. Walker.
2. Elvira married Charles Old.

Brothers and sisters of Pleasant Nelson:
1. John Nelson — of him Nathan Vaught wrote "a bro. of P. Nelson so favourabily known here; he John came in about 1818 a carpinter did not marry while here moved to Shelby county in 1823 and married but had no children."
2. William Daniel Nelson, born about 1784 in Halifax Co., Va. See below.
3. No information on others.

Source: Nathan Vaught, "Youth and Old Age," pages 86, 100; Greenwood Cemetery tombstone inscriptions; information furnished by John O. Bronson, Jr., Wye Mills, Maryland.

WILLIAM DANIEL NELSON
Served as private in Capt. William Dooley's company; born 1784 in Halifax Co., Va., died 11 Oct. 1836 in Maury County, married 3 June 1814 in Maury to Naomi Jaggers, born 1798 in S. C., died July 1866 in Maury County. He was the son of John Nelson.

Children of William D. Nelson:
1. Albert Gallatin Nelson, born 3 Aug. 1816 in Maury, died 27 July 1884 in Chickasaw County, Miss., married 22 May 1838 to Lucinda Wallace Hill.
2. James Madison Nelson, born 13 March 1821 in Maury County, died 6 Aug. 1899 in Cherry Hill, Washington County, Texas, married Mrs. Margaret M. Rains.
3. William D. Nelson, a minor in 1850.
4. Esther Nelson.
5. Naomi Nelson (believed to have married James Howard)
6. Hannah Nelson.
7. No information on others, he had nine children. (Either his daughter Esther or Hannah married a Rains and was living in Hardin County, Ky., in 1870.)

Source: Information sent by descendant John O. Bronson, Jr., Wye Mills, Maryland with information from Bounty Land application of Naomi Nelson; Biographical Sketch of James M. Nelson in Souvenir of Texas, 1889, pages 633-634; based on notes by Albert Lucius Sutherland and Wade Hampton Sutherland, grandsons of A. G. Nelson above.

GEORGE NEWMAN
Served as private in Capt. William Dooley's company. No further information.

AGRIPPA NICHOLS
Served in Capt. Samuel B. McKnight's company. Still in the county in 1820. No further information.

JOHN NICHOLS
Served in Capt. Benjamin Reynolds company. No further information. [Maury County Will Book A-1, page 241, has will of John Nickles, 25 Feb. 1816, which mentions daughters Peggy and Kizzy; son Robert Nickles; Robert Chafen and wife Amelia.]

JOHN NICHOLSON
Commissioned lieutenant in 27th Regiment 1811. No further information.

JOHN NICHOLSON
Served in Capt. Benjamin Reynolds company. No further information. [The will of John Nicholson was recorded 8 Jan. 1824 in Will Book C-1, page 143; he mentions his mother Jane Nicholson, sisters Elizabeth Zollicoffer and Mary Swanson; also mentions Maria Walker, Calvin Nicholson and Alfred Nicholson. A chancery court suit titled Swanson versus Zollicoffer, 1843, Box S-3, shows that George Nicholson married Jane Pope, the later was 87 at the time the suit was filed, and that they had the following children: Elizabeth (Betsy) who married John J. Zollicoffer; Mary (Polly) who married James Swanson; Osburn Nicholson; John Nicholson, who died many years ago.] [George Nicholson's will is recorded Book C-1, page 139, and he mentions his wife Jane, daughter Elizabeth Zollicoffer, daughter Polly Swanson, son John Nicholson, and grandchildren Maria Walker and Alfred Nicholson.]

JOHN NICHOLSON
Served in Capt. Bird S. Hurt's company. No further information.

JOHN NICKERSON
Served in Capt. John Chisholm's company. No further information.

+JAMES NIXON
Served in Capt. Bird S. Hurt's company. Died 4 Jan. 1815.

JOHN NIXON
Served in Capt. Bird S. Hurt's company. No further information.

ROBERT B. NIXON
Served in Capt. Bird S. Hurt's company. No further information.

WILLIAM NIXON
Served in Capt. James McMahan's company. No further information.

THOMAS NOKES
Served in Capt. John Gordon's company. No further information.

ROBERT NORMAN
Served in Capt. Andrew Patterson's 1st Regiment Tennessee Militia, from 12 Oct. 1814 until discharged 12 July 1815. Applied for pension 6 Feb. 1851 at Marshall County, Tenn. Had lived in Bedford County. Born 1777 in N. C., died 10 Oct. 1855 in Perry County, Tenn., married 28 Dec. 1816 to Martha (Patsy) Coffee born 1795 in Ga., died 7 Feb. 1852. He was born in N. C., after his father's death, his mother, Nellie Norman, came with Robert to Tennessee. Received bounty land warrant 32052-80-55.

Children of Robert Norman:
1. Thomas N. Norman, born 25 Dec. 1817, died 14 July 1852, married Maria Phillips.
continued on next page

Children of Robert Norman, continued:

2. James C. Norman, born 18 April 1818 in Bedford County, married Mary (Polly) Grammer and Sarah J. Gibson.
3. Mary Jane Norman, born 26 Sept. 1819 died 30 Aug. 1852, married James Shelton Butler, born 1810, died 1890.
4. Eliza E. Norman, born 29 Nov. 1821 married William Noblett on 11 April 1839. (He vouched that he had known Robert Norman for about 18 years and was present when Robert Norman died in Perry County, Tenn.)
5. William Allen Norman, born 4 Aug. 1823 in Maury County, died 24 Oct. 1895, married 30 Dec. 1849 to Mary Ann Gibson, born 6 Oct. 1829 died 20 March 1879.
6. Elizabeth P. Norman, born 29 Dec. 1827 married _____ Craig.
7. Martha Ann Norman, born 26 Oct. 1829 married A. Hugh Guthrie.
8. Robert Porter Norman, born 16 March 1836, died 20 Nov. 1900, married Mary Lucretia Phillips, born 1840, died 1925.

Source: Information from descendant Mrs. James A. Thomas, Morrow, Georgia, who wrote that the Bible records were in his pension file.

JOHN P. NORVELL
Commissioned captain of volunteer infantry company in 1812. No further information.

JOHN P. NOWLIN
Served in Capt. James McMahan's company. No further information.

JAMES OGDEN
Served in Capt. Andrew McCarty's company. No further information.

DAVID OGLIVIE
Commissioned captain of cavalry in militia in 1813. Western Chronicle, 25 Aug. 1814, has notice that he is the captain of a company in the 5th Brigade of Maury County militia. Died early in 1816. Will Book B-1, page 168, has an inventory of his estate 24 Aug. 1816 and Elizabeth Oglivie was the administratrix. Will Book C-1, page 427, has "A list of notes, money, and property delivered to us by John Hodges, received of A. Lewis in Virginia where Ogilvie died..." Elizabeth P. Oglivie is still in Maury County by the 1820 census and her household includes two young males and one female, possibly her children.

ELISHA OGLEVY
Served as corporal in Capt. Robert Campbell's company. Name also found as Oglesby in our early records. Elisha Oglesby married Polly Pride on 8 Dec. 1816 in Maury County. Maury County Court Minutes 25 Feb. 1814, page 110: Burwell Kannon and Joseph Brown were appointed guardian for Elisha Oglesby, Richard Oglesby, Polly Oblesby, Celia Oglesby, minor orphans of James Oglesby, late of Maury County.

HEZEKIAH OLIVER
War of 1812 soldier. Born 1787 in Virginia, died 1867 in Maury County, came to Maury County in 1825; married 1822 to Mahala Lewis, born 1800, died 1840.

Children of Hezekiah Oliver:

1. Dr. Hilary L. Oliver, born 8 Dec. 1828, died 27 Jan. 1900, buried Pleasant Mount Cemetery; married Valderia A. _____.
2. Jane Oliver married Josiah Mitchell.
3. No information on other children.

Source: Soldiers of the War of 1812 Buried in Tennessee, page 86; Century Review of Maury County, page 260; Goodspeed's History of Maury County; tombstone inscriptions from "They Passed. This Way."

JAMES ORR
Served in Capt. James McMahan's company. [This is believed to be James Orr, born 5 Nov. 1787, died 13 Oct. 1876, who married 29 July 1809 to Elizabeth Lowrance, daughter of Jacob and Rebecca Beard Lowrance. Jacob Lowrance was a soldier in the American Revolution. James Orr is buried in the Bear Creek Cumberland Presbyterian Church Cemetery in Marshall County. His wife Elizabeth, born 23 Nov. 1787, died 22 Feb. 1863, is also buried there. His stone says "He was an elder in Bear Creek Cumberland Presbyterian Church 62 years". Source: "Maury County Neighbors" by Marise P. Lightfoot and Evelyn B. Shackelford, page 52.]

JOHN ORRICK
Served in Capt. Robert Campbell's company. No further information.

DAVID ORTON
Appointed constable in Maury County in 1807. No further information.

ABNER OSBURN
Served in Capt. James McMahan's company. No further information.

JOHN OXFORD
Served in Capt. John Looney's company. No further information.

JOHN PACE
Commissioned ensign in rifle company 27th Regiment in 1814. No further information.

ROBERT PARK
Served in Capt. James McMahan's company. No further information.

CHARLES PARKER
Served in Capt. Robert Campbell's company. No further information.

HUGH PARKS
Served in Capt. James McMahan's company. No further information.

WILLIAM PARKS
Maury County Deed Book G-1, page 543, on 4 Jan. 1819 William Parks sold to Davis Kilcrease of the Illinois territory 160 acres which Parks got "from Government for his services in the late war" in Illinois.

WILLIAM PARR
Commissioned lieutenant in 27th Regiment in 1811. No further information.

GEORGE PATTERSON
Served in Capt. Robert Campbell's company. No further information.

JACOB PATTERSON
Served as blacksmith for Capt. James McMahan's company. No further information.

JAMES PATTERSON
Served in Capt. John Gordon's company. No further information. [Maury County Deed Book M-1, page 446, 25 Dec. 1824: James McMurry of Lauderdale County, Ala., sells 120 acres to James Patterson of Maury, land on Cedar Creek. Deed Book E-1, page 354, mentions James Henderson Patterson of Smith County, Tenn. James M. Patterson, born 8 Jan. 1829 in Maury, was the son of James and Mary Reed Patterson of Maury, and was a member of Tennessee State Senate from Marshall County, Tenn.] [James Patterson, Rev. War soldier, lived in Maury County and among his children was James Patterson, born 1795.]

ELIAS PATTON
Served as private in Capt. William Dooley's company. No further information.

ISAAC PATTON
Captain of a Williamson County company, Col. Thomas McCrory's regiment from 4 Oct. 1813 to 4 Jan. 1814. Born 14 Feb. 1777 in S. C., son of a soldier in the American Revolution, who died in service. His mother, left with six sons, moved to Kentucky where she died in 1797. Isaac Patton came to Tennessee and remained in Davidson County until 1801, then "I married a lady of my own name a distant relative" and settled in Williamson County. "In the fall of 1812 there was a call on Tennessee for troops to march to the Creek Nation under General Jackson. I at that time being the oldest captain in the regiment was first ordered...I was near four months in service." His wife Ann Patton died 16 May 1826. He married 29 Nov. 1827 to Ann Henley Byars, sister of Major James F. Byars of Maury County. About 1833 he moved to Maury County and settled on Rutherford Creek. Later moved to Texas.

Children of Isaac Patton:
1. Eliza Patton born 3 July 1802 married Dr. George Barnett.
2. Alexander Patton born 1 Dec. 1803
3. Rebecca Patton born 16 Jan. 1806 [married a Lockridge]
4. John Works Patton born 16 Feb. 1808, married Malinda Pickins 30 Oct. 1827.
5. Polly Patton born 27 Aug. 1810 (Mary Ann) married 8 Dec. 1832 to Dossey Atkinson
6. Margaret M. Patton married Jessie B. Atkinson

Source: Patton information contributed by Virginia W. Alexander, including a Bible Record and a Biographical Sketch written by Isaac Patton.

MOSES PATTON
Served as private in Capt. William Dooley's company. No further information.

DANIEL PAYNE
Served as corporal in Capt. James McMahan's company. No further information.

ROBERT PAYNE
Served in Capt. John Looney's company. No further information.

WILLIAM PEEBLES
Served in Capt. Andrew McCarty's company. No further information.

ALEXANDER PEERY
Served in Capt. James McMahan's company. [This man is believed to be the son of James Peery, Sr., soldier of the American Revolution who settled in Hickman County. The following information is about this family.]

James Peery, Sr., born in England, came to Virginia as young man and served in the Revolution under General Morgan, died 1829.

Children of James Peery, Sr.:
1. George Peery, fought at Battle of New Orleans
2. James Peery, Jr.
3. Robert Peery (triplet), fought at Battle of New Orleans
4. Alexander Peery (triplet), fought at Battle of New Orleans
5. William Peery (triplet), fought at Battle of New Orleans

Source: Kate Derryberry Leeper, "Family and Military Records from Spence's History of Hickman County, Tennessee," pages 88 and 89.

JAMES PEERY
Served in Capt. Samuel Ashmore's company. No further information.

JOHN PEERY
Served in Capt. James McMahan's company. No further information. [Maury County marriages John Peery to Rebecca Dickey, 18 July 1816.]

JOHN PEERY
Served in Capt. Samuel Ashmore's company. No further information.

WILLIAM PEERY
Served in Capt. James McMahan's company. [As this company fought at the Battle of New Orleans, and William Peery of Hickman County is known to have been in that battle, this is possibly William Peery, son of James Peery, Sr. Refer to entry of Alexander Peery. He and his triplet brothers Robert and Alexander all died between the ages of 50 and 60. William later moved to Mississippi where he died. A son W. D. Peery was State Senator of Mississippi. Source: Kate Derryberry Leeper, "Family and Military Records from Spence's History of Hickman County, Tenn." p. 89.]

WILLIAM PENNINGTON
Served in Capt. James McMahan's company. No further information.

JOSEPH PERKINS
Served in Capt. John Looney's company. No further information.

SAM PERRY
Mentioned in the John Bell Diary as having been in his company. No further information.

PETER
Waiter to Capt. James McMahan. No further information.

CAPTAIN JAMES P. PETERS
Believed to have served in N. C. as he did not come to Maury County until about 1819, service not determined. Raleigh Register, 5 April 1810, James Peters of Wake County, N. C., married 22 March 1810 to Rebecca Boddie of Nash county, she was born 1791. He was the son of James Peters (old Father Peters of Spring Hill) and his wife Lucy Parker of Virginia. James P. Peters later moved to West Tennessee.

Children of James P. Peters:
1. Susannah Hill Peters married Col. William Arthur.
2. Thomas Hill Peters.
3. Dr. George Boddie Peters, born 1812, died 29 April 1889 in Memphis, married Narcissa Williams, Evelina Louisa McNeal McDowell, and Jessie Helen McKissack.
4. Ann Elizabeth Peters, born 1819, married Benjamin Franklin Young; lived in Texas.
5. John Buxton Peters, born 1817, died 1864 Camden, Ark., married Paralee Jackson.
6. Lucy Peters.
7. Mary Peters.
8. James Peters.
9. Rebecca Peters.
10. Ellen Pauline Peters, born 1832, married Dr. William Green Wright of Pine Bluff, Arkansas.

Brothers and sisters of James P. Peters:
1. Susan Peters, baptized 1771, died 1840; married Paul Jeffreys, James Thompson, and Spivy McKissack.
2. Nancy Peters married Simon Turner.
3. Others but names not found.

Source: Boddie and Allied Families, page 35; Will of James Peters in Maury County recorded 18 Sept. 1829; Deed Book H-1, page 85; Memphis Appeal, 30 Apr. 1889.

ELIAS PEYTON

Served as corporal in Capt. Robert Campbell's company. On 23 Nov. 1814 he was assigned to work on the road leading from Columbia to intersect with the Doublehead Trace at or north of the little spring on Elk River Ridge. His age was given as between 26 and 45 on the 1820 census. [Conflicting information found on this man. He is found on 1850 census of Maury County as age 44.]

HENRY PEYTON

Served in Capt. Benjamin Reynolds' company. On 19 March 1811 he was appointed overseer of road leading from Columbia to Bigby Creek called the McGee Road. He married Elizabeth Due 5 Oct. 1826. His age given as 62 on 1850 census.

Children of Henry Peyton:
1. Amanda C. Peyton, age 17 in 1850, married 6 July 1849 John W. Stewart.
2. Thomas B. Peyton, age 14 in 1850.
3. Laura L. Peyton, age 10 in 1850.
4. Others, but no information.

Source: 1850 census of Maury County; Maury County Court Minutes for 1811; Maury County marriage records.

MOSES PEYTON

Commissioned captain of 27th Regiment in 1814. On 23 Nov. 1814 he was assigned to work on road leading from Columbia to intersect with Doublehead Trace at or north of a little spring on the Elk River Ridge. He will be found listed on the 1830 census of Maury County.

BEVERLY PHILLIPS

Served in Capt. James McMahan's company. No further information.

ALEXANDER PICKARD

Served in Capt. James McMahan's company, Dyer's Regiment of Mounted Gunmen. In 1830 he was living in Mt. Pleasant and had apparently applied for a pension because of some injury in service. James L. Edwards of the Pension Office wrote James K. Polk: "Alexander Pickard does not appear to have been disabled while in the performance of military duty. The injury alleged to have been received arose while he was on furlough. The law does not allow pensions in such cases. His claim has of course been rejected. The papers will remain on our files." [Will of John Pickard, recorded 15 Sept. 1829 in Maury County, mentions the following children: Isaac, John, Ruth, Catharine, Sally, Alexander, Young S., Aron, Margaret, Rebecca, Jane, Delila, Mary, Mahaley, and Rhoda.]

CRAIG PICKARD

Served in Capt. James McMahan's company. No further information.

ISAAC PICKARD

Served in Capt. James McMahan's company. No further information. (Refer to John Pickard's will in Alexander Pickard entry.)

ABSALOM PICKENS

Served in Capt. John Chisholm's company. No further information. [On one roll the surname appears to be Perkins.]

JOHN PICKENS

Commissioned lieutenant in 46th Regiment 1814. No further information.

JOSEPH PICKENS

Served in Capt. John Gordon's company. No further information.

WILLIAM GABRIEL PICKENS

The following obituary was in May 1871 issue of The Christian Montly, edited and published by J. M. Pickens, Mountain Home, Lawrence County, Alabama from 1870 to 1871. (Two bound volumes deposited with the Library of the School of Religion, Butler University, Indianapolis, Indiana, 1945.) "Died at Mountain Home, Alabama, February 9th, 1871, William G. Pickens, aged seventy-six years, eleven months and twenty days.

"The deceased was born in Abbeville District, South Carolina, February 20, 1794, and removed with his father's family to Maury County, Tennessee, about the year 1806 and in the early settlement of that country. In obedience to his country's call and while quite young, he served in General Jackson's army in the war with the Indians and participated in a number of its hardes fought battles.

"On November 7, 1816, he was married to Charlotte Bruce and continued to reside in his adopted State and near the homestead of his father till near two years before his death when he removed to Mountain Home, Alabama.

"He became a member of the Christian Church early in the Reformation, practiced virtue and maintained a high degree of integrity and honor. Though a man of more than ordinary intellect and possessing an education superior to that usually afforded in the days of his youth, he was quiet and retired, loved his home and preferred industrial pursuits to the more noisy spheres of life. His memory is fondly cherished by family and friends and not least by her who was his faithful companion through more than fifty years; but age and infirmity admonish that she too must follow soon."

Born 20 Feb. 1794 in Abbeville District, S. C., died 9 Feb. 1871 in Mountain Home, Lawrence County, Alabama; son of Abrem Pickens (forn 1755-1775 in VA. or S. C., died 1815-Maury County, Tenn.) and his wife Elizabeth Patterson (died about 1828). Abrem Pickens was the son of Gabriel Pickens and his wife Zerubiah (maiden name might be Smith). Elizabeth Patterson was the daughter of John Patterson and his wife Margaret Baskin. (This Patterson family is from Georgia near the S. C. line.) William G. Pickens married 7 Nov. 1816 in Maury County to Charlotte Bruce, daughter of John Bruce and his wife Ruth Adair.

Children of William Gabriel Pickens:
1. James Madison Pickens, born 6 Feb. 1836, died 3 Feb. 1881 in Lawrence Co., Ala., married 25 Sept. 1866 to Mary Catherine Williams. J. M. Pickens at one time was candidate for Governor of Alabama.
2. Sarah Frances Pickens, never married, buried in Thorp Spring, Granbury, Texas.
3. Josephine Arimenta Pickens, born 18 Aug. 1842 in Maury, died 18 June 1920, buried Glenwood Cemetery, Houston, Texas; married 2 Oct. 1866 to William Henry Treadwell
4. Benjamin Franklin Pickens, died 9 April 1857, married 6 Aug. 1842 in Marshall County, Tenn., to Malissa Cruse.
5. Thomas Jefferson Pickens, born 1821, died 1903, married 30 Oct. 1849 in Maury to Elizabeth Guest Bailey.
6. Anderson Oliver Perry Pickens, born 1827, lived in Lawrence County, Alabama, was member of Alabama Legislature; married 5 Sept. 1857 to Mary Stewart, Rankin County, Miss.
7. William Jasper Pickens, married 14 Oct. 1852 Rebecca Stewart, Hinds County, Miss.
8. John Bruce Pickens, born 1830.
9. Charlotte Elizabeth Pickens, born 1834 (attended Columbia Institute).

Children of Abrem Pickens, brothers and sisters of William G. Pickens:
1. Margaret Pickens married Robert Henderson; lived in Bedford County, Tenn.
2. Jane A. Pickens married 13 Sept. 1822 in Maury County to Cawsby Scott.
3. Elizabeth Pickens, married 20 May 1817 in Maury County to Samuel McCall.
4. Hannah Malvina Pickens married 19 May 1839 to Stephen M. Vaden in Marshall County, Tenn.
5. John P. Pickens married 21 Nov. 1837 in Maury County to Martha Gilliam.
6. Thomas R. Pickens married 18 July 1849 in Hinds County, Mississippi, to Elizabeth Bryant.

Children of Gabriel and Zerubiah Pickens:
1. Margaret Pickens married William Bole; lived in Old Ninety-Six District, S. C.
2. Abrem Pickens, father of William Gabriel Pickens.
3. William Pickens, born 5 Oct. 1748 in Augusta County, Va., married Jane Hamilton, died 6 May 1835 in Maury County; lived on Globe Creek. His children were: John G., William Hamilton, Matthew Galaspy, Margaret, Elizabeth Ann and James S. Pickens.
4. Johnathan Pickens, Sr., born about 1745-50 in Augusta County, Va., died about 1832 in Hardin County, Tenn. His children were Johnathan Pickens, Jr., Gabriel Pickens, and four daughters, names not known.

Source: Information sent by John Dorroh, Houston, Texas, based on "The Pickens Families of the South" by Rev. E. M. Sharp of Memphis.

WILLIAM PICKENS
Served in Capt. Samuel Ashmore's company. [Possibly the service record for William Gabriel Pickens in last entry.]

ABNER PILLOW
Enlisted 4 Oct. 1813 as first lieutenant and aide in Brig. Gen. Isaac Roberts' West Tennessee Militia. Born 23 Jan. 1784 in N. C., died 1860, buried Rose Hill in Columbia; son of John Pillow and Ursula Johnson. He married 31 March 1808 in Williamson County to Mary S. (Polly) Thomas, born 20 July 1788, died 1828.

Children of Abner Pillow:
1. William H. Pillow, born 15 April 1809, died 1864, married 1837 to Elizabeth T. Porter.
2. Mary Tom Pillow, born 23 March 1811.
3. A. H. Pillow, born 18 July 1816.
4. Anthony L. Pillow, born 7 Oct. 1819, died 14 July 1904, buried Rose Hill, married 14 Jan. 1847 to Mary F. Young, born 1827, died 1873.
5. James W. Pillow, born 12 April 1822 died 1853, buried Rose Hill. Married Cordelia Parilee Moore.
6. C. B. Pillow, born 17 April 1825.

Brothers and sisters of Abner Pillow:
1. Colonel William Pillow, see entry.
2. Gideon Pillow, Sr., see entry.
3. John Pillow, see entry.
4. Mordecai Pillow married Mary Johnson 8 Aug. 1808 in Rockingham Co., N. C., daughter of Gideon Johnson, Jr.
5. Barbary Pillow.
6. No information on others.

Source: Maury County Cousins, 536; Goodspeed's History of Maury County, page 948; tombstone inscriptions from "They Passed This Way."

CLAIBORNE PILLOW
Served in Capt. Bird S. Hurt's company, enlisted 13 Nov. 1814; on 7 Jan. 1815 was sergeant major. He died 31 Dec. 1844; son of William Pillow, Sr. He married 22 Sept. 1815 in Maury County to Jane Chambers. His obituary said he left a large family.

Children of Claiborne Pillow:
1. Julia Ann, born 1819, married 1845 to Jeremiah Temple.
2. Claiborne, born about 1826, married Emily Ginger in 1842.
3. John H., born about 1828.
4. Sarah E., born about 1831.
continued on next page

Children of Claiborne Pillow, continued:
5. Narcissa A., born about 1838.
6. Benjamin, born 1842.
7. Possibly others, but no information.

Brothers and sisters of Claiborne Pillow:
1. Sarah Pillow, born 1780 in Virginia.
2. William Pillow, Jr., born 1796 in Va.
3. Willis Pillow
4. Lucy Pillow, born 1795
5. Mary Jane Pillow [believed to be the one who married William Rucker 1827]
6. Emily Pillow, born 1797, married 1822 to Hugh A. McMackin.
7. Allen Pillow, born about 1790 in Va. [Sister Sarah says she had a brother and that "it was before the birth of a younger brother that was born on the 23 March 1789". This is believed to be his birthdate.] Died 12 Oct. 1861.
8. [Richard Dearing Pillow may have been another child, but not yet proved.]
9. No information on others.

Source: James Washington Matthews Diary, entry for 12 Oct. 1861; Pillow versus Robinson, filed 27 Aug. 1839 in circuit court; 8 July 1831, Wm. P. Sowell attachment on property of Sarah, Lucy, and Claburn Pillow; Pension application of Zachariah Butler, Rev. War, W341; St. John's Episcopal Church marriage records in manuscript section State Library and Archives; newspaper clipping, no date, Lizzie Porter papers in Maury County Historical Society; Tennessee Democrat, 9 Jan. 1845. William Pillow, Sr., has been accepted as Rev. War soldier by DAR and possibly additional information on his family will be in his file in the DAR Library.

GIDEON PILLOW
Served as private in Capt. Murray's company, Col. William Pillow's regiment West Tennessee Militia. His stone in Rose Hill Cemetery is quite worn but the inscription seems to be born Sept. 1771 or 1774, died 20 or 26 Feb. 1830; marriage license issued 22 Jan. 1803 in Davidson County to marry Annie Payne, born 20 Feb. 177?, died 10 April 1864. (Another source gives her deathdate as 9 April 1864.) Son of John Pillow and Ursula Johnson.

Children of Gideon Pillow:
1. Granville A. Pillow, born about 1805 died 1868, married 1833 Olive D. Cheatham.
2. Gideon Johnson Pillow, born 8 June 1806 in Williamson County (now Maury), died 8 Oct. 1878 in Helena, Arkansas, buried Elmwood Cemetery, Memphis; general in Mexican War and Confederate general in Civil War; married (1) Mary Martin, born 1812, died 1869; (2) 27 Nov. 1872 Mrs. Maria Eliza Dickson Trigg of New Orleans.
3. Jerome B. Pillow, born 12 May 1809, died 16 Sept. 1891, buried Rose Hill in Columbia, married 1833 Martha W. Harris and married 1835 to Elvira Dale.
4. Cynthia Holland Pillow, born 1810, died 16 Sept. 1892, married (1) 1832 to John E. Saunders; (2) 1845 Governor Aaron V. Brown.
5. Narcissa Pillow, born 17 Jan. 1811, died 28 April 1883, married 1828 to George W. Martin.
6. Amanda Pillow married 1839 to West Humphreys.

Source: Maury County marriage records; tombstone inscriptions "They Passed This Way"; Whig and Tribune, Jackson, Tenn., 7 Dec. 1872; Davidson County marriage records; Columbia Herald, 8 Oct. 1869, 5 Nov. 1869; Nashville Republican Banner, 28 Aug. 1868.

The following comes from a manuscript entitled "The Birth, Parentage, Family and Ancestry of General Gideon J. Pillow, His Early Life, Education, and Selection of a Profession":

"John Pillow had five sons, William, Gideon, John, Mordecai, and Abner, all of whom grew up amidst the hardships, perils and privations incident to the Frontier settlements to that State. For many years they were constantly engaged in the Indian Wars which for so long a time retarded the settlement of that part of the country. These five brothers were distinguished for activity and fearless intrepidty in their conflicts with the Indians. William Pillow, a Colonel, and commanding under Gen. Jackson, was greatly distinguished in the War of 1812, and while gallantly pursuing the routed foe at the battle of Talladega, being in advance of his Regiment was shot through the body, from which wound he was ever afterwards disabled. He died in 186? at the advanced age of 103 years.

"Abner Pillow had a fierce and terrible combat with a fierce and athletic Indian in the water of Duck River. Both parties had emptied their rifles and then grappled in deadly conflict in the water about four feet deep, Abner armed with a sharp butcher knife, and the Indian with a tomahawk. In the midst of the struggle both parties went under the water. While in deadly grapple under the water, a plunge of Abner's butcher knife into the heart of the Indian decided the battle.

"Gideon Pillow and his four brothers were all in the battle of Nickajack, south of the Tennessee River. The Indians killed and scalped a beautiful young girl at the spring of John Pillow, seven miles south of Nashville. The whole male population of the country for miles around was roused and organized and followed the trail of the retreating Indians. They reached the Tennessee River only _____(illegible) after the Indians had crossed. These brave and determined men made rafts of dry cane, found scattered about in the canebrakes by tying the cane into bundles with papaw bark. Upon these bundles they laid their rifles and ammunition and swam the river pushing the bundles before them. There was with this party a man, John Steele, who could not swim. Gideon Pillow swam the river pushing the raft before him with John Steele holding to the waistband of his drawers. Having crossed the river the party followed the trail to the Indian town..."

JOHN PILLOW

Served as private in Capt. David Mason's militia cavalry company in Williamson Count, enlisting 18 June 1812, was sent home sick 31 July 1812. This man lived briefly in Maury County and later moved to Giles County. He is buried in Old Brick Church Cemetery there. Born Rockingham County, N. C., 25 March 1781, died 20 July 1854. Marriage bond dated 20 May 1806 in Williamson County to marry Polly Fitzpatrick. Also at Brick Church Cemetery is stone for Mary Pillow, wife of John Pillow, who died 2 Oct. 1850 age 63 years. She was born in Stokes Co., N. C.

WILLIAM PILLOW

Enlisted as private 28 Jan. 1814 in Capt. Andrew McCarty's company, served until May 1814. No further information. [This is believed to be William Pillow, Jr., son of the elder William Pillow, Rev. War soldier. No proof.]

COLONEL WILLIAM PILLOW

Lt. Colonel, enlisted 21 Nov. 1812 in 2d Regiment Volunteer Infantry, promoted from Lt. Col. on 26 Sept. 1813 by order of General Andrew Jackson, wounded 9 Nov. 1813. Born 1772 in Guilford Co., N.C., died Maury County 1868; married (2) 19 Dec. 1812 in Williamson County to Portia Thomas. (The name of his first wife has never been ascertained despite diligent research by local researchers.)

Children of Colonel William Pillow:
1. Marcus L. Pillow, died 1877 at the age of 65 in Nashville, buried in Rose Hill.
2. Lachlan F. Pillow, died 1856 in Maury County.
3. Mary Eliza Pillow, born about 1815 married 8 Jan. 1833 to Nathaniel F. Smith.
4. William Bonaparte Pillow, married 25 Dec. 1822 in Lauderdale County, Ala., to Emily L. Chisholm, she died 13 Nov. 1837. [William B. Pillow married Narcissa Terry 16 May 1842 in Maury County.]
continued on next page

Children of Colonel William Pillow, continued:

5. Anthony Nathaniel Pillow, born about 1826. His father wrote in his will in 185? a clause disinheriting him because of his abusive treatment and cruelty to him. No further information.

6. [Napoleon Bonaparte Pillow — said to be his son; not mentioned in will. Historian Frank H. Smith wrote: "Napoleon Bonaparte (Poney or Bone) Pillow] son of the old Indian fighter Col. William, who lived near head of Little Bigby Creek, died aged 107. Bone joined Co. A, 9th Bn. Cavalry at organization of the command, taken prisoner at Fort Donelson 16 Feb. 1862; took oath and joined the Federal Army (14th Michigan?); died at the George Martin place two miles on Mt. Pleasant pike just after the war in abject poverty." This was written in 1907. No further information.]

Columbia Herald, dated 12 Nov. 1869: "WOULDN'T FALL BACK—Very few of the young men of this generation know much about the late Col. William Pillow, although he has been dead more than a year, and passed a life having more remarkable events crowded into it than any other man in the county. He was 100 years old when he died; having been born before Humboldt and the real Napoleon. During all his early manhood his was a soldier's life, fighting Indians and enduring the hardships of frontier life. There are enough incidents, of a historical nature, to fill a huge book, and yet so quiet and unpretentious was his life near Bigbyville, that no one knew when they met him the road that they were passing one who was in many respects a "grand man".

"He had the fine sensitive instincts of a woman united to a lionic courage, and the purity of honor of a young girl. He possessed sinews of iron and even up to his death, he walked as martially upright as old Hickory himself. The 8th day of Nov. last Sunday recalls to mind one of the incidents of his life.

"A number of years ago Nimrod Porter, Esquire, probably then a candidate for some office, met Col. Pillow on the square one day, and in a smiling way said, "Col. Pillow do you remember the 8th of November, the 8th of November 1813?" "Yes, very well, the day of the battle of Talladega." The circumstances thus recalled by these two old warriors are these:

"On the 7th of Nov. 1813, Col. Pillow commanded a regiment of Tennessee troops under old Hickory. Gen. Jackson's aid-de-camp, Capt. Sinclair, rode up to Col. P. and ordered him to go up a certain ravine, while the main army under the General would take a different route.

""If you meet the enemy," said Capt. S., "fall back immediately." The Colonel replied emphatically, "I'll do no such thing—I will not fall back." Away went the Captain and promptly General Jackson rode up furiously and demanded in a stern tone, "Col. Pillow, what is this I hear—do you refuse to obey my orders?"

""Yes, sir, I will not fall back in retreat after I once become engaged in fight—I will not leave my wounded men on the field to be scalped by the demons. But, General, I will 'hold them off' till you come up."

The face of Jackson melted in an instant from inflexible rigidity into a bland smile of pleasure, and his porcupine hair smoothed down, as he said quickly, "All right, Colonel, all right, just fight 'em till I come up. All right."

"They met the Indians the next day and the world knows the result. Some time after this event on a certain occasion, Gen. Jackson became very violent at some reports (section here is illegible) and said he would cowhide any man who started the report. "No, you won't," said Gen. Roberts of Rutherford Creek, "You will do no such thing. You will not cowhide this man, he is not to be cowhided by mortal man. "It's Colonel Pillow." It is hardly necessary to say no more was head of cowhiding

Colonel William Pillow, continued:

The following are abstracted notes from the Pension Application of Colonel William Pillow loaned by Mrs. Marise P. Lightfoot:

On 10 Sept. 1849, Robert M. Martin, M. D., and R. C. K. Martin, M. D., made a report that placed Pillow on the pension roll for having received a wound from a rifle ball "which entered the left 'hypochondriac' region and passing through the 'abdomen' was lodged in the right side, just above the crest of the 'ilium' from which place it was cut out by the Surgeon of the Army, who attended him when wounded; the wound has caused and now causes great pain and contraction of the abdominal muscles and general debility; was wounded 'while in the line of his duty, and in the said service, on or about the 9th day of Nov. in the yr 1813 at a place called 'Talladega' in the (then) Territory of the Creek Indians and is not only still disabled in consequence of the said injury.

Col. Pillow was dropped from the pension roll by the act of Feb. 1862. Took oath of allegiance on 10 Jan. 1864 and was reinstated 10 Jan. 1866 at the age of 96 when he said he did not bear arms nor in any manner encouraged rebels or sympathize with their cause.

From his pension record, Col. Pillow lived briefly in 1840s in Madison Co., Tenn. For further information on his Indian fighting days, refer to Ramsey's Annals of Tennessee, pages 474, 477, 485, 486, 612, 513, 615.

REUBEN PINTON
War of 1812 pension living in Columbia in 1875. No further information. (Mentioned in Columbia Herald and Mail, 17 Sept. 1875.)

ENOS PIPKIN
Enlisted as private 28 Sept. 1814 in Capt. James McMahan's company, 1st Tennessee Mounted Gunmen. Born 1772, died 1852; son of Philip Pikin of Pitt County; married Betsy Dill, license issued 13 Feb. 1804 in Davidson County, Tenn. His wife was the daughter of Jobe Dill, who by 1817 was in Miss. In May 1836 Enos Pipkin and wife Elizabeth were selling land they owned in Hickman County, Kentucky.

Children of Enos Pipkin:
1. Asa, eldest, moved to Arkansas then Utah.
2. Philip, second son, born 6 Oct. 1811, died 8 July 1865, married Mary Ann White, by 1847 they are in Madison County, Tenn.
3. Stewart Pipkin.
4. Enos D. Pipkin, went to Greene County, Missouri, where he died.
5. Grief E. Pipkin, born 10 June 1819, married 30 April Diane (Dicey) Sargent.
6. Parisea Pipkin, married William Rainey, lived in Missouri and Kentucky.
7. Martha Pipkin, married William Head, lived in Arkansas and Missouri; she was born about 1835.
8. Mary D. Pipkin married John B. Davidson.
9. Elizabeth Pipkin married John Head.
10. Tabitha Pipkin, born about 1820.
11. Tempy or Duranda Pipkin.
12. Susie Pipkin.
13. John P. Pipkin, age 19 in 1850.
14. Thomas P. Pipkin, age 17 in 1850.

Source: Information supplied by Gladys Jones (Mrs. Willis), Williamsport, Tenn., descendant.

BENJAMIN POLK

Served in Capt. James McMahan's company. Born 1 Jan. 1790, died 2 June 1840 in San Augustine, Texas; son of "Devil John" Polk; married 26 Sept. 1816 to Margaret R. Moore, born 10 Oct. 1797, daughter of James and Catherine Moore.

Children of Benjamin Polk:
1. Elizabeth Ann Polk, born 1817 Maury, died 1841, married Henry Brooks.
2. James Moore Polk, born 1820 died 1840, never married.
3. John Polk, born 12 May 1822, died 1 June 1822.
4. Lucius B. Polk, born 1823, died 1910 married Maggie Miller.
5. Viola Catherine Polk, born 1825 died 1840.
6. Franklin Armstead Polk, born 1827 died 1843.
7. Mary Ophelia Polk born 1829 died 1836.
8. John Thaddeus Polk, born March 1832 died Oct. 1832.
9. Margaret Jane Polk, born 1833, married Wyatt F. Teel of Texas.
10. Robert Green Polk, born 1836, died 1852.
11. Sarah Robina Polk, born 1838, married Joseph Burleson and John C. Pritchett.

Source: "The Polks of N. C. and Tennessee" by Mrs. Frank Angellotti, pages 268, 269.

EVAN SHELBY POLK

Commissioned ensign in 46th Regiment 1814; served in Capt. James McMahan's company. Son of John Polk (Devil John, born 1767 N. C., died 24 May 1845 in Maury County) and his first wife Elizabeth Alderson (born 1766, died 24 Nov. 1829.) Evan S. Polk was born 16 Dec. 1791 in Va., died 23 Oct. 1878 in Huntsville, Arkansas, buried there; married 18 July 1818 to Jane Miller of Carter's Creek, born 17 April 1804, died 29 March 1872, Huntsville, Arkansas, buried there. He also served as corporal in Capt. Henry Newland's company.

Children of Evan S. Polk:
1. Thomas Calvin Polk, born 27 April 1820, died in infancy.
2. William Vincent Polk, born 9 March 1822, died 1893, married Elizabeth Long.
3. Mary Elizabeth Polk, born 5 Nov. 1824, died 22 Nov. 1867, married (1)____Sanders (2) Dr. Isaac B. McReynolds. She is buried at Huntsville, Ark.
4. John Shelby Polk, born 9 Nov. 1827, died 1884, married Dorcas Lear Armstrong.
5. Lonzy Frances Polk, born 14 Sept. 1830, died in childhood.
6. Robert Bruce Polk, born 23 Feb. 1836, died 12 May 1876, never married.
7. Benjamin Rufus Polk, born 3 June 1833 in Maury County, died 3 July 1869, married 1853 to Fanny Berry, sister of Governor of Arkansas.
8. Viola Tranquilla Polk, born at Huntsville, Ark., 22 June 1838, died Fayetteville Ark., 1 Oct. 1911, married 1853 to Charles Burton Sanders.
9. Martha Jane Polk, born 1840, died 1859, married Young Beard.
10. Charles King Polk, born 1843, died 1917, married Drusilla Williams.
11. James Knox Polk, born 1849, died in infancy.

Brothers and sisters of Evan S. Polk:
1. Benjamin D. A. Polk, born 1 Jan. 1790, deceased by 1845.
2. Nancy Polk, married Ethelbert Kirby.
3. Robert Polk, born 1792, died 4 Aug. 1840.
4. Elizabeth Polk, born 1796 died 1856, married second cousin Robert Campbell.
5. John Polk, born 25 Oct. 1798, died 14 Feb. 1864 in Madison Co., Texas, married (1) Cynthia Springs Polk; (2) Mrs. Mary Floyd McIlhenny, (3) Nancy Newsome.
6. Franklin Armstead Polk, born 10 April 1804, died in Maury County 2 June 1887, married (1) Mary Eliza Stevens and (2) Emeline Winifred Lane Hancock.

Source: "The Polks of North Carolina and Tennessee", pages 218, 219, 268, 269.

JOHN POLK
Served in Capt. Samuel Ashmore's company. [Two men of this name in county at the same time; impossible to determine the soldier. The following information is on both of these men.]

John Polk - son of "Devil" John Polk; born 25 Oct. 1798 in western Virginia, died in Madison Co., Texas, 14 Feb. 1864; married (1) in Tipton Co., Tenn., 28 Oct. 1825 to his first cousin Cynthia Springs Polk, born 1801, died 1855, daughter of Charles and Margaret Baxter Polk; (2) 1856 Mrs. Mary Floyd McIlhenny, died 22 June 1859; (3) 1861 to Nancy Newsome, born 1842, died 1865.

Children of John Polk:
1. Isaac Carlo Polk, born 15 Oct. 1826, died 18 March 1852, never married.
2. Margaret Olivia Polk, born 22 April 1829, married 1846 to Col. James Marcus Burleson, who died 1895 in Texas.
3. Elizabeth Jerome Polk, born 31 Jan. 1831, died in Texas 3 Sept. 1900, married Col. John H. Broocks.
4. Eugenia Polk, born 27 July 1834, died 24 Jan. 1864 in Texas, married 1855 to Dr. Thomas Biser Davenport.
5. John De Kalb Polk, born 10 Nov. 1839, married 1857 to Elizabeth Bills.
6. Benjamin Carlo Polk, born 20 Feb. 1843 in Texas, died in western Texas after the Civil War. Never married.
7. Betty Georgiana (twin), born 18 July 1857, married about 1881 Frank Hudgeons.
8. Erasmus (twin) Polk, born 18 July 1857, died in infancy.
9. Almonte Lee Polk, born 12 Sept. 1863, married 1894 Frank L. Wilder of Texas.

Source: "The Polks of North Carolina and Tennessee", pages 33-36.

John Polk (Devil John)
Son of Capt. John Polk; born 1767 in N. C., died 24 May 1845 in Maury County; he was originally buried in family cemetery on Carter's Creek Pike, but in recent years he was moved to the St. John's Church Cemetery. He married (1) Elizabeth Alderson, born 1766, died 24 Nov. 1829; and (2) Mrs. Rebecca Briggs, widow. His children are listed under his son Evan S. Polk. Soldier of the American Revolution.

Source: "The Polks of North Carolina and Tennessee", pages 218, 219.

John Polk
Son of Charles Polk, grandson of Captain John Polk; nephew of Devil John' born in Mecklenburg Co., N. C., about 1782, died in Nacogdoches Co., Texas 1866; married Elizabeth Allen, who died at 70 years. Moved to Texas in 1840.

Children of John Polk:
1. Charles Grandison Polk, born 12 March 1811 in Maury County.
2. William Allen Polk, born in Maury in 1813, married Martha Barrett.
3. Margaret Benigna Polk, born 4 May 1819, died 1899, married Dr. William S. Massey.
4. Amanda M. Polk, born April 1821 in Tenn., died 1912, married the Rev. Robert Overton Watkins.
5. Emily B. Polk, born 25 Feb. 1827, died 1875, married Josiah Taylor Childers.
6. Nancy Polk, married 1850 to Norman P. Branch.
7. Victoria Polk, married 28 Jan. 1856 to William Birdwell, lived in Texas.

Source: "The Polks of North Carolina and Tennessee", pages 264, 265.

RICHARD POLK
Served as corporal in Lt. Joseph Mason's company, enlisted 26 Sept. 1813, discharged 10 Dec. 1813. No further information.

ROBERT POLK
Served as ensign in Tennessee militia; mentioned in Buell's history of Andrew
Jackson; later served as Indian agent. Born about 1792, died 4 Aug. 1840, son of
Devil John Polk. Married Melvina Porter. Two of his children were mentioned as
devisees of his father's estate. No further information.

Source: "The Polks of North Carolina and Tennessee", 218, 219.

SAMUEL POLK
Took oath as inspector of cotton for Maury County in March 1809; appointed justice
of the peace in 1810. Born 1772, died 1827; married 25 Dec. 1794 in Mecklenburg
Co., N. C., to JANE KNOX, born 1776, died 1852. His wife is the one for whom our
D.A.R. chapter is named. He was the son of Ezekiel Polk (1747-1824), soldier of
the American Revolution, and his first wife Maria Wilson (died 1791).

Children of Samuel Polk:
1. James Knox Polk, born 1795, died 1849, 11th PRESIDENT OF THE UNITED STATES,
   married Sarah Childress, born 1803, died 1891.
2. Jane Maria Polk, born 1798, died 1876, married James Walker, born 1792, died
   1864. Their home, which still stands in Columbia, was named Rally Hill because
   some of the soldiers "rallied" or encamped on the hillside there before marchin
   to Fayetteville, Tenn., to join the army, during the War of 1812. The home was
   not built here until much later, however.
3. Lydia Eliza Polk, born 1800, died 1864, married Silas M. Caldwell.
4. Franklin E. Polk, born 1802, died 1831.
5. Marshall T. Polk, born 1805, died 1831, married Laura T. Wilson.
6. John Lee Polk, born 1807, died 1831.
7. Naomi Leetch Polk, born 1809, died 1836, married Adlai O. Harris, 1800-1862.
8. Ophelia C. Polk, born 1812 died 1851, married John B. Hays, 1796-1863.
9. William Hawkins Polk, born 1815, died 1862; married (1) Belinda Dickenson;
   (2) Mary Corse; (3) Lucy Williams.
10. Samuel Washington Polk, born 1817, died 1839.

Source: "The Polks of North Carolina and Tennessee", pages 221, 222.

WILLIAM POLK
Commissioned captain in 27th Regiment in 1808; son of Ezekiel Polk, brother of
Samuel Polk. Full name is given as William Wilson Polk, born 1776, died 8 Oct. 184
in Walnut Ben, Phillips Co., Ark., married Elizabeth Dodd. In 1820 he moved to
Hardeman County, Tenn.

Children of William Polk:
1. Laura Weston Polk, born 1805 in Maury, died 1879 in Madison Co., Tenn., married
   Chatman Manly and Abner Taylor.
2. Clarissa Polk, born 1806 in Maury, died 1844, married Andrew Taylor.
3. Mary Wilson Polk, born 1808 in Maury, died 1871, married Wardlow Howard.
4. Caroline Polk, born in Maury, died 1829 in Fayette Co., Tenn., married John
   Wirt.
5. Olivia Marbury Polk, born 1811 in Maury, died in Missouri in 1850, married
   Daniel Dorsey Berry.

Brothers and sisters of William Polk:
1. Thomas Polk, born 5 Dec. 1770 in Tryon Co., N. C., died 1 Nov. 1814 in Roberts
   County, Tenn., married Abigail Irvin.
2. Matilda Golden Polk (twin), born 5 Dec. 1770, married John Campbell and
   Philip Jenkins.
3. Samuel Polk, born 5 July 1772, married Jane Knox.
4. John Polk, born 1774.
continued on next page

Brothers and sisters of William Polk, continued:
5. Clarissa Polk, born 25 Dec. 1782, died 8 Dec. 1846, married Thomas McNeal.
6. Mary Polk, born 1784, died about 1830 in Bolivar, married about 1814 to Thomas Jones Hardeman.
7. Louisa Polk, born about 1787, died 20 Dec. 1869 Bolivar, married Charles Rufus Neely and Clinton C. Collier, M. D.
8. Several infants by Ezekiel Polk's second marriage died and are buried in a cemetery near Pineville, N. C.
9. (Half) Charles Perry Polk, born 27 Oct. 1813.
10. (Half) Eugenia Polk, born in Maury, died 1895 in Oklahoma, married Alexander Neilson.

Source: "The Polks of North Carolina and Tennessee", pages 141, 145, 220, 221, 223.

WILLIAM POLK
Served in Capt. Samuel Ashmore's company. Cannot be identified, might be the same as the William Polk of previous entry.

WILLIAM POLK
Enlisted 26 Sept. 1813 in Lt. Joseph Mason's company; discharged 10 Dec. 1813. No further information.

WILLIAM POLLOCK
Maury Democrat, 28 May 1891: "William Pollock, age 98, lives at Napier...still entertains visitors with the part he took at the battle of New Orleans...has son-in-law Col. John Floyd, 72, who has killed as many as 500 deer." Drew pension for his service. Born 3 Oct. 1797, still living in 1891. (A woman who died just a few years ago remembered attending his funeral at Napier). He married 29 April 1819 to Sarah Hymer, born 18 May 1793.

Children of William Pollock:
1. Mary Stanton Pollock, born 1 April 1820.
2. Susannah Wilson, born 3 Sept. 1821.
3. Elisha Kirkman Pollock, born 6 Sept. 1823, died 1 July 1863 at Chattanooga, Tenn.
4. John Wesley Pollock, born 5 July 1825, buried at Clifton, Tenn., married Rebecca
5. Eveline Jane Pollock, born 22 April 1827, died 25 Oct. 1852, married ____ Morris.
6. Henrietta Catherine Pollock, born 4 March 1829, died 20 Aug. 1849, married ____ Morris.
7. William Irvin Pollock, born 4 Sept. 1830.
8. Sarah Carolina Pollock, born 11 Feb. 1832, died 6 May 1855, married ____ Lee.
9. Alexander Newton Pollock, born 2 Feb. 1834.
10. Martha Ann Pollock, born 12 Dec. 1835.
11. Eliar Jones Pollock, born 17 June 1838, died 14 June 1852.
12. Eliza Ellen Pollock, born 15 June 1841, died 5 Sept. 1886, married John Allen Walker, born 8 Dec. 1842, died 27 Jan. 1929, son of George Isom Walker.
13. James Marion Pollock, born 20 Oct. 1843, died 4 June 1862 in Chicago, Illinois.

Source: Pollock Family Bible contributed by Imogene R. Parsley (Mrs. W. B.) of Knoxville, Tennessee.

JOSEPH B. PORTER
First clerk of Maury County in 1807. Born 7 Dec. 1770, died 21 Oct. 1823, married Elizabeth Thomas, born 3 Jan. 1772, died 26 Dec. 1832, buried in Lytles Creek Cemetery. Son of Reese Porter (born 26 Feb. 1744, died 15 Feb. 1821) and his wife Jean Brown, he was soldier in the American Revolution.
continued on next page

Children of Joseph B. Porter:

1. Isaac Newton Porter, born 17 Oct. 1802, died 7 (?) Oct. 1825—considered the handsomest man in the county; murdered by the Hardins.
2. Elias Humphreys Porter, born 1 May 1815, died 3 May 1851, buried Lytles Creek Cemetery; marriage bond dated 1 Sept. 1835 to marry Ann W. Shaw.
3. Parry Washington Porter, marriage bond dated 9 Feb. 1832 to marry Jane M. Looney. He died 7 Nov. 1856 near Memphis.
4. Thomas Jefferson Porter. In the old Winchester Cemetery in Memphis, before it was destroyed, this tombstone was there for Genl. Thomas J. Porter, of Columbia, Tenn., "This tomb contains the remains of Thomas Porter and his son E. Porter," "Thomas J. Porter died 30 Aug. 1843."
5. Elizabeth Porter married Robert Caruthers.
6. John T. Porter, later of Madison Co., Tenn.
7. James Madison Porter.
8. Joseph Young Porter.

Brothers and sisters of Joseph B. Porter:

1. William Porter, born 3 March 1769, died 24 Dec. 1843 of palsy, married Jane Bradshaw.
2. John Richard Porter, born 18 June 1773, married Martha Hobson, daughter of Lawson Hobson. (Hobson's will shows that his daughter Martha married John Porter.)
3. Reese Porter, born 1 July 1776, married Sarah Whitsett.
4. James B. Porter, Cumberland Presbyterian minister, born 26 Feb. 1779 in Guilford Co., N. C., died 13 Dec. 1854, buried in Spring Hill Cemetery; married (1) Polly G. Hudson, died 21 June 1818, age 28 years 3 months 10 days, buried in Mt. Moriah Cemetery, Giles County; (2) Mrs. Frances Doherty Bond. (Nashville Whig and Tennessee Advertiser, 4 July 1818: Mrs. Polly G. Porter, wife of Rev. James B. Porter, age 29, died on the 25th ultimo of pulmonary disease.)
5. David Washington Porter, born 4 March 1782, married Martha Rennick Crawford, lived in Giles County.
6. Dr. Elias Porter, born 18 Aug. 1783, died 20 Sept. 1811, never married, buried at Mt. Moriah Cemetery, Giles County.
7. Thomas Craighead Porter, born 20 July 1787, married Deborah_____, lived in Giles County.

Source: Porter Bible in Maury County Cousins; Beard's Ministers of the Cumberland Presbyterian Church, Vol. 2, page 70; DAR papers of Reese Porter; will of Reese Porter; will of Joseph B. Porter in Maury County; tombstone inscriptions from "They Passed This Way"; National Banner and Nashville Daily Advertiser, 9 Jan. 1833.

NIMROD PORTER

Enlisted as private 4 Oct. 1813 in Capt. William Dooley's company, Col. Thomas McCrory's regiment. He wrote in his diary in later years, "I returned from the War of 1812 on the __Feby 1814." Born 13 Jan. 1792, died 30 May 1872 in Maury County; served as sheriff of Maury County for about 25 years; married Billa M. Hamon, daughter of Abraham and M. Hamon, born 1800, died 8 Feb. 1836, age 36. He was the son of William Porter (born 3 March 1769, died 24 Dec. 1843) and his wife Jane Bradshaw (who died 19 May 1836, National Banner, 27 May 1836.)

Children of Nimrod Porter:

1. Mary Anne Hamon Porter, born 15 Nov. 1818, died 26 Oct. 1867, buried Webster Cemetery. She married (1) 10 Nov. 1841 to Henry L. Booker, born 9 Aug. 1814, died 31 March 1841; (2) 23 Oct. 1844, William Jonathan Webster, born 1811, died 1859.
2. Nimrod Hamon Porter, born 25 March 1822, died 17 March 1842, student in Knoxville at his death; buried in Bradshaw Cemetery on Lytles Creek, Maury County.

continued on next page

Children of Nimrod Porter, continued:
3. William Bradshaw Porter, born 19 April 1820, died 29 April 1887.4
4. Martha Jane Porter, born 20 Oct. 1827, married 19 Dec. 1847 at Zion to
   William D. Mayes (he died in Water Valley, Miss. of snakebite in 1872).
5. Thomas Leroy Porter, born 14 Aug. 1834, died 19 May 1924, married Fannie
   Webster.
6. One account says he was the father of ten children, however, only the names of
   five are recorded in the family Bible.

Source: Porter Bible in Maury County Cousins, 223-225; diary of Nimrod Porter, a
copy of which is in State Library and Archives, Nashville; Columbia Herald, 28
June 1872. Nimrod Porter was the ancestor of the late Frances Moore Stephenson,
member of Jane Knox Chapter.

REESE PORTER
Service for him given as serving in Capt. Nathan Davis Militia Infantry. (Service
is in question). Born 7 Jan. 1795, died 15 March 1822; married 22 May 1816 to
Mary Hamilton Thomas, born 26 Sept. 1803 or 1808, died May 1873.

Children of Reese Porter:
1. Nimrod Reese, killed 21 April 1847 at Cerro Gordo, never married.
2. Two other children, no information.

Brothers and sisters of Reese Porter: (Children of Wm. Porter and Jane Bradshaw)
1. Nimrod Porter, born 1792 N. C., married Dilla Hamon.
2. Hugh Bradshaw Porter, born 16 Dec. 1790, died 26 Dec. 1866, married Rachel
   Roberts. (See addenda)
3. John "Jack" Porter, born 24 ? Dec. 1798.
4. Jane B. Porter, born 30 Dec. 1800, died 30 Aug. 1874, buried Elmwood Cemetery,
   Memphis, married James T. Crofford.

Source: Tombstone inscriptions "They Passed This Way"; Pension application of
Mary T. Porter on Nimrod R. Porter's Mexican War service; Maury County marriage
records; Nathan Vaught's sketch of William Porter.

DR. SAMUEL SHAW PORTER
Wife Catherine (sic) Porter drew pension in 1883 in Williamsport as widow of War of
1812 soldier. Served elsewhere as did not come to Maury County until 1826. Born
3 Feb. 1793, died 25 Jan. 1873, buried Williamsport Cemetery; son of David Porter
(born in Ireland County Antrim) and his wife Flora Brownfield. Married 23 Feb. 1826
at Lexington, Ky., to Jane W. Moore, born 29 Aug. 1799, died 5 Feb. 1828, buried at
Zion Cemetery. Married (2) Katherine Todd (cousin of first wife), born 17 July 1817
died 28 July 1895.

Children of S. S. Porter:
1. Flora, born 8 April 1827, married A. H. Nicks and moved to Missouri. Only
   child by first marriage.
2. William Todd Porter, born 1836, died 1901.
3. Samuel S. Porter, born 1843, died 1929.
4. Possibly others, but no further information.

Source: Tombstone inscriptions from "They Passed This Way"; letter written by
S. S. Porter, dated 7 Oct. 1859.

WILLIAM PORTER
Commissioned lieutenant 27 Regiment in 1812; commissioned captain 51st Regiment
in 1814. No identification of this man.

WILLIAM PORTER
Served in Capt. Samuel B. McKnight's company. No further information.

JOHN POWELL
Served in Capt. John Looney's company. No further information.

JOHN A. POWELL
Served in Capt. Benjamin Reynolds company. Married 23 July 1818 in Maury County to Charlotte Lane, daughter of William and Winnefred Lane. [Maury County marriages also show John A. Powell marriage to Susan Arnold, 8 Sept. 1814—date of bond.]

Children of John A. Powell:
1. William B. Powell, born 18 Nov. 1819 in Maury, married Phebe E. Stanfield, daughter of Thomas S. Stanfield. Lived in Mississippi then Texas.
2. J. W. Powell.
3. Fletcher Powell.
4. John I. Powell.
5. George Powell.
6. Eliza Powell married W. D. Coots.
7. Fanny Powell married Leonard Lane.

Source: Biographies and Memories of McLennan County, Texas, Lewis Publishing Company, page 835, furnished by Jane Luna (Mrs. John W.).

ISHAM POWELL
Served in Capt. Andrew McCarty's company. No further information.

ISHAM POWELL
Served in Capt. Samuel B. McKnight's company. No further information. [A man by the name of Isom Powell made bond to marry Sally Knox 13 July 1814 in Maury County; one Isom Powell in Maury County was the son of Lewis Powell, son of Ambrose Powell. Refer to chancery court case Smith vs Brown, 1834.] *

LEMUEL PREWETT
Appointed justice of the peace for Maury County; settled at Cave Spring in 1806; in 1818 he and his twelve children moved to Monroe County, Miss. He was a Baptist minister for many years. Died in Mississippi in 1845. Served as justice of the peace from 1807 until 1812. Married (1) Catey_____ (2) Elizabeth, widow of Amos Johnston.

Children of Lemuel Prewett:
1. Phoebe Prewett, first white child born in Maury County, born about 1806, died in Mississippi in 1870s.
2. Elisha Dyer Prewett, married 31 March 1818 to Polly McGee and 10 Aug. 1824 to Elizabeth Wilkes.
3. Abner Prewett, oldest child, died at eighty.
4. Kirk Prewett married 7 April 1818 to Elizabeth Harris.
5. Mark Prewett marriage bond to marry Sarah D. Wilkes 12 Jan. 1828.
6. Larkin Prewett married 12 Dec. 1820 to Polly Love.
7. No information on other children; Jeremiah and John are believe to be the name of two of these children.

Source: Maury County marriage records; Columbia Herald and Mail, 1 June 1877.

ABNER PREWETT
Served in Creek War; son of Lemuel Prewett, living in 1846 in Mississippi; died in his eighties. Married Eliza Jane McGee, daughter of the Rev. Thomas McGee, brother of Chiles McGee. Name of only one child known: Austin L. Prewett.
*Isom Powell, age 59, found on 1850 Census of Wayne County; possibly the same.

ELISHA DYER PREWETT

Served in Creek War; died 1876; married (1) Mary G. (Polly) McGee, daughter of the
Rev. Thomas McGee; (2) 10 Aug. 1824 Elizabeth Wilkes; son of Lemuel and Catey
Prewett.

Columbia Herald and Mail, 1 June 1877:
"... The wagon-train had reached and camped at Jumper's Spring, a few miles from the
Horseshoe, Dyer Prewett had been violently attacked with fever, and was then lying
unconscious. When the train started on their return, his brother Abner and a few
friends remained with him, he having sent word by returning friends to his father,
and expecting every day to see his brother breathe his last, his fever became typ-
hoid, with no medicine and no supplies, it was decided a gloomy prospect.

"An old Indian doctor commenced with teas of roots and herbs, and there he set in
stoical silence, day and night, by Dyer's pallet, occasionally administering his
teas. Some week or two passed in that way, when one day the old doctor thought he
discovered perspiration, he bent over and watched intently, then jumped up, much
excited, and said, "White man get well."

"There was no return of consciousness, but the doctor got into a profuse sweat. After while his brother having no supplies for the sick, commenced the long return to
Fort Deposit. A friend would lead while Abner rode, holding his brother before him,
as helpless as an infant; when he seemed much exhausted, they would gently take him
down, and lay him on a blanket, and so changing and resting each other, by easy
stages, they reached Fort Deposit.

"A few days after their arrival, their father, with a strong led-horses, reached the
fort. When Dyer heard his father's voice, he gradually regained consciousness. He
often stated afterwards that he had no recollection of anything after the train left
nor did he recollect one thing of that long 200 to 300 miles to the fort, not until
he heard his father's voice.

"Getting some supplies at the fort, they remained a few days and then by easy
stages his father leading the strong horse and Abner riding and holding Dyer before
him, letting him rest when too exhausted to go on, they reached home, took him down,
carried him into the house, and placed him under the care of his mother. He was
still perfectly helpless. It was several months before he regained sufficient
strength to go out of the house and yard. He found then his hearing impaired, which
he never regained..."

BAYLISS EARL PRINCE

Buried in the James Holland Cemetery in Maury County and his stone reads "He served
his country with credit to himself as an officer in the Creek War and the Battle of
New Orleans." He died August 1825. He was captain of a company but men in his
company are not Maury County men—appear to be men from Montgomery County, Tenn.
He was related to the Holland family—Sarah Gilbert Holland, wife of James Holland,
was the daughter of William Gilbert. One of William Gilbert's daughters married
Dr. Robert Prince.

Source: Memorabilia of Her Family, by Mrs. S. S. I. Cochran, 1881, copy of this
manuscript in State Library and Archives, Nashville.

GILBERT PRINCE

Served in Capt. John Looney's company. No further information. [A man of this
name will be found on the 1820 census of Lawrence County, Tenn.]

HENRY PRITCHARD

Served in Capt. Bird S. Hurt's company. No further information.

JAMES PRITCHARD
Served in Capt. Robert Campbell's company. No further information.

JOHN PRUEIT
Served in Capt. Benjamin Reynolds company. No further information. [This man may be correctly John Prewett, believed to be son of Lemuel Prewett.]

PETER PRYOR
Commissioned ensign in 46th Regiment in 1813. [Man of this name also served in Capt. C. E. McEwen's company, Williamson County troops.]

ELISHA PULLEN
Served in Captain Samuel Ashmore's company. Born 11 May 1781, died 4 Oct. 1868, buried New Famie Cemetery on Valley Creek Road; married (1) Ann Richardson, daught: of Thomas and Jane Willis Richardson, she died 29 April 1843. He is known to have fought at Horseshoe Bend; made a second marriage and had several children by that marriage.

Children of Elisha Pullen:
1. Thomas Pullen, buried at McCain's.
2. No information on other children.

JOHN QUEEN
Served in Capt. James McMahan's company. Married 30 April 1816 in Maury County to Mary Campbell.

BURWELL B. QUIMBY
Served in Capt. Bird S. Hurt's company; also served as first sergeant in Capt. Robert Campbell's company. Born between 1775 and 1794, possibly N. C., married Susannah Rains, born between 1770 and 1780 in Davidson County, Tenn. She is buried in Mt. Olivet in Nashville. She wad daughter of Capt. Johnathan H. Rains, born 1743, died 26 March 1834, and his wife Christianna Gowen, born 1752, died 24 March 1826, buried in Mt. Olivet Cemetery, Nashville. The following was included in his record in the National Archives: "I certify that Burwell B. Quimby, a private, in my company of militia has served on an expedition and fought the Creek Indians under the command of Maj. General Andrew Jackson three months and fifteen days and is here by honorably discharged. 10 May 1814, Fayetteville, signed Robert Steele, 4th Regiment." He is listed on the 1830 census of Lawrence County, Tenn.

Children of Burwell B. Quimby:
1. Caroline Quimby, born 1807 in Davidson County, died between 1879 and 1882, married William Warmath.
2. Caswell K. Quimby, born 1808 in Davidson County, died 27 April 1889 in Bradley County; married 7 July 1831 Classie Hopper.
3. Barbara Quimby, married 28 May 1846 to John De Mumbreun on 28 May 1846 in Davidson County, Tenn.
4. Christiana R. Quimby, born 1826, died 10 May 1837.
5. John R. Quimby.
6. No information on other children; had 12 children in all.

Source: Information from the family records of Mrs. Joy Quimby Stearns.

+JESSE RADFORD
Mustered 28 Sept. 1814 in Capt. Glen Owens company, Col. Robert Dyer, "died 7 Jan. 1815 in captivity". Will Book B, page 123, has his inventory taken 10 Apr. 1816 and it included "a discharge fro three months and 4 days, $69.40; amount of property lost in battle—$31." Hannah Radford was a buyer of items at his sale. County is still paying for schooling of his sons, Jesse and John Radford, in 1820. 18 Oct. 1819 county made contract for education of Anderson, John and Jesse, his minor orphans. Jesse Radford signed petition in 1809 as living in Suck Island area.

RICHARD RAIL

In Jan. 1824 he petitions the Maury County court asking to be exempted from working on road: "being afflicted with a rupture which frequently renders him unable to labour and is very distressing, yet he is liable to be proceeded against and harassed by the overseers of road who admit of no excuse from delinquents. He is willing to show to your worships the certificates of Dr. Hogg who examined him respecting his said disability and by which he obtained his discharge from military duty by his Excellency Gov. Carroll while in a subordinate command..." Born 5 Feb. 1776, died 23 August 1851, buried in Rail Cemetery on Leeper's Creek; married Susanna Adkisson born 4 Oct. 1787, died 31 May 1844, buried Rail Cemetery.

Children of Richard Rail:
1. Susan married John Wesley Hill.
2. Richard Rail, Jr.
3. Reddick (or Redric) Rail married 1836 to Lucinda Humphrey.
4. Thomas Rail married Anna Goodman 1826.
5. Sally Rail married 1826 to Lemuel Nickens.
6. Thomas Rail.
7. No information on others.

Source: Rail Cemetery inscriptions from "They Passed This Way"; 1850 census of Maury; Maury County marriages; information from Mrs. Priscilla Hill, Tracy, Calif.

+JOHN RAMSEY

Served in Capt. Samuel B. McKnight's company; died 8 Nov. 1813. No further information.

JOHN DUNWOODY RAMSEY

Served in Capt. Bird S. Hurt's company. Born 25 Oct. 1795, S. C., died 26 June 187 buried Camp Ground Cemetery at Culleoka; married 25 Sept. 1822 to Elizabeth Kennedy born 25 Nov. 1792, Ky., died 16 Feb. 1880. He drew a pension at the age of 77. (Columbia Herald, 29 April 1873). Wife Elizabeth was on the 1883 pension list—not her deathdate on stone is 1880. He was the son of Thomas Ramsey, died 31 Aug. 1841

Brothers and sisters of John D. Ramsey:
1. Esther Lamirah Ramsey, married Alexander S. Henderson.
2. Rufus Giles Ramsey.
3. Harriet Narcissa Ramsey married 1831 William Simonton of Lawrence County.
4. Tirzah Catharine.
5. James Marshal Ramsey.
6. William Henderson Ramsey.
7. Duncan Brown Ramsey, born 23 Dec. 1826.

Source: Historic Ebenezer by Charles C. and Virginia W. Alexander, pages 27, 28.

JOSHUA RAMSEY

Commissioned lieutenant in 27th Regiment 1808; marriage bond to Peggy Thomas dated 21 Oct. 1817. No further information.

ROBERT RAMSEY

Served in Capt. John Looney's company. No further information. (Two men by this name in the county, impossible to determine the soldier. One Robert Ramsey, born 1 Jan. 1787, died 30 May 1866, married Elizabeth Caskey 9 Nov. 1819, she died 30 April 1842 at the age of forty-two, buried Ramsey Cemetery at Campbell Station. One Robert Ramsey and his wife Jane were members of Reese's Chapel and were dismissed from membership in 1834. No further information.)

WILLIAM G. RAMSEY
Served in Capt. John Looney's company. No further information.

WILLIAM H. RAMSEY
Served in Capt. James McMahan's company. No further information.

RICKS A. RANDOLPH
Served in Capt. John Chisholm's company. No further information.

HENRY READ
Served in Capt. James McMahan's company. No further information.

SION RECORD
Reported to be War of 1812 soldier. [Several men of this name, all related, in the county and impossible to determine the soldier. The following information will be on these men.]

Sion S. Record - born 27 Sept. 1793, died 26 Sept. 1821. Buried in Record Cemetery in Marshall County.

Sion P. Record - deceased by 31 Dec. 1823 when his property was sold. Buyers at his sale included Mary Record, Sherwood P. Record, John W. Record, George W. Record, and James C. Record.

Sion Record - born about 1780 in Tenn., died between 1825 and 1830, will dated 7 Oct. 1826; wife Penelope; children: Polly Green, Mahala Pickens, Comfort Glasscock, Nelly Weaver, John, James Ballard, William, and Candress (or Condra). Will Book D, page 208.

Sion Record - son of John and Mary Record; John Record's will 20 July 1814 is recorded in Will Book B, page 19, and mentions his children: Elizabeth Hunter (wife of Elisha), John, Jr., Sion, "all my children", and "one to be born" after his death.

ABIJAH REDDING
Commissioned captain in 27th Regiment in 1814. Marriage bond dated 5 Jan. 1809 to marry Mahala Mitchell.

CHARLES REECE
Served in Capt. John Gordon's company. No further information.

ROBERT D. REECE
Served in Capt. John Looney's company. No further information.

GEORGE REED
Served in Capt. Benjamin Reynolds company. No further information.

JAMES REED
Served in militia, commissioned captain 1814 in the 27th Regiment. No further information.

ROBERT REED
Served as private in Capt. William Dooley's company. No further information.

ROBERT REED
Served in Capt. John Chisholm's company. No further information. [On one roll the name appears to be Weed).

ROBERT REID
Served in Capt. John Gordon's company. No further information.

JOEL REESE

Commissioned captain in 27th Regiment in 1813. Appointed constable of Maury County in June 1809. Son of James Reese, Sr. (born 1744, died 17 Nov. 1828, Rev. War soldier) and his wife Elizabeth Brevard (died 27 Aug. 1831.) He married 5 Nov. 1803 in Sumner County, Tenn., to Sarah Ramsey.

Brothers and sisters of Joel Reese:
1. Thomas b. Reese married 1794 to Margaret Thompson.
2. Assenath Reese married Edward Hudson.
3. George Reese.
4. Sarah Reese, born 1778 died 1839, married Silas Alexander.
5. Ruth Reese married 1808 to Andrew McCarty.
6. Elizabeth Reese married Franklin Houston.
7. Flavia Reese married 1803 Daniel Woods.
8. James H. Reese married 1805 to Rebecca Simpson.
9. Susannah Reese married James Stockard.

Source: Historic Ebenezer, page 25.

ELIJAH REEVES

Served in Capt. Samuel Ashmore's company. Whig and Tribune, Jackson, Tenn.,: Elijah Rieves, age 81, died in Maury County, May 6. Columbia Herald, 10 May 1872: Died last Monday. Columbia Herald, 15 Dec. 1871: lived in District 27, drew pension. Columbia Herald and Mail, 11 May 1877: Reives and brother were pensioners. He was son of Reuben Rieves (died 1816) and his wife Hannah. This branch of the family spelled the name Reeves. He married 14 July 1819 (date of bond) in Maury County to Polly Stallings, born 1800 in Georgia. On the 1850 census of the county the following were living in their household: Mary, age 16; Angeline, age 14; and Wiley, age 12.

Brothers and sisters of Elijah Reeves:
1. Thomas Rieves.
2. Joel Rieves.
3. No information on others.

Children of Elijah Reeves:
1. Mary Jane married Hugh Griffin.
2. No information on others.

LEVI REEVES

Served in Capt. Robert Campbell's company. No further information.

PETER REEVES

Served in Capt. Andrew McCarty's company. No further information.

WILLIAM S. REEVES

Served in Capt. Andrew McCarty's company. No further information.

JOHN RENFRO

Served in Capt. John Looney's company. No further information. [Several men of this name lived in county at the same time. The following information will be on those men.]

John Renfro - long a citizen of this county died 5 Sept. 1844; wife and children survive. (Tennessee Democrat, 14 Sept. 1844.) Renfro Bible give the following as his children:

1. George Washington Renfro, born 7 Feb. 1837.
2. John Franklin Renfro, born 23 Nov. 1840, died 4 Aug. 1866.
3. Hugh Marshal Renfro, born 22 March 1842, died 9 Nov. 1871.
4. Rosco Porter Renfro, born 19 Dec. 1843.
5. William Renfro, born 15 July 1836, died July 1863 (died as Confederate soldier)
6. Possibly others, but no further information.   (continued)

John Renfro, continued:

John Renfro - "Old Mr. John Renfro, who died several years ago at a great age was one of the first settlers of Birbyville." Columbia Herald, 15 April 1870.

John Renfro - found on 1850 census of the county age 61, born in Virginia, lived in Bigbyville area; wife Nancy, born in Kentucky, age 56; children in household were Rufus, 26; Wilkerson, 18; and James, 17.

John Renfro "is dead" - entry made 17 Feb. 1868 in James Washington Matthews diary.

John Renfro marriage bond dated 30 May 1822 to marry Rachel Rankin.

John Renfro - son of William Renfro (born 1734, died 1830 in Maury, Rev. War soldier) and his wife Chloe_____. (Information from Mrs. Marise P. Lightfoot.)

John Renfro - deceased, widow was Susan. (Circuit Court minutes 21 Jan. 1845.)

THOMAS REUBY
Commissioned lieutenant in 27th Regiment in 1809. No further information.

BENJAMIN REYNOLDS
Served as captain of the 39th Regiment, United States Infantry. On 27 March 1814 at the Battle of Horseshoe Bend on the Tallapoosa River he was "severely wounded, the ball entering in the left groin, and ranging downwards passed through back part of thigh, producing an incapacity of using that leg". William Purris, late Surgeon, 39th Infantry signed the certificate. After 18 Jan. 1833 he was paid pension at the Agency of the State of Mississippi. Senator John Williams of Knoxville, late colonel of 39th Infantry, was his endorser.

Benjamin Reynolds, captain, 27th Regiment Tennessee Militia; represented Maury County in State Senate 1819-21, 1823-1829; democrat; enlisted 21 Nov. 1812 under Colonel Thomas Hart Benton of 39th Regiment. In 1830 he was appointed Chickasaw Agent, State of Alabama, moved to Franklin County, Alabama. He also served in legislature of Alabama, 1839-1841; was Presidential Elector in 1840.

On 7 June 1840, Tishomingo Co., Mississippi, Benjamin Reynolds, Stephen W. Smith, William Ira Weems, Alexander Dugger and Stephen A. Hale met at Carrollsville and after spending the greater portion of the day drinking and shooting at a mark, returned to their respective homes, having agreed to meet the next day and hunt together. Meeting according to agreement at the home of Smith, the parties became involved in an argument and Reynolds shot Smith, inflicting a mortal wound from which he died in a few hours. Reynolds was indicted by the grand jury for murder in the first degree with Hale and Dugger as accessories. The parties were later acquitted by the circuit court. (From History of Old Tishomingo County, Miss., compiled and edited by Fan Alexander Cochran, 1972.) Regarding this incident, the parties involved were all originally from Maury County except Stephen A. Hale.

Benjamin Reynolds was born 1785 in Orange Co., Va., or Fayette Co., Ky., died about 1842-43 in Franklin County, Alabama. He was the eldest son of Aaron Reynolds (born 1753 died 1833) and his first wife Catherine Chambers of Orange Co., Va. and Fayette Co., Ky. Catherine, probably died in Tennessee about 1809—refer to Hugh Griffin entry regarding Aaron Reynolds.

Benjamin Reynolds was in Maury County, Tenn., before 1808 when he served on road duty. He married in Kentucky to Catherine Allen, daughter of James Allen, Sr., (born 1755, died 1830) and Mary Tomlinson (born 1757, died 1820) of Fayette Co., Ky., and Maury County, Tenn. She was daughter of William Tomlinson of Fayette or Scott Co., Ky. James Allen, Sr., and Aaron Reynolds are buried side by side in Shane's graveyard, Campbell Station in Maury County. Stones were discovered Nov. 1973.

Benjamin Reynolds, continued:

Children of Benjamin Reynolds:
1. James Allen Reynolds, born about 1808 in Maury County, died before 1837 in Franklin Co., Ala., married 21 Sept. 1829 in Maury to Cynthia Ann Williams.
2. Chambers Reynolds, born about 1810 in Maury County, married Lavinia Cowan of Alabama.
3. Catherine Reynolds, born about 1812 in Maury County, married Alexander Dugger on 27 June 1830 in Maury County. (This is Alexander Dugger who was involved with Reynolds in the Tishomingo County, Miss., incident.)
4. Son, born about 1814 in Maury, died before 1830 in Maury.
5. Lemuel Montgomery Reynolds, born about 1815-16 in Maury, living 1840 in Franklin County, Ala. He was named for Maj. Lemuel P. Montgomery killed at Horseshoe.
6. Benjamin Reynolds II, born about 1818 in Maury County, killed 1846 in Mexican War, married Cornelia Ann Avery.
7. Nancy Reynolds, born about 1820 in Maury County, married Francis Mastin Green.
8. Thomas I. Reynolds, born about 1823 in Maury County, living 1850 in Franklin County, Alabama in household of his mother Catherine; married Sarah Turberville.
9. [Marandy Reynolds married JulianCarter, moved to Texas.]
10. Possibly others, no further information.

Brothers and sisters of Benjamin Reynolds:
1. Mary Reynolds, born about 1787 at Fayette Co., Ky., married Joseph or Jacob Landess.
2. Catherine "Kit" Reynolds, born 3 Nov. 1789 Fayette Co., Ky., died March 1873, Lynnville, Giles County, Tenn., married John M. Emerson (born 1768 Va., died 26 Nov. 1854) on 25 Nov. 1806 at Scott Co., Ky. (John H. Emerson was War of 1812 soldier, see his entry.)
3. Elizabeth "Betsy" Reynolds, born about 1793 Woodford or Scott County, Ky., married James Allen, Jr., on 12 March 1812 in Maury County, Tenn.
4. Amos Reynolds, born about 1795 in Scott Co., Ky., married Cordelia Miller on 15 April 1821 in Maury County, Tenn.
5. Sarah "Sallie" Reynolds, born about 1798 in Scott Co., Ky., died before March 1876 in Maury, married 22 Jan. 1824 in Maury to Hugh Griffin, born 1790, died 1873, also in War of 1812. (Refer to his entry)
6. Son, born about 1799 (twin?)
7. Son, born about 1799 (twin?)
8. Thomas C. Reynolds, born about 1801 in Scott Co., Ky., died 1834-40 in Maury County, married Lucy L. Williford on 1 March 1826, daughter of Prof. William L. Williford, early Maury County educator.
9. James Reynolds, born about 1803 in Scott Co., Ky., died 1879 in Giles County, Tenn., married Elizabeth E. Jackson, born 1811, died 186 5, daughter of Isham Jackson, on 2 July 1828 in Maury County.
10. Lidia Reynolds, born about 1807 in Tennessee, married Noah Herald on 16 Sept. 1826 in Maury County, living 1850 in Monroe County, Tenn.
11. Rachel Reynolds, born about 1809 in Tennessee, married 18 Sept. 1826 to Wiley E. Farrar.

Source: Information from files of Monte Hugh Knight, great-nephew of Benjamin Reynolds, based on his research of the Reynolds family.

JOHN REYNOLDS
Commissioned lieutenant in 27th Regiment in 1809. No further information.

WILLIAM REYNOLDS
Served in Capt. James McMahan's company. No further information.

ISAAC RHODES
Served as private in Capt. William Dooley's company. No further information.

THOMAS RHODES
Served in Capt. John Gordon's company. Married 29 July 1819 to Elizabeth Hardin
in Maury County. Still in the county and found on 1824 tax list.

JAMES RICE
Commissioned ensign in 27th Regiment 1814; served in Capt. Benjamin Reynolds'
company. No further information.

JOEL RICE
Served as private in Capt. William Dooley's company. Son of Ebenezer Rice (born
about 1756 in Vermont, died June 1831 in Maury County, Rev. War soldier). Ebenezer
Rice's will is recorded in Will Book E-1, page 384, and his wife is given as
Henrietta (impossible to determine if she was mother of Joel or not). Joel Rice
married 18 Nov. 1819 in Maury County to Mary Brown. He is found on the 1850
Census of White County, Illinois, age 51 or 57, born in Vermont. His wife was
Mariah, age 36, born in Indiana. The following were listed in his household and
presumably were his children:
1. Able Rice, age 23.
2. Nancy J. Rice, age 14.
3. Toliver Rice, age 12.
4. Louisa Rice, age 9.
5. Charles Rice, age 6.
6. Mary A. Rice, age 3.
7. Mariah J. Rice, age 2.
8. (Sarah A. Miller age 14 was living in household. All children in household
   were born in Illinois.)

Brothers and sisters of Joel Rice (from father's will):
1. Ebenezer Rice, Jr., married Catsy Baldridge, daughter of Capt. John Baldridge.
2. Sally Rice married _____Mayson.
3. Abel Rice.
4. Patsy Rice married Allen Moore.
5. Rowland Rice, died 1815, married Fereby _____, and had daughter Sally and son
   Ebenezer Rice.

[Davidson County, Tenn., Wills and Inventories, Vol. 2, page 5, July 1794—Joel
Rice of Davidson County gives power of attorney to trusty brother Elisha Rice to
sell property he is entitled to as heir of John Rice, late of Nashville.]

[Davidson County, Tenn., Superior Court Minutes, 1803-1806: page 191; Elisha,
Nathan, William H. and Joel Rice, heirs of John Rice, mentions land granted jointly
to John and Harrioll Rice.]

+ROWLAND RICE
Served as private in Capt. Newlin's company; died 1815. He is buried near Fort
Williams, Alabama, about 15 miles southwest of Childersburg, Alabama. His estate w.
settled in Maury County, and court minutes for Nov. 1815 show Pherila Rice as his
widow. Will for his father establishes his children. Wife's name is also found as
Fereby.

Children of Rowland Rice:
1. Sally Rice.
2. Ebenezer Rice.

Source: Research from files of Virginia W. Alexander and Marise P. Lightfoot;
Will Book E-1, page 384; burials at Fort Williams, Alabama; miscellaneous court
minutes. [Able Rice, private in Capt. Newlin's company, is also buried at Fort
Williams. We had no way to determine if this were the Abel Rice mentioned in the
will of Ebenezer Rice or not.]

NICHOLAS RICE
Served in Capt. Bird S. Hurt's company. He owned land on Fountain Creek in 1827.
(Deed Book M-1, page 501), died June 1856 aged about 78, born in Virginia. His
wife Jane Rice died Jan. 1858 aged about 74, born in Georgia. They are buried in the
Rice Cemetery south of Sampbell's Station in Maury County.

SOLOMON RICE
Served in Capt. William Dooley's company. No further information.

NATHANIEL RICHARD
Served in Capt. John Looney's company. No further information.

ALLEN RICHARDSON
Served in Capt. Samuel Ashmore's company. Born 22 Feb. 1797, died 11 Nov. 1865;
enlisted 28 Jan. 1814 as corporal. Married Elizabeth R. Boaz 15 March 1835, daugh-
ter of William Boaz of Pittsylvania Co., Va. He was first married to Rebecca Bailey
He is buried in New Ramey Cemetery near Culleoka, Tenn. He was born in Wilkes Co.,
Ga., son of Thomas Richardson.

Source: Information from Marise P. Lightfoot and Barry Brown.

AMOS RICHARDSON
Enlisted 21 Dec. 1812 as private in Capt. John Kennedy's company; also served in
Capt. Benjamin Reynolds company. He married Polly Richardson, daughter of William
Richardson.

WILEY P. RICHARDSON
Born about 1791 in Georgia, son of John and Sintha Richardson of Stiversville. He
served in War of 1812 under Col. William Pillow His father's will was executed
25 Feb. 1839. Married 18 Dec. 1816 to Nancy P. Crofton.

Brothers and sisters of Wiley P. Richardson:
1. Sterling R. Richardson.
2. Carrol Richardson, born 1810-20, moved to Texas after 1840.
3. John W. Richardson, born 1 Nov. 1817, died 5 Feb. 1888, married (1) 9 Dec. 1841
   Lucy Vincent; (2) 14 Oct. 1869 to Mrs. Nancy Sellars Pewett.
4. Thomas H. B. Richardson.
5. Robert Richardson.
6. Polly Richardson married before 1830 to _____ Croffort.
7. Anna Richardson married Henry B. Cannon 6 April 1823.
8. Lucinda Richardson married Rollin Hester 11 Dec. 1828.
9. Huldah Richardson married 18 Dec. 1828 to Edward Covey.
10. Winney Richardson married 24 June 1829 to William O. Fleming.

Source: Information from files of Marise P. Lightfoot.

WILLIAM RICHARDSON
Served in Capt. Benjamin Reynolds company. No further information. [Marise P.
Lightfoot reported that the only William Richardson in her files who was old enough
to have served was William Richardson, brother of "old" Thomas and John. This
William was born before 1775 according to 1820 census and his oldest child was
born about 1800. This William Richardson died before 19 June 1827 leaving widow
Keziah, who esecuted her will 24 Oct. 1848. Their children are the ones given
following.]

Children of William and Keziah Richardson:
1. James M., born 1804-1810, oldest son, married Lucy_____ before 1830. he died
   before 30 June 1848. (continued on next page)

Children of William Richardson, continued:
2. Polly Richardson, born 1794-1800, married before 1820 Amos Richardson, above.
3. William W. Richardson, second son, born 1808 in Georgia, living in 1860 with his widowed sister in law Lucy Richardson.
4. John M. Richardson, third son, born about 1810, married 24 Jan. 1832 to Emily J. Scott.
5. Thomas T. Richardson, fourth and youngest son, born 1812-15, married (1) Cinthia Hewett, 19 Oct. 1831; (2) Parthenia Pullen, first coursin, daughter of Elisha and Anna Pullen.

Source: Information from the files and research of Marise P. Lightfoot.

WILLIS RICHARDSON
Served in Capt. Samuel Ashmore's company; served in Capt. Benjamin Reynolds company; son of Thomas Richardson of Wilkes Co., Ga., who died in Stiversville in 1815 and his wife Jane Willis. He married Peggy P. Pickens.

Brothers and sisters of Willis Richardson:
1. Amos Richardson.
2. Allen Richardson married Rebecca Bailey and Elizabeth Boaz.
3. Thomas Richardson, born circa 1794-1804, died before 11 Oct. 1831.
4. Jane (Jinny) Richardson married Matthew G. Pickens, moved to Wayne Co., Tenn.
5. Hulda Richardson married Permenas Howard.
6. Frances Richardson married Constantine Davis and moved to Giles County.
7. Lovey Richardson married Solomon Davis.
8. Lucretia (Cresy) Richardson married Howard Cannon.
9. Anna Richardson born 7 March 1790 died 29 April 1843, married Elisha Pullen.

Source: Will of Thomas Richardson, Will Book B-1, page 16, dated 18 May 1815; information from files of Marise P. Lightfoot and Barry Brown.

MATTHIAS RICHESON
Commissioned lieutenant in 51s Regiment in 1814. No further information.

CAPTAIN WILLIAM RICHMAN
Patrolee in Capt. James Byres' company Sept. 1808. His name will be found on 1811 tax list; lived in neighborhood of the Double Branches and Sanford Road. No further information.

(UNKNOWN) RICKETTS
Mary Ricketts, widow of War of 1812 soldier, drew pension in Columbia in 1883. [1850 Census for Lewis County shows William Ricketts, age 58, born N. C., with wife Mary, age 43, born in N. C. Members of the household, presumably their children, were Sarah E., age 26; Elizabeth A., age 20; Andrew M., age 12; and Thomas M., age 10.]

JOHN RIDGEWAY
Served in Capt. John Gordon's company. No further information.

JONATHAN RIDGEWAY
Served in Capt. John Gordon's company. No further information.

VINCENT RIDLEY
Served as sergeant and lieutenant in Capt. Benjamin Reynolds company; served in Samuel B. McKnight's company as first lieutenant; discharged 11 Dec. 1813. He was son of George Ridley (born 1737, died 1835 in Nashville, Revolutionary War soldier) and his wife Sally Vincent (born 1754, died 1836. He married 28 Dec. 1799 in Davidson County to Lydia Everett, age 71 on 1850 census of Maury County. He was born 26 June 1778, died 19 Nov. 1852. (continued on next page)

Children of Vincent Ridley:
1. George M. Ridley, born 24 Oct. 1800.
2. Betsy Ridley, born 15 Sept. 1802.
3. Thomas Ridley, born 15 Sept. 1804.
4. John T. Ridley, born 22 June 1806.
5. Winefred Ridley, born 6 March 1808.
6. Rufus Ridley, born 3 March 1811.
7. Sarah Hay Ridley, born 1816.
8. [Young Ridley, age 20, son of Vincent Ridley, died in Kentucky. Columbia Observer, 17 Sept. 1840. Name not given in Bible.]

Source: 1850 census of Maury County; Ridley Bible in Maury County Cousins No. 1, page 68; Edythe Rucker Whitley, Roster and Soldiers, The Tennessee Society of the Daughters of the American Revolution 1960-1970, Vol. 2, page 655.

Brothers and sisters of Vincent Ridley:
1. Beverly Ridley, born 23 July 1762, married Annie Sullivan and Elizabeth Gooch.
2. George Ridley, born 11 Jan. 1764.
3. John Ridley, born 5 June 1765 married a German lady.
4. William Ridley, born 2 Feb. 1767; all his family killed by Indians.
5. Patsy Ridley, born 13 March 1770 married James Wright.
6. Betsy Ridley, born 13 Feb. 1772, married William Smith and _____ McNubb (?).
7. Sally Ridley, born 28 Nov. 1773, married Maj. John Buchanan.
8. Lettie Ridley, born 24 Jan. 1776, married James Roberts.
9. Thomas Ridley, born 16 Feb. 1780, married Margaret Harwood.
10. Moses Ridley, born 6 June 1782 married Kate Howard.
11. James Ridley, born 24 May 1784, married Amy Hampton.
12. Abigail Ridley, born 26 Apr. 1786 married Dr. Charles Mulcherin.
13. Winfred, born 7 Feb. 1789, married Thomas Garrett.
14. Samuel Jones Ridley, born 1 Oct. 1791, married Sally Hay.
15. Henry Ridley, born 29 May 1794, married Elizabeth Allison.

Source: Edythe Rucker Whitley, Roster and Soldiers, The Tennessee Society of the Daughters of the American Revolution 1960-1970, Vol. 2, page 655.

ANDREW RILEY
Commissioned captain in 27th Regiment in 1808; appointed constable Dec. 1808 in Maury County. No further information.

DANIEL ROANE
Service not determined. Nashville Union and American, 19 April 1873: Daniel Roane, War of 1812 soldier, died in Maury County on the 10th instant. He was from Orange County, N. C.

Children of Daniel Roane:
1. William Roane married Permelia Chandler.
2. No information on others.

Source: Moore Questionnaire of E. S. Roan. (Name spelled both ways.)

ISAAC ROBERTS
Often called "The Father of Maury County".
Born 1 March 1764, died 19 Feb. 1816 in Maury County. (Birthplace given as Pennsylvania.) Quoting from the American Historical Magazine:

"Largely owing to his death so early in the State's history and to his opposition to what Goldwin Smith calls 'the tyrannous egotism of Andrew Jackson', scant justice has been done the memory of this pioneer. His grave is at his old settlement, three miles north by east from Columbia, Tenn., on the Nashville pike.

Isaac Roberts, continued:

"Some of his old commissions and letters are now in the possession of his grand-daughter Mrs. Joseph H. Fussell of Columbia, Tenn. The oldest I have seen is dated 14 Nov.1789, from Gov. Johnston of North Carolina and appoints Isaac Roberts, Esquir to be "First Major of the Davidson Regiment of militia.""

"The next commission is dated 15 Dec. 1790 by Governor Blount, the territorial governor, and appoints him "First Major of the Regiment of Militia of Davidson County.""

"This appointment also appears from page 231, this magazine for 1897, July, Governor Blount's Journal there published. On June 10, 1791, he was appointed by Governor Blount "Lieutenant Colonel of Davidson County in the place of Elijah Robertson promoted.""

"The next commission is Oct. 27, 1792, to be a Lt. Col. Commandant of said Regiment. On Oct. 4, 1796, this appointment was confirmed for the new State by Gov. John Sevier's commission appointing him to the same rank. On Sept. 20, 1804, Governor Sevier commissioned him Brigadier General of the Fifth Brigade of Tennessee. So he had held important military trusts under N. C., the Territory, and the State. His differences with Jackson in the Creek campaigns, his siding with the troops in their construction of the terms of their service, his court-martial—all are parts of the history of the Creek War."

Isaac Roberts was the first chairman of the Maury County Quarterly Court and lived on a tract of land which lies east of the Nashville Pike and his land extended from the mouth of Bear Creek to the Double Branches. His home, near the Double Branch Road, burned 2 Dec. 1950.

He married Mary Johnston, born 17 May 1772, died 15 March 1844, died 15 March 1844.

Children of Isaac Roberts:
1. Elijah Roberts, born 15 Nov. 1790, died 2 Feb. 1816.
2. Polly Roberts, (Mary Jane), born 5 Aug. 1794, died 25 Aug. 1818, married Peter Imloy Voorhies.
3. Nancy Roberts married Samuel Hawkins.
4. Rachel Roberts, born 11 Feb. 1805, died 6 April 1859, married Hugh B. Porter.
5. Persia Roberts.
6. Patsey Roberts.
7. Mark Roberts.
8. John Roberts.
9. Moses Roberts.
10. William Roberts, born 28 Dec. 1810, died 1854, married Martha E. Smith 1837.

Letters pertaining to his court-martial were published in recent years in "Frank H. Smith's History of Maury County, Tennessee," by the Maury County Historical Society.

The following letter was copied by Marise P. Lightfoot from the Draper Manuscripts, Reel 6XX19 (microfilm):

Columbia, Tennessee
November 12, 1845

Mr. L. C. Draper

Sir: After my respects to you I will proceed to give you all the information that I have been able to obtain relative to my father General Isaac Roberts. I feat that I will not be able to give you all the information that you would like to have. My father was the son of Roger Roberts who was of English descent. My father was born in Mereland March 1st 1764 and when quite young his father emigrated to Pennsylvania (continued)

Isaac Roberts, continued:

near Red Stone Old Fort   My father when quite young took an active part in the
Indian War then going on. He remove to Tennessee Davidson County in the year 1786 or
7. I understand from Col. Brown that he was a member of the Legislature of Tennes-
see but do not know the date. He was among the first settlers in Davidson County.
He was maryed to Mary Johnson November 5, 1789   he was commissioned Major of the
Davidson County militia December 15, 1790   he was commissioned Major of the Davids
County militia December 15, 1790, then commissioned Lefttenant Col. the 25 Oct.1792
and Brigadier General September 20, 1804.

He had many hardships to endure while engaged in the army but I am unable to give
you any information relative to what was done in the army as I was quite young.
My mother died the 15th day of March 1844 of the epidemic that raged in this section
of country called the errispules or putrid sore throat.

My father located seventy five thousand acres of land in Carroll County in West
Tennessee in 1797 in the name of Mimicun Hunt of North Carolina for which he was
entitled to 25,000 acres as his location interest which was done in three weeks.

He remove in 1806 to Maury County near Columbia and settled on a tract of land that
was given to my mother by her uncle James Robertson where he lived until his death
which was the 19th day of February, 1816. He was among the first settlers in Maury
when the cane grew very thick, was one of the commissioners that laid off the town
of Columbia and participated in all the Indian troubles of his day, died of the
epidemic called cold plague.

He was not a professor of religion but allways bore the name of a good citizen a
kind neibor a good husband a kind parent and indulgent master, a brave high minded
man that never shrunk from any responsibility when his country called for his
services but was always foremost in time of danger, served his country many times
in driving the Indians from our frontier.

He was the father of 12 children, 8 of whom are now living and I am the youngest
son. My oldest brother Mark R. Roberts lives in Texas on Red River I think in
Miller County. If you could get a letter to him he could give you more information
than I can as he was with my father in the Creek War. I will write to him and request him to write to you. I have examined all the old papers that I can find and
find none that _____ be of service to you.

Abner Pillow of Summer County in this state was aid to my father if you will write
to him he will give you some information relative to the part my father took in
the Creek War. I send you a letter that is written by Col. Brown that will give
you some information.

My father was an energetic man and laid up sufficient of this worlds goods for
his ofspring to live independent on but unfortunately they have not taken care of
it. I should be glad to hear from you frequently how you are getting along with
your work.

                    Respectfully yours William T. Roberts.

Nathan Vaught, "Youth and Old Age", pages 62, 63: "Genl. Isaac Roberts (came) in
1807. On the north side of the River. A Farmer, 2½ miles northeast from Town.
Had five sons, to wit, Elish, Mark R., John, Fisk, and William; had three
daughters, Mrs. Peter I. Voorhies, Mrs. Hugh B. Porter, Mrs. John or Jack Porter.

According to legend, General Roberts was buried in his uniform and with his sword.
His grave and cemetery has been vandalized in recent years.

MARK ROBERTS
Served under his father Gen. Isaac Roberts during Creek War; later lived in Texas.
No further information. (Those interested in line might refer to Maury County Deed
Book H-1, page 419, which gives the heirs of Isaac Roberts.)

(UNKNOWN) ROBINSON
Mary Robinson, widow of War of 1812 soldier, drew pension in 1883 in Spring Hill.
No further information.

CAPTAIN CHARLES ROBINSON
Service not determined, but said to be soldier, however according to 1850 census he
was born 1802. He married Edna Bissell. They are buried in unmarked graves on the
Emory Harmon farm on Kincaid Road—the site of the two graves is known.

Children of Charles Robinson:
1. Margaret Robinson married Alec Harmon.
2. William Robinson married 1847 to Lucy Ann Chumley; she married 2nd in 1858 to
   Jeremiah Tucker.
3. No information on other children.

Source: Information from Mrs. Floyd Mills, descendent, and from Century Review of
Maury County, page 284.

WILLIAM RODGERS
Served in Capt. James McMahan's company. No further information.

WILLIAM RODGERS
Commissioned captain in 51st Regiment in 1814. No further information. [There is
a divorce action dated Dec. 1820 for a William Rogers versus Nancy Rogers. Jacob
Rogers was his security and John Mills was his witness.] [William Rodgers marriage
bond to marry Nancy Caldwell, 23 Jan. 1817, with James Mills bondsman.]

SAMUEL ROGERS
Commissioned lieutenant of infantry comapny, 27th Regiment 1814; served in Captain
Benjamin Reynolds company. [A Samuel J. Rogers and wife Sarah are mentioned in
a division of estate of George Davidson early in Maury County.]

SOLOMON ROGERS
Served in Captain Benjamin Reynolds company. No further information.

DAVID ROGERS
Served in Capt. Bird S. Hurt's company. No further information.

JACOB ROOKS
Enlisted 20 Sept. 1814 as private in Capt. James Kincaid's company, Col. A. Loury.
On 1820 census his age is given as between 26 and 45, with his wife between 16-26.
Marriage bond issues 24 Nov. 1810 to marry Elizabeth Asque with William Asque as
bondsman. He recorded his stock mark April 1825 in Maury County. A ford on Duck
River was known as Jacob Rooks upper ford and Hanna's Mill was built here—the court
had to order Rooks to permit him to let it be built. Names of his children not
known.

Frank H. Smith wrote of him (page 65): "Jacob Rooks lived up river about 12 miles,
above Sowell's upper mill. Soldier of War of 1812? Soldier in Seminole War? Good
education, great reader, especially of history, and biography, very polite. Indian-
like features. Was married when he settled in Maury. Man of remarkably fine sense

"After death of wife, Jacob withdrew from society and very rarely left home. When
he did, with a rifle. Then made his own clothes, weaving the cloth, cooked, washed,
churned &c. Jacob had one son. Son married and raised family. Son sent his boy '

Jacob Rooks, continued:

live with Jacob. Boy never left without permission and much devoted to grandfather. One afternoon boy asked to visit his father. Wooden lock (homemade) on door. Boy hid key outside. Found it next morning, undisturbed. Entering room, found Jacob had died during night. Jacob lying dressed, stretched full length, arms folded, ready for coffin. No suspicion of violence. Jacob man of powerful will—supposed to have much gold and silver hid in cedars, never found. Jacob's son was an axe-handle maker, gunsmith, and general mechanic..."

Blind item in Columbia Herald, 29 April 1870: "Several years ago one of the strangest human creatures we have ever heard of lived in the vicinity of the old Hammer Mill (now owned by the hospitable and excellent Col. Sowell). His name is that of a tribe of birds, cousins to the crows, and very inappropriately named, because the birds in question always go in immense droves and the old gentleman was so misanthropic he lived alone and died alone. His little grandson went to see him as usual, one cold winter day, and found him stark and cold in death. The old man was very unfortunately constituted and none of his children could live with him. He would sometimes take his rifle and start off through the woods, and be gone months, and years. Not a word would his family hear of him until some day he would quietly and unexpectedly return, with a little concern as if he had only been gone on a day's hunt. Not a word as to his travels would ever escape his lips."

JAMES ROSS
Served in Capt. Robert Campbell's company. Marriage bond dated 13 July 1814 to marry Nancy Pritchett. No further information.

(UNKNOWN) ROUNDTREE
Mary Roundtree, widow, drew pension in 1883 in Columbia. No further information.

WILEY ROY
Born Caroline Co., Virginia, 12 Oct. 1787, died in Maury County 27 August 1870 at the home of Col. W. M. Voorhies. "Came to Tennessee in 1808; volunteer in the Creek War in 1814; at Battle of Horseshoe Bend; Methodist."

Source: Columbia Herald, 2 Sept. 1870.

(UNKNOWN) RUCKER
Maria Rucker, widow of War of 1812 soldier, drew pension in Columbia in 1883.

JAMES RUDD
Served in Capt. John Looney's company. No further information.

CAPTAIN RUSH
Rush was captain of a militia company in Maury County in 1807. No further information.

ALBERT RUSSELL
Lt. Colonel in volunteer militia in 1793; member of House of Delegates 1789-1793; also served in the American Revolution; born 1755 in Pennsylvania; died 1818 in Huntsville, Albama; married Anne Frances Hooe. Lived at Spring Hill in Maury County and his home was known as Anne's Bower and was located where the Tennessee Orphans Home is today.

Children of Albert Russell:
1. Susan Catherine Russell married Dr. Alexander Erskine.

Source: 1812 Ancestor Index, National Society, United States Daughters of 1812, page 440.

ARNOLD RUSSELL
Served in Capt. John Gordon's company. No further information. [One researcher believed this might be the same Arnold Russell, War of 1812 soldier, who moved to Yazoo County, Miss. He was born 3 April 1796 in Davidson County, Tenn., and was the son of James Russell, Revolutionary War soldier. No information on this man.]

DAVID RUSSELL
Served as private in Capt. William Dooley's company. No further information.

DAVID RUSSELL.
Commissioned major in 27th Regiment in 1811. No further information.

JAMES RUSSELL
Served in Capt. John Gordon's company. No further information.

WILLIAM RUST
Was in the Battle of New Orleans according to family history. Born 1792 in Granville County, N. C., died in Randolph, Illinois. Came to Maury County about 1811, married 3 Jan. 1811 Nancy McGeehee. He was the son of Matthew Rust (died 1808-1809 in Granville Co., N. C., who married 2 July 1791 in Granville County to Pricilla Mills. Matthew Rust was the son of John Rust and his wife Sarah (Sally) Daniels.

Children of William Rust:
1. James Wesley Rust, born 1813.
2. John Rust, born 1816.
3. George Rust, born 1817.
4. William Rust, born 1821.
5. Harvey Rust, born 1823.
6. Mary Rust, born 1825.
7. Ruth (?) Rust, born 1827.

Brothers and sisters of William Rust:
1. James Rust, born 1804 in Granville Co., N. C., married Lucy_____.
2. John S. Rust, born 1801 or 1805 in Granville Co., N. C., married Nancy Cook; he is buried in Gibson County, Tenn.
3. Charnock Rust, born 1798 in Granville Co., N. C., married Avarilla Stone on 15 March 1820, died 1832, buried in Lindsey Cemetery, Maury County, Tenn.
4. Mary C. Rust (Polly), born 1796 in Granville Co., N. C., married ____ Raycroft.
5. Boswell Rust, born 1806, Granville Co., N. C., married Lucy Rust, widow of brother James Rust.

Source: Family information belonging to Mrs. Reuben Algood, Columbia, Tenn.

WILLIAM RUST
Served in Captain Bird S. Hurt's company. This is believed to be the service record for the previous entry.

JAMES RUTLEDGE
Commissioned captain 27th Regiment in 1808; appointed patrolee for Columbia in Sept. 1808. No further information. [Marriage bond dated 16 Jan. 1811 to marry Nancy Armstrong.]

SAMUEL J. RUTLEDGE
Served in Capt. Benjamin Reynolds company. Born about 1785 in N. C., married Bethia R. Carter 26 Dec. 1823 in Maury County; left will in Maury County in 1855.

Children of Samuel J. Rutledge:
1. William R. (or K.) Rutledge, born 1824.
2. Orphia J. Rutledge, born 1825, married John W. Mitchell and lived in Wayne Co.
continued on next page

Children of Samuel J. Rutledge, continued:
3. John C. Rutledge, born 1829, married Malissy and Elizabeth Lynn. (?)
4. Martha R. Rutledge, born 1831, married E. Roberts.
5. Robert Gideon Rutledge, born 1834, married Sarah Angeline Keaton.
6. Matilda Rutledge, born 1838.
7. Mary Rutledge, born 1841.
8. Amaline C. Rutledge, born 1843.

Source: Information from Mrs. Charles C. Alexander, Columbia, and Mrs. C. E. Waterhouse, El Paso, Texas.

SAMUEL RUTLEDGE
Served as private in Capt. William Dooley's company. No further information.

WILLIAM RUTLEDGE
Commissioned captain of 27th Regiment in 1811. No further information.

WILLIAM RUTLEDGE
Served as private in Capt. William Dooley's company. No further information.
[Marriage bond to Sarah Sims, dated 10 Dec. 1809] [Marriage bond to Margaret C. Reid dated 21 Dec. 1814] [Marriage license issued to Martha W. Moody, 23 Dec. 1820.]

+DAVID SANDERS
Service not determined. "Died at N. Orleans under Maj. Genl. Carrol Division in the Service of the United States against the Tories of Great Britain." Entry found in Rock Creek Baptist Church Minutes, March 1815.

JAMES TURNER SANFORD
Qualified as justice of the peace of Maury County Sept. 1809, served as county court chairman for several years; born 1770, died 13 Dec. 1830, buried in Jackson College Cemetery; always called Colonel Sanford; married Winneford Speight Turner, born 17 April 1775, died 16 Dec. 1844. Maury County Minute Book 9, page 116, July 1825 mentions Captain Sanford's company, Ephraim Erwin being constable of company.

Children of James T. Sanford:
1. Robert J. Sanford, married 22 May 1823 to Eliza J. Yancy and 4 March 1850 to Mariah W. Yancy, moved to Mississippi.
2. Karen Hackett (one source) or Happuch (another source) Sanford, born 1809, died 20 June 1832, buried Jackson College Cemetery, married Dr. G. T. Greenfield
3. Winnefred Sanford, born 1 June 1812, died 11 April 1831, Jackson College Cemetery, married James T. Holland on 7 June 1827.
4. Susan E. Sanford married _____ Riley (or Reilly).
5. Mary Brown Sanford, born 7 March 1807, died 22 Feb. 1851, married 11 Nov. 1834 to Absolum Thompson.
6. William A. Sanford, born 19 March 1817, died 15 July 1855, buried Rose Hill, married 20 June 1895 to Eliza A. Garland.
7. Ann Sanford, died 29 Aug. 1832 in Madison County, Alabama, at 19, married 30 June 1831 to Dr. William H. Glasscock.
8. Sarah Sanford, died young.
9. Betsy Sanford, died young.
10. [George W. Sanford sometimes given as a child. Circuit court minutes say James T. Sanford had seven children; so this one must have died in infancy.]

Source: Circuit Court Minutes 1844-1846, page 230; tombstone inscriptions from "They Passed This Way"; family information from Mrs. Robert Ikard, Columbia, Tenn., descendant. This family is mentioned frequently in James Norman Smith's Memoirs, which are on file in the Maury County Public Library.

DEMPSEY SARGENT

Service not determined; Charlotte Sargent of Williamsport drew pension as widow of War of 1812 soldier in 1883. He was born about 1792 in N. C., died around 1863 in Maury County; son of James Sargent (born about 1765, died about 1845 in Maury) and his wife Rachel Phelps of Caswell County, N. C. (married 4 August 1791). The family came from North Carolina to Maury County before 1840. Dempsey Sargent married (1) 1815 in Caswell County, N. C., to Miss A. M. Burton; (2) Miss Charlotte Cook, born 1811.

Children of Dempsey Sargent by first marriage:

1. Jesse Frank Sargent, born 12 Nov. 1818 in N. C., died 20 Jan. 1892, never married; Confederate soldier.
2. John M. Sargent, born 1820, died 1907, never married; buried Mt. Nebo in Maury County; went to Holmes County, Miss., and was wholesale merchant in Lexington, Miss.
3. Thomas Sargent, never married, buried Mt. Nebo in Maury County; lived in Holmes County, Miss. at time father's estate was settled.
4. Lucy Ann Sargent, born 1826 in N. C., married 19 Dec. 1843 in Maury County to James Brinn.
5. Samuel D. Sargent, born about 1828; it is believed he never married. Family history marked him as "wanderer".
6. Elizabeth (Beth) Sargent, born 1829 in Tennessee, married Edward B. McKennon.
7. Dicie Sargent, born 14 Jan. 1816 in N. C., married 30 April 1840 in Maury County to Grief E. Pipkin, born 10 June 1819. She is buried at Mt. Nebo.

Children of Dempsey Sargent by second marriage:

1. Susan Sargent, born 1837, married James Allen of Perry County, Tenn.
2. James William Sargent, born 1839, died 1922, married Sally Nichols, born 1852, died 1925.
3. Robert Wilson Sargent, born 10 Jan. 1840, died 10 April 1906, married Laura Nichols, sister of Sally Nichols above.
4. Trizzie (or Triza) Sargent, born 1842, married Solomon Crafton.
5. Francis Marion Sargent, born 1844, died 1920; never married.
6. Virginia Sargent, born 1846, married Lee Johnson.

Source: Heirs and distributees of Dempsey Sargent in chancery court records; "Major Sargents and their Minors" by Agnes Sargent Harpole, pages 8-13; interview on 10 Nov. 1968 with Mrs. Willie S. McBride, now deceased, by Jill K. Garrett and Virginia W. Alexander. She said: "My father was Robert Wilson Sargent, Southern soldier in the Civil War. My grandfather was Dempsey Sargent who died while father was away in Civil War, fought in War of 1812." At the time of the interview she was 92 years old. She died November 1970 at 93 according to her obituary.

DAVID SARVEN

Born 7 Dec. 1787, New Jersey; died 6 May 1880, buried in Rose Hill Cemetery; drew pension for his service. He is believed by descendants to have been the son of David Edward Sarven, who died 29 May 1849. He married 3 Sept. 1808 to Maria Straut, born 9 Oct. 1790, died 21 June 1873, buried in Rose Hill, Columbia. He came to Columbia in 1856.

Children of David Sarven:

1. James David Sarven, born 1 Nov. 1816, died 4 April 1900, married 27 Nov. 1844 to Abigail Davis Norton, died 4 Aug. 1899.
2. John Sarven, born 22 March 1819, died 5 Dec. 1863, married 4 Jan. 1847 to Sarah Elizabeth Norton, who died in 1899.

Source: Information furnished by descendant Mrs. Mary Lee Park, descendant of David Sarven.

AUGUSTUS B. SAUNDERS

Served in Capt. James McMahan's company. [Service also found for Capt. Archibald McKinney's company from Sept. 1813 to May 1814.] Born 1791 in N. C., died 25 Feb. 1842 in Jackson, Miss., had moved to Wilkinson Co., Miss., by 1821. Married after 1818 to Hannah Walker, born 6 March 1796 Rockingham Co., N. C., died around 1840 in Jackson, Miss. He was son of James Saunders (born 1769) and his first wife. Hannah was the daughter of Allen Walker of Hickman County, Tenn.

Children of Augustus B. Saunders:
1. Esther Caroline Saunders, born 8 July 1824 in Lawrence Co., Miss., died 19 Dec. 1881 in Wilkinson Co., Miss.; married 13 June 1844 as fourth wife John Whitaker.
2. No information on others if any.

Brothers and sisters of Augustus B. Saunders:
1. Winnefred Saunders.
2. Nancy Saunders.

Half-brothers and sisters by father's second marriage to Levisa Bowen:
1. Samuel A. Saunders.
2. John H. Saunders.
3. Will Bowen Saunders.
4. Tabitha Mary Saunders married (1)____Perdue (2) B. W. Harris.

Source: James E. Saunders, The Saunders Family in the U. S., 1890, pages 5, 6; and information from John H. Stockett, Baton Rouge, La.

BARTLETT SCOTT

Served in Capt. Nail's company, Hart's Battalion. Died 25 June 1876 at age 81 in Maury County.

Source: Columbia Herald and Mail, 21 July 1876.

JACOB SCOTT

Appointed justice of the peace in Maury County in 1812. No further information.

JAMES SCOTT

Appointed constable in Maury County in 1812. No further information.

JOSEPH SCOTT

Served in Capt. John Looney's company. No further information.

NATHANIEL SCOTT

Commissioned ensign in 46th Regiment in 1812. No further information.

ROBERT SCOTT

Commissioned captain in 27th Regiment in 1809. No further information.

BENNETT SEAGRAVES

Served as drummer in Capt. Ebenezer Kilpatrick's company. His age is given as between 26 and 45 on 1820 census of Maury. It is believed he might be son of Jacob and Alinar Seagraves—Jacob was soldier in American Revolution. On 1820 census the following all live in Snow Creek area of Maury County: Bennett, Isaac (26 to 45), William (26-45), and Jacob Seagraves (over 45). Century Review, page 237, says that the Seagraves family came early from North Carolina.

THOMAS SEAGRAVES

Service not established. Estate being settled in 1815 with Sarah Seagraves as the administratrix. Feb. 1816 his orphan children were Harvey Seagraves, Jefferson Seagraves and Alfred Seagraves. John Lindsey and Jesse Evans appointed to look out for their home.

VINCENT SEAGRAVES
Maury County Deed Book B-1, page 158, Vincent Segraves of Maury gives power of attorney to Horatio Depriest of Maury to convey and deed 160 acres in Missouri Territory this "being my bounty land". Land was given by U. S. "for enlistment as soldier during late war". Vincent Seagraves married Dosha, heir of George W. Martin, deceased.

Source: Maury County, Tennessee, Deed Abstracts, Vol. 1, Books A, B, and C, by Virginia W. Alexander and Rose H. Priest, pages 42, 43.

ROWELL SEATON
Service not determined. Married 15 July 1815 to Martha Yeates. Maury County Will Book A-1, page 157, Rowell Seaton petitions court Aug. 1815, mentions that he and his wife Martha, formerly Martha Yeates married Daniel Yeates, who died 1 Feb. 1815.

RYAN SEATON
War of 1812 soldier, was at New Orleans. Born N. C., lived in both Maury and Giles counties; married in N. C., to a Miss Stinson.

Children of Ryan Seaton:
1. John Green Seaton, second child, born 15 May 1840 in Maury County.
2. Four other children, no further information.

Souce: Hale and Merritt, Tennessee and Tennesseans, page 1385.

LEROY SECREST
Commissioned ensign in 46th Regiment in 1813; commissioned lieutenant in 46th Regiment in 1814. No further information.

JAMES SELLARS
Appointed justice of the peace in 1810. No further information.

JOHN SELLERS
Served in Capt. Samuel Ashmore's company. His will (unrecorded in books) shows that he died 18 Feb. 1824 and he names sons John and Ebenezer; the executors were to be wife Elizabeth and William Hart. Witnesses to will were James Cathey, James Isom, and Andrew Blair.

IARD SELLARS
Commissioned captain 1808 in 27th Regiment. Deed Book N-1, page 290, on 23 Dec. 1809, Lard Sellers sold to Thomas Hudspeth the slaves Harry and Rachel for $400. Witnesses were Sam Watkins and James Hudspeth.

ROBERT SELLERS
Justice of the peace in 1810 and 1811. No further information. [One Robert Seller who was in the county early married Sallie_____, and they had son Luke Sellers.]

THOMAS SESSON
Served in Capt. Robert Campbell's company. No further information. [Name appears to be Summers on the payroll of this company.]

WILLIAM SESSON
Served in Capt. Robert Campbell's company. In 1811 he had land on Wally's Creek, a branch of Rutherford Creek. Henry Sessions or Cisson was early settler in this area and on 12 June 1810 there was a petition about a road called Sandford Road, which was in area of Double Branches and Wallice's Creek, and those who signed included: Henry, Thomas, William, John, James, and Eldridge Sessions. No further information.

GEORGE SEWELL
Served in Capt. Andrew McCarty's company. No further information.

JOHN SHARP
Served in Capt. John Looney's company. No further information.

NEHEMIAH SHARP
Served in Capt. Bird S. Hurt's company. Born about 1784 in Pennsylvania; married 15 Sept. 1807 in Williamson County to Milly Clayton, her age given as 63 on 1850 census. He was son of John Sharp who settled between 1800-1810 on Big Swan Creek in what is now Lewis County.

Children of Nehemiah Sharp.
1. Levi Sharp, born about 1826.
2. No information on the others.

Brothers and sisters of Nehemiah Sharp:
1. William Sharp, age given as over 45 in 1820.
2. Edward Sharp.
3. Samuel Sharp.
5. Joshua Sharp.

Source: 1850 Census of Lewis County; Williamson County marriages: Goodsped's History of Lewis County, Tenn., page 802.

GEORGE M. SHAW
Served in Capt. Samuel B. McKnight's company. [Middle initial in question.] No further information.

JAMES SHAW
Served in Capt. James McMahan's company. No further information. [James Shaw was a War of 1812 soldier in Marshall County; marriage bond dated 12 March 1823 in Maury to marry Betsy Shaw. See Hale and Merritt, Tennessee and Tennesseans, Vol. III, page 807.]

SAMUEL SHAW
Commissioned lieutenant in 51st Regiment 1814. Made a verbal will in Maury County 10 July 1818; witnesses to his will were Hugh Shaw and Levi Shaw; executors were David Craig, William Shaw and Hugh Shaw. He married Jane (Jeany) Gordon 7 July 1803 in Orange County, N. C.

Children of Samuel Shaw:
1. Nancy Shaw.
2. Will of Jane Shaw mentions "my children".
3. James and William Shaw were possibly the other children as Jesse M. Gordon made report as guardian of the minor heirs of Samuel Shaw, deceased, James and William Shaw. Later a report was made by David Craig, acting executor of Samuel Shaw, Jr., deceased of the estate of John Shaw, minor heir of said Shaw, deceased, "for use and repair done to a Deaburn wagon to convey said John Shaw to Danville, Ky., and home."

Source: Maury County, Tennessee, Wills and Settlements, 1807-1824, compiled by Jill K. Garrett and Marise P. Lightfoot, pages 46, 72, 81, 82.

JOHN H. SHELBY
His will is recorded in Maury County Will Book B-1, page 25, in form of a letter, which follows on next page.

John H. Shelby, continued: Clarkesville
                                                    .24 Nov. 1814

Dear Mother. I have a few words to say to you respecting the situation I am now in
and will be in when I get home. I am at this time well clothed but I shall take the
greater part of them with me. Mother, You know the wool I left in your possession.
I want you to have me two complete suits made, one a dark mixed, the other just like
the black patron farther has got and the westcoat like the white streaked patron if
now you know C. Farriss cannot weave like the patron get T. C. Farris to weave it___.
and I will pay him so send to my and it will be done complete.

I request you to pay yourself out of my wool for your work and for the cotton you
make use of. Some of my money that is in the hands of T. C. Farris to get indego
and cossess to the work of all the blue the cloth I got of Miss Campbell was black
wool and when it gets wet it stains my cloths as black as it is nearly.

Give my complements to sister Polly and tell her I make a present of that cow and
calf to John Wiley that is due me on Cathy's Creek as my part to help buy her a
house, but in the main time you give her my corn and tell her I shall want a complete
slive cotton of flax shirt.

A few words to farther.
Dear Farther. I am started to meet a vetern for where the cannons will soar and the
bullits come perhaps it may be my toll to fall in the defense of our liberty and I
say my wish respecting my land is that after Thomas P. Shelby gets his fifty acres
off my west fork land that I am due him then divide the rest of the tracts between
him and Isaac Shelby and my Duck river land I shall give to my nephew Wright.

A few words from Clarey. She wishes to be visited by her friends while we are ab-
sent and for the Lords sake tell George W. Shelby come and stay until we return he
can with the help of friends here get out little crop of 7 or 8 acres planted perhaps our friends has drew an idea that we draughted and are going off with reluctance
but you must give over that idea. We volunteered ourselves at first and second
sargents. We done this because we considered this tour more favourable than the
next and we have not repented what we have done but a cannon ball can take us as
easy as some that is in camps and crying to go and see their poor wives. We have
had one man made an example for deserting, he had to ride trukton twenty minutes.

Give my complements to Captain J. G. Smith and Capt. Greenfield and all the
neighbors particularly Capt. J. Michael.
                              Farewell
                                  John H. Shelby
Witnesses: Evin Shelby, William Shelby and Eli Shelby.

(The writer John H. Shelby was the son of Thomas Shelby.)

JOHN P. SHELBURNE
Served in Captain David Mason's militia cavalry company. Marriage bond dated
15 July 1814 Williamson County to marry Nancy Duncan. Lived briefly in Maury.

JOHN M. SHELL
Served in Capt. John Gordon's company. No further information.

(UNKNOWN) SHEPPARD
Martha N. Sheppard drew pension in 1883 in Mt. Pleasant as widow of War of 1812
soldier. No further information.

+BENJAMIN SHIPLEY
Commissioned ensign in light infantry company, 46th Regiment in 1813. Will Book B-1,
page 129, 19 Feb. 1815: "the service money of Benjamin Shipley for three months
continued on next page

Benjamin Shipley, continued:
tour against the Creek Indians as an insighn." Deed Book G-1, page 68: Benjamin
Shipley's land adjoined Davis Kilcrease's land on Rutherford Creek. Maury County
Court Minutes, 20 Feb. 1815, letters of administration were given to Jane Shipley
and Samuel Wasson. No further information.

+ANDREW SHOEMAKE
Served as private in Capt. Bird S. Hurt's company. Died 2 Jan. 1815.

+MICHAEL SHOLFER
Service not determined. "Died at N. Orleans under Maj. Genl. Carrol Division in the
Service of the United States against the Tories of Great Britain." Entry found in
Rock Creek Baptist Church Minutes, March 1815.

THOMAS SHORT
Served in Capt. John Gordon's company. No further information.

JOHN M. SHULL
Served in Capt. John Gordon's company. No further information. [Name also appears
to be Shell.]

ROBERT SIBLEY
Commissioned ensign in 27th Regiment in 1814 from Maury County. No further information.

FLEMMON R. SIMMONS
Commissioned ensign in 27th Regiment in 1809, lived in Bear Creek area of the
county. Marriage bond in Maury dated 31 March 1810 to marry Polly Kilchrist.

ABEL SIMPSON
Served in Capt. Robert Campbell's company. Simpson's Horse Mill was in the vicinity
of Rutherford Creek and was established quite early. Marriage bond dated 18 Dec.
1814 to marry Polly Gordon.

WILLIAM SIMPSON
Commissioned lieutenant in 27th Regiment in 1808; served also in Capt. John Looney's
company. No further information. [Marriage bond dated 29 July 1809 to marry
Elizabeth Stephenson.]

JOHN SIMS
Commissioned captain in 27th Regiment in 1812. No further information. [This man
is believed to be the son of Col. William Sims, Rev. War soldier, who settled early
in Mt. Pleasant area.]

HUGH SINCLAIR
Served in Capt. James McMahan's company. No further information.

JACOB SKIPPER
Served in Capt. Robert Campbell's company. No further information.

ANDREW SMITH
Served in Capt. Bird S. Hurt's company. No further information.

BENJAMIN SMITH
Appointed justice of the peace early in Maury County, resigned December 1809. [Two
men of this name in early Maury County. One lived in 1814 on the Natchez Trace
in the county. The other was the brother of James T. Smith and came about 1806 and
had land on Flat Creek. See the Memoirs of James Norman Smith for more detail on
this Smith family.]

JACOB SMITH
Served in Capt. Samuel Ashmore's company. No further information.

+JAMES HENRY SMITH
Killed at the Battle of New Orleans, one of the two men from Maury County killed there. Service not determined. Refer to James Moore entry.

JAMES NORMAN SMITH
In his memoirs he wrote that he volunteered for service in War of 1812 and was elected first lieutenant of a company of cavalry militia. Those to serve were chosen by lottery and he was not drawn. Born 1787, died 1875, son of James T. Smith and his first wife Constance Ford, who died July 1812. James T. Smith was a soldier in the American Revolution. He taught school about 1810 on Carter's Creek and had thirty students, among whom was James K. Polk. He married (1) Sarah "Sallie" Jenkins, daughter of Philip Jenkins, she died 1819; he married (2) 7 Feb. 1825 to Elizabeth H. Morehead.

Children of James Norman Smith:
1. Constance Ann Smith, born Nov. 1812, died 1813.
2. James Brown Smith, born 1816.
3. Jane Catherine Smith, born 1817, married 1837 Francis S. Latham.
4. Sarah Ann Smith, born 1 March 1826.
5. Mary Morehead Smith, born and died 1827.
6. Elizabeth Hungerford Smith, born 1 Aug. 1814, married William Calhoon.
7. No information on others, if any.

Brothers and sisters of James Norman Smith:
1. Annie Ford Smith, born 1 August 1785.
2. Richard Smith, born 24 Sept. 1787, died in Salisbury, N. C., before family came to Tennessee.
3. Charles A. Smith, born 14 Sept. 1789, twin to James Norman Smith, married Elizabeth Lanier of Warren County, Ky. and Mrs. Mary T. Morehead.
4. Elizabeth Ford Smith, born 23 March 1792.

Source: Memoirs of James Norman Smith, microfilm copy in Maury County Public Library. He later lived in Tipton Co., Tenn., and Gonzales County, Texas.

JOHN SMITH
Served in Capt. Robert Campbell's company. No further information. [At one point the last name appeared to be Singleton.]

JOHN SMITH
Served in Capt. James McMahan's company. No further information.

JOHN SMITH
Served in Capt. Bird S. Hurt's company. No further information.

JOHN W. SMITH
Service not determined. Born 23 Oct. 1792 in N. C., died 28 June 1845 in Culleoka, buried Friendship Cemetery; married 12 Feb. 1823 to Nancy Toombs, born 1805 in Tenn., died after 1880 and buried in Arkansas. She was the daughter of Edmund Toombs and his wife Sabra.

Children of John W. Smith:
1. David W. Smith, born 23 Sept. 1824 in Maury, died 28 April 1903 in Maury, married 1851 to Nancy Minerva Brown.
2. William Brown Smith, born 17 Nov. 1826, Maury, died 25 May 1901, married 1848 to Elizabeth M. A. Brown.
3. Elijah H. Smith, Confederate soldier, born 1832, died Oct. 1862.
continued on next page

Children of John W. Smith, continued:
4. Jesse H. Smith, born 1837, died 28 July 1864 in Yankee prison.
5. John H. Smith, born 1838, died 17 March 1862, prisoner at Fort Dix.
6. James Smith, born 1840, Union soldier, later lived in Lawrence County, Tenn.
7. Elisha D. Smith, Confederate soldier, born 1842, died after 1908, married Margaret A. Wiley and Betsy Purdom.
8. Wiley "Eli" Smith, born 16 March 1844, died 25 April 1895, married Eliza Jane Collins.
9. Nancy Smith, born 1846.

Source: Family records of Mrs. Reuben Algood, Columbia, Tenn.

MATHIAS SMITH
Served in Capt. James McMahan's company. No further information.

MOSES SMITH
Commissioned captain in 27th Regiment in 1808.
McFerrin's History of Methodism, Vol. III, page 60: "Moses Smith only continued in the traveling connection for a short time; located and settled near Mt. Pleasant, Maury County, Tenn., where he long lived, an active supporter of the institution of the church. On his land was erected a house of worship and camp ground where many souls were brought to Jesus. He died in Illinois a few years since. He has left a very reputable posterity. He was connected with a large and reputable family and left an untarnished reputation."

Maury County Deed Book T, page 232, dated 16 June 1815—John Smith of Williamson County, Tenn., deeds land to Moses Smith of Maury for natural good will and affection...and the further consideration of his agreeing and promising to maintain his mother Catherine Smith land where Moses Smith now resides." (Also F-1, page 237.) Maury County Deed Book S, page 624, 18 March 1836, Moses Smith of McCorpin Co., Ill. deeds to J. C. and Samuel Smith of Maury County, Tenn.

Portrait and Biographical Record of McCorpin County, Ill., Chicago, 1891, page 896 Elisha Smith, living here, son of Moses Smith (born Pennsylvania) and Pamelia Aiken (born N. C.) to Macupin County from Tennessee in 1835 and the parents spent the rest of their days there. Moses and Pamelia Smith were the parents of seven children, four sons and three daughters. Elisha was the third in order of birth, being born in Muray (sic) County, Tenn., 29 March 1817. Elisha came to Illinois with family in 1835 and was married in N. Otter Township 20 July 1837 to Susan A. Eaves, a daughter of Benjamin and Elizabeth Clark Eaves, the former native of N. C. and the latter of Pennsylvania. Elisha and his wife had fifteen children.

Moses Smith and Pamelia Aiken were married in 1808. In Hunter's Cemetery at Mt. Pleasant is the grave of Catherine Smith, died 13 June 1851 or 1854, aged 78 years. and this is believed to be his mother.

Estate of Moses Smith filed 1845 in Carlinville, Illinois.

Association of Methodist Historical Society, Lake Junaluska, N. C., letter dated 18 Oct. 1862 to Mrs. Evelyn B. Shackelford: "Moses Smith admitted on trial 1820 i Tennessee Conference, appointed to Duck River in the Nashville District. In 1821 he remained on trial and appointed to Buffalo in same district. The next year admitted to full connection and ordained elder..."

Source: Research contributed by Mrs. Evelyn B. Shackelford, Mt. Pleasant.

The following is a deposition made June 1834 at the house of Eli Neelley in the circuit court lawsuit Chiles McGee versus Archibald Gilchrist. Robert Neelley, S

Moses Smith, continued:

a witness, says he owned land adjoining Chiles McGee which he bought from Henry Hunter and I sold it to Hugh Gilbreath, bought land in 1811 from Hunter and the deed to the land was made by Henry Hunter and Eliga Hunter. In the year 1806 John Smith requested John Hunter to run the south boundary of his 1000 acres as he wanted to settle his son Moses Smith on the southwest corner, but Hunter was not an authorized surveyor. Moses Smith's son John settled on the southwest corner, cleared and put up a fence. Malcom Gilchrist some time after ran his father's tract in 1807 and old man Gilchrist moved out and settled on his tract and settled his on-in-law McMillan on the northeast corner in 1813 the plaintiff, McGee, purchased the balance of the Smith tract. Later the suit says that Moses Smith was the son of John Smith, the grantor, and settled on it in 1806. (The underlined phrase is believed to be an error on the part of the clerk, as elsewhere it says twice that Moses Smith was the son of John Smith.)

North Carolina Warrant 201, for ten pounds, James Campbell got land of 1000 acres on south side of Duck River on east fork of Big Tom Bigby beginning at the west boundaries of Andrew Hunt's land and mentions James Gillaspie's northwest corner, signed 27 Nov. 1792. (This was land grant for the land in question in this lawsuit.)

SAMUEL SMITH
Served in Capt. James McMahan's company. No further information. [A Captain Samuel Smith lived in the Bear Creek-Flat Creek area of the county as found on early road minutes.]

STEPHEN SMITH
Served in Capt. Robert Campbell's company. [This man is believed to be Stephen Wood Smith, but no proof that he is the soldier. The following information is on Stephen W. Smith.]
Stephen Wood Smith - born 1792 in Virginia, died 1840 in Tishomingo County, Miss., married 1824 in Maury County to Nancy Catherine Weems, daughter of William Weems who married 1791 in Orange Co., N. C., to Mary Kendrick. . . . . He was the son of Samuel Smith and Sallie Wood of Maury County. He was murdered on 7 June 1840 by Benjamin Reynolds, and was first person killed in Tishomingo County.

Brothers and sisters of Stephen W. Smith:
1. John Smith.
2. Elizabeth Smith.
3. Possibly others, but no information.

Source: Information from the files of Monte H. Knight, Columbia, Tennessee.

THOMAS SMITH
Served in Capt. James McMahan's company; killed 24 Jan. 1814. On 16 Aug. 1819 the Maury County court made appropriation for tuition for "three children minor heirs of Thomas O. Smith, deceased, and two children minor heirs of Jesse Mays, deceased, both of whom fell in the late war." Will Book A-1, page 197, his estate was sold 3 Oct. 1815 and the widow Sarah Smith was administratrix.

WILLIAM SMITH
Served in Capt. Bird S. Hurt's company. No further information.

HEZEKIAH POWELL SMITHSON
War of 1812 soldier; born 1791 in Pittsylvania Co., Va., died 13 Feb. 1871, buried in Lexington, Alabama; married 31 Oct. 1810, Danville, Pittsylvania Co., Va., to Henrietta Carter, born 1795 in Virginia, daughter of Presley Carter and Anne Waddell. He was the son of Francis Smithson and Lucretia Powell.

continued on next page

Children of Hezekiah P. Smithson:
1. Hezekiah Powell Smithson, Jr., born in Va., married Melinda Locke.
2. Eliza Carter Smithson, mard (1) 2 March 1837 Benjamin Slayden; (2) John Trotter; (3) _____ Walker.
3. Henrietta Smithson, born in Virginia.
4. Paten Smithson, married 27 May 1846 to Perlina Brooks.
5. John Greene Smithson, born 10 June 1820 Pittsylvania Co., Va., died 2 Jan. 1893 in Giles Co., Tenn., married 18 Feb. 1841 to Ann Vaughan Ladd.
6. Nathaniel Smithson, born in Virginia.
7. William Q. A. Smithson, born in Va., married 8 May 1847 to Nancy A. Trotter.
8. Henry C. Smithson, born in VA., married 1 July 1849 to Mary Brooks.
9. Sarah Smithson, born in Tenn.
10. Marion Smithson, born in Tenn.

Brothers and sisters of Hezekiah P. Smithson:
1. Mary Smithson, born 1795 in Pittsylvania Co., Va.

Source: Family information furnished by Martha Gladish, Lawrenceburg, Tenn., and Dorothy Kelley (Mrs. J. T.), member of Jane Knox Chapter.

PHILIP SOUTH
Served in Capt. John Looney's company. No further information.

WILLIAM SPARKMAN
Served as corporal in Capt. James McMahan's company. He enlisted in Maury on 15 Sept. 1814, discharged at Nashville, April 1815; married Hertford Co., N. C., on 3 Dec. 1789 to Rosanna Williams. He died 15 March 1832. Widow Rosanna Sparkman made claim for bounty land in 1855 in Williamson County. He was the son of William Sparkman of Bertie County, N. C.

Children of William Sparkman:
1. Mary Sparkman married _____ Walker.
2. Selah Sparkman.
3. Seth Sparkman.
4. Williams Sparkman.
5. Elizabeth Sparkman, born 1802, married Aaron Vestal.
6. Charles Robertson Sparkman.
7. James Colden Sparkman.
8. Delana Sparkman.
9. Thomas Washington Sparkman.

Source: Information furnished by Mrs. Lecy Dobbins, descendant.

THOMAS SPEAK
Served in Capt. John Looney's company. No further information.

JOHN SPENCER
Appointed justice of the peace in 1807; first sheriff of Maury County. He settled 3/4 mile east of Columbia. His will was probated 14 Jan. 1827 in Tuscaloosa, Ala. (Will Book 1, pages 27-32).

Children of John Spencer:
1. Zilman Spencer.
2. John Spencer.
3. Benjamin Franklin Spencer.
4. Mary Spencer married _____ Walker.
5. Elizabeth Spencer married _____ Barker.
6. Nancy Spencer married Edward B. Elliott.

continued on next page

Children of John Spencer, continued:
7. Sarah Spencer married Thomas Windham.
8. Rebecca Spencer married _____ Williams.

Source: Information furnished by Virginia W. Alexander from her research.

THOMAS SPENCER
Served in Capt. Bird S. Hurt's company. Born 25 Jan. 1780, died 25 Dec. 1863, buried Wayland Cemetery, Lawrence County, Tenn., married Elizabeth Wayland, born 24 Feb. 1799, died 27 March 1876.

ZILMAN SPENCER
Deputy sheriff in 1807 under his father John Spencer; appointed deputy again in Dec. 1809. He was twice married and the following children were by his first marriage.

Children of Zilman Spencer:
1. Eliza Spencer.
2. John Spencer.
3. Louisa Spencer.
4. No information on any other children.

Source: Will of John Spencer, Tuscaloosa, Alabama, Book 1, pages 27-32; Nathan Vaught, "Youth and Old Age", pages 42, 62.

JOSEPH SPURLOCK
Served in Capt. John Looney's company. No further information.

SAMUEL SRYGLEY
Commissioned ensign 27th Regiment in 1808; served as sergeant in Capt. James McMahan's company, enlisted 22 Jan. 1815. Born 1749, died 1815; married 1808 to Rachel McClus (aged between 26 and 45 on 1820 census). Court minutes of 21 Feb. 1814 refer to Samuel Srygley's house on the "Pulaskey" Road. On 15 May 1815 provisions were made for Rachel, widow of Samuel Srygley. On April 1838 a deed of conveyance from Rachel Srygley, Joseph J. Srygley, James M. Srygley and John D. Rice and wife Elizabeth A. Rice for 65 acres sold is registered in Maury County. Maury County marriage records show that John D. Rice married 30 Sept. 1834 to Elizabeth Srygley.

GEORGE B. STAGGS
Drew pension in 1883 as soldier in War of 1812, was wounded in left foot.

MARTIN STAKS
Served in Capt. Benjamin Reynolds company. No further information.

WILLIAM STANDIFER
Served in Capt. John Gordon's company. No further information.

THOMAS STANFIELD
Served in Capt. John Looney's company. No further information. [Marriage bond dated 21 Aug. 1810 in Maury to marry Rachel Burns with George Burns as bondsman.]

WILLIAM STANFIELD
Commissioned ensign in 27th Regiment in 1813; lieutenant in 51st Regiment in 1814. No further information. [Marriage bond dated 24 May 1814 in Maury to marry Sally Bolin.]

AARON STEEL
Served in Capt. Samuel B. McKnight's company. No further information. [Nathan

continued on next page

Aaron Steel, continued:
Vaught, "Youth and Old Age," page 66, says Aaron Steel married Katharine Fawsett, daughter of Richard Fawsett. A marriage bond in Maury dated 6 March 1819 for one Aaron Steel to marry Nancy Davis.]

MICHAEL STEELE
Served in Capt. Samuel B. McKnight's company. In 1809 was assigned to work on the road known as Fountain Creek Road leading to the upper ford on McCutchan Trace. [Marriage bond dated 23 Jan. 1833 for one Michael Steele to marry Mary A. Pursel.]

ROBERT STEELE
Commissioned first major of 27th Regiment in 1808. No further information. No further information.

(UNKNOWN) STOCKARD
Mary Stockard of Columbia drew pension in 1883 as widow of War of 1812 soldier.

THOMAS STONE
Served in Capt. James McMahan's company. No further information. [Marriage bond dated 12 March 1814 to marry Nancy Dogan.]

JOHN STOKES
Served in Capt. John Looney's company. No further information. [Marriage bond dated 21 Dec. 1821 in Williamson County to marry Peggy Tatum.]

VINSON STORY
Served in Capt. Andrew McCarty's company. Married 29 July 1818 in Maury County to Jane Ausman. He is still in the county in 1820.

SAMUEL STRICKLAND
Served in Capt. Bird S. Hurt's company. No further information. (Samuel Stricklin of Maury County drew pension for his service and pension was suspended in 1832.)

DUNCAN STUART
Served in Capt. Andrew McCarty's company. No further information.

ELIJAH SULLIVAN
Served in Capt. Bird S. Hurt's company. No further information.

+NATHAN SUNDERLAND (also found as SOUTHERLAND)
Maury County Will Book B-1, page 165, dated 19 Aug. 1816, "his services for a tour of 12 months as a regular soldier in the service of the U. S." Feb. 1816 court minutes mention his orphan children: "Nathan Southerland died in the army, one child proper object of charity, child too young for schooling."

The following comes from "Roster of Soldiers and Patriots of the American Revolution Buried in Tennessee, 1974," compiled by Lucy Womack Bates, page 306: Mary Ann Reeves Sunderland (widow), born 26 June 1800, married 8 June 1817 in Hickman County to her second husband Edward Nunnelee, Rev. War soldier. She drew pension on Nathaniel Sunderland, War of 1812, and Edward Nunnelee, Rev. War.

Nashville Republican Banner, 13 Jan. 1874, shows that Mary A. Nunnelee of Centerville was still drawing a pension.

Columbia Herald and Mail, 24 March 1876: Old aunt Polly Nunneley, the widow of a Revolutionary soldier, now living in Centerville in her 94th year, is knitting a pair of socks for the Centennial.

JOHN SUTHERLAND
Served in Capt. Samuel B. McKnight's company. Will Book B-1, page 127, inventory of his estate taken 19 May 1817 and included was "one discharge for three months eleven days, $26.88."

THOMAS SUTHERLAND
Served in Capt. Bird S. Hurt's company. No further information.

ISAIAH SUTHERN
Served in Capt. John Chisholm's company. The following tombstone was found in the Blackburn Cemetery on Leiper's Creek: "Matilda Southern, wife of Isaiah Southern, Jan. 1783 - Sept. 1846, wife and mother...member of Baptist Church."

Source: "They Passed This Way", B-5.

RICHARD TAIT
Served in Capt. John Gordon's company. No further information.

(UNKNOWN) TATUM
Sarah B. Tatum, widow of War of 1812 soldier, drew pension in 1883 at Santa Fe.

ALLEN TAYLOR
Served in Capt. Benjamin Reynolds company. Married 3 Sept. 1818 in Maury County to Polly Thornton. Age given as between 26-45 on 1820 census.

DEMPSEY TAYLOR
Served as corporal in Capt. Samuel B. McKnight's company. Probate deeds, 13 March 1835, page 126, mention Dempsey D. Taylor and wife Nancy. Circuit court minutes 1825-1834, show that he married a daughter of Peter Herald.

MAHAJAH TAYLOR
Served in Capt. Robert Campbell's company. No further information.

REDEN TAYLOR
Served in Capt. Samuel B. McKnight's company. Age given as between 16 and 26 on 1820 census.

SAMUEL TAYLOR
Appointed constable in Maury County March 1809. No further information.

THOMAS TAYLOR
Commissioned ensign in 46th Regiment in 1812. No further information.

GEORGE TERRILL
Served in Capt. James McMahan's company. Still in Maury County on 1820 census. No further information.

JOHN THACKER
Served in Capt. Bird S. Hurt's company. No further information.

÷BARNA THOMAS
Feb. 1816 court minutes: "Barna Thomas died returning from the service of his country, left four boys and two girls." Court appoints Elisha Thomas and Ames Johnston to look out for suitable homes for children.

BENJAMIN THOMAS
Maury Intelligencer, 15 Feb. 1849: Was too young for Revolution, but took part in battle against savages of Miami 20 Aug. 1794. Born 25 Jan. 1768 in Maryland, died Feb. 1849 in Maury County; married 25 Oct. 1800 Amelia Thomas, died 8 Oct. 1837; he was brother in law of Joseph Brown. He came to Maury County and settled early on

Benjamin Thomas, continued:
Lytles Creek; elder in First Presbyterian Church; settled on Mooreville Pike, put
up cabins to shelter his family, then a neat two story brick house which was still
standing in 1878 and was owned by William Moore.

Children of Benjamin Thomas:
1. Alfred W. Thomas, born 1801, died 1877, married Lucy, daughter of Robert Smith.

Source: Nathan Vaught, "Youth and Old Age", page 62; Century Review of Maury
County, pages 122, 251.

GEORGE THOMAS
Served in Capt. Benjamin Reynolds company. No further information.

JOB H. THOMAS
Served in Capt. William Dooley's company as private. No further information. Was
still in the county by 1820 census.

(UNKNOWN) THOMPSON
Sarah Thompson, widow of War of 1812 soldier, drew pension at Santa Fe in 1883.

FLEMING B. THOMPSON
Served in Capt. John Looney's company. No further information.

HENRY THOMPSON
Served in Capt. John Gordon's company. No further information.

JOHN THOMPSON
Commissioned lieutenant of rifle company, 27th Regiment in 1814.

WILLIAM THOMPSON
Served in 7th N. C. Militia. Born 20 March 1796 in Rutherford Co., N. C., or in
Spartanburg Co., S. C., died 25 March 1888, buried in Jerusalem Cemetery in Pickens
County, Ga.; married 17 May 1818 in Rutherford County, N. C., to Nancy Henderson,
born 1800 in Rutherford County, N. C., died 25 June 1890, buried Jerusalem Cemetery,
Pickens County, Ga. She was daughter of William Henderson, born 1770 in Va., died
1852-53 in Rutherford Co., N. C.

William Thompson applied for Bounty Land due him for his service and stated that he
enlisted at Rutherford County, N. C., was a school teacher and farmer at time of his
enlistment. He moved to Forsyth County, Ga., in 1835, where he lived until 1845,
when he moved to Murray Co., Ga., then to Walker Co., Ga., then to Bartow Co., Ga.,
or Cherokee Co., Ga., where he was living in 1850. When Pickens County was created
from Cherokee, he was living in the part of Cherokee that became Pickens. His des-
cription at time of enlistment was 5 ft. 10 or 11, black eyes, light hair and complexion. He said that Andrew Thompson and Samuel Thompson served with him. Elijah
Thompson was also mentioned. Relationship to any of these unknown. Jos. Cloud was
bondsman for William when he and Nancy married.

Children of William Thompson:
1. Lewis Thompson, born 24 April 1821 Rutherford Co., N. C., died 11 Jan. 1913 in
   Pickens Co., Ga., married 1858 to Elizabeth Ann Stewart.
2. Rebecca Thompson, born 1825 in Rutherford Co., N. C., married 1851 in Walker
   County, Ga., Ephriam Alex. Holland.
3. Mary K. (Polly) Thompson, born 1829 in Rutherford Co., N. C., died 1916 in
   Whitfield Co., Ga., married James Holland.
4. Margaret Fealove Thompson, born 1832 in Rutherford Co., N. C., died 26 Dec.
   1925, married Leander Childers.

continued on next page

Children of William Thompson, continued:

5. William Thompson, born 1 Aug. 1833 in Rutherford Co., N. C., died 6 Aug. 1906 in Pickens Co., Ga., married Nancyan Barrons and Kissiah Cross

6. Bayless Thompson, born 30 Dec. 1835 in Forsyth Co., Ga., died 14 Dec. 1918 in Pickens Co., Ga., buried Talking Rock Cemetery; married Sarah Findley.

7. Elijah Thompson, born 20 Oct. 1837 Forsythe Co., Ga., died 8 Nov. 1924, Pickens Co., Ga., buried Talking Rock Cemetery; married Rebecca Parks.

Source: Family information from Virginia W. Alexander, descendant, member of Jane Knox Chapter.

WILLIAM W. THOMPSON

Commissioned captain 5th brigade of cavalry 1809; lieutenant colonel 5th Brigade in 1812. No further information. Register of Maury County Dec. 1809.

JOHN THORPE

Maury County Deed Book H-1, page 310, 24 April 1819, "selling land in Illinois which got for services in late war." Land was located in Section 26, Township 5. A man of this same name will be found on 1840 census of Hardin County, Tenn.

WILLIAM TOLLY

Served in Capt. James McMahan's company. No further information.

JOHN TOMBS or TOOMBS

Columbia Herald, 25 April 1873: John Tombs, now 83, War of 1812 pensioner. Born 8 Dec. 1791 in Virginia, died 4 March 1875 in Maury, buried Friendship Cemetery; married 26 Nov. 1812 in Maury to Catherine Weems, born 5 Feb. 1794, died 20 Feb. 1881, buried at Friendship. He was son of Edmund Tombs, born Amelia Co., Va., who died 1830, will recorded in Maury County, and his wife Sabra, who died in Maury County in 1852.

Children of John Toombs:

1. William Wiley Toombs, born 1813, married Eliza Renfro and Mary Perry.
2. Anthony M. Toombs, born 1815, married Caroline Young on 16 July 1835.
3. John H. Toombs, born 6 Jan. 1819, died 24 Oct. 1893, married Elizabeth P. Hill.
4. Mary A. Toombs, married 28 July 1849 to James R. Goad.
5. Nancy Toombs married Martin Hardin on 22 Oct. 1845.

Brothers and sisters of John Toombs:

1. William, born Richmond, Va., married 28 May 1808 in Maury to Betsy Duff.
2. Susannah, born in Va., married 16 March 1809 in Williamson County to Isaac Long.
3. Joseph, born in Virginia.
4. Dicy, born in Va., married 10 June 1809 in Maury to John Davis.
5. James, born 1804 in Tenn., married 11 March 1824 in Maury to Cinderalla Benton.
6. Garner McConnico, born about 1804 (?), in Tenn., married 1823 to Katherine Smith, after 1880 lived in Arkansas.
7. Nancy, born 1807, Tenn., married 12 Feb. 1823 to John W. Smith.

Source: Family information contributed by Mrs. Reuben Algood, Columbia, descendant.

HENRY TOMLINSON

Served as corporal in Capt. Samuel B. McKnight's company. No further information.

JAMES TOMLINSON

Served in Capt. Bird S. Hurt's company. [marriage bond dated 5 Aug. 1822 to marry Martha Gannaway in Maury County.]

JESSE TOMLINSON
Enlisted in Capt. Benjamin Reynolds company, 2d Tennessee Volunteers 1 Dec. 1812.
Born 14 Feb. 1772, died 17 March 1841 in Franklin County, Alabama, married 31 Oct.
1800 in Scott Co., Ky., to Nancy Allen, daughter of James and Mary Tomlinson Allen.
She was born 22 June 1783.

Children of Jesse Tomlinson:
1. Charles Allen Tomlinson, born 12 June 1808 in Scott County, Ky., died 26 Aug.
   1892, Culleoka, Tenn., married 7 Dec. 1838 to Sally D. Foster.
2. No information on other children, had eleven children.

Source: Information from Mrs. Leonard Gibson, Culleoka, Tennessee.

BERRY TONEY
Served in Capt. Bird S. Hurt's company. No further information.

JOHN TOONES
Commissioned ensign in 46th Regiment in 1812. [This is believed to be John Toombs;
see previous entry.]

EDWARD TRENOR
Served in Capt. John Looney's company. No further information.

HENRY TRUETT
Henry Truett served in Capt. John Gordon's company, which had many Hickman County
men, and it is not known if Truett ever lived in Maury County. He was born in N.C.
and died 1833 in Hickman County where he settled early. He married Sarah Clampett,
born in Delaware, died 1840.

Children of Henry M. Truett:
1. Alpheus Truett, born 17 May 1823 in Hickman County, married 1849 to Roena A.
   Beard.
2. James M. Truett.
3. No information on other children; twelve children in all.

Source: Goodspeed's History of Williamson County, page 1015.

PETER TRUNSTON
Served in Capt. James McMahan's company. No further information.

DAVID TUK
Served in Capt. Benjamin Reynolds company. [Name hard to read and was in question.]

HUGH TURNBOW
Served in Capt. Andrew McCarty's company. Born about 1793 in South Carolina, married
Mary (Polly) Powell, born about 1797 in N. C., daughter of Lewis Powell. They
later lived in Wayne County, Tenn.

Children of Hugh Turnbow (from 1850 census):
1. Elizabeth Turnbow, born about 1826.
2. Hugh Turnbow, born about 1823.
3. Jackson Turnbow, born about 1823.
4. Ambrose Turnbow, born about 1838.
5. No information on other children.

Source: 1850 Census of Wayne County, Tenn.

JESSE TURNER
Commissioned ensign in 27th Regiment in 1809. No further information.

ROBERT TURNER
Served in Capt. Samuel Ashmore's company. No further information.

WILLIAM TURNER
Served in Capt. Bird S. Hurt's company; also served in Capt. Samuel Ashmore's company. Born 15 May 1792, died 18 June 1865, buried at Haynes Cemetery, soldier of War of 1812 on his tombstone; married Martha Caudle, born 12 March 1800, died 1 Aug. 1886. Marriage bond dated 22 Nov. 1814 to marry Christian Caudle. Pension.

DAVID TUTTLE
Commissioned ensign 27th Regiment in 1812. No further information.

JESSE TYNER
Served in Capt. Benjamin Reynolds company. No further information.

JESSE TYNER
Served in Capt. Bird S. Hurt's company. No further information.

LEWIS TYNER
Served in Capt. Benjamin Reynolds company. No further information.

JERRY TYREE
Served in Capt. Samuel Ashmore's company. No further information.

JOHN VASHERS
Commissioned ensign in 27th Regiment in 1811, no further information.

RICHARD VINSON
Served in Capt. Samuel B. McKnight's company. No further information.

DAVID VOORHIES
Served in Capt. John Looney's company. Born 1794 in N. C., married in Maury County 13 Nov. 1817 to Elizabeth McBride, born 1798 in Rockingham Co., N. C., daughter of Isaiah and Jane McClain McBride. In 1818-19 they moved to Wayne County, Tenn., and she died between 1840 and 1850. He was still living in 1860.

Children of David Voorhies:
1. John Voorhies, born 1819.
2. Samuel W. Voorhies, born 1824, married Sophia T. _____.
3. James Voorhies, born 1827.
4. Rebecca Voorhies, born 1828.
5. Mary Voorhies, born 1830.
6. Eliza Voorhies, born 1832, married 1 Jan. 1860 to Joseph H. Jones in Wayne Co.
7. Thomas Voorhies, born 1833/34 married Eliza J. _____. In 1860 living in Wayne County and in 1880 in Lewis County.
8. Two other children, but no information.

Source: Pages 8 and 9, The McBride Family History, by Robert M. McBride.

JOHN VOORHIES
Born N. C., died 24 April 1865; son of Aaron Voorhies who settled early in Maury County. Married Mary Chaffin, who died 24 July 1874. Marriage in Maury County dated 17 Sept. 1816 and her name given as Polly Chappen.

Children of John Voorhies:
1. Angeline Voorhies.
continued on following page

Children of John Voorhies, continued:
2. Robert Voorhies.
3. Rebecca Voorhies.
4. Aaron Voorhies.
5. Margaret Melissa Voorhies, born 24 Oct. 1825, married 24 July 1844 to James Craig.
6. Jasper Newton Voorhies.
7. Martha Voorhies.
8. Mary Jane Voorhies.
9. David Voorhies.
10. John Voorhies.

Source: Goodspeed's History of Hickman County, page 912.

WILLIAM VOSS
Served in Capt. James McMahan's company. No further information.

DABNEY WADE
Commissioned coronet in 5th Brigade cavalry in 1812; he also received license to kee an ordinary in Maury County in 1812. Maury County Deed Book F-1, page 246, shows that he married Nancy Turner, widow of William Turner. Had land on Rutherford Creek and died about 1822.

WILLIAM J. WADE
Commissioned captain in light infantry company, 27th Regiment in 1812. No further information. William J. Wade was security for Dabney Wade when he got license to keep an ordinary.

JOHN WAGGONER
Served in Capt. Robert Campbell's company. No further information.

JOHN WAGGONER
Served in Capt. James McMahan's company. No further information.

LEWIS C. WAGGONER
Drew pension at Spring Hill in 1883 as surviving soldier of War of 1812, was wounde in right side, neck and shoulders. [Lewis C. Waggoner married Mary A. Walker on 29 Aug. 1839 in Williamson County.]

MICHAEL WALDROP
Served in Capt. A. McKinney's company, cavalry, Col. R. H. Dyer, Williamson County troops from 24 Sept. 1813 to 18 May 1814. Marriage bond to marry Rebecca Brown 8 Jan. 1810.

JAMES WALKER
Served in Capt. John Gordon's company. No further information. [This is believed NOT to be the James Walker who was living in Columbia at this time.]

JOEL WALKER
Served as private in Capt. McKamey's company, Col. John Brown's regiment, East Tennessee Militia from 1 Jan. 1814 to 20 May 1814. Died 14 Oct. 1876 at the age of 93 years in Columbia and buried in Greenwood Cemetery. He was married to Mary R. Born Fluvanna County, Virginia.

Children of Joel Walker:
1. Joseph A. Walker.
2. No information on other children.

Source: Obituary in Columbia Herald and Mail, Oct. 1876.

SYLVESTER WALKER
Reported to us as War of 1812 soldier. No further information.

THOMAS WALKER
Commissioned captain in 27th Regiment in 1813 and in 51st Regiment in 1814. [No information. Several men of this name lived in county at about the same period. The following information will be on those men.]

Thomas Walker, Sr. - believed to have been born in Ireland, will recorded 5 Jan. 1824 in Maury County. Mentions the following children: Thomas, John, Joseph, Andrew, Jane, Nixen, and Joseph. Mentions also a deed of gift recorded in Chester County, S. C. (Will Book C-1, page 132)

Thomas Walker, Jr., born 2 Dec. 1786, died 20 April 1875 in Maury County, Tenn., married 3 Jan. 1813 to Anneliza Walker; son of Thomas Walker, Sr., and Anzela _____. (Information from Mrs. Kay Adams, Portage, Indiana.)

Thomas Walker married Bethana Woolard and they were the parents of Anneliza Walker, born 16 Sept. 1822 in Tenn., married 1848 Jefferson Harrison Kirkpatrick. (Information from Mrs. Kay Adams, Portage, Ind.)

Thomas Walker settled in Cathey's Creek area of Maury County and will be found on 1850 census of county at the age of 77 years. (Maury Democrat 2 April 1908.)

Griffith Walker, son of Thomas Walker, lived at Williamsport at early date. (11 Feb. 1892). Old Squire Thomas Walker lived four miles west of Columbia, had daughter who married a Mr. Brown, who lived at Williamsport.

WASHINGTON WALKER
Served in Capt. William Dooley's company. Born in Virginia, died 29 Sept. 1813. H settled in Maury County near Love's Mill on Fountain Creek. (Maury Democrat, 8 Aug. 1889). Will Book A-1, page 246, mentions wife Elizabeth, brothers and sisters except Suey Ganoway and her heirs, his friend Joseph Brown to be executor. No children. Equity records show that his widow married Moore Lumpkins in 1816.

Brothers and sisters of Washington Walker:
1. Charles Walker, died before his brother.
2. Jane Walker, died 1832-3.
3. Warren Walker, died before 1804.
4. Martha Walker died about 1819 married Robert Self.
5. Elizabeth Walker married Samuel Fitch.
6. Frances Walker married Alexander Legrand of Campbell Co., Va.
7. Druscilla (Lucy) Walker married Edmond Gannaway and lived in Monroe Co. Miss.

Sources: Gannaway vs Walker, 1842, chancery court records. At another place his brothers and sisters given as Martha, Fanny, James, Warren, Charles, Jane, Judith, Elizabeth, and Drucilla.

WILLIAM WALKER
Served in Capt. John Gordon's company. No further information.

HEZEKIAH WARD
Served in Capt. Samuel Ashmore's company, muster 28 Jan. 1814, discharged 10 May 1814. Born 10 March 1795, died 10 May 1836, buried in Greenwood Cemetery. He was a carpenter in Columbia. Married Elizabeth Ridley, born 15 Sept. 1802, died 17 Jul. 1847. His marriage bond was issued 2 May 1822 and James K. Polk was his bondsman. His wife is also buried at Greenwood Cemetery.

Children of Hezekiah Ward:
1. Vincent R. Ward, 25 Jan. 1823 - 7 Aug. 1838, Greenwood Cemetery. (continued)

198

Children of Hezekiah Ward, continued:
2. Judge Hillary Ward - later moved to Pulaski.
3. Hezekiah Ward married 22 July 1852 to Josephine E. Craig.
4. Rufus Ward.
5. Evelyn Ward married _____ Dawson.
6. Eliza Ann Ward married _____ Rogers.
7. Mary E. Ward married 14 April 1847 to Jesse A. Dawson.

Source: Nathan Vaught, "Youth and Old Age", page 73; "They Passed This Way", page D-11. Also refer to Frank H. Smith's History of Maury County for an account of death of Vincent Ward. Columbia Herald, 30 June 1871.

JAMES WARD
Served in Capt. Samuel Ashmore's company. No further information.

WILLIAM WARD (or WARE)
Served in Capt. Robert Campbell's company. No further information.

+ELI WAROT
Served in Capt. Bird S. Hurt's company. Died 31 Dec. 1814.

JOHN D. WARREN
Served as private in Capt. Glen Owen's Tennessee Mounted Gunmen from 28 Sept. 1814 to 28 March 1815. He drew pension in 1883. He was born about 1800 in N. C., and is buried at Mt. Carmel Cemetery, Duplex, Tenn., no marker; married 1817 in Williamson County to Mary Crouch (age 45, born in Virginia, on 1850 census). He was a founding member of New Hope Methodist Church at Hurt's Cross Roads in Maury County.

Children of John D. Warren:
1. William Warren, born 1836, married Bell Waddy.
2. Robert Burr Warren, born 1843, died 1913, married Molly Burney, daughter of Arch and Sally Glover Burney.
3. Edward A. Warren, born 17 April 1827, died 1912, married Emaline Padgett, born 1837, died 1907.
4. Thomas A. Warren, born 1840, died 1917, married Sallie Christman.
5. S. M. Warren, born 1838.
6. N. W. Warren, born 1830 (female)
7. M. H. Warren, born 1832 (female)
8. J. W. Warren, born 1834 (female)

Information from Mrs. John C. Derryberry, descendant of John D. Warren; 1850 census of Maury County; Williamson County Marriage Records; Williamson County Burials, page 212, compiled by Williamson County Historical Society.

The following article of interest appeared in Columbia Herald and Mail, 22 Sept. 1876: Capt. John D. Warren, Rally Hill, is now the only surviving soldier of the War of 1812 in this portion of the county. The Capt., with the exception of being somewhat deaf, is still hale and hearty. He enlisted in Williamson County in Capt. Glenn Owen's company, who lived on West Harpeth Creek, near the old Baptist Church that stood near Capt. John Bowden's. James (or Jones) Hardeman was 1st lieutenant. He was the uncle of Thos. and Nick Hardeman. Andrew Spratt was 2d lieutenant. He lived near Bethseda. David Moore was ensign. He was in the 1st Battalion, 1st Regiment, Col. Dyer, commanding. They were mounted volunteers in General Coffee's Brigade. Lauderdale was Lt. Col. of the regiment and Gibson was the Major.

The Capt. was in the capture of Pensacola, and was in the battle on the 23rd December at New Orleans, the recollection of which is still vivid. The Capt. says they were mixed up and partially surrounded by the British. Capt. McMahan said he would

John D. Warren, continued:

die before he would retreat. He and his 1st Lieutenant Brooks were both killed. Lt. Col. Lauderdale was also killed and Gibson was wounded and captured twice during the night. The battle was obstinately disputed. The Americans fought with desperate valor, and resisted with clubbed rifle the British bayonets.

The British were principally grenadiers with tall bearskin caps, the flower of the British army, who had fought for years in Spain against the French, under such leaders as Massena, Soult, Suckett and Napoleon. The Capt. was taken prisoner and put on the 74-gun ship Plantagenet, and transferred to the Bedford and then to the Norge. There were eleven 74 gunships present. The Bedford was full of wounded afte. the battle of the 8th. In two hours after the battle the news of the decisive battl. was signaled to the ships. The Capt. was a prisoner forty days.

ROBERT GRAY WASHINGTON
Commissioned captain in cavalry company 5th Brigade 1811. No further information.

LEWIS WATTS
Drew pension in Columbia in 1883 as surviving soldier of the War of 1812. No further information.

ISAIAH WEATHERLY
Served in Capt. Robert Campbell's company. No further information.

(UNKNOWN) WEBSTER
Martha Webster, widow of War of 1812 soldier, drew pension in Columbia in 1883. No further information.

THOMAS WEEMS
Appointed constable March 1809 in Maury County; resigned Dec. 1809. No further information.

JAMES WELCH
Commissioned second major in 27th Regiment in 1808. No further information.

JAMES WELCH
Appointed patrolee for Columbia in Sept. 1808. No further information. In 1809 was given license to keep ordinary in the county.

CAPTAIN THOMAS WELLS
Captain of a company during War of 1812; born 1 March 1782 died 4 June 1860 in Maury and buried in Wells Cemetery on Port Royal Road. Banks Wells and John Glenn were executors of his estate in Sept. 1860.

DAVID WHARTON
Served as corporal in Capt. James McMahan's company. No further information.

DAVID WHARTON (or WHORTON)
Served in Capt. John Chisholm's company. No further information.

JOHN WHITAKER
Commissioned lieutenant in 27th Regiment in 1814. Appointed constable of Maury County in March 1810 and renewed in March 1811. Born 13 March 1785, died 10 August 1834; married Elizabeth Love, born 1791, daughter of David and Mary Draper Love. Whitaker's Path, an early road in the county, was named for him.

Children of John Whitaker:
1. Mark Whitaker married 5 Sept. 1833 to Harriet Holt.
2. Pauline Whitaker married Washinton Hardy.
continued on next page

Children of John Whitaker, continued:
3. John Whitaker.
4. Susie Whitaker, born 1825, died 13 Feb. 1885.
5. Thomas Jefferson Whitaker married 1842 to Mary A. L. S. Myrick.
6. David Love Whitaker, lived in Arkansas.
7. William Love Whitaker, born 1821 died 1884, married Susan Patton.
8. Larkin Whitaker, born 1831 died 1906, married Adeline Wilson.

Source: Maury County Cousins, page 447.

ALFRED M. WHITE
Commissioned ensign in 27th Regiment in 1812; served as second sergeant in Capt.
James McMahan's company. No further information.

BENJAMIN WHITE
Served in Capt. Andrew McCarty's company. Was described as Benjamin White, planter,
in 1817. He was still here by 1820 census.

EDWARD WHITE
Served in Capt. William Dooley's company. No further information.

JAMES WHITE
Served in Capt. Benjamin Reynolds company. No further information.

JAMES WHITE
Served in Capt. Robert Campbell's company. No further information.

JAMES WHITE
Served in Capt. Samuel B. McKnight's company as sergeant. No further information.

JAMES WHITE
Commissioned lieutenant in 5th Brigade of Cavalry in 1809. No further information.
[One early James White who lived in Maury County was a soldier of the Revolution
according to his obituary reported in National Banner and Nashville Daily Advertiser
of 6 July 1832.]

MEDY WHITE
Enlisted 28 Sept. 1814 in Capt. Cuthbert Hudson's company as a private and was discharged 28 March 1815. [Maury County Cousins, page 432: Media White married Mary
Penelope _____ and they were the parents of Luke Sumner White, born 31 May 1820,
died Feb. 1892, of Maury County.]

THOMAS WHITE
Served in Capt. Samuel Ashmore's company. No further information.

ABRAHAM WHITESIDE
Commissioned lieutenant of volunteer company, 51st Regiment in 1814. No further
information.

ABRAHAM WHITESIDE
Served in Capt. Bird S. Hurt's company. No further information.

ABRAHAM WHITESIDE
Commissioned constable in 1808 with Thomas Whiteside and Edward McCafferty as his
bondsmen.

[Two men named Abraham Whiteside lived at the same period in Maury County. The
following information will be on these two men; it was impossible to determine
which man had the above service records.]

Dr. Abraham Whiteside
Born 1778, died 1821, married 6 Aug. 1809 to Ruth M. Davidson, who died 1847 at the age of 56. Both are buried in Greenwood Cemetery. He was the son of Thomas Whiteside, born in Ireland, died 1823, and his wife Mary Jenkin. His widow later married Edward H. Chaffin of Columbia.

Children of Abraham Whiteside:
1. Richard C. Whiteside, born 1810, died 1852, buried in Greenwood Cemetery. Only child.

Brothers and sisters of Abraham Whiteside:
1. Jenkins, born 1772, died 1822, never married; noted lawyer.
2. William, born 1774, died 1848, married Blanche Shelton.
3. James, born 1767, died 1845, married Mary Entrican.
4. David Whiteside, born 1785, died 1859, married three times.
5. Thomas Whiteside, born 1794, died 1840-50; never married.

Source: DAR Roster No. 1, page 774; tombstone inscriptions from "They Passed This Way".

Abraham Whiteside
The other man of this name lived in the Cathey's Creek area of the county and will be found on the 1823 tax list in this section.

SAMUEL WHITESIDE
Commissioned captain in 51st Regiment in 1814. [A man of this name signed a petition to establish Maury County in 1807. 1850 Census shows him to be 73 years old, born in S. C., married Cynthia Farris, born 1786 died 1830, marriage license issued in Davidson County on 23 Oct. 1896.]

THOMAS WHITSON
Served in Capt. James McMahan's company. He was the son of William and Ann Whitson, originally from Buncombe County, N. C. The father's will is first one recorded in Maury County, Book A-1, page 1. The mother died in 1829 and lived on Knob Creek.

Brothers and sisters of Thomas Whitson:
1. John Whitson.
2. Joseph Whitson.
3. George Whitson.
4. James Whitson, lived in Alabama.
5. Mary M. Whitson married ____Hardin and lived in Hardin County, Tenn.
6. William Whitson (said to have moved to La. or Arkansas)
7. Samuel Whitson, moved to Hickman County.
8. Sarah Whitson married Wesley Witherspoon.
9. Rebecca Whitson married Edmund L. Williams.

Source: Hardin versus Edmonds, 1835, chancery court records unpublished.

ALEXANDER F. WILEY
Born 1790, buried in Harder Cemetery, Cedar Creek, Perry County, Tenn. Served as private in Capt. Peter Searcy's company, Col. Amos Pipkin's regiment from 20 June 1814 to 20 Dec. 1814 as substitute for John Wiley. Also served in Capt. John Gordon company, 24 Sept. 1813 and discharged 10 May 1814. He was son of Robert Wiley. He married 1822 to Sally Farris, born 1797.

Children of Alexander F. Wiley:
1. John Wiley
2. Caleb Wiley
3. William Wiley
continued on next page

Children of Alexander F. Wiley, continued:
4. Jane Wiley
5. Sarah Wiley
6. Mary Lou Ann Wiley

Brothers and sisters of Alexander F. Wiley:
1. John Wiley
2. Thomas Wiley
3. Robert Wiley
4. William Wiley
5. Moses Wiley
6. Andrew Wiley
7. Polly Wiley
8. Margaret Wiley
9. Sarah Wiley

Source: Family information from Don Richardson, Linden, Tenn.; Robert Wiley's will recorded Jan. 1824 in Maury County; National Banner and Nashville Whig, 2 Sept. 1830, Sarah Wiley, wife of Robert Wiley, deceased, died 10 Aug. 1830 in Maury County at age of 73 years.

JOHN WILKS
Served in Capt. William Dooley's company. [This is believed to be the John Wilks born 8 May 1780, died 14 Dec. 1834, who married 6 May 1818 in Maury County to Francis Butt, born 22 Sept. 1795, died 19 Jan. 1878, daughter of Radford Butt. The following are the children of this John Wilks.]

Children of John Wilks:
1. Mary Ann Eliza Wilks, born 17 Feb. 1819.
2. Nancy Francis, born 24 June 1820.
3. Archelaus Butt Wilks, born 26 Aug. 1822, died 7 Oct. 1898.
4. William James Wilks, born 11 April 1829, died 28 June 1863.
5. M. Ellinnora, born 30 Jan. 1831, died 18 Jan. 1893, married _____ Shaw.
6. Harriet Melisse, born 19 March 1833, died 1900.
7. Elizabeth Lipscomb Wilks, born 5 May 1835.

Source: Bible record in Maury County Cousins; Maury County marriage records.

MINOR WILKES
Commissioned ensign in 27th Regiment in 1814. No further information.

WILLIAM WILKES
Served in Capt. Bird S. Hurt's company. No further information.

JACOB WILLIAMS
Served in Capt. James McMahan's company. No further information.

JAMES WILLIAMS
Commissioned captain in 27th Regiment in 1809. No further information.

JAMES WILLIAMS
Service not determined. Columbia Herald 15 Dec. 1871, lost mind year or so ago, lived in District 27, drew pension, wife died several years ago. Columbia Herald and Mail, 17 March 1876: James Williams of Rock Springs died 11 March 1876 of paralysis, War of 1812 soldier.

Children of James Williams:
1. J. N. Williams
2. No information on other children.

JOHN WILLIAMS
Served in Capt. James McMahan's company. No further information.

JOHN WILLIAMS
Served in Capt. William Dooley's company. No further informaion.

JOHN WILLIAMS
Served in Capt. Bird S. Hurt's company. No further information.

JOHN E. WILLIAMS
War of 1812 soldier, service not determined. Was soldier under Jackson "although
little more than a boy" at Horseshoe Bend. Born Sept. 1796, died 20 April 1851,
buried Williamsport Cemetery; married Rachel Harbison Ayers. Son of Edward Williams
(born 1766 died 1835) and his wife Dorcas Edwards of Sumner County.

Children of John Edward Williams:
1. Martha Ann Williams, married Samuel S. Bobo.
2. Margaret Jane Williams.
3. Rachel Harbison Williams married Timothy I. Nunnelee.
4. John James Williams, born 14 Dec. 1829 at Williamsport, married 1863 to
   Victoria Felicia Robertson. Lawyer.
5. Dorcas Edwards Williams.
6. Edward Mumford Williams.
7. Elizabeth Gantt Williams.
8. Cynthia Ann Williams.
9. Child died in infancy.

Brothers and sisters of John Edward Williams:
1. Sarah (Sally) Williams, deceased by 1835, a great beauty, married William Edward
2. Nathan Williams.
3. Elisha Williams.
4. Dorcas (Tobitha) Williams married James Ayers.
5. Mahala Williams married Joseph Allen and went to Missouri.
6. Mary Elizabeth Williams married George Gantt.
7. Margaret Williams married John Smoot.
8. Martha (Patsy) Williams married Isaac Faris.

Brothers and sisters of John Edward Williams by father's second marriage to
Mrs. Elizabeth Coleman Alderson, widow of John Starke Alderson:
1. Edward Williams, Jr., born 1820, died 1890; married (1) Dorothy Darby, born
   27 July 1820, died 20 Sept. 1843; (2) Eleanor Elizabeth Dedman, born 16 May
   1828, died 23 April 1850; (3) 1851 Lily Ann McConnico, born 1831, died 1866;
   (4) Roberta Porter, born 1845, died 1909.

Source: John Trotwood Moore, The Volunteer State, Vol. II, page 780; Columbia
Herald, 4 July 1873; and family information contributed by Mrs. Mary Lee Park.

JOSHUA WILLIAMS
Appointed justice of the peace of Maury County in 1807; born 14 Sept. 1762, died
22 Sept. 1831, buried on Snow Creek, sheriff of Buncombe County, N. C., from 1800 to
1803; captain of militia company in 1807 north of Duck River; married Sarah Davidson, born 30 July 1773, died 8 Dec. 1853.

Source: Soldiers of the War of 1812 Buried in Tennessee, page 122.

SAMUEL H. WILLIAMS
Sheriff of Buncombe Co., N. C., 1804; second sheriff of Maury County; served in
2nd Division of Maury County militia; born 27 June 1768, married 24 April 1835 in
Maury County, married Ruth Davidson, born 7 Nov. 1777, died 23 May 1849. (continued)

Children of Samuel Humphreys Williams:
1. Maria Ruth, born 1812, died 1867, married 24 Sept. 1835 Barclay Martin.
2. Sarah Quincy, born 1818, died 1850, married 24 Sept. 1835 to Matt Martin.
3. Lavinia married Gardner Frierson.
4. Jane married John L. Smith.
5. Lucretia married James Jones, he ran Jones Academy in 1870s.
6. Rachel married John H. Stratton.
7. Mary, married Dr. J. W. S. Frierson.
8. Margaret married John D. Fleming.

Source: Family records of Miss Emma Porter Armstrong, Columbia.

WILLIAM WILLIAMS
Served in Capt. James McMahan's company. No further information. [marriage bond dated 12 Sept. 1809 to marry Nancy Smith.] [Letters of administration on estate of William Williams given to Martha Williams 22 Feb. 1815.]

WILLIAM WILLIAMS
William Williams, Sr., son of Amy Williams, before his death lived at Pleasant Grove in Maury County and was "late a soldier in the army of U.S." and got bounty land in Arkansas, circa 1829. John Campbell was administrator of his estate.

RUSSELL McCORD WILLIAMSON
Thought to be a soldier; later known as colonel; moved to Mississippi, but died in Columbia in 1845. Married 2 Oct. 1827 to Sarah K. Lindsey, daughter of the Rev. John Lindsey. Children not known, if any. Son of Green Williamson (born 1768, died 1819) and his wife Patsy H. (died 10 Sept. 1854 at 77 years, buried at Greenwoo Cemetery.

Brothers and sisters of R. M. Williamson:
1. William H. Williamson, born 9 April 1797, died 1 Oct. 1825, murdered by the Hardin brothers.
2. Sallie Williamson married David Martin and P. D. Franklin.
3. Sackey Williamson married _____ Burney.
4. Elizabeth P. Williamson married 22 Oct. 1823 Washington Keys.
5. Ann Williamson married James Brown.
6. Martha A. Williamson married 2 April 1833 to Samuel M. Neeley.
7. Mariah Williamson married 31 Jan. 1837 to George W. C. Maxwell.

Source: Nathan VAught, "Youth and Old Age", page 65, 66, 77; tombstone inscriptions from "They Passed This Way"; Tennessee Democrat, 6 March 1845.

SAMUEL WILLIAMSON
Service not determined; born 1786 in N. C., died 1860 in Maury County; married Judith Woodfin, born 1790, died 1873.

Source: Soldiers of the War of 1812 Buried in Tennessee, page 122.

MAJOR WILLIS
Served in Capt. John Chisholm's company. Married Mary Jones. On 1823 tax list he is living in the Bear Creek area.

Children of Major Willis:
1. Seaborn Willis, born in N. C., married Elizabeth Southall, daughter of John and Judie Flippen Southall of Williamson County.
2. No information on others.

Source: Moore Questionnaire of W. M. Willis in State Archives; Century Review of Maury County 235.

+SAMUEL WILLIS
Served in Capt. Samuel Ashmore's company, R. C. Napier's regiment, muster 28 **Jan.**
1814, died 10 April 1814. Maury County Will Book B-1, page 91, 16 June 1814, provision made for his widow and family. Piety Willis, presumably his wife, was the administratrix of his estate.

Source: Maury County Will Book B-1, pages, 9, 24, 27, 54, 91.

ABEL WILSON
Served in Capt. Bird S. Hurt's company. In 1809 lived in Carter's Creek area of the county.

HARDIN WILSON
Commissioned captain in 46th Regiment in 1812. Paid taxes on land on Cedar Creek.

HIRAM I. WILSON
Served in War of 1812 from Giles County; later about 1835 lived in Maury County; died Marshall County, Tenn., in 1848. He was known to have a brother Boyd Wilson. No further information.

JAMES WILSON
Served in Capt. Andrew McCarty's company. No further information.

JOEL WILSON
Served in Capt. Samuel B. McKnight's company. No further information.

JOHN WILSON
Served in Capt. Bird S. Hurt's company. No further information.

JOHN WILSON
Served in Capt. Bird S. Hurt's company. No further information. [One of these men named John Wilson in War of 1812 was son of Cornelius Wilson, Rev. War soldier. The following information will be on that John Wilson.]

John Wilson*
Born 1788 Abbeville District, S. C., died 1860 in Independence Texas, married Celia Campbell 27 Feb. 1810 in Williamson County, Tenn. She died before 1845. He was son of Cornelius Wilson, born about 1764, died 22 June 1822. His mother's name was Anney, and she died 18 Jan. 1824. John Wilson lived in the Bear Creek Area.

Children of John Wilson:
1. William Cahal Wilson, born 7 Jan. 1833 in Maury County, died 6 Sept. 1927 in Abbeville, Miss., married 8 Jan. 1861 Mary Wilmina Elizabeth Morgan in Abbeville, Miss.
2. Other children, but no information.

Brothers and sisters of John Wilson:
1. Elizabeth Wilson, died 1834, married 22 Jan. 1810 Jeremiah Trainum.
2. Mary Bird "Polly" Wilson, born 1793, died 1869, married 30 Oct. 1813 to Thomas Hardison.
3. Alexander Wilson, born about 1794, died 6 July 1834, married 30 Sept. 1815 in Williamson County to Nancy Fuzell.
4. Henry Stephens Wilson, born 13 June 1802, married 15 May 1823 to Sarah Caldwell.
5. Nancy, no further information.

Source: Information from Maury County records contributed by Jane Luna (Mrs. John), member of Jane Knox Chapter.
*It has been established that this is the John Wilson who served in Capt. Bird S. Hurt's company.

NAPIER WILSON

Service not established. Columbia Herald and Mail, 26 March 1875: Napier Wilson died last week, War of 1812 soldier, buried Greenwood Cemetery. Married Elizabeth Gill, born 12 Oct. 1796, died 7 Sept. 1834, buried Greenwood Cemetery. Her grave is marked, his is not, but an old listing of cemetery shows that he is buried next to her.

Children of Napier Wilson:
1. Junius, born 3 Sept. 1822, died 22 Oct. 1892, married _____ Haley.
2. Elmira Helen, born 29 Aug. 1826, died 14 April 1909, married I. M. Powell. (At father's death she was the only survivor)
3. Eliza A. Wilson married E. Kuhn.
4. About two other daughters, no information.

Source: Nathan Vaught, "Youth and Old Age", page 107; tombstone inscriptions from "They Passed This Way".

JOSEPH WINGFIELD

Served in Capt. John Jackson's company, West Tennessee militia. His age is given as between 26-45 on 1820 census; he died 1838 when Ephraim McRady was given an administrator's bond on his estate 29 Nov. 1838. His wife Lucy (aged 77 on 1850 census and born in Virginia) left will, dated 11 June 1855, and said she was entitled to a bounty warrant for 88 acres as late husband served as private in Capt. John Jackson's company, West Tennessee militia, late War of 1812. Wingfield came to Maury County about 1828 and was a carpenter according to Nathan Vaught.

Children of Joseph Wingfield:
1. Son, no further information.
2. Son, no further information.
3. No further information.
4. Sarah Margaret Wingfield, born about 1810, married 11 Feb. 1826 to Ephraim McCrady.
5. Daughter married R. S. Orton.
6. Mary D. Wingfield, born about 1808, married 3 Feb. 1837 to Chesley P. Bynum.
7. Daughter married _____ Smith.

Source: Nathan Vaught, page 102; 1850 census of Maury County; Maury County marriage records.

PHILIP P. WINN

Commissioned captain 1811 in 27th Regiment. Married in Virginia to the oldest daughter of William Sims and Judith Cross. He lived on Big Bigby and was a prominent man in the early days of Maury County. He was supposed to have died March 1843 during the big snow and was buried three miles south of Mt. Pleasant on the Military Road. On 7 Aug. 1841 an inquisition into his sanity was held and he was found to be of unsound mind, "but peaceable and inoffensive and harmless and docile and friendly."

Children of Philip P. Winn:
1. William M. Winn.
2. No information on others.

Brothers and sisters of Philip P. Winn:
1. William Winn, never married, lived in Maury County number of years.
2. John Winn, lived in Rutherford Co., Tenn., dying there in 1816, father of 17 children.
3. Richard Winn, born 1750, died 1818, Revolutionary War soldier and General in N. C. militia after the Revolution.
Source: Frank H. Smith's History of Maury County, Tenn., pages 348-349.

RICHARD WINN
Revolutionary War soldier and general in S. C. militia after the Revolution. Born
1750 in Fauquier County, Va., died 19 Dec. 1818 in Maury County. His grave was not
marked until recent years when a memorial stone was placed to him in Greenwood
Cemetery in Columbia. Served as member of Congress from S. C. He married Susan
Priscilla McKinney.

Children of Richard Winn:
1. Minor Winn, first born child, studied law under Andrew Jackson; died at Hermi-
   tage in 1799.
2. Benjamin Winn, M. D., married Mary C._____and lived in Florida.
3. Thomas Winn, M. D., lived in Maury County but returned to S. C. and died there
   unmarried.
4. Richard Winn, never married, buried with father and mother in old family
   cemetery near Sawdust. Grave was never marked.
5. William Winn, never married, died in Weakley County while on visit to his
   brother Samuel.
6. Samuel Winn, born 1796, died 5 Jan. 1868. Married 23 Dec. 1817 to Sarah
   McKenzie.
7. Susan Priscilla, born 1793, died 8 Oct. 1852, married Elijah Blocker.
8. Sophia Winn married Dr. Bratton of S. C.
9. Margaret Winn, died before 1856, married Dr. Evans or Ivins.
10. Mary Winn married Thomas Sims.
11. No information on the 11th child.

Source: Frank H. Smith's History of Maury County, pages 338-349.

SAMUEL WINN
Served at New Orleans. Born 1796, died 5 Jan. 1868 in Weakley County, Tenn. Son of
Richard and Priscilla Winn. Married 23 Dec. 1817 to Sarah McKenzie, daughter of
Col. John McKenzie.

Children of Samuel Winn:
1. Gabriella C. Winn married _____Jackson; lived in Henry County, Tenn.
2. Six other children, no information.

Source: Frank H. Smith's History of Maury County, Tenn., pages 348-349.

THOMAS WINN
Served in War of 1812; no service record established. Died in S. C.

WILLIAM WINN
Served as officer in War of 1812; no service record established. Son of Richard
and Priscilla Winn, died in Weakley County while on visit to brother Samuel Winn.

WILSON WINN
Served in Capt. John Gordon's company. No further information.

BENJAMIN WINSTEAD
Served in Capt. Bird S. Hurt's company. No further information.

CHURCHELL WOLLARD
Served in Capt. James McMahan's company. Wife Nancy, widow, drew pension at Santa
Fe in 1883. He was born 10 March 1792, died 18 Nov. 1867. He married Nancy Fox,
born 3 Jan. 1806. He was the son of Willoughby Wollard and his wife Rebeckah.

Children of Churchell Wollard:
1. Mary Ann Wollard, born 24 Aug. 1822.
2. Martha W. Wollard, born 4 June 1827.
   continued on next page

Children of Churchell Wollard, continued:
3. Manda H., born 4 Sept. 1828.
4. Joseph Franklin Wollard, born 21 June 1834, died 1 Sept. 1851.
5. Margaret Sarah Wollard, born 13 June 1836.
6. James Henry, born 5 Sept. 1838, died 31 Aug. 1851.
7. William Bartley, born 26 April 1841.
8. Hugh Fox Wollard, born 23 June 1842, died 5 Feb. 1861.
9. Churchel Marion Wollard, born 4 April 1845.
10. Nancy Leonar, born 13 June 1851, died 13 Sept. 1906.
11. Elija Nelson Wollard, born 29 April 1848, died 7 March 1926, married Mary
    Catherine Ladd Bird, daughter of Peter and Marticia Ladd.

Brothers and sisters of Churchell Wollard:
1. William Wollard, born 5 Oct. 1794.
2. Seth Wollard, born 18 July 1797.
3. Athilla Wollard, born 15 Oct. 1799.
4. Elizabeth Wollard, born 25 July 1802.
5. James Wollard, born 16 Dec. 1804.
6. Winne Wollard, born 1 Oct. 1807. (Winifred)
7. Mary Vines Wollard.

Source: Wollard Bible Records contributed by Marise P. Lightfoot.

NATHANIEL WOLLARD
Served in Capt. James McMahan's company. Born 6 Aug. 1792 in Wadkins Falls, N. C.,
died 1 Sept. 1863, murdered in Missouri where he had moved by Northern sympathizers
who shot him in face, ransacked his home and stole all his livestock; married 1816
Margaret Hardison. Son of John Wollard.

Children of Nathaniel Wollard:
1. Sarah, born 1817, married Moses Bennett.
2. Rebecca, born 1819, married Dr. George Davison.
3. Frances, born 1820, died 1840, married Ben Henson, Mr. Prater and Robert Welch.
4. Margaret, born 1825 married Robert O. Randles.
5. Elizabeth, born 1827, married James Edmisson.
6. Delilah, born 1831, married Richard C. Newport, step-brother.
7. Harriet, died in infancy.

Children by second marriage in 1841 to Mrs. Margaret Abel Newport:
1. Louisa Polk, born 1842, died 1847.
2. Nathaniel Jackson, born 1844, died 1914, married Alice Caroline Randles.
3. Silas Benton, born 1846, married Pamelia Price.
4. James Moses Robert, born 1849, married Sarah Frances Miller.

Brothers and sisters of Nathaniel Wollard:
1. Silas Wollard, aged between 26 and 45 on 1820 census; married Lucretia_____,
   died 12 Oct. 1854 at age 69, buried in Humphrey Hardison Cemetery.
2. (Half) Simon Wollard.
3. (Half) Nimrod Wollard.
4. No information on others.

Source: Maury County Cousins, pages 487-489; tombstone inscriptions from "They
Passed This Way".

WILLIAM WOLLARD
Served in Capt. James McMahan's company. [Quite possibly the brother of Churchel—se
his entry.]

DANIEL WOOD
Commissioned captain in militia company in 1807; lived on Little Bigby. No further information.

JOHN WOOD
Served in Capt. Bird S. Hurt's company. No further information.

SWAYNE W. WOOLIARD
Served in Capt. Bird S. Hurt's company. No further information.

PETER WOOLSEY
Maury County Will Book C-1, page 142: Recorded 8 Jan. 1824, will of Peter Woosley, "late of the U. S. Army" well beloved friend Sarah Venable the 160 acres of land due me from the U. S. and her daughter Jane Venable. Friend William Venable to be executor. Signed 18 Nov. 1818. Witnesses were Polly Myers and Elizabeth Venable.

DANIEL WOOTIN
Served in Capt. John Looney's company. No further information.

ABRAHAM WORHTINGTON
Served in Capt. James McMahan's company. No further information.

CHRISTOPHER WRIGHT
Served in Capt. John Gordon's company. No further information.

JOHN WRIGHT
Served in Capt. Andrew McCarty's company. No further information.

JOHN WRIGHT
Served in Capt. Robert Campbell's company. No further information.

[Several men of this name in early Maury County. One John Wright married Nancy McIntire and had son Archibald Wright.] [Francis Wright settled in Maury County in 1808 and had sons John, Francis, and Robert and son-in-law Roberty McCarty or Mc-Carter; Francis Wright's will was proved 1809.] [One John Wright died in Maury County in 1833, left wife Permelia Anne and children Robert and Leanna. Source: Headley vs Wright, chancery court, 1835-40.]

SAMUEL WRIGHT
Served in Capt. John Looney's company. No further information.

ABSOLEM YARBOROUGH
Served in Capt. John Looney's company. No further information.

+JESSE YARBOROUGH
Maury County Will Book A-1, page 236: Inventory of Jesse Yarborough, deceased, made 19 April 1815, included "his services to New Orleans in the late expedition." Signed by Absalem Yarborough.

+DANIEL YEATES
Maury County Will Book A-1, page 157: Daniel Yeates died 1 Feb. 1815; since his death his wife Martha married Roswell Seaton; Martha had remarried by August 1815. Feb. 1816 court minutes direct John Lindsey, Esquire, and James Hill to look out for homes for children of "Danl Yeates died in the service."

Children of Daniel Yeates:
1. Mariah Yeates.
2. James Yeates.
3. William Yeates.
4. John Yeates.
5. Sarah Yeates.

EBENEZER YOUNG
Served in Capt. Bird S. Hurt's company. No further information.

JAMES YOUNG
Served in Capt. John Gordon's company. No further information.

JOHN YOUNG
Served in Capt. Andrew McCarty's company. No further information.

NATHANIEL YOUNG
Commissioned captain in 51st Regiment in 1814. Born 1777 in S. C., and when in Maury lived on Green's Lick Creek; married his cousin Jemima Young, born 1777 in S. C.

Children of Nathaniel Young:
1. Nathaniel Young, Jr., born 16 Sept. 1807 in Maury, died in Hickman County; married Elizabeth Young, born 1810.

Source: Spence's History of Hickman County, pages 359-360.

SAMUEL YOUNG
Served in Capt. John Gordon's company. No further information.

GEORGE ZOLLICOFFER
Appointed constable 1808 in Maury County. Married 18 Dec. 1810 in Williamson County to Abigail Nicholson. His age is given as between 26 and 45 on 1820 census.

JOHN JACOB ZOLLICOFFER
Came to Maury County about 1808 and was member of court at one time. Born 13 July 1775, died 17 August 1840 in Maury County; son of George Zollicoffer (1738-1815) and his wife Anna Lindsey (born 1753); married (1) Martha Kirk, born 30 March 1786, died 11 June 1815, daughter of Isaac Kirk of North Carolina; (2) 25 Nov. 1818 to Elizabeth Nicholson, daughter of George Nicholson, a cousin of his first wife.

Children of John J. Zollicoffer by first marriage:
1. Leanna, born 1804, died 1848, married 1822 to Nathaniel Williams of Maury.
2. Frederick, born 1806, died 1874, married 1830 Elizabeth Love of Maury County.
3. Ann Maria, born 1808, died 1854, married 1827 to James Swanson, Jr., ot Tenn.
4. Felix Kirk, born 1812, died 1862, Confederate General, married Louisa Pocahontas Gordon.

Children of John J. Zollicoffer by his second marriage:
1. John Leonidas, born 1820, married about 1856 to Harriet_____.
2. George Nicholson, born 1823, died unmarried and a Confederate prisoner at Terre Haute, Indiana.
3. Maria Johanna, born 1825, married 1846 to Dr. William Matthew Wheeler.

Source: The Zollie Tree, pages 142-3; Octavia Zollicoffer Bond, "Family Chronicle and Kinship Bood".

ADDENDA

This section contains additional information on some soldiers previously listed or soldiers whose names were given in too late for inclusion in proper order.

LITTLETON ABERNATHY — page 1
From "Memorial and Biographical History of McLennan Co., Texas", page 848-849:
John F. Abernathy, born in Tenn. 1 Jan. 1826, was son of Robert G. and Martha Fry

Littleton Abernathy, continued:
Abernathy. Robert G. lived in Maury, later in Giles County. Grandfather Abernathy a Scot, born in N. C., married the daughter of Peter Forney and moved to Maury. He served in Revolution. Children: M. P., Ephraim, Littleton, Robert G., Saina, Derucia, and Susan. (Note: this would make Littleton the son of David Abernathy).

From "The Abernathys, Alexanders, Forneys and Sims," by Mable R. McClure, Enid, Oklahoma, 1934: David Abernathy, born Dinwiddie Co., Va., 29 July 1752, died Giles County, married Christina Forney 27 May 1780, daughter of Jacob and Marie Forney, sister of General Peter Forney and Major Abram Forney. She was born 1762, died 1842. Children were Milton, Ephraim, Littleton, John Young, Robert G., Sina, Drucilla, Dionysia, and Susan.

.Contributed by Virginia W. Alexander, Columbia.

JAMES BELL — page 10, John Bell entry.
The will of James Bell is recorded in Lewis County, Tennessee, in 1845, and he gives his brothers and sisters:

1. Elizabeth Bell.
2. Darcus Bell married Joseph Peyton.
3. Starling Bell.
4. Sarah Bell.
5. Polly Bell.
6. Florence Bell.
7. Thomas Bell.
8. Stevenson Bell.
9. John Bell.

CAPTAIN JOHN PORTER BLACKBURN

Served in War of 1812, son of Captain Ambrose Blackburn and his wife Frances Elizabeth Jones; born N. C., moved to Texas in 1853 and is buried in Blackburn Cemetery near Killeen, Texas; married 21 Jan. 1819 in Maury County to Nancy Church-well. His will is recorded in Lewis County (refer to Maury County Neighbors).

Children of John Porter Blackburn:
1. Merriweather Whitley.
2. Frances married ___Chalk.
3. Rosara.
4. Valera married ___McClanahan.
5. E. J.
6. Ella (or Ellen D.) married ___Hensley.
7. Elias H.
8. John C. G.
9. William H.
10. Richard T.
11. Elizabeth J., born 1828, died 1906, married E. J. Ricketts and Alfred Polk.

Source: The Polks of North Carolina and Tennessee, page 44; Maury County Neighbors, page 97.

HARRISON BLACKGRAVES

Appointed constable 1808 in Maury County. No further information.

ANDREW COWSERT

Served as farrier to Capt. Archibald McKinney's company 24 Sept. 1813, to May 1814. His will was settled October 1826 in Williamson County; he is buried at Brick Church Cemetery in Maury and the inscription on his stone has about shaled away. He had son named James Andrew and possibly one named John F. No information on other children.

BENJAMIN EMERSON
Served in War of 1812 in N. C., came to Maury County in 1823 from Chatham County, North Carolina; died 1846 in Marshall County.

Source: Letter from Joe C. Harris, Florence, Alabama, great-great-grandson.

WILLIAM LANE — page 114
Chancery court case Dugger vs Clane, 1848:
Additional information on this man: William Lane was deceased by 1848. His children were: (or distributees)

1. Emaline married 27 June 1832 to Stephen M. Hancock.
2. Frances married William F. Blanton.
3. William M. Lane, deceased by 1848.
4. James Lane, deceased by 1848, married Phoebe_____. Lived in Mississippi.
5. Thomas C. Lane.
6. Samuel C. Lane.
7. Sarah Lane married William Smith. [Marriage records show Sarah Lane married 4 May 1820 to Francis Smith; Mary Lane marriage license issued 14 July 1817 to marry William Smith.]
8. Nancy Lane married William Williams and lived in Madison County, Miss.
9. Charlotte Lane married 23 July 1818 in Maury to John A. Powell; living in La. at time of lawsuit.
10. Louisa Lane married John W. Hancock, living in Missouri at time of lawsuit.

CAPTAIN DANIEL M. McKENNON
According to Nat Jones' history of Maury County, page 19, he was a soldier in the War of 1812; son of John and Elizabeth McKennon, born 8 Oct. 1791 in S. C., died in Maury 28 Jan. 1865; married Prudence Blackburn, daughter of Edward and Patsy Blackburn of Virginia, born 6 March 1806, died 17 Dec. 1862.

Children of Daniel McKennon:
1. Daniel Boone, born 1837, died 1911.
2. George Nichols McKennon, born 1833, died 1910, married Mary Louise Kinzer.
3. G. B. McKennon.
4. No information on others if any.

Source: Maury Democrat, 26 Jan. 1911; Century Review of Maury County, page 303; Confederate Soldiers and Patriots of Maury County, pages 225, 226.

JOHN MOREHEAD — page 138
He was the son of Arch Morehead; inventory of his estate was made in Maury County in 1813, he died before the divorce.

HUGH BRADSHAW PORTER
Was Lt. Col. of volunteer militia in 1826; cannot determine if he had service in War of 1812 or not. Born 16 Dec. 1796, died 26 Dec. 1866; married Rachel Roberts, born 11 Feb. 1805, died 6 April 1859; son of William Porter.

Children of Hugh B. Porter:
1. William R., killed 21 May 1861 by William Reynolds; married 5 Aug. 1845 to Sarah Elizabeth Leftwich.
2. Reese Porter, age 24 in 1850, died near Huntingdon, Tennessee; married sister of J. Mack Cabler. (Frank H. Smith's history of Maury County, page 64.)
3. Persia Porter married Henry Osborn.
4. Mary J., married 10 April 1844 James Akin.
continued on next page.

Children of Hugh B. Porter, continued:

6. Elizabeth B. Porter, married 8 May 1850 to James Akin.
7. Hugh B., Jr., born 28 Oct. 1824, died 4 July 1848.
8. Nimrod Pike Porter, born 31 Aug. 1828, died 6 Oct. 1852.
9. Rachel Pocahontas, born 15 Oct. 1830, died 24 March 1844.
10. Sterling Robertson Porter, born 7 Dec. 1834, died 6 March 1863, married 12 Nov. 1856 to Margaret Roberts.
11. No further information.

Source: Tombstone inscriptions from "They Passed This Way", C-51; Nathan Vaught, "Youth and Old Age".

JOHN ROBERTS

Served in Capt. John Chisholm's company. No further information.

MARK ROBERTS - page 175

Served as private in Capt. William Dooley's company. No further information.

CHARLES THOMAS ROGERS

Enlisted 20 Dec. 1813 in Williamson County in Capt. Matthew Johnson's company, Col. Nicholas T. Perkins' regiment. In the fight at Enotochapco Creek 24 Jan. 1814 he was wounded in the right arm and discharged from service 8 Feb. 1814. born about 1795 in Wake Co., N. C., and died at South Harpeth, Williamson County, 23 Sept. 1824, death was caused indirectly by his old wound. He married Elizabeth Hutton at Fall Creek, Rutherford Co., Tenn., 9 April 1817, daughter of John M. Hutton.

Children of Charles Thomas Rogers:

1. John Henry Rogers, born March 1818
2. Zane Mira Rogers, married ____ Allen.
3. Mark Washington Rogers, born 19 Oct. 1822 in Maury County, married 11 Sept. 1844 Weakley County to Sarah Tabitha Mitchell.
4. James Williams Rogers, died 1863.

Source: "The Polks of North Carolina and Tennessee," pages 51, 52.

NATHANIEL HARRISON STEELE

Commissioned Lieutenant 1810 in the militia. No further information.

JESSE OVERTON TATE

Served in 39th Regiment of Infantry. Born 1784 in Caswell County, N. C., died 13 May 1845 in Rogersville, Lauderdale County, Alabama; son of Capt. Waddy Tate (born 1741, died 1789) and his wife Nancy Ann Simpson (born 1750, died 1795). The name of his wife is not known.

Children of Jesse O. Tate:

1. Jerome Benton Tate, born 1822, died 1862, married Elizabeth Grisham, 23 July 1845.
2. Mary Ann Tate, born 1828, died 1873, married Jesse Nelson Grisham 2 Aug. 1851.
3. Jesse Overton Tate, Jr., born 1830, died 1900, married Eliza Ann Grisham on 6 Jan. 1851.

Brothers and sisters of Jesse O. Tate:

1. Susannah Tate.
2. William Tate.
3. Richard Tate.
4. Zachariah Tate.
5. Ede Tate.
6. Zedekiah Tate.

continued on next page

Jesse Overton Tate, continued:

Memorial Service for Lt. Jesse Overton Tate – A memorial service for First Lt. Jesse Overton Tate was held 26 May 1975 at Harvey Cemetery, Rogersville, Alabama, where a memorial marker was placed by his great, great grandson Andrew Frank Tate, Jr., of Pulaski, Tennessee. Lt. Jesse Overton Tate was a veteran of the War of 1812 and the Seminole War. The Rev. William L. McDonald, former minister of Mt. Bethel Methodist Church, the church where the early Tate family attended services, gave the invocation. Iliff Lavern Tate, District Attorney of Lauderdale County, and a great, great grandson delivered the memorial address. Retired Colonel Sidney Frank Tate, Jr., of the United States Army placed a wreath of flowers at the memorial. An honor guard from the American Legion Post in Florence, Alabama, participated in the memorial service.

Memorial to Jesse Overton Tate
by Andrew Frank Tate, Jr. (to be read at the memorial service)
"Jesse Overton Tate was born in 1784 in Caswell County, North Carolina, the son of Captain Waddy Tate and Nancy Ann Simpson Tate. His father, Captain Waddy Tate, was the son of John Tate and Lucy Waddy Tate of St. Peter's Parish, New Kent County, Virginia. St. Peter's Parish Church was the church where the Dandridge family and Tate family attended services. Martha Dandridge, later the wife of George Washington, the first President, also attended services here. His mother, Nancy Ann Simpson Tate was the daughter of Richard Simpson, Jr., and Mary Kincheloe Simpson of Fairfax Co., Virginia.

"Captain Waddy Tate participated in the Revolutionary War having been appointed captain of the Militia of the First Battalion in 1776 from Caswell and Guilford Counties, N. C. Soon after the Revolution in 1789 Captain Waddy Tate died and a few years later his wife leaving Jesse Overton Tate and his brother Zedekiah Tate and sister Ede Tate orphans. The grandmother of these orphans, Mary Kincheloe Simpson, reared them until her death in 1797 when she named them one legatee in her will.

"In the early 1800s Jesse Overton Tate and Zedekiah Tate migrated to the Alabama Territory from North Carolina. Zedekiah Tate is listed as an early surveyor of Madison County, Alabama. He married Mildred Rountree in 1810.

"August 3, 1812, Jesse Overton Tate was ordered by the War Department to report to Colonel John Williams at Nashville, Tennessee, as a second lieutenant in the 39th Regiment of Infantry. Lieutenant Tate was listed with Lieutenant Vance Green in Fayetteville, Tenn., 3 Dec. 1813 with the 39th Regiment of Infantry. On 20 Feb. 1815 he was promoted by President James Madison to the office of first lieutenant in the 39th regiment of infantry, to rank as such from 20 May 1814 for his services to the United States in the war with Great Britain and in the Seminole War.

"After the War of 1812 Jesse Overton Tate came back to the Alabama Territory and it is soon declared a state in 1819. Zedekiah Tate became the first Tax Collector of Lauderdale County with his brother Jesse Overton Tate as surety. They both were commissioned justices of the peace. Jesse Overton Tate was first commissioned a justice of the peace 15 Nov. 1823 and served as such until his death in 1845, a period of over twenty years. There are countless signatures of Jesse O. Tate in the old books at the courthouse in Florence, Alabama, where he has witnessed marriages, wills, contracts, and estate settlements.

"Jesse Overton Tate had three children who were all unmarried at his death 13 May 1845. All three of his children married into the Grisham family. His son, Jerome Benton Tate, married Elizabeth Grisham. His son, Jesse Overton Tate, Jr., married Eliza Ann Grisham. His daughter, Mary Ann Tate, married Jesse Nelson Grisham. Jerome Benton Tate was killed at the Battle of Shiloh in the Civil War and is buried there. Jesse Overton Tate, Jr., also served in the Civil War. Many, many descendants of Jesse Overton Tate have served in every war the United States has waged since

Jesse Overton Tate, continued:
his service in the War of 1812."

Information contributed by Andrew Frank Tate, Jr., Pulaski, Tennessee.

FORT WILLIAMS BURIALS

The following are the graves of War of 1812 soldiers buried near Fort Williams,
Alabama, about 15 miles southwest of Childersburg, Alabama. Those men known to have
been from Maury County have been listed previously, but it is possible that some of
these men were from our county and have not been included before.

ELIJAH BRIGHT — Private, Newlin's company, 1st West Tennessee Militia.
ANDREW CAHOON — Private, Newlin's company, 1st West Tennessee Militia.
THOMAS DAWSON — Private, Newlin's company, 1st West Tennessee Militia.
ABLE DOCKERY — Private, Newlin's company, 1st West Tennessee Militia.
JAMES ELLIS — Private, Newlin's company, 1st West Tennessee Militia.
JOHN FRENCH — Private, Newlin's company, 1st West Tennessee Militia.
ROBERT GIASCO — Private, Newlin's company, 1st West Tennessee Militia.
JAMES HAMILTON — Private, Newlin's company, 1st West Tennessee Militia, 21 Sept. 1814.
RICHARD HILL — Private, Newlin's company, 1st West Tennessee Militia.
CALEB HORTON — Private, Newlin's company, 1st West Tennessee Militia.
WILLIAM P. HARDIN — Private, Newlin's company, 1st West Tennessee Militia, died
    20 Sept. 1814.
THOMAS J. JOHNSON — First lieutenant, Newlin's Company, 1st West Tennessee Militia,
    died 6 Nov. 1814.
JOSHUA IATON — Private, Newlin's Company, 1st West Tennessee Militia.
DAVID McANTS — Private, Newlin's Company, 1st West Tennessee Militia.
JAMES McCOY — Private, Newlin's Company, 1st West Tennessee Militia, died 13 Oct.
    1814.
ARCHIBALD NAIL — Private, Newlin's Company, 1st West Tennessee Militia, died
    20 Sept. 1814.
ABLE RICE — Private, Newlin's Company, 1st West Tennessee Militia.
ROWLING RICE — Private, Newlin's Company, 1st West Tennessee Militia, died 20 Sept.
    1814.
JEFFREY REFFEW — Private, Newlin's Company, 1st West Tennessee Militia.
SPENCER ROGERS — Private, Newlin's Company, 1st West Tennessee Militia.
ALFRED SIMS — Private, Newlin's Company, 1st West Tennessee Militia, died 20 Sept.
    1814.
HENRY SAWRY — Private, Newlin's Company, 1st West Tennessee Militia.
PARIS TRACY — Private, Newlin's Company, 1st West Tennessee Militia, died 20 Sept.
    1814.
MOSES THOMPSON — Private, Newlin's Company, 1st West Tennessee Militia, died
    24 Sept. 1814.

BENJAMIN GHOLSON

The following sketch was written by a descendant, Mrs. Ruth French, Prineville, Oregon:

The wedding of Benjamin Gholson and Jane Ganaway took place 31 August 1815 in Maury County, Tenn. The groom, son of Francis and Mary Craig Gholson, was twenty-two years old. He was born 17 Dec. 1793 in Scott County, Kentucky. The newlyweds set up housekeeping in Tennessee. Their first child, Elizabeth, was born there 8 Sept. 1816.

By 1827 the growing family was living in Woodstock Township of Schuyler County, Ill. On 24 Sept. 1831 Benjamin Gholson witnessed the paper deeding land for the first church in the Township. The land was given by Isaac Naught, who would become Elizabeth's father-in-law when she married John Naught 20 July 1834.

Benjamin Gholson fought in the Black Hawk War (1831) under Capt. Daniel Matheny. Reportedly the local men joined with a group of Rangers from Springfield in which young A. Lincoln served.

Again the family moved on west. The Iowa Territorial Census of 1836 has the following entry:

Des Moines County

Head of House	Male over 21	Male under 21	Female over 21	Female under 21
Golston, Benjamin	2	1	6	1

There is record of a Benjamin Gholson residing in Henry Co., Iowa, after the above census. Henry County was formed from part of Des Moines County.

The Gholsons along with their married children (except for two) joined a wagon train leaving Iowa on 29 March 1853. After six months on the trail they reached Oregon 29 Sept. 1853. Benjamin filed a Land Claim in Polk County, Oregon, in the fertile Williamette Valley. He lived only briefly two years on his new farm, dying two months and two days after his sixty-second birthday 19 Feb. 1856.

The Probate record lists Benjamin's legal heirs as: "Jain Gholson, Elizabeth Naug Martha Massey, Manerva Mathena, Lydia McQueen, Edmun Gholson, Jain Hamilton, Rosan Darr, James Gholson, Emely Gholson residing in the territory of Oregon and Alvina Roortz, Mary McFall residing in Harrison County in the State of Missouri."

(Mrs. French noted that she was descended from Benjamin through his daughter Elizabeth Gholson Naught. Her daughter Sarah Frances Naught married the young pilot of the wagon train, Nathaniel Wallace. Their youngest daughter, Anna Laura, was her grandmother.)

DR. ZEBENA CURTIS CONKEY

Served in War of 1812. Born 3 July 1796 in N. Y., died 17 Feb. 1862 at LaGrange, Fayette Co., Tenn., buried Oxford Cemetery, Oxford, Miss., married 18 Dec. 1828 in Maury County, Tenn., to Sarah Minerva Brown, born 7 July 1811 in Maury County, died 24 March 1850 Oxford, Miss., buried Oxford Cemetery. He was charter member of First Presbyterian Church, Oxford, Miss., 1838. Mrs. Sarah H. Conkey was a new member in 1852. He was the son of Joshua Conkey and Millicent Bridge. He married secondly on 25 May 1852 to Sarah H. Thomas in Maury County.

Children of Dr. Conkey:
1. Joseph Joshua Conkey, born 11 Oct. 1829 in Maury, died 30 Sept. 1859 in Tunica, Miss.
2. Sarah Ann Millicent Conkey, born 21 July 1831, died 10 Oct. 1834.
3. Jane Elizabeth Conkey, born 12 Oct. 1833, died 22 Sept. 1898 in Oxford, Miss., married 14 Dec. 1854 to Henry Edward Roscoe.
   continued on next page

Children of Dr. Conkey, continued:

4. Mary Amanda Conkey, born 23 Dec. 1835, died 27 July 1869 at Bailey Springs, Alabama, married the Rev. Richard Hugh Whitehead.
5. James Brown Conkey, born 17 Jan. 1838, died 30 Sept. 1839.
6. Sarah Amelia Conkey, born 30 July 1841, died 5 July 1842.
7. Clara Zebena Conkey, born 2 May 1843 in Oxford, Miss., died 4 Feb. 1882 in Naples, Italy, married J. A. Jahier.
8. Minerva Helen Conkey, born 28 Aug. 1845 in Oxford, Miss., died after 1899 at Clearwater, Pinellas County, Florida.

Source: Information contributed by Mrs. Helen Rugeley, Austin, Texas. She also included another sketch on Dr. Conkey which tells more of his War of 1812 service:

"Dr. Zebina Conkey, born in New York state and one of a large family, son of Joshua Conkey and his wife Millicent Bridge of Deerfield, Ma. Joshua enlisted 1775 at the age of 15 from Pelhammas a drummer. He served under different commands throughout the war; died at Canton, N. Y., in 1840. (See Lineage Book N. S. D.A.R., Vol. XI, 1895, pp.45-46, #10108.) Joshua was the son of Joseph Conkey who was also a soldier in the Revolution. Dr. Z. Curtis Conkey ran away as a boy and enlisted in the War of 1812, and was captured and imprisoned by the British. He graduated from Jefferson Medical College and went South as a young man. He had pronounced musical talents, possessing a fine basso voice and in his youth played the violin and flute. A man of great charity both in words and deeds, he was a great student and devoted himself to his large and lucrative medical practice. Ten children." (Only eight listed.)

Here in Maury County Dr. Conkey was appointed the first postmaster of Bigbyville about 1830.

THOMAS McNEAL
Additional information on this soldier contributed by descendant Mrs. Helen H. Rugeley, Austin, Texas.

"Thomas McNeal was born 19 June 1771, probably in Mecklenburg Co., N. C., and died 2 July 1830 in Hardeman County, Tenn. On 2 Sept. 1803 in Mecklenburg Co., he married Clarissa (1782-1846), the daughter of Col. Ezekiel Polk and his first wife Mary Wilson.

"The name of the father of Thomas McNeal has not yet been discovered by this compiler, but apparently he died before 26 Sept. 1775 when Martha McNeal made her will in Mecklenburg Co. (Will Book B, page 54). This will directs that her daughter Prudence and her son Thomas be sent to her sister Susannah Polk. Several North Carolina histories record that Thomas Polk married Susannah Spratt/Sprott.

"The will of "Thomas Sprot" (Abstract of NC Wills, J. B. Grimes, p. 356) dated 15 Jan. 1757 in Anson Co., NC, names (among others) his daughters Susannah Polk and Martha Sprot; to the latter he gave land on Sugar/Sugaw Creek. The brothers Thomas and Ezekiel Polk also owned land on that creek in Mecklenburg Co., so the young people no doubt were acquainted early in life. Thomas McNeal married the daughter of the brother of his uncle-in-law.

"Thomas and Clarissa McNeal accompanied her father when he left Mecklenburg Co. for greener pastures to the west. Their first child was born 6 Sept. 1804 in Williamson Co., Tenn., a part that now is northeastern Maury Co. ("Colonel Ezekial Polk: Pioneer and Patriarch", Charles Grier Sellers Jr. in William and Mary College Quarterly, 3rd Series, Vol. X, p. 94). On 29 Dec. 1807, Ezekiel Polk gave them 400 acres on Richland Creek. (Alexander & Priest, Maury County Deed Abstracts, Vol. 1, p. 4). In 1812 Thomas McNeal was taxed for 400 acres on Carter's Creek (Historic

Thomas McNeal, continued:

Maury, Vol. VIII, p. 19), but he seems to have acquired 200 more: on the 1818 Maury Co. Tax List, North Side of Duck River, appears "McNide (?) Thos." with 600 acres, one white poll and five black polls (Historic Maury, Vol. VIII, p. 161. McNide is probably a misreading of McNeal.)

"In 1821 his father-in-law moved west again (to the area now known as Hardeman County), and Thomas McNeal soon followed, settling on the Hatchie River north on present-day Bolivar, on land bought from Peter Swanson in 1821. On this land were located Hatchie Town and the first cemetery. The first court was held in the McNeal home, but later the county seat was moved to Bolivar on land deeded by William Ramsey and Ezekiel Polk. (Family Findings, Vol. V, No. 3, July 1973, Hardeman Co. Sesquicentennial Issue).

McNeal's property and political activity (he "took a prominent part in organizing the new county of Maury in 1807") proved to be a liability in the War of 1812, however. He "had to enter Jackson's army as a private in 1813, because the prejudices of the members of his company 'against men of wealth and tallents' prevented his expected election as captain." (Sellers in "Colonel Ezekiel Polk" cited above.) It is believed that Thomas's father-in-law, Ezekiel Polk, intervened with Jackson in his behalf, obtaining a commission for him as captain in the militia by the end of the War of 1812. (Letter from Virginia McDaniel Bowman, County Historian, Franklin, Tenn.)

"Thomas McNeal is listed as private with pay of $8 per month on the "Pay Roll of a Company of Mounted Gunmen commanded by Capt. James McMahan on the Regiment Commanded by Nicholas T. Perkins" for the period 18 Dec. 1813-15 Feb. 1814. (Historic Maury, Vol. IX, p. 197.)

His box tomb in Polk Cemetery at Bolivar, Hardeman Co., Tenn., reads: "Sacred to the memory of Cap. Thomas McNeal, born June 19th AD 1771. Died July 2nd AD 1830. Aged 59 years and 13 days. An affectionate husband and father—in his friendships benevolent and sincere."

"The children of Thomas and Clarissa (Polk) McNeal were:

"1. Ezekiel Polk married Ann Williams.
 2. Mary Eliza married Mark R. Roberts.
 3. Prudence Tate married Maj. John Houston Bills.
 4. Albert Thomas married Mary Jane Dunlap.
 5. Jane Frances married Dr. David Franklin Brown. : (Ancestor of Mrs. Rigeley.)
 6. Samuel L. (Lycurgus ?), did not marry.
 7. Evelina Louisa, married 1. Erosman (Erasmus?) McDowell, 2. Dr. George Peddie Peters.
 8. William Wallace married Elizabeth Walker Berry."

DANIEL DAVIS
War of 1812 soldier; born 1794 in Pittsylvania Co., Va., died 1820; son of William Davis, of Virginia, who died 1835; married Lydia Boaz, daughter of Shadrach Boaz, born 1795 died 1863.

Children of Daniel Davis:
1. William B. Davis, born 1816 in Pittsylvania Co., Va., married 19 March 1835 in Maury County to Mary M. Cole, daughter of the Rev. Joshua and Elizabeth Smith Cole; born 1815, died 1882.
2. No information on other children.

Source: Ansearchin' News, Summer 1975, page 84, publication of the Tennessee Genealogical Society, Memphis, Tenn.

JOHN LOONEY
Refer to earlier listing on page 118. Florence Times-Tri Cities Daily, 17 Nov. 1974:
"HISTORICAL LOONEY HOUSE TO BE DEDICATED—When John Looney and his son Henry came to
Alabama in 1813 to fight in the Creek Indian War with General Andrew Jackson, they
found the beautiful mountains and valleys of St. Clair County much to their liking.

"After the war, John returned to Maury County, Tenn., sold his property there, and
came back to Alabama to homestead two "forties" in beautiful Beaver Valley. He, with
his sons Henry, Asa and Jack, felled trees, planed them, squared, notched and hauled
the logs to a spot on little Beaver Creek. They erected a two-story log home with
dogtrots on each level and massive timbers that graduated from 18 inches deep at the
bottom log to 12 inches deep at the uppermost log. The logs were so perfectly rect-
angular that very little clay was need to daub the house. By Feb. 25, 1818, the
Looney family, including wife Rebecca and seven children from one to 21 were living
in Beaver Valley.

"Shortly after the house was completed the creek overflowed its banks and mosquitoes
became a serious problem, so the Looney's disassembled and moved the structure to
higher ground on the other side of what is now Greensport Road. Here it stands today

"After two years of careful restoration, the St. Clair Historical Society will
dedicate and open the house to the public Nov. 23 and 24...The Looney House is 4.8
miles from the Ashville Court House. The way will be clearly marked along Hwy. 231
and Greensport Road. Smoke will be signalling a welcome from the two fireplaces of
handmade brick."

Hardison, Abner, 85; Charles, 86; John, 86; Joshua, 86.
Hardy, Coleman, 86.
Hargrove, 86.
Harper, Moses D., 87.
Harris, David, 87; Edmund, 87; Reuben, 87.
Hart, Henry, 87; John, 87; Joseph, 87.
Hascell, Elias, 88.
Hastings, Henry, 88.
Hatchett, John, 88.
Hawkins, Grant, 88.
Hays, Andrew, 88; George, 88; Jonathan, 88; Joseph, 88.
Helms, William, 88.
Henderson, James, 88, 89; Joseph, 89; Nathaniel, 89; William, 89.
Hendricks, Abner, 89; John, 89.
Henley, Caleb, 89; William, 89.
Herald, John, 89.
Herndon, Joseph, 89.
Herring, Solomon, 90.
Hester, Abraham, 90.
Hicks, Elijah, 90; John, 91.
Higdon, 91.
Higgs, James, 91.
Hill, Alexander, 91; Richard, 215; Robert, 91; William K., 91.
Hillis, John, 92; Samuel, 92.
Hindsley, Michael, 92.
Hines, David, 93.
Hinnegan, James, 93.
Hodge, John, 93; William, 93.
Hogan, Anderson, 93; Benjamin, 93; Isaiah, 94; John, 94.
Holcomb, Daniel, 94.
Holding, Sam, 94.
Hollaway, Edward, 94.
Hollis (Holace), James, 94; Silas, 94.
Holmes, James, 94; Lewis (Levin), 94.
Hood, Delanson W., 94; John, 94.
Hope, Eli, 94.
Hopkins, Holmes H., 95; Jason, 95; Neal, 95.
Hopson, Henry, 93, 95; Isaac, 95; John, 95.
Horton, Caleb, 215.
Hossey - see Jossey also-95.
House, William, 95.
Howell, Caleb, 95; John, 95; Malachi, 95; Stephen H., 95.
Howard, Allen, 95; Permenus, 95; Shadrick, 96; William, 96.
Hubbell, William B., 96.
Hud, Thomas, 96.
Huddleston, Daniel, 96; John, 96.
Hudson, Edward B., 96.
Huey, James, 96; John, 96.

Huffstaller, Solomon, 96.
Hughes, Buddet, 96; David, 96; Kibble T., 96.
Humphrey, Daniel, 97.
Hunt, Oliver, 97.
Hunter, Aaron, 97; John, 97; Nicholas, 97.
Hurst, Kemp W., 98.
Hurt, Bird S., 98.
Hutchinson, John, 98.
Hutton, Patrick, 98.

Isom, Arthur T., 98; George, 98; James, 99.

Jackson, Bobby, 99; Branch, 99; Daniel, 99.
Jacobs, Nathaniel, 99.
Jaggers, John, 99; Simon, 99.
Jarrel, David, 99.
Jenkins, Simeon, 99; Walter S., 99.
Jennings, John, 100.
Jobe, Abraham, 100; James, 100.
Johnson, Johnston, Abner, 100; Abner H., 100; Alexander, 100; Amos, 101; Elijah, 101; Garrett, 101; Isham, 101; James, 101; John, 101; John, 102; Robert, 102; Samuel, 102; Simon, 102; Thomas, 103, 215; William, 103.
Jones, Abner, 103; Alfred, 103; Caroline, 104; Benjamin, 104; Hezekiah, 104; John, 104; Samuel, 104; Thomas, 104; William, 105; Willis, 105.
Jordan, James, 106; Benjamin 106; William, 106.
Jossey, James, 106.
Judd, Diana, 106.

Kellam, Henry, 107; John, 107.
Kelly, Edward, 107; Joh, 107; Joshua, 107; William, 107.
Kelsey, Robert G., 107.
Kenamore, William, 107.
Kendrick, Jesse, 108; John, 108.
Kennedy, Andrew, 108; Evander, 108; Eli, 108; James, 108; John M., 108; Parthenia, 108; William, 109.
Kenner, Eli, 109.
Kerr, Robert, 109; William, 109.
Kilcrease, Davis, 109; John, 109; William, 109.
Kilpatrick, Ebenezer, 110; Felix, 110.
Kile, James, 110.
Kincaid, Joseph, 111.
Kindle, William, 111.
King, Abner, 111; Avery, 111.

www.ingramcontent.com/pod-product-compliance
Lightning Source LLC
Chambersburg PA
CBHW021901020426
42334CB00013B/430